AGING AND HUMAN VISUAL FUNCTION

MODERN AGING RESEARCH

Series Editors

Richard C. Adelman
Jay Roberts

George T. Baker III
Vincent J. Cristofalo

AGING AND HUMAN VISUAL FUNCTION

Editors

Robert Sekuler
Departments of Psychology, Ophthalmology, Neurobiology/Physiology
Northwestern University
Evanston, Illinois

Donald Kline
Department of Psychology
University of Notre Dame
Notre Dame, Indiana

Key Dismukes
Committee on Vision
Assembly of Behavioral and Social Sciences
National Research Council
Washington, D.C.

Alan R. Liss, Inc., New York

Address all Inquiries to the Publisher
Alan R. Liss, Inc., 150 Fifth Avenue, New York, NY 10011

Library of Congress Cataloging in Publication Data

Main entry under title:

Aging and human visual function.

(Modern aging research ; v. 2)
Revised papers originally presented at a symposium sponsored by the Committee on Vision of the National Research Council, held Mar. 31–Apr. 1, 1980 in Washington, D.C.
Includes bibliographies and index.
1. Vision disorders — Age factors — Congresses.
2. Visual pathways — Aging — Congresses.
I. Dismukes, Key. II. Sekuler, Robert.
III. Kline, Donald. IV. National Research Council (U.S.). Committee on Vision.
[DNLM: 1. Vision — Physiology — Congresses.
2. Aging — Congresses. W1 M0117 v.2 / WW 103 A267 1980
RE48.2.A5A35   618.97'77   82-7172
ISBN 0-8451-2301-7   AACR2

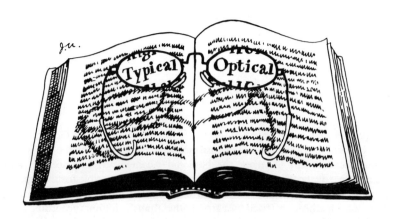

TYPICAL OPTICAL
By John Updike

In the days of my youth
*   'mid many a caper*
I drew with my nose
*   a mere inch from the paper,*
but now that I'm older
*   and life has grown hard*
I find I can't focus
*   inside of a yard.*

First pill-bottle labels
*   and telephone books*
began to go under
*   to my dirty looks,*
then want ads and box scores
*   succumbed to the plague*
of the bafflingly quite
*   unresolvably vague.*

In the days of my youth
*   I devoured John Donne,*
George Meredith, et al.,
*   in eight-point Granjon.*
Now long in the lens,
*   my poor eyeballs enfold*
no print any subtler
*   than sans-serif bold.*

The project that is the subject of this report was approved by the Governing Board of the National Research Council, whose members are drawn from the councils of the National Academy of Sciences, the National Academy of Engineering, and the Institute of Medicine. The members of the committee responsible for the report were chosen for their special competences and with regard for appropriate balance.

This report has been reviewed by a group other than the authors according to procedures approved by a Report Review Committee consisting of members of the National Academy of Sciences, the National Academy of Engineering, and the Institute of Medicine.

The National Research Council was established by the National Academy of Sciences in 1916 to associate the broad community of science and technology with the Academy's purposes of furthering knowledge and of advising the federal government. The Council operates in accordance with general policies determined by the Academy under the authority of its congressional charter of 1863, which establishes the Academy as a private, nonprofit, self-governing membership corporation. The Council has become the principal operating agency of both the National Academy of Sciences and the National Academy of Engineering in the conduct of their services to the government, the public, and the scientific and engineering communities. It is administered jointly by both Academies and the Institute of Medicine. The National Academy of Engineering and the Institute of Medicine were established in 1964 and 1970, respectively, under the charter of the National Academy of Sciences.

This study was supported by a consortium of agencies through the Office of Naval Research Contract N 00014–75–C–0406 to the National Academy of Sciences.

Committee on Vision of the National Research Council

Members*

Derek H. Fender, Chair, Jorgensen Laboratory of Information Science, California Institute of Technology

Robert Sekuler, Chair-Elect, Departments of Psychology, Ophthalmology, Neurobiology/Physiology, Northwestern University

Dorothea Jameson, Past-Chair, Department of Psychology, University of Pennsylvania

Anthony Adams, School of Optometry, University of California, Berkeley

Eliot L. Berson, Berman-Gund Laboratory for the Study of Retinal Degenerations, Harvard Medical School

John E. Dowling, Department of Biology, Harvard University

Julian Hochberg, Department of Psychology, Columbia University

Ken Nakayama, Smith-Kettlewell Institute of Visual Sciences

Luis M. Proenza, Department of Zoology, University of Georgia

Harry Snyder, Department of Industrial Engineering and Operations Research, Virginia Polytechnic Institute and State University

Sponsor Representatives

Constance W. Atwell, National Eye Institute

Allen Dittman, Department of Education

Terrence Dolan, National Science Foundation

James Goodson, Department of the Navy

Leonard Jakubczak, National Institute on Aging

Arthur Jampolsky, American Academy of Ophthalmology

Walton Jones, National Aeronautics and Space Administration

Bruce Leibrecht, Department of the Army

Donald Pitts, American Optometric Association

Vernon Putz-Anderson, National Institute for Occupational Safety and Health

Thomas Tredici, Department of the Air Force

Staff

Key Dismukes, Study Director

Barbara S. Brown, Research Assistant

Llyn M. Ellison, Administrative Secretary

*As of December 1981.

Contents

Contributors and Participants

*Endre A. Balazs [45]
  Department of Ophthalmology, Research Division, College of Physicians and Surgeons, Columbia University, 630 West 168th Street, New York, NY 10032

*James E. Birren [7]
  Andrus Gerontology Center, University of Southern California, University Park, Los Angeles, CA 90007

*Jack Botwinick
  Department of Psychology, Washington University, St. Louis, MO 63130

*Laurence G. Branch [279]
  Department of Social Medicine and Health Policy, Division of Aging, Harvard School of Public Health, 641 Huntington Avenue, Boston, MA 02115

Kenneth R. Brizzee [79]
  Department of Neurobiology, Tulane University; Delta Regional Primate Research Center, Covington, LA 70433

*John H. Carter [121]
  New England College of Optometry, 424 Beacon Street, Boston, MA 02115

*Peter Comalli
  Department of Psychology, Temple University, Philadelphia, PA 19122

*Jack Daubs
  Department of Epidemiology, Harvard School of Public Health, 641 Huntington Avenue, Boston, MA 02115

Janet L. Denlinger [45]
  Department of Ophthalmology, Research Division, College of Physicians and Surgeons, Columbia University, 630 West 168th Street, New York, NY 10032

*Key Dismukes [xv, 3]
  Committee on Vision, National Research Council, 2101 Constitution Avenue, Washington, D.C. 20418

*Jay Enoch
  School of Optometry, University of California, Berkeley, CA 94720

Eleanor E. Faye [301]
  The Lighthouse, The New York Association for the Blind, 121 E. 60th Street, New York, NY 10022

*Participants at Symposium on Aging and Human Visual Function.
The number in brackets following each contributor's name indicates the opening page of that author's article.

*James Fozard
Division of Extended Care, Veterans Administration, Washington, D.C.

*David A. Greenberg [279]
Center for Aging and Vision, New England College of Optometry, 424 Beacon Street, Boston, MA 02115

*William J. Hoyer [245]
Department of Psychology, Syracuse University, Syracuse, NY 13210

*Leonard Jakubczak
National Institute on Aging, National Institutes of Heath, Bethesda, MD 20205

Horton A. Johnson [79]
Department of Pathology, Tulane University, New Orleans, LA 70112

*Donald W. Kline [xv, 3, 231]
Department of Psychology, University of Notre Dame, Notre Dame, IN 46556

*Toichiro Kuwabara
National Eye Institute, National Institutes of Health, Bethesda, MD 20205

*Herschel Leibowitz
Department of Psychology, Pennsylvania State University, University Park, PA 16802

*R. John Leigh [173]
Department of Neurology, Johns Hopkins Hospital, Baltimore, MD 21218

*Sidney Lerman
Department of Ophthalmology, Emory University School of Medicine, Atlanta, GA 30322

Michael F. Marmor [59]
Division of Ophthalmology, School of Medicine, Stanford University, Stanford, CA 94305; Ophthalmology Section, Veterans Administration Medical Center, 3801 Miranda Avenue, Palo Alto, CA 94305

*Kalidas Nandy
Geriatrics Center, Veterans Administration, Bedford, Massachusetts, 01730

*David Newsome
National Eye Institute, National Institutes of Health, Bethesda, MD 20205

*J. Mark Ordy [79]
Department of Pharmacology, Pennwalt Corporation, 755 Jefferson Road, Rochester, NY 14623

Cynthia Owsley [185]
Department of Psychology, Northwestern University, Evanston, IL 60201

*William V. Padula [315]
American Foundation for the Blind, Inc., 15 W. 16th Street, New York, NY 10011

*Leon A. Pastalan [323]
Department of Architecture and Urban Planning, The University of Michigan, Ann Arbor, MI 48109

*Donald G. Pitts [131]
College of Optometry, University of Houston, Houston, TX 77004

Dana J. Plude [245]
Aging and Mental Performance Laboratory, Veterans Administration Out-patient Clinic, 17 Court Street, Boston, MA 02108

*Robert Reinecke
Wills Eye Hospital, 9th and Walnut Streets, Philadelphia, PA 19107

*Barry Robinson [335]
American Association of Retired Persons, 1909 K Street NW, Washington, D.C. 20037

Frank J. Schieber [231]
Department of Psychology, University of Notre Dame, Notre Dame, IN 46556

*Robert Sekuler [xv, 3, 185]
Departments of Psychology, Ophthalmology, Neurobiology/Physiology, Northwestern University, Evanston, IL 60201

*Abraham Spector [27]
Department of Ophthalmology, College of Physicians and Surgeons, Columbia University, 630 West 168th Street, New York, NY 10032

*Martha Storandt [269]
Department of Psychology, Washington University, St. Louis, MO 63130

*David A. Walsh [203]
Department of Psychology, University of Southern California, University Park, Los Angeles, CA 90007

*R.A. Weale [161]
Department of Visual Science, Institute of Ophthalmology, University of London, Judd Street, London WC1H 9QS, England

M. Virtrue Williams [7]
Andrus Gerontology Center, University of Southern California, University Park, Los Angeles, CA 90007

Preface

Aging and Human Visual Function, a symposium sponsored by the Committee on Vision of the National Research Council, took place from March 31 – April 1, 1980 in Washington, D.C. Revised and edited papers from this symposium constitute the core of this volume. An additional paper was solicited from Michael Marmor. The editors have added an overview and interstitial material to provide a framework for the topics discussed. Some of the papers have been updated to include recent research data.

The Committee gratefully acknowledges the major contribution to this symposium by its research assistant, Michelle Eabon. Ms. Eabon undertook an enormous amount of work in arranging the symposium to be a pleasant and productive interaction for the participants. Production of these proceedings was effectively assisted by Llyn Ellison, also on the committee staff.

Funds for this symposium were provided from the general budget of the Committee on Vision, which is supported by the Departments of the Army, Navy, and Air Force, the National Aeronautics and Space Administration, the National Science Foundation, the National Eye Institute, the Office of Special Education, the National Institute on Aging, the National Institute for Occupational Safety and Health, the American Optometric Association, and the American Academy of Ophthalmology. Supplementary funding for the symposium was provided by the National Institute on Aging.

The Committee on Vision is a standing committee of the National Research Council. The committee provides analysis and advice on scientific issues and applied problems involving vision. It also attempts to stimulate the development of visual science and to provide a forum in which basic and applied scientists, engineers, and clinicians can interact. Working groups of the committee study questions that may involve engineering and equipment, physiological and physical optics, neurophysiology, psychophysics, perception, environmental effects on vision, and treatment of visual disorders.

Robert Sekuler
Donald Kline
Key Dismukes

I. OVERVIEW

Aging and Human Visual Function, pages 3–6
© 1982 Alan R. Liss, Inc., 150 Fifth Avenue, New York, NY 10011

Social Issues, Human Needs, and Opportunities for Research on the Effects of Age on Vision: An Overview

Donald Kline, Robert Sekuler, and Key Dismukes

We can interact with our environment effectively only if we can detect, interpret, and respond to sensory information. The loss of sensory abilities severely impairs performance of even the simplest everyday tasks. This is particularly true of visual loss. Unfortunately, the decline of vision with age is a common fact of life. Some people experience severe deterioration of vision with age, and virtually everyone must adjust to some reduction in visual function as he or she gets older. Given the universality of aging and the increasing numbers of older persons in our society, the causes and consequences of visual aging must concern us all.

Both the number and proportion of older people in our society are increasing. In 1900 there were 3.1 million people in the United States over the age of 65 and they made up about 4.1% of the population. By 1980 there were more than 23 million people over 65 and they represented 11% of the population. It is estimated that by 2020, 15.5% of the U.S. population will be over 65 [Siegel, 1980]. This demographic trend is expected to have a major social impact, particularly in such areas as the delivery of health-related services.

The prevalence of many forms of ocular pathology rises sharply with age. Greenberg and Branch (this volume) review data suggesting that among persons over 65, cataracts and glaucoma are roughly eight times more common than in the general population and retinal disorders are six times more common. Roughly 5% of persons over 65 have visual impairments severe enough to prevent them from reading newspaper print even with corrective spectacles. Greenberg and Branch point out that existing data on prevalence and incidence of visual impairment are not very reliable and probably underrepresent the magnitude of this problem.

Fortunately, most people do not experience severe visual impairment, but anyone who lives long enough will encounter a decline in visual functions sufficient to influence their performance of daily tasks to some degree. Losses in both static and dynamic visual acuity are common among older persons. Weale [1961] estimated that the older retina receives only about one-third as much light as does its younger counterpart because of changes in the optical media. The rate of recovery from glare is significantly protracted in older persons [Reading, 1968]. Age also produces decrements in visual field size, visual search performance, and contrast sensitivity (see reviews by Carter and Pitts, this volume); these deteriorations undoubtedly contribute to the decline experienced by older people in performance of everyday tasks such as automobile driving [Panek et al, 1977]. Visual losses can also adversely affect social and psychological well-being. Anderson and Palmore [1974] reported that individuals with poor vision (not correctable to better than 20/50) in both eyes tend to have reduced feelings of self-worth, diminished emotional security, and restricted leisure, group, and work activities. It is little wonder that at least one poll has found the loss of vision second only to cancer as a dreaded consequence of aging [cf Cogan, 1979].

Although visual decline is clearly associated with age, we do not know a great deal about the processes involved and we understand even less well their impact on the lives of older persons. The symposium upon which this book is based was intended to review what is currently known about visual changes with age and to examine the effects of these changes on an individual's well-being. We also wished to explore the gaps in our knowledge in order to better delineate the needs for research in both basic and applied aspects of age-related alterations in visual function.

We hope that alerting vision scientists to some opportunities and needs associated with studying the effects of age on vision will encourage them to undertake research in this field. In order for this research to be effective, vision scientists need to be aware that there are special problems associated with the study of aging. These problems are encountered at various levels: the optics of the aging eye, psychophysical methodology, experimental design in attempting to separate cohort differences from age differences, etc. Such practical problems as finding and working with elderly subjects are also encountered. Storandt (this volume) discusses a number of the problems that vision scientists face in entering this field. An unanticipated outcome of the symposium was identifying the need for additional training of professionals in certain areas: For example, students in the vision science are generally given little exposure to gerontological or epidemiological issues.

The lines between many disciplines must be crossed in order to effectively study the effects of age on visual functions and performances. Unfortunately, interaction among professionals from different disciplines has been limited in this field. A major aim of the symposium was to bring together professionals to learn about work and issues outside their own disciplines. Contributors to the symposium came from anatomy, ophthalmology, optometry, physiology, neurology, psychology, epidemiology, gerontology, and architecture. We hoped that this interaction would eventually lead to interdisciplinary research, which is sorely needed. For example, although the effects of age on such basic visual functions as acuity and light-dark adaptation have been described fairly well at the phenomenological level, we can say very little about the anatomical and physiological bases of these effects. Attempts to relate the effects of age on visual function to structural alterations should be encouraged, but caution is needed in this effort. Psychophysicists and physiologists have often erred by prematurely and simplistically assuming causal relationships among phenomena at different levels of brain organization. The relations between the effects of age on visual structures and on visual functions are likely to be highly complex.

There is especial need in the study of vision and aging for interaction between clinicians and visual scientists. Increased interaction might reveal new opportunities for applying basic science techniques—for instance, psychophysical measures—to clinical problems [cf Proenza et al, 1981]. Clinical data may be of considerable value to basic research scientists. Unfortunately, these data are often not in a form useful for research. Greenberg and Branch (this volume) point out the need for standardizing conditions and reports of clinical measurement of visual functions. Attention must also be given to selecting valid measurements that have functional relevance.

The study of vision and aging cannot be disentangled from its social implications. Unfortunately, there has been little interaction between those concerned with the delivery of social services and those in the vision science community. Greater familiarity with the daily living problems encountered by persons with deteriorating vision might influence vision scientists to develop and emphasize research relevant to those problems. The papers of Padula and Pastalan (this volume) demonstrate many opportunities for applied vision research that would contribute to the well-being both of the elderly and of younger people with visual impairment. One potentially fruitful approach would be to establish teams composed of vision scientists, clinicians, and service deliverers (eg, rehabilitation counselors) who would collaborate toward applied research on the problems of vision and aging.

The study of vision and aging is in an early stage of development. Most of the challenges it presents remain to be faced. Current research focuses on the changes that age produces in the structure and function of the visual system and on ocular pathologies associated with aging. The symposium pointed to several research issues that need more attention. Approaches are needed for relating the changes with age observed in visual structures, basic sensory functions, and perceptual processes. This effort would be facilitated by multivariate techniques such as concomitant measurement of sensory-perceptual functions and electrophysiological activity. The contributions of health, nutrition, experience, and other environmental variables to age differences observed in visual performance need to be explored more deeply. There has been little research on the effects of visual decline on individual well-being and daily living. We need to determine the extent to which individuals can compensate for a decline in visual functions and whether these compensatory skills can be taught. Related to these problems is an urgent need to develop techniques for assessing the performance of visual tasks. There is an enormous gap between an individual's ability to perform the visual functions measured in the laboratory or clinic and his or her ability to perform real-world tasks. Perhaps most important is an overriding need for explicit theories to guide research into the nature, causes, and consequences of visual changes with age.

Research on vision and aging presents an interesting set of questions. In addition, this research can improve our understanding of basic visual processes and contribute to the advancement of general theories for vision. For example, age-related changes in vision can be used as natural experiments providing data unobtainable in laboratory experiments. Theories of visual and perceptual function should be examined for compatibility with observed age differences in visual function and task performance.

We have grouped the papers of this book into five broad themes: anatomical and physiological alterations, changes in basic visual functions, changes in perception and information processing, methodological issues, and the human impact of visual changes with age. None of these sections is intended as a comprehensive treatment of the area. More exhaustive treatments, particularly of ocular pathology, can be found in books written for specialty audiences. This book is intended to illustrate the work and issues in each of these five areas in order to give the reader a sense of the scope of the problems involved in vision and aging. A diversity of style and emphasis will be noticed among the sections of this book. That diversity reflects in part the different approaches taken in the several fields involved in the study of vision and aging and illustrates one of the problems of interdisciplinary communication. We hope that this book will assist readers in beginning their own exploration of the interrelations of these topics and of the possibility of developing better interdisciplinary approaches.

REFERENCES

Anderson B, Palmore E (1974) Longitudinal evaluation of ocular function. In E Palmore (Ed) "Normal aging." Durham, NC: Duke University Press.

Cogan DG (1979) Summary and Conclusions. In SS Han and DH Coons (Eds) "Special senses in aging." Ann Arbor: University of Michigan Press.

Panek PE, Barrett GV, Sterns HL, Alexander RA (1977) A review of age changes in perceptual information ability with regard to driving. Exp Aging Res 3(6):387–449.

Reading V (1968) Disability glare and age. Vision Res 8:207–214.

Siegel JS (1980) Recent and prospective trends for the elderly population and some implications for health care. In SG Haynes and M Feinleib (Eds) "Second conference on the epidemiology of aging." Washington, DC: US Dept of Health and Human Services (NIH Publication No 80969).

Aging and Human Visual Function, pages 7–19
© 1982 Alan R. Liss, Inc., 150 Fifth Avenue, New York, NY 10011

A Perspective on Aging and Visual Function

James E. Birren and M. Virtrue Williams

HISTORY

Researchers from many disciplines have noted for over 100 years that visual dysfunctions are associated with advancing age. The early literature reflects the tendency to characterize visual change with age in terms of a single factor, the lens. In the last century, the length of life was largely viewed as adventitious. Aging was looked on not as an organized set of phenomena but rather as a collection of random assaults, possibly because the main causes of death then were infectious diseases.

In the 1870s Frances Galton organized a health exposition in London through which passed thousands of people on whom many different anthropometric measurements were made; among these were measurements of visual and auditory acuity and speed of movement. There were not, however, many academicians who emulated this approach of putting visual function in the context of other functions of the organism. The earlier literature on age and vision was reviewed by Jonas Friedenwald [1942], who made an attempt to place issues of age and vision in a "life sciences" context. His review appeared in the book "Problems of Ageing," edited by E.V. Cowdry. This book reflected the emergence during the 1930s of a life science, or gerontological, point of view in which various phenomena of aging were examined for underlying processes. Friedenwald presented his 1942 literature review under the title "The Eye"; his work reflected a residual 19th century emphasis on the eye as a peripheral structure much like a camera, having specialized parts, some of which show defects with advancing age. In the last century and even up until 1940, research literature emphasized the anatomical changes with age in the specialized structures of the eye: the cornea, lens, vitreous humor, retina and other components. Later investigations were made on functional aspects of vision such as size of the visual field, dark adaptation, and visual flicker fusion.

Friedenwald reviewed five studies from the last century on the relation of visual acuity to age. The studies as a group indicated a rather uniform decline in visual acuity with advancing age. Some of these studies made attempts to exclude the contributions of identifiable disease from the relationship of visual acuity to age. Friendenwald also attempted to determine whether the useful life span of vision was longer or shorter than the potential life span of the organism. "Total loss of function of the eye, i.e., blindness, may be taken as equivalent to death of the organ" [p 536]. Using 1916 census data, he compared survival of visual function with survival of individuals. He inferred that the potential life span for vision was longer than the life span of the organism and that the number of survivors with vision would not reach zero before the age of 120 to 130 years. He noted, however, that the census data probably underestimated the amount of blindness. He also pointed out that blind persons were less likely to survive, although he did not estimate the extent of this influence. Clearly, if disease exists in an individual, it may be expressed in impaired vision, a shorter length of remaining life, and in increasing liability to accidents. Therefore, it is difficult to separate quantitatively the effects of age-related disease, the greater disposition of blind persons to accidents, and any intrinsic relation between age and visual function. Longitudinal studies of cohorts of individuals are the only sources of data that can separate these effects in greater detail. Unfortunately, such studies on representative populations have not been undertaken.

Prior to 1900, the literature on vision and aging focused mainly on specific visual defects arising from disease, primarily cataracts, glaucoma, and diseases of the cornea. With the growth of ophthalmology, much of the early literature relates to reports of surgical operations in clinical settings. Early ophthalmology journals devote more space to reports on the young diseased eye than on the aged eye, although Knapp [1881] reported, as a result of his analysis of 700 cataract extractions, that older patients responded well to cataract surgery. Also, Baker [1885] reported successful removals of cataracts in old persons. Changes in the lens were discussed by Smith [1879], who believed that at about age 50 there is a change in the shape of the lens. In 1886 he also reported on the relationship between primary glaucoma and age in 1000 cases. Fewer than 1% of the affected individuals were under the age of 20, and the percentage increased each decade until the seventh, when it appeared to diminish. He believed that the probability of developing glaucoma between the ages of 60 and 70 was twice as great as it was between 40 and 50. Smith also made observations about the relations of age to six differences in cornea alterations (1880).

The accommodative capacity of the lens to focus on near and far objects has been studied systematically with relation to age. Greater muscular effort is required to obtain focus when the lens becomes rigid, as it does with age. The older fibers apparently constitute the center of the lens and the young fibers are added at the periphery or on top of the older layers. The periphery or surface of the lens is softer and more pliable and is the portion of the lens involved in accommodation. Bernstein [1932] thought that individual differences in accommodation were related to length of life and reported a positive correlation between longevity and accommodation, Whether this correlation reflects a fundamental biological process is open to question: Bernstein's correlation between accommodation and length of life was obtained at a time when the average length of life was much shorter. Now, many persons live long after their accommodative power has been largely lost. If accommodation were in some way intrinsically related to length of life, accommodative power should increasingly extend into the later years as the average length of life increased, and there appears to be no evidence for this.

Weiss [1959] in his interpretation of the early literature concluded that maximum accommodation of the lens decreases from age 5, when it is about 20 diopters, until age 60, when it is about one-half diopter. It is possible that the increasing rigidity of the lens with age is an isolated phenomenon related to the lens's unique morphology and not to aging of the rest of the organism. If so, lens rigidity may be only an annoying accompaniment of old age much like balding or grayness of the hair, which are not indicators of life-threatening processes.

In addition to Friedenwald [1942] and Weiss [1959], Weale [1963] and Fozard et al [1977] have provided useful reviews of literature and discussion of issues.

EPIDEMIOLOGY

Data from a range of sources and historical periods shows increasing visual dysfunction with age in the population. Admittedly, population surveys of vision may be criticized on several bases, such as sampling criteria of subject selection, failure to specify the characteristics of health and demographic characteristics of the subjects, inadequate number of subjects, and lack of standardized measurements. However, it would be grossly inappropriate to deny that visual dysfunctions increase with age to a level constituting a serious issue for many older persons and warranting the attention of both applied and basic investigators.

The Journal of Visual Impairment and Blindness has published a number of statistical briefs giving us some estimates of the extent of severe visual dysfunction in the population. Two sources of data have been compared in the Journal. One is from a 16-state model reporting areas and concerns of the legally blind. The definition of blindness in this case was 20/200 being power vision in the better eye with best correction or the widest angle of the visual field being no greater than 20°. The other data source was the National Center for Health Statistics, which conducted an interview survey of national households. In this case, severe visual impairment was defined as the inability to read newsprint. Using the model reporting area with its criterion of distance vision, it was found that 73% of the legally blind were over the age of 45 years. Using the other criterion of severe visual impairment, that used by the National Center for Health

Statistics (reading newsprint), about 91% of the severely visually impaired were over the age of 45 years. In 1971, the estimated number of severely visually impaired persons in the .United States was 1,306,000. Of these, over two-thirds (68%) were above the age of 65—about 884,000 persons in contrast to 422,000 under the age of 65. Using the criterion of the 16-state model reporting area of the legally blind, it was estimated that 46% of the legally blind were over the age of 65 years.

Thus, at least half of the population with severe visual dysfunction are over the age of 65, although that age group accounts for only about 11% of the total population. Of those over 65, those defined as visually impaired or legally blind are much more likely to be female than male. In part, this statistic may be attributable to the higher proportion of women in the over-65 age group. However, if vision is linked with primary processes governing longevity, as Friendenwald [1942] held, then one would expect a higher proportion of severe visual dysfunction in males than in females of the same age.

On the other hand, if one examines the population of persons reporting visual loss as the main cause of their limitation in activity, one finds a preponderance of men. Rather than different levels of visual dysfunction in the sexes, this finding may reflect different expectations about adequate behavior in work situations compared with home or school situations. Perhaps working-age males more readily consider themselves visually handicapped than do females of the same age. The same impairment may differentially handicap an individual depending upon social demands [Peterson et al, 1978]. Clearly, the physical and social circumstances of the individual are important in determining the extent to which visual impairment is disabling.

In considering projections of the number of severely visually impaired persons in the population, one should note that the proportion of the very aged is increasing. Between 1977 and 2000, the population of individuals aged 75 to 84 years was projected to increase by 56%, but those over the age of 85 were projected to increase by 84%. Given the higher incidence of legal blindness or severe visual impairment with age, a very large number of older persons with visual dysfunction may be anticipated. By the year 2000, the estimated number of legally blind persons over 65 will be 367,000 and the number of persons with severe impairment, 1,756,000.

Not only is visual impairment clearly associated with age, it is also associated with family income. Severe visual impairment per 1000 persons aged 65 and over was found to be about twice as frequent in families with annual incomes of less than $3000 as in families with annual incomes of $10,000 or more [Kirschner and Peterson, 1979].

Although age is the single best demographic predictor of blindness, it is clear that income is also a strong indicator. A third indicator can be derived from the association of visual impairment with other physical impairments, including deafness, speech impairment, learning disability, and paralysis. A visually impaired person *under* 65 is most likely to have visual impairment alone, whereas in the *over*-65 group, visual impairment is twice as likely to be associated with other physical or sensory impairments as it is to occur alone [Kirschner and Peterson, 1979]. Obviously, in the design of environments for older persons, one must consider visual impairment in the context of other coexisting impairments.

The present brief discussion of the demography of visual impairment of the elderly was designed to present a perspective on visual function and age and does not consider specific diseases. Many factors contribute to the effects of age, including exposure to occupational hazards during the work life, which may be of especial concern with the low-income group. Another consideration not possible to develop at length here, is the demographic effect of the occurrence of visual impairments in persons who die early in life and are thus removed from the population of older adults who can be studied. Visual impairment can be associated with a variety of diseases, many of which can shorten the length of life significantly. The effect of such selection on observed visual impairment rates with age is not clear. Consider, for example, the sometimes-expressed opinion that the wide use of antibiotics allows less biologically fit individuals to survive to the later years. If the use of antibiotics allows less biologically fit individuals to survive to the later years. If the use of antibiotics is a factor in survival, then one might expect to find increasing age-specific visual impairment in the older years as the older population becomes less fit. At present, epidemiological data are insufficient to draw inferences as to whether visual impairment is increasing or decreasing in specific age groups. Future studies might evaluate an accumulation hypothesis in which visual impairment accumulates in the upper age groups, in comparison with a hypothesis of an intrinsic age relationship with visual impairment dependent upon a dynamic physiological process.

Relationships between mental status and vision were explored in a small pilot study in which there appeared to be an association between mental impairment and poor vision [Snyder et al, 1976]. It was not resolved whether poor mental status results from the visual impairment or whether both are related to a third unidentified variable, such as degenerative disease, which may be differentially related to sex, social class, and occupational subgroups.

AGING AND THE NEUROSCIENCE OF VISION

Vision is a behavior, a complex function of neural structures, biochemistry, physiology, and learning. Therefore, understanding the relation of visual functioning to age requires integrative efforts from many disciplines. A neuroscience approach to vision can expect eventually to answer the question "How is visual behavior organized?" Introducing the additional variable of age, however, implies change over time and the question becomes more complex: "How does visual behavior, over time, become organized?" Such a question seems unlikely to be answered in terms of the earlier, highly specific studies of age and vision and in terms of the view of vision as a passive transfer of light images to the brain. A contemporary neuroscience approach, however, appears promising as a way of going beyond the conforming effects of the methods and knowledge of single disciplines.

With the exception of researchers specifically interested in behavior, 19th century scientists took acuity as the measure of visual function. The predominant model of vision remained that of René Descartes' "camera obscura." Explanations for loss of visual acuity with age were sought in the poor optics of the camera itself, ie, the eye. A catalog of what appeared to be normal age-related changes, such as reduction in pupil diameter and restriction of accommodation, followed such investigation. The need to distinguish incipient pathology from a primary senile change has spurred detailed analysis, such as protein analysis of the lens and cornea and detailed study of animal retinal change, and much of this work continues with modern biochemical and anatomical methods.

An exhaustive enumeration of all the age changes found in the visual system would be prohibitively long. It is, perhaps, safe to state that each level of the visual system does show some type of decline in functioning, and these changes are discussed in detail in later chapters. In sum, several types of change appear across age in the visual system: a loss in the amount and fidelity of light transmission to the retina, a loss in the responsiveness and number of the retinal receptors and neurons at later stages in the visual pathway and in efferent visual control systems, and a loss of integrity of support tissues and cells, eg, basement membranes and vascular structures. From a neuroscience point of view, one of the more interesting recent findings is by Govoni and co-workers [1977], who reported a loss with age of retinal dopamine receptor sensitivity in the retinas of rats. This finding may suggest a general trend of decline with age in the dopaminergic system in which the retinal changes parallel those in the rest of the nervous system. Finch and co-workers [see Finch, 1977] have reported several age changes in the dopaminergic system in the substantia nigra of the mouse.

As mentioned earlier, one of the first major studies of visual performance across the life span was by Sir Francis Galton. Analysis of this data by Koga and Morant [1923] in many ways anticipated modern trends in research on visual function with age. Koga and Morant concluded that while there was a significant decline in visual acuity with age, it could not account for lower performance of the old in a visual reaction-time task. This has been a general trend of findings of age and vision: Specific deficits do not account for the overall performance decrements.

In an article on the eye and age—a topic much more circumscribed than vision and age—Weale [1978] stated, "Precisely because the advances are far and wide, it may be prudent to select—quite arbitrarily—a small number of widely differing fields which may help to illustrate some of the ideas which it may be useful to explore" (p 1). Clearly, if that is the prudent approach for the eye and age, it must be seen as even more prudent for the study of vision. Our general thesis is that the field of visual research in aging has followed a path from the specific to the general and from the particulate to the interactive. To be sure, there are counterexamples to such a broad statement, but the trend will in all probability continue, for several reasons.

The second third of this century has seen a lessening of the expectation for a rigid localization of function within the central nervous system. This view has been replaced by one which sees the brain as highly interactive. In a similar vein, since 1960 the Cartesian view of vision, which depicted the brain as a passive recipient of the pictures from its camera eye, has declined as a research model. Neurobehavioral work such as that by Hubel and Wiesel [1959] has led to new theories on the nature of vision and behavior. Schneider's Two Visual Systems model in neuroanatomy, Neisser's Information Processing approach, and Gibson's [1966] Perceptual Systems models illustrate conceptual developments since 1960.

The import of these new conceptual frameworks to the study of age and vision can be illustrated by several examples. Dru et al [1975] investigated visual recovery of function in young and old hooded rats, using an extension of the procedures of Held and Hein's investigation of early visual experience in young kittens. Dru demonstrated that recovery of visual discrimination function in the adult does not require both visual and motor experience during the recovery period. An important finding was that the plasticity necessary for functional recovery extended into the rat's senescent period. Equally important was the demonstration that visual discrimination needs both pattern stimuli—hence activity of the classic visual pathway—and movement—hence activity of kinesthetic and vestibular pathways. By implication, visual effects might be influenced by the impairment of neural function in systems not involved in the classic visual system. Furthermore, since age decrements in postural balance are known to occur because of compromised blood flow through the vertebral arteries and to the inner ear, assaults on visual system integrity may have exacerbated the effects of lowered efficiency of secondary sensory input.

The effect of changing theoretical models in psychology on understanding vision and age is illustrated in a series of studies by Walsh and co-workers [Hertzog et al, 1976; Walsh, 1976; Walsh et al, 1978; Walsh and Thompson, 1978; Walsh et al, 1979]. These studies along with work by other laboratories, notably Kline's [Kline and Birren, 1975; Kline and Szafran, 1975] have pointed to a series of visual processing stages, each showing the disturbing effects of age. Neisser's model [1967], Sequential Information Processing, was expanded and demonstrated experimentally by Turvey [1973]. This model is interesting in part because of its close association with physiological theories of visual information processing [Brietmeyer and Ganz, 1976; Brietmeyer, 1980]. The model holds that a number of stages in the information processing sequence are functional correlates of visual anatomical processes.

Thus for each of the visual information processing stages investigated, changes have been shown to occur for older groups in reliable and predictable ways. The information-processing model has allowed the tracing of age changes in vision from the eye, with its age-associated structural changes, into central visual structures. The pattern of change found in this manner is such that Williams [1979] has suggested that all the slowing in visual reaction time reported by Galton (discussed above) can be attributed to a pattern of diffuse slowing across discrete stages of visual information processing. However, the nature of the organization of these changes remains to be described.

Early interest in visual changes with age was largely concerned with changes in acuity and it was expected that loss of acuity with age was a result of changes in the optical properties of the eye. Weale [1975], in an insightful analysis, attempted to account for the loss of acuity, as measured by the Snellen Chart, on the basis of known changes in the eye. Estimates of cell loss in receptors were included in his analysis. He was unable to account for age-related loss in acuity by this analysis. Weal concluded that explaining the acuity loss requires a decrease in functional cells through at least four and possibly as many as seven stages of visual processing. Weale made the restrictive assumption that the cell loss is uniform in rate and diffuse in character. This is a reasonable initial assumption, but if it is incorrect, the organization of functional loss with age becomes a moot question if the changes extend beyond the retina.

Our view is that the combination of historic trend and our grasp of the nature of aging itself makes a systematic neuroscience approach to vision inevitable. While it is necessary to understand specific functional components of the visual system, behavior (and hence vision) requires cross-classification of numerous internal and external sensory cues. One might expect breakdowns of specific systems in disease states, but it now seems improbable that only one system would age while others remained invariant. Therefore, a clear picture of age change is best sought in the interactions of systems.

AGE, VISION, AND ENVIRONMENTAL INTERACTIONS

Whether a visual dysfunction results in an impairment depends in part on the environmental demands on an individual. A blind person living in a circumscribed neighborhood is less likely to be limited in activity than is a person required to take a bus and cross many geographic barriers. The social and physical context of visual impairment is as important as the dysfunction itself. The consequences of change in vision, as in other age-related changes, must be viewed in terms of the reciprocal effects between one's visual status and the physical and social environment.

The visual system, as with other tissues, is subject to such influences as circulation and nutrition. The retina, morphologically a part of the brain, may also show intrinsic characteristics in common with other vital tissues and may be used to develop an index or measure of biological age. Increasingly, measurements of visual function are being made on individuals in relation to other functions, and it is important to review some of the data that have been fathered on a wide range of functions in individuals of a broad age range. One group of studies has examined sensory functions and behavioral capacities such as memory and reasoning, as well as physiological variables in a wide range of individuals. Measures of hearing, vision, reaction time, respiratory vital capacity, and blood pressure have been found to be highly correlated with age.

Dirken and his colleagues [Dirken, 1972] analyzed results of a battery of measurements requiring about 1¼ hour for each person. A cluster of measurements showed a multiple correlation of 0.87 with chronological age. These included auditory pitch ceiling, figure comprehension, choice reaction time, accuracy in semantic categorization, maximum breathing frequency, maximum systolic pressure, aerobic capacity, and forced expiratory volume. Included in the study sample were 316 male industrial workers aged 30 to 70 years. The investigators developed an index that was highly related to chronological age and that could presumably serve as a predictor of the functional capacities of individuals in a work context. Remarkably parallel findings were obtained by Heron and Chown [1967], who made sensory, behavioral, and physiological measurements of 540 men and women ranging in age from 20 to 70. In both studies there was remarkable convergence of evidence that psychological and physiological variables are closely linked in their relationship with age.

Since limitations of sensory function in older persons are likely to occur together with changes in cognitive capacity, our perspective on an individual's adaptation to the environment requires that we examine visual change together with a constellation of changes related to the central nervous system, both as to cause and as to consequence. Thus a broad natural science view of the relationships between visual function and age is required.

Important issues remain in creating environments for the impaired aged in which the consequences of their visual and other concurrent disabilities are minimized. Research is needed to identify those characteristics of the environment and of individuals that lead to optimum functioning. Studies of the contrasts between successfully adapting and poorly adapting older adults with visual dysfunctions may be useful. While it is possible that individuals who adapt poorly to their environments may have concurrent multiple impairments of the nervous system, it is also possible that the effects of multiple impairments are minimized by self-confident individuals living in a socially supportive environment. If the environmental demands on impaired older persons are excessive, then not only will the aged fail to develop necessary skills, but also they may regress. Visual dysfunctions in older persons, then, are expected to have different outcomes depending on the interaction between the social and physical environment in concert with the motivational, affective, and cognitive qualities of the individual. There are two sets needing further analysis of issues: the characteristics of the social and physical environments of older persons and the nature of the organization of behavior.

Visual memory is one of the visual system that can most affect the life of an older person. Renewed interest in Tolman's original concept of cognitive maps has led to the demonstration that a spatial-visual matrix guides a person through the environment. It is clear from the work of several investigators [Lynch, 1960; Neisser, 1967] that internal representations of the environment are not simple Cartesian topographic transformations of visual-location information, but rather include a variety of usage, aesthetic, and emotive data related to the person's environment. Recent research suggests that these maps not only represent topographic distortion due to a variety of historical influences on the individual, but they can be influenced by the person's visual-spatial ability. In a series of studies by Krauss and her co-workers [Krauss and Quayhagen, 1977; Awad et al, 1979; Krauss et al, 1980; Stafford and Krauss, 1980], the complex interrelation of visual-spatial ability and spatial memory has been shown to result in dramatic impact on an older individual's use of the physical environment. Whereas maintenance of cognitive skill results in an expanded concept and increased use of physical space, a decline in skill results in decreased use of personal space and reduced social and physical interaction.

There are both research and service opportunities in trying to maximize effective adaptation and minimize chronic maladaptive consequences of visual dysfunction. Helping older individuals to disengage from personal and contextual restraints is a relatively new subject.

Sorting out the various environmental and concurrent physiological changes associated with advancing age is a slow empirical process that involves some issues not commonly found in experimental studies. For one thing, many aspects of humans and their environments change with advancing age. Because of the large number of variables, investigators may perceive no organization to the changes and essentially adopt a "noise" explanation holding that with age, the organism undergoes a random degradation of function. For some phenomena this may indeed be the case and furthermore, accidents may occur whose consequences accumulate over time but cannot be predicted as to timing or magnitude. Other instances may involve a cluster of age changes that rest upon a common metabolic process. Advances in neurochemical methodology may soon give us insight into age changes in general and in particular, regional metabolism of the brain, including that involved in sensory functions [Sokoloff, 1979].

We should be sensitive to the possibility of independent aging phenomena that coexist in the aging organism. These may be called *age co-existing independent phenomena*. Other functions may show mutual effects and may be called *age co-existing dependent phenomena*. If both cataract formation and muscular degeneration were age co-existing dependent phenomena, then removal of a lens would have little chance to benefit the patient. The fact that lens removal alone restores vision to many persons shows that changes in the lens and the retina are not closely interdependent on a single underlying physiological process with age.

Another important point is that an entire cohort of newborns does not survive into later years. Selective mortality may influence associations obtained between variables at high ages compared with those for low age groups. Since the composition of the population available for study changes with time, primary phenomena of aging may be distorted or masked. Perception and adaptation involve the entirety of the organism to which the eyes are attached.

SUMMARY

Changes in visual function with age appear to be tied to many concurrent anatomical, physiological, and psychological processes. For this reason the model or approach of the neurosciences may be used to advantage in this field. Clearly an explosion of knowledge is occurring in the neurosciences, a field in which students of morphology, biochemistry, physiology, and behavior interact. It would seem that vision research is moving toward the type of science that has evolved in the second half of this century, in which the significance of anatomical description is derived largely from its contribution to the mutual understanding of physiological, biochemical, and behavioral function. In turn, each of the sciences is gradually converging on the principles of organizational structure and function.

Science, like all human enterprise, is a social process and one can at best point out its apparent path. In this paper we have noted the social, humanitarian, and scientific imperatives that are now leading to a new interest in the field of aging and vision. We have also attempted to delineate what we believe are current trends in the structure of scientific theory and practice. This structure is leading to interactive models of behavior and physiology, individual and environmental. It has inevitably produced collaboration among neuroscientists in different fields. We believe that these trends are productive and will continue.

This volume reviews a wide sample of current work in the field of vision and aging. To be sure, each field has unique interests. However, it is our belief that the interactive trend in science and the cross-disciplinary dissemination of information represented by this volume will inevitably lead to more collaborative and significant research in the study of vision and aging.

REFERENCES

Awad AZ, McCormick DJ, Ohta RJ, Krauss IK (1979) Neighborhood knowledge of the elderly: Psychological and environmental correlates. Presented at Gerontological Society Annual Meeting, Washington.

Baker AR (1885) A report of twenty-seven consecutive cases of senile cataract operated on by the Von Graefe modified linear extraction. Ophthal 2:15–21.

Bernstein, F (1932) Alterssicktigkeit and Lebenserwartung. Forsch Fortschr 8:272–273.

Birren JE, Bernstein L (1978) Health and aging in our society: Perspectives on mortality and the emergence of geriatrics. Trans Assoc Life Insur Med Dir Am 62:135–152.

Brietmeyer B (1980) Unmasking visual masking: A look at the "why" behind the veil of the "how." Psychol Rev 87:52–69.

Brietmeyer BG, & Ganz, L (1976) Implication of sustained and transient channels for theories of visual pattern masking, saccadic suppresion, and information processing. Psychol Rev 83:1–36.

Dirken, JM (Ed) (1972) "Functional Age of Industrial Workers." Groningen: Walters–Nordhoff.

Dru D, Walker JP, Walker JP (1975) Self-produced locomotion restores visual capacity after striate lesions. Science 187:265–266.

Finch CE (1977) Neuroendocrine and autonomic aspects of aging. In Finch CE and Hayflick L (Eds) "Handbook of the Biology of Aging." New York: Van Nostrand, pp 262–274.

Fozard JL, Wolf E, Bell B, McFarland RA, and Podolsky S (1977) Visual perception and communication. In Birren JE and Schaie KW (Eds) "Handbook of the Psychology of Aging." New York: Van Nostrand, pp 497–534.

Friedenwald JS (1942) The eye. In Cowdry EV (Ed) "Problems of Ageing." Baltimore: Williams and Wilkins, pp 535–555.

Gibson JJ (1966) "The Senses Considered as Perceptual Systems." Boston: Houghton Mifflin.

Govoni S, Loddo P, Spano PF, Trabucchi M (1977) Dopamine receptor sensitivity in brain and retina of rats during aging. Brain Res 138:565–570.

Heron A, Chown S (1967) "Age and Function." London: Churchill.

Hertzog CK, Williams MV, Walsh DA (1976) The effect of practice on age differences in central perceptual processing. J Gerontol 31:428–433.

Hubel DH, Wiesel, TN (1959) Receptive fields of single neurons in the cat's striate cortex. J Physiol 148:579–591.

Kirchner C, Peterson R (1979) The latest data on visual disability from NCHS. Vis Impair Blind April:151–153.

Kline DW, Birren JE (1975) Age differences in backward monoptic visual masking. Exp Aging Res 1:17–25.

Kline DW, and Szafran J (1975) Age differences in backward monoptic visual noise masking. J Gerontol 30:307–311.

Knapp H (1881) Report of seven hundred cataract extractions. With historical and critical remarks, particularly on the peripheral opening of the capsule. Arch Ophthalmol 10:295.

Koga Y, Morant GM (1923) On the degree of association between reaction times in the case of different senses. Biometrika 15:346–372.

Krauss IK, Quayhagen M (1977) Components of spatial cognition. Presented at: Gerontological Society Annual Meeting, San Francisco.

Krauss IK, Quayhagen M, Schaie KW (1980) Spatial rotation in the elderly: Performance factors. J Gerontol 35:199–206.

Lynch K (1960) "The Image of the City." Boston: MIT Press.

Neisser U (1967) "Cognitive Psychology." New York: Appleton.

Peterson R, Lowman C, Kirchner C (1978) Visual handicap: Statistical data on a social process. Vis Impair Blind Dec:419–421.

Smith P (1879) "Glaucoma: Its Causes, Symptoms, Pathology, and Treatment." London: Churchill.

Snyder LH, Pyrek J, Smith KA (1976) Vision and mental function of the elderly. Gerontologist 16(6):491–495.

Sokoloff L (1979) Effects of normal aging on cerebral circulation and energy metabolism. In Hoffmeister F and Müller C (Eds) "Brain Function in Old Age: EValuation of Changes and Disorders." Berlin: Springer-Verlag, pp 367–380.

Stafford JL, Krauss IK (1980) Spatial ability and environmental knowledge among the elderly. Presented at Western Psychological Association Annual Meeting, Honolulu.

Turvey MT (1973) On peripheral and central processes in vision: Inferences from an information-processing analysis on masking with pattern stimuli. Psychol Rev 80:1–52.

U.S. Dept Health, Education, and Welfare (1971) "Prevalence of Selected Impairments." Washington, D.C.: DHEW Publication No (HRA), 75–1526.

Walsh DA (1976) Age differences in central perceptual processing: A dichoptic backward masking investigation. J Gerontol 31:181–188.

Walsh DA, Thompson LW (1978) Age differences in visual sensory memory. J Gerontol 33:383–387.

Walsh DA, Till RE, Williams MV (1978) Age differences in peripheral perceptual processing: A monoptic backward masking investigation. J Exp Psychol [Hum Percept] 4:232–243.

Walsh DA, Hertzog CK, Williams MV (1979) Age-related differences in two stages of central perceptual processes: The effects of short target durations and criterion differences. J Gerontol 34:241–243.

Weale RA (1963) "The Aging Eye." London: Lewis.

Weiss AP (1959) Sensory Functions. In Birren JI (Ed) "Handbook of Aging and the Individual." Chicago: Univ of Chicago Press, pp 503–542.

Williams MV (1979) Age differences in speed of information processing. Presented at American Psychological Association 87th Annual Convention, New York.

II. ANATOMICAL AND PHYSIOLOGICAL CHANGES IN THE VISUAL SYSTEM

Aging and Human Visual Function, pages 23–26
© 1982 Alan R. Liss, Inc., 150 Fifth Avenue, New York, NY 10011

Introduction

Because aging is usually related to a single independent variable—the passage of time—it is easy to consider aging as though it were a unitary process. But examining how the various tissues of the eye change as we grow older reminds us that each tissue ages in its own way and according to its own timetable. The idiosyncratic character of aging in each tissue is related to that tissue's structure and position within the eye.

Dr. Balazs uses a dramatic metaphor in his paper to distinguish between aging in closed and open systems: "Neuronal cells of the retina do not accumulate aging pigment (lipofuscin) and do not show any signs of aging. They instead commit suicide. But in the central nervous system we know that many ganglion cells . . . show the accumulation of those waste pigments. But in the retina we don't see [such accumulation] at all except in the pigmented epithelial cells."

The lens of the eye ages as a system that is basically closed. Since the lens does not lose cells as it ages, at any one moment during its life span, the lens contains cell cohorts of all ages. Its nucleus consists of cells that it has had since early fetal life, while its cortex consists of recent additions.

The changing optical interfaces among these cohorts alter the lens's image-forming ability. It is not hard to imagine that the laws governing the aging of such a closed system might differ from those governing other types of systems. For example, the lens has to live with its own errors. Cells that become dysplastic or oxidized remain an integral part of the lens for that lifetime. As a result, once damage has been suffered and optical performance altered, there is relatively little opportunity for the tissue to rid itself of the offending cells.

This process contrasts with the first-in, first-out principle that governs the aging of photoreceptors. In this system, the rod outer segments in the mammalian sensory retina consist of a stack of discs containing the photosensitive molecules, rhodopsin. Depending upon the light conditions and metabolic status of the organism, over the course of several weeks, a disc is first created at the proximal portion of the outer segment and then moves up in the stack todward the distal end of the outer segment. Over time, older discs are sloughed off at the top of the stack and are phagocytized in the pigment epithelium. Thus the complement of discs present at any one moment during the lifetime of the sensory cell is altogether different from the complement of discs present 6 months earlier. This is the remarkable renewal process that characterizes aging in the open system of the sensory retina [Young, 1981].

The renewal process allows the retina to rid itself of mistakes or the effects of some environmental insults. For example, if the organism had a vitamin-A deficient diet over a short time, the rhodopsin-deficient discs produced during that period would eventually be replaced by "better" ones. Of course, when it ages, this kind of open system has special properties: It is particularly dependent on neighboring tissues for housekeeping—eg, the garbage collection service of the pigment epithelium.

What are the implications of ocular changes for visual function? Seeing requires that light be transmitted through the eye's media to the photoreceptors. Seeing also requires that an image of reasonable spatial definition be formed on the photoreceptor array. Since the tissues and fluids through which light must pass age at different rates and in different ways, the net effect of their aging is an aggregation of several, independent processes. In other words, changes in visual function with aging do not result from a single coherent change in ocular tissue or fluid. Instead, the visual capabilities of any aging eye depend upon the sum of a series of variables acting together. Since we have only an imperfect understanding of any one of these variables, it should be no surprise that our understanding of their combined action is very far from adequate.

We learn an important lesson by recognizing that ocular aging is the sum of several independent age-related processes. The lesson is that changes in visual function are likely to be task dependent: Age may not affect all visual functions uniformly. Consider this example: Under many circumstances, the eye has to satisfy two competing and often incompatible requirements, the need for images of good spatial resolution and the need to maximize light-gathering ability. The trade-offs between these two goals are described in several sources, including Walls [1967]. Biological conditions that impair one visual function may not impair another; in fact, age-related ocular changes that *enhance* image formation may *impair* the simple capacity for detecting light. The miotic pupil of the aging eye can have precisely these two opposed effects. This is just one extreme example of a basic point: Visual functions need not age in lockstep with one another—aging may be differential.

Ocular aging can also exhibit another kind of heterogeneity, a geographical one. Suppose that only some restricted part of a tissue is affected by some age-related process. Because of their spatially heterogeneous blood supply, different parts of the retinal tissue may appear to age differentially. This possibility suggests the usefulness of a perimetric approach to visual functions and, more particularly, the use of spatially localized probes.

Although interesting and useful within their own realms, the approaches to aging of ocular tissue represented in this section have limited applicability to studies of visual function. In particular, the techniques used to study the retina, lens, and vitreous are difficult to integrate within experiments that actually measure vision in individual intact human or animal observers. To understand visual function, we need techniques to assess these tissues in observers on whom psychophysical measurements are being made. Now we are limited to correlations between anatomical or biochemical measurements of tissues in animals or humans other than those on whom psychophysical measurements are made.

The required techniques are quite different from those now available to investigators. For example, to make maximum sense of psychophysical data on older human observers, it is necessary to quantify the optical properties of tissues in the eyes of the very observers being tested. This calls for the development of new, noninvasive clinical tools for use by psychophysicists interested in changes in visual function with aging. The development of these tools will require a collaborative effort among the psychophysicists, the clinicians, and the basic scientists who study the anatomy and physiology of ocular tissues.

Another theme in this section of the volume is the difficulty of distinguishing between normal aging and what traditionally has been considered pathology. It has been noted by some that aging is a default variable—in other words, "aging effects" are limited to those that cannot be ascribed to known diseases. But leaving this philosophical issue aside for the moment, we are faced with more immediate issues relating to healthy aging and disease in ocular tissue. For example, are oxidative changes in a noncataractous eye qualitatively similar to the changes in an eye with a cataract? Is the difference between the diseased lens and a normal old lens simply a matter of *quantity* of tissue change?

Most attempts to relate visual function and physiological age-related changes depend upon correlational methods. The limitations of correlation methods in general are well known. But in vision research correlational methods acquire several additional burdens. One very significant limitation to the correlational approach has not been mentioned before and deserves comment here. To make the argument concrete, let us suppose that some substrate is proposed as a neural correlate for a particular change in visual function. At the neural level the most common putative substrate is a loss in the number of neurons at a particular site in the visual system. In one guise or another, cell loss is one of the most widely used explanatory constructs in work on vision and aging. An important assumption, although rarely articulated, stands implicitly at the core of such explanatory constructs. Some psychophysical linking hypothesis [Brindley, 1970] is required before one can translate changes at the neuronal level into statements at the behavioral level. In particular, asserting that cell loss causes a particular change in vision requires the assumption of a particular connection between behavior at the neural level and a change in vision. Unfortunately, people interested in visual function and aging almost never state explicitly how functions depends on cell number or cell density. Under what circumstances should a loss of n cells out of some population significantly alter some visual function? Under what conditions will it not?

We cannot make progress in relating visual function to the behavior of populations of neurons until we are able to offer intelligent guesses as to the relevant aspects of the population behavior. In other words, statements about cell loss are too vague without appropriately detailed psychophysical linking hypotheses. Although we do not champion one particular linking hypothesis over another, the sort of detailed hypothesis we have in mind relating cell loss to change in visual function, can be seen in the paper by Frisen and Frisen [1976]. We hope that as studies of vision and aging become more sophisticated and analytic, detailed linking hypotheses will emerge.

REFERENCES

Brindley, G. (1970) "Physiology of the Retina and Visual Pathway." Baltimore: Williams & Wilkins.

Frisen, L., Frisen, M. (1976) A simple relationship between the probability distribution of visual acuity and the density of retinal output channels. Acta Ophthalmol. 54:437–444.

Walls, C. (1967) "The Vertebrate Eye and Its Adaptive Radiation." New York: Hafner.

Young, R. (1981) A theory of central retinal disease. In Sears (ed) "Future Directions in Ophthalmic Research." New Haven: Yale University Press, 237–270.

Aging and Human Visual Function, pages 27–43
© 1982 Alan R. Liss, Inc., 150 Fifth Avenue, New York, NY 10011

Aging of the Lens and Cataract Formation

Abraham Spector

The lens is an attractive tissue for the study of aging. Its morphological and biochemical characteristics are ideally suited for examination of the impact of time on biological processes. Since cataract, the loss of lens transparency, is predominantly a disease of older individuals, it frequently has been suggested that cataract is an age-dependent disease process. In this brief review, some aspects of the lens related to aging and disease will be considered. First, the unique morphological and biological character of the tissue will be discussed; second, consideration of some of the age-dependent changes that occur in the tissue will be examined; and finally, the question of whether cataract in the elderly is an extension of the normal aging process will be considered.

The lens is completely isolated from the remainder of the organism, being avascular and entirely enclosed by a collagen glycoprotein elastic basement membrane, the capsule (Fig. 1). This membrane acts more as a supporting wrapper than as a molecular barrier, since low molecular weight components such as sugars, amino acids, and lactate appear to pass freely across the capsule. The lens is suspended by zonular fibers in a fluid and gel-like environment, on the anterior side by the rapidly replenished aqueous humor and on the posterior side by the relatively static vitreous humor.

A single layer of epithelial cells is present immediately beneath the capsule on the anterior side of the tissue. These cells are nondividing in the central area in the region of the optical axis. However, approaching the equatorial region (see Fig. 1), mitosis is initiated. In the equatorial regions of the organ located at the three and nine o'clock positions, the epithelial cells differentiate into fiber cells growing out toward the anterior and posterior poles, and abut at the suture lines. With the commencement of the formation of the fiber cells, there is an accelerated production of most of the characteristic structural lens proteins, the appearance of gamma crystallin, and the initiation of degradation of the cell nuclei. The mature lens fibers resulting from this process have lost their nuclei and most mitochondria and other intracellular bodies. The long hexagonally shaped fibers are in intimate contact with each other. Ball and socket and ridge

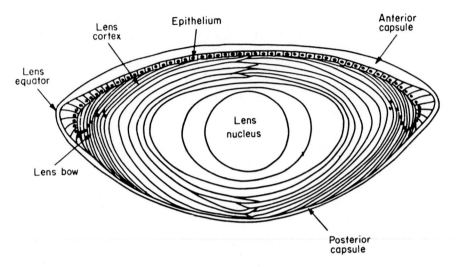

Fig. 1.   Diagrammatic section of the lens. [From van Heyningen, 1961.]

and valley-like interdigitations can be observed [Kuwabara, 1975]. A large part of the fiber membrane appears to be involved in gap junctions that are probably in the open state, allowing communication between the multiple fiber layers of the structure [Goodenough et al, 1978].

The avascular nature of the tissue emphasizes the dependency of the lens upon its environment. All nutrients must be obtained from the surrounding fluids and all waste products must be eliminated into the same fluids.

The differentiation of epithelial cells to fiber cells continues throughout life although the rate decreases markedly shortly after birth. Since the lens is encapsulated, no cells are lost. As each new fiber cell is produced, it displaces the previously formed fibers inward toward the center of the lens. In some species this leads to a tight packing of fibers into the central region, the nucleus, of the tissue, and results in marked loss of H_2O. In the bovine lens, the protein concentration of the inner fibers may be as high as 65%–70% in contrast to the usual 35% in newly formed fibers. In the human lens this dehydration does not occur to any marked extent and the protein concentration may, at most, rise in the central region to approximately 40%. This may reflect a concomitant increase in the volume of the tissue. A consequence of this process of inward packing of the fiber cells is that the center of the lens represents the older fibers, cells produced during embryonic and early postnatal life. The youngest fibers are at the periphery. Thus there is a gradient of young-to-old fiber cells as one moves from the outer surface to the center of the tissue.

There is a preservation not only of cells but of macromolecules as well. With the pyknosis of the nucleus and the breakdown of mRNA, the fiber cell loses its ability to synthesize new protein [Wannemacher and Spector, 1968]. Thus the protein observed in the central region of the older lens represents macromolecules synthesized in early life. In the normal lens, little proteolytic digestion is observed. The lens is therefore an ideal tissue for the study of aging, for examination of time-dependent changes in gene expression and post-translational reactions, and for investigation of changes at the molecular level. It is also an attractive tissue for exploration of the impact of time on cell structure, on membrane integrity, and the dynamic aspects involved with differentiation of the epithelial cells to their fiber cell counterparts.

Not only is there a loss of the machinery to synthesize protein but other metabolic processes cease to function in the central region of the tissue [Ohrloff, 1978; Ohrloff et al, 1979]. Most enzymes are concentrated in the outer perimeter of the tissue, decreasing markedly as one moves towards the inner nuclear region. Certain transport functions such as Na^+,K^+ ATPase are observed predominantly in the epithelial layer [Bonting and DePont, 1979].

The impression that emerges from these observations is that of an isolated organ with an active metabolism in its outer perimeter maintaining a precarious homeostasis of the inner nuclear region. The maintenance of native constituents for many decades, the inability to replace either damaged cells or chemically altered macromolecules, the unique high concentration of protein organized in an orderly manner to prevent light scattering and the loss of transparency all attest to the delicate equilibrium that exists in this tissue. With aging, the stress on this system increases. The mass of inert fiber cells and their constituents increases and metabolic activity decreases in the outer regions of the tissue, the superficial cortex, and the epithelium. This situation creates a tissue increasingly susceptible to irreparable damage and disease.

MOLECULAR CHANGES DURING AGING

A number of changes occur in the lens with aging. At birth the human lens has a net weight of approximately 90 mg. The organ increases rapidly in size during the first few years of life and then appears to grow at a relatively linear rate [Garner and Spector, 1978]. In older individuals the lens may have a weight of approximately 250 mg or more. In the order of 90% of the dry weight of the lens is contributed by protein. The dry weight of the human lens demonstrates an apparent linear increase of approximately 0.4 mg per year after an early rapid growth period [Garner and Spector, 1978]. It is interesting to note that the increase in the dry weight of the water-soluble fraction appears to occur at the same rate as the total dry weight. Thus the total soluble fraction remains constant with aging and the water insoluble fraction contributes an increasing fraction of the total dry weight expanding from approximately 1% in the very young lens to more than 50% in the 70-year-old normal lens. This dramatic change is accompanied by a gradual loss of lens transparency.

The size of the protein aggregates in the lens change with age. Studies with alpha crystallin, one of the major cytoplasmic fiber cell proteins, have demonstrated that only the newly synthesized macromolecule is physically homogeneous [Stauffer et al, 1974; Spector et al, 1976]. Almost immediately after synthesis, physical heterogeneity expressed as an increase in size is observed [Spector and Katz, 1965; Spector, 1972]. Thus the macromolecule increases in mass from approximately 700,000 daltons to an average mass of 1×10^6, and species having greater than 50×10^6 daltons are observed. It is primarily in the nuclear region of the lens that the transformation to this high molecular weight (HMW) species occurs. Thus in 8-year-old steer lenses, more than one-third of the total alpha crystallin in the nuclear region has an aggregate size greater than 50×10^6 daltons. In the outer cortical region, little HMW alpha crystallin is observed. While some size changes may occur in the other lens protein fractions, they do not appear to be of the magnitude observed for alpha crystallin.

It is interesting to find that the water-insoluble protein in the bovine lens appears to be derived primarily from alpha crystallin although small amounts of other lens proteins are present. Such observations have led to the suggestion that the water-insoluble fraction may develop primarily from the HMW alpha crystallin fraction [Spector, 1972; Roy and Spector, 1976a].

The generation of HMW and some insoluble species probably contributes to a decrease in the transparency of the lens [Sigelman et al, 1974; Spector et al, 1974]. The giant aggregates, those greater than 50×10^6 daltons, have a different refractive index from their environment, act as scatter points of light, and, when present in random array and in sufficient concentration, may seriously affect the passage of light through the tissue [Sigelman et al, 1974; Spector et al, 1974]. This concept is supported by light scatter theory [Benedek, 1971].

The cytoplasmic protein of the lens fiber cells is composed of three major protein groups designated alpha, beta, and gamma crystallins. The alpha crystallin is the largest macromolecule; beta contains aggregates ranging from 3×10^4 to 20×10^4; and gamma crystallin is composed of monomeric proteins averaging from 19×10^4 to 24×10^4 in size [Harding and Dilley, 1976; Kabasawa et al, 1977]. In normal human lens the generation of HMW protein aggregates also occurs, is age dependent, and is localized primarily in the nuclear region but is much more complex than in the bovine lens [Sigelman et al, 1974; Spector et al, 1974]. Most of the cytoplasmic lens proteins probably contribute to this fraction, which in older lenses may represent approximately 10% of the total protein. Interestingly, the water-insoluble protein in the human lens is also found to have a composition similar to that of the HMW protein, again suggesting a relationship between these two fractions. It is important to recognize that the observed changes in size of either alpha crystallin in the normal bovine lens or the soluble proteins in the human lens are not caused by covalent bonding; rather, the interactions leading to both atypical components are caused by electrostatic and hydrophobic interactions.

Examination of the water-soluble proteins in the normal human lenses shows a number of interesting, age-related changes. Studies with alpha crystallin indicate that in the nuclear region of the lens, the low molecular weight species (0.7×10^6 to 1.0×10^6 daltons) disappear [Roy and Spector, 1976b]. Analyses of the composition of alpha crystallin suggest a dramatic increase in the number of different polypeptides comprising the aggregate structure. An increase in negative charge is also observed. Thus, while newly formed alpha crystallin may contain two or three polypeptides, with aging, ten chains are observed [Roy and Spector, 1976c]. The origin of these changes in net charge is not understood, deamidation of asparagine and glutamine groups may be partially responsible. Similar charge changes are also observed in the beta and gamma crystallin groups.

Not only are there dramatic age-dependent changes in charge distribution of the lens polypeptides, but other fundamental changes are also observed. The relative abundance of the polypeptides and proteins of the soluble lens proteins changes with age [Garner and Spector, 1979]. This is dramatically shown in Figure 2A. At birth, the 20,000-dalton population is the major species, while lenses older than 10 years have a 22,000-dalton population as the major component. A low molecular weight species in the 10,000-dalton range gradually accumulates with time. The latter polypeptide has been shown to be composed of degradation products of larger components. Analyses of the data suggest that there are three relatively well-defined periods into which the development of the lens can be divided. There is the first period occupying the first few years of life, in which large changes in relative abundance occur. Little protein degradation is observed in this period but sharply changing rates of protein synthesis are found. Little insoluble protein is observed and what is present represents primarily the membrane components. Sharp decreases in both the 20,000-dalton species and the 27,000 dalton-species occur, and there is a rapid increase in the 22,000-dalton population. In the second stage, from approximately 5 to 40 years of age, the soluble protein remains constant and only gradual changes in relative abundance are observed. Finally, in the third stage, from 40 years on, there is little change in either the soluble protein or the relative abundance of the polypeptides. The changes in composition reflect modification in synthesis, insolubilization, and degradation of the different classes of polypeptide as well as leakage from the lens. The overall contribution of each factor is complex. It

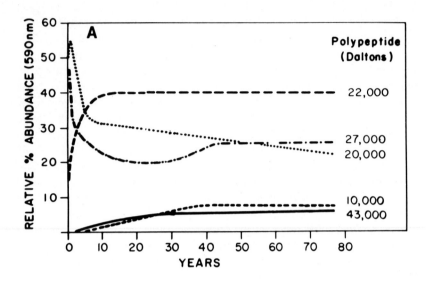

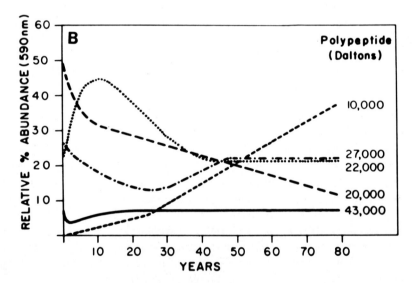

Fig. 2. Comparison of subunits of polypeptide distribution of normal human lenses in the water-soluble (A) and water-insoluble (B) fractions. Because the lines denote the best fit to experimental data with approximately ± 10% error, the total percentage at given ages does not always equal 100.

should be noted that the change in relative abundance of the polypeptides of the insoluble fraction (Fig. 2B) does not generally reflect the changes in the soluble fraction.

A few further points should be made with respect to these data. First, it is now clear that the pattern of lens protein synthesis changes with age, leading to significant alteration in the relative protein synthesis as well as the appearance in some cases of new synthetic products [Roy and Spector, 1976b]. Second, the dramatic increase in the 10,000-dalton species in the insoluble fraction is not due simply to degradation of soluble polypeptides but probably to degradation of insoluble species as well. Finally, a comment with respect to the 43,000-dalton component: This polypeptide does not appear in the cytosol fraction isolated from lenses of young donors. Its release into the soluble phase can be produced by physical shock or the addition of EGTA to the extracting medium [Spector et al, 1979]. Rupture of the lens fibers by osmotic shock results in the isolation of a soluble fraction containing little 43,000-dalton material.

Changes in protein composition with aging occur in the lens fiber membranes as well [Roy et al, 1979]. Thus, while in young human lens membrane, a 26,000-dalton polypeptide is predominant, with aging, the relative abundance of the 26,000-dalton species decreases and a 22,000-dalton component becomes a second major component. The origin of the 22,000-dalton species is obscure. While it appears to be somewhat similar to the 26,000-dalton component, very recent word suggests that it may arise not only by degradation of the larger polypeptide but also by direct synthesis [Garner et al, 1980]. The effect of this age-dependent change in composition upon membrane function is unknown at present.

All amino acids utilized for synthesis of animal protein require amino acids which are in the L-configuration. With time, however, transformation from the L-configuration to the D-form may occur. This transformation is called racemization. A technique for measuring the aging of biological material is based upon the racemization of amino acids (particularly aspartic acid). Examination of human lens protein indeed indicates that an age-dependent racemization of lens protein occurs [Masters et al , 1977; Garner and Spector, 1978]. It can be seen from Figure 3 that while no change in the D:L Asp ratio occurs in the soluble protein fraction, a linear age-dependent racemization contributes to perturbing the native protein structure, causing aggregation and insolubilization. With aging, the lens yellows and also generates nontryptophan-like fluorescence [Spector et al, 1975]. It is now clear that the yellowing is related to oxidation since reduction with borohydride eliminates much of the age-dependent increase in absorbtion in the 300–450 nm range [Garcia-Castineiras et al, 1979]. The nontryptophan fluorescence does not appear to be associated with the yellowing since it is hardly affected by the borohydride reduction.

Changes occur with aging in other constituents besides protein, such as lipophilic species important in membrane structure and function. The cholesterol content of the lens doubles between approximately 25 and 75 years of age [Broekhuyse, 1973]. Spingomyelin increases fourfold between 3 and 80 years. Phosphatidyl choline and phosphotidyl ethanolamine decrease with age. Supposedly, all of these components are located primarily in the membrane fractions of the organ. Changes in the composition of such lipid species can have marked effects upon the characteristics of the membrane, altering permeability and metabolic properties.

All of the changes in lens biology described above occur with aging of the normal human lens: generation of HMW protein, increase in insoluble protein, changes in polypeptide and protein composition, increase in negative charge, racemization, generation of yellow chromophors, increase in nontryptophan fluorescence, decrcase in metabolic activity, and changes in lipid composition. Unquestionably some of these changes affect transparency and possibly accommodation. The young lens is crystal clear in spite of its high protein concentration. With aging, transparency of the tissue decreases and increased light scatter is observed [Spector et al, 1974]. The visual system appears to be able to accept this distortion of incoming information without significant loss of visual acuity. However, if the light scatter increases beyond a particular threshold, it appears that deterioration of vision occurs. The changes in lens biology associated with the development of cataract appear to include certain additional chemical alterations not found in the normal aging lens. The lens may be increasingly susceptible to factors causing such change because of the age-dependent alterations described above.

MOLECULAR CHANGES DURING CATARACTOGENESIS

Let us examine some of the unusual aspects of cataract that appear to be separate from the normal aging process. In many types of cataracts there is an accelerated process of insolubilization. While investigation of such cataracts suggests no apparent change in the overall rate of racemization, examination of the water-insoluble fraction of cataractous lenses clearly indicates a decreased level of racemization. Such observations confirm the conclusion that a more rapid transformation of water-soluble protein to an insoluble form has occurred. Examination of the D:L ratios of individual polypeptides suggests that the accelerated rate of insolubilization is not the same for all polypeptides (see Fig. 3). Such observations suggest that possibly different insolubilization mechanisms may be involved in cataract. It can be argued that while a normal lens of a given age has a certain amount of insoluble and HMW protein and this amount is increased in cataracts, normal lenses of older ages have a level of such protein equivalent to the younger cataract lens. This observation is undoubtedly correct. However, the characteristics of the insoluble protein have changed. In the normal lens, all of the HMW and water-insoluble protein appears to be held together noncovalently. In cataract, this is definitively altered. Covalent linkage between the polypeptides of the insoluble fraction are now observed. Such changes may cause the HMW and insoluble proteins to become more effective scattering agents. Thus not simply the quantity but the nature of the HMW and insoluble protein is of importance.

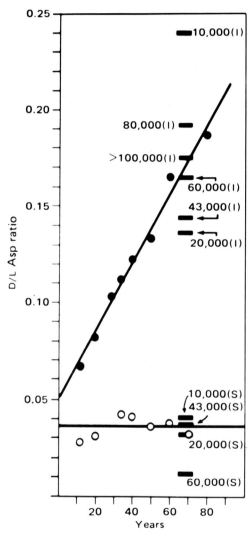

Fig. 3. Comparison of the rate of racemization of aspartic acid found in the total water insoluble (●) and total water soluble (○) fraction of normal human lenses. Polypeptides isolated from the soluble (S) or insoluble (I) fractions of cataractous lenses are denoted by the bars.

Let us consider some of the experiments that have led to these conclusions and to further implications concerning the process of cataract. When the water-insoluble material was alkylated to protect the SH groups and then analyzed by adding the material to a cylindrical gel and separating the components on the basis of charge differences in the presence of a detergent, sodium dodecyl sulfate (SDS), the results shown in Figure 4 were obtained. With the material from

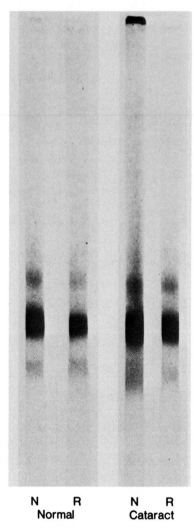

N   R   N   R
Normal   Cataract

Fig. 4. Sodium dodecyl sulfate, agarose-polacrylamide electrophoresis of water-insoluble protein: before (N) and after (R) reduction with 2-mercaptoethanol.

normal lenses, no large covalent linked polymers were observed and no change in gel pattern was produced by reduction of possible disulfide linkages with 2-mercaptoethanol. However, with the water-insoluble fraction from cataractous lenses, a marked difference was obtained. A HMW component was observed that does not penetrate the gel and disappears upon reduction. No other unusual bands were found. The disulfide interchain linkages are present only in the material from cataractous lenses. If the alkylated water-insoluble proteins from normal and severe cataracts solubilized by compounds such as urea are passed through a Sephadex G200 column in the presence of 7.2M urea, isolation of the S-S linked HMW aggregates can be achieved [Spector et al, 1979]. The results are shown in Figure 5. The first peak contains species greater than 1×10^6 to 5×10^6 daltons. It has doubled in relative abundance in the cataractous lens based on absorbance and protein content determined by amino acid analysis. Examination of this material indicates that most of the thiol is present as disulfide in the cataract preparation. It is this peak that contains the HMW S-S linked polymers. Upon reduction, the HMW band observed by SDS gel electrophoresis was eliminated. Only trace amounts of disulfides are present in the material isolated from normal lens. In the normal preparation, the peak 1 material appears to be composed of heterogeneous components that on agarose gel electrophoresis give a diffuse streaky pattern. Amino acid analysis indicates only small amounts

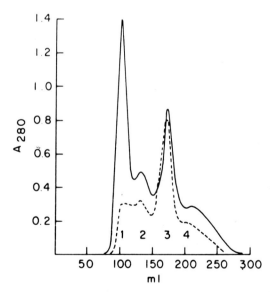

Fig. 5. Sephadex G-200 chromatographic profile of urea-solubilized alkylated water-insoluble proteins from normal (- - -) and cataractous (—) lenses. The column was run in 7.2M urea, 10% acetic acid at room temperature.

of protein. This material is also present in the cataractous lens. Disulfide linkages probably of the interchain type are found in all the other fractions of the water insoluble protein from cataractous lenses shown in Figure 5. Thus oxidation of thiol groups appears to be of major importance in the development of cataracts.

Further purification of the disulfide linked polymers indicates that they contain a number of polypeptides with sizes characteristic of cytosol components as well as a 43,000-dalton species representing up to 20% of the total material. This 43,000-dalton polypeptide was isolated and purified by gel filtration and gel electrophoresis after release into the soluble fraction. A rabbit antiserum was produced to this antigen by multiple subcutaneous injections of the polypeptide. Radial immunodiffusion and Ouchterlony double diffusion experiments indicated that this antibody was monospecific for the 43,000-dalton species isolated from either the HMW S-S linked aggregates or from the water-soluble or -insoluble fractions [Garner et al, 1979]. When indirect immunofluorescent staining techniques were used to localize the 43,000-dalton species in frozen lens sections, the species was found to be present in the normal lens in the region of the lens fiber membrane (Fig. 6) [Spector et al, 1979]. Thus, from these observations as well as other studies, it would appear that the 43,000-dalton species is an extrinsic membrane component. (It should be noted that the anti-43,000 dalton species

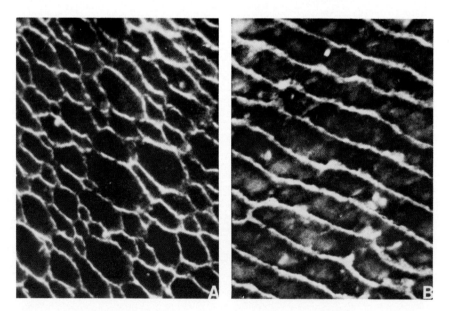

Fig. 6. Immunofluorescence of human lens sections treated with anti-43,000-dalton polypeptide and fluorescein conjugated goat antiserum to rabbit immunoglobulin. Cortical sections: (A) cross section and (B) longitudinal section.

does not react with muscle actin. The polypeptide also has a markedly different amino acid composition from actin.) Furthermore, since most of the S-S linked HMW aggregates can be bound to a Sepharose 4B affinity column prepared with the anti-43,000 dalton component, it is clear that this polypeptide is present in most HMW aggregates. Other studies indicate that these aggregates contain significant levels of cytosol polypeptide as well. It would therefore appear that there is an interaction between cytosol and membrane components, resulting in the formation of S-S linked HMW aggregates.

A model depicting our view of these aggregates is shown in Figure 7. The 43,000-dalton polypeptide is depicted as extrinsically bound to the membrane probably via Ca^{2+} ions. In cataract, the polypeptide acts as a nucleation site for aggregation. Its thiol groups are oxidized gradually, forming a large disulfide-linked aggregate that may entrap other polypeptides. From other observations, some of which are reported elsewhere in this volume, it seems probable that other membrane-cytosol disulfide interactions that involve intrinsic membrane components and low molecular weight thiols such as gluthathione also occur.

There is little question that the formation of these disulfide-linked aggregates associated with both extrinsic and intrinsic polypeptides, as well as the concom-

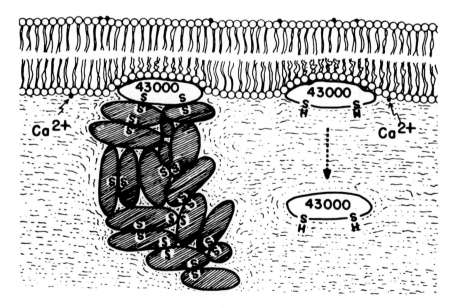

Fig. 7. Model of extrinsic 43,000-dalton membrane polypeptide acting as a nucleation site for the formation of large disulfide-linked protein aggregates. It is also demonstrated that the polypeptide can be easily detached from the membrane (by homogenization or EGTA).

itant gradual breakdown of membrane structure, can lead to definitive loss of transparency. The uniform index of refraction required for transparency is disrupted, scatter increases, and, as the region of the lens involved with such reactions enlarges, macroscopic areas of opacity would develop.

It can be argued that the S-S linked aggregates involving the 43,000-dalton polypeptide are not formed at the membrane but develop after release of the polypeptide from the membrane. Examination of the soluble protein fraction obtained after release of the 43,000-dalton polypeptide from the membrane indicates that this polypeptide can be isolated primarily in the beta crystallin region (10×10^4 to 20×10^4 daltons). However, if aqueous preparations of the soluble protein are passed through an anti-43,000-dalton polypeptide column only, the 43,000-polypeptide binds. Since low ionic strength solutions were utilized, it is unlikely that dissociation of already formed complexes would occur. Thus it would appear that the 43,000-dalton material aggregates upon release to sizes in the beta crystallin range but does not interact with other cytosol polypeptides. Such experiments as well as immunofluorescent studies support the argument that it is at the membrane that the 43,000-polypeptide binds cytosol protein forming the S-S linked complex.

It is probable that the initiating events triggering the oxidative reactions that lead to the formation of the S-S linked aggregate involve alteration in membrane structure leading to increased interaction between cytoplasmic and membrane components. How might this occur? In order to obtain some insight into this problem, an investigation was undertaken of the oxidative state of membrane polypeptides [Garner and Spector, 1980]. Normal and cataractous lenses ranging in age from 60 to 65 years as well as a group of young normal lenses from 12- to 20-year-old individuals were examined. The cataracts were moderate to severe and involved both cortical and nuclear regions. In the young normal lens, no oxidation was found in either cytosol or membrane polypeptides. However, in the older normal lenses, while the cytosol polypeptides were not oxidized, significant oxidation was observed in the membrane: 25% of the methionine was in the sulfoxide form and 50% of the cysteine was in the disulfide form. In the cataracts, extensive oxidation was found not only in the membrane fraction but throughout the lens. Thus it would appear that oxidative insult to the fiber cell membrane precedes the development of cataract. This membrane-localized oxidation appears to develop in older, apparently normal lenses. Recent studies with cataracts localized in either the nuclear or cortical regions demonstrate the complexity of the mechanisms involved in cataract formation. With both nuclear and cortical cataracts, extensive oxidation was found in both the transparent and opaque regions. This oxidation was observed in both the membrane and cytosol regions. Such observations would suggest that oxidation, while a necessary condition for cataract, may not be a sufficient condition. However, it should be noted that only in the opaque regions were significant concentrations of disulfide-linked HMW aggregates and cytosol polypeptide disulfide linked to membrane observed. Thus oxidative perturbation leading to formation of scattering elements is required for the loss of transparency.

The type of oxidation observed in cataract suggests that powerful oxidants not normally encountered in biological material may be involved. Recently, H_2O_2 has been detected in remarkably high levels in the aqueous fluid of some patients with cataract by Spector and W.H. Garner (Table I). In 7 of 17 cataract cases, H_2O_2 levels ranging from 45 to 663 nmoles/ml were observed. While it is difficult to obtain fresh aqueous from normal eyes, in a small population of patients with disorders other than senile cataract, an average aqueous H_2O_2 value of 24 ± 7 nmoles/ml (n = 5) was found. Furthermore, a significant correlation

TABLE I. Determination of Human Aqueous H_2O_2 Values From Selected Putative Normal and Cataractous Patients*

Age	Sex	Aqueous H_2O_2 (μM)	Lens H_2O_2 (μM)	Cataract Type
2	M	14[a]	38	Clear
44	M	31[b]	31	I, CxE[+1], SCP[30%], NS—yellow
46	M	32	5	I, CxE[+2], CxA[+2], CxP[+2], SCP[5%], NS—yellow
49	M	39	80	I, SCA, NS—light yellow
52	M	22	6	I, CxE[+4], CxA[+4], CxP[+4]
54	F	148	94	I, CxE[+4], CxA[+4], CxP[+4], N[+1], NS—dark yellow
56	F	29[a]	—	Clear
57	F	18	20	I, CxA[+2], CxP[+4], NS—brown
58	F	15	10	I, CxE[+4], CxP[+1], NS—light yellow
61	F	31[b]	39	I, CxE[+1], CxP[+1], N[20%], NS—dark yellow
61	F	16	29	I, N[10%-20%], NS—yellow
66	F	67	—	I, CxA[+1]
66	M	80	28	I, CxE[+3], CxA[+2], CxP[+2], NS—yellow
67	M	663	97	I, CxE[+4], CxA[+4], CxP[+4], NS—dark yellow
67	M	110	34	I, CxE[+1], NS—yellow
69	F	20	10	I, CxE[+4], CxA[+3], CxP[+3], NS—brown
73	F	45	60	I, CxE[+2], CxP[+1], NS—yellow
73	F	22	7	I, CxE[+4], CxP[+1], NS—yellow
73	F	65	69	I, CxE[+2], CxA[+2], NS—yellow
74	F	15	18	I, CxE[+1], CxP[+1], NS—dark yellow
75	F	19[b]	30	I, CxE[+4], CxA[+3], N[+1], NS—yellow
81	F	11	31	I, CxE[+2], CxA[+2], CxP[+2], NS—yellow

*H_2O_2 concentrations were determined either by the 2,6-dichloroindolphenol procedure [Mapson, 1945] or by the electrochemical oxidation at a platinum electrode (YSI Model 27 Industrial Analyzer). Cataract classification is according to method of [Chylack, 1978]. Because of the necessity to obtain very fresh samples due to the transient nature of H_2O_2, the term "normal" relates to patients with the following characteristics:
[a]Clear lenses from patients with retinal blastoma or glaucoma.
[b]Cataractous lenses from patients with documented diabetic history. Diabetic cataract formation appears from present experimental evidence to arise from causative factors different from those for senile cataractous lenses.

was observed between aqueous and lenticular peroxide levels. The results imply that H_2O_2 may be one of the agents involved in the oxidation of the lens.

The lens has a number of defenses against oxidative insult. For example, catalase and glutathione peroxidase metabolize H_2O_2. Superoxide, a potent oxidant that can be generated by photochemical reactions, is metabolized by superoxide dismutase. Glutathione in conjunction with glutathione reductase represents a powerful recycling system fueled by NADPH generated primarily by the active hexose monophosphate shunt found in the lens. This system is not only capable of reducing disulfide bonds but can quench powerful photochemically produced oxidants such as singlet oxygen. In most cases these defenses to oxidation are concentrated in a narrow band of superficial cells surrounding the central mass of the tissue. The inner regions of the tissue are vulnerable to oxidative insult since little glutathione or metabolic activity is found in this region.

It is probable that aging increases the susceptibility of the lens to oxidative insult. With lesser levels of key antioxidative enzymes, cofactors, and glutathione, the tissue is less capable of protecting itself from a hostile environment. Thus the lens is susceptible to oxidative insult leading to disulfide-linked aggregates, membrane breakdown, light scatter, and finally opacity.

It can be concluded that the unique morphology and chemistry of the tissue lead to many of the age-dependent changes that occur in the biology of the lens. It would appear that while these changes may not be directly responsible for the formation of cataract, they increase the susceptibility of the organ to oxidative insult, which may be a major initiating factor in the development of cataract.

REFERENCES

Benedek GB (1971) Theory of transparency of the eye. Appl Optics 10:459.

Bonting SL, DePont JJHHM (1979) Cation transport in the lens and the Na-K activated ATPase system. Docum Ophthalmol 18:41–49.

Broekhuyse RM (1973) Membrane lipids and proteins in ageing lens and cataract. Ciba Found Symp 19:136–149.

Chylack, LJ, Jr. (1978) Classification of human cataracts. Arch Ophthal 96:888–892.

Farnsworth PN, Shyne SE, Burke PA, Fasano AV (1980) Cellular maturation of human lens fibers. In Srivastava SK (Ed) "Developments in Biochemistry: Red Blood Cell and Lens Metabolism," Vol 9. New York: Elsevier, pp 45–48.

Garcia-Castineiras S, Dillon J, Spector A (1979) Effects of reduction on absorption and fluorescence of human lens protein. Exp Eye Res 29:573–575.

Garner MH, Spector A (1980) Selective oxidation of cysteine and methionine in normal and senile cataractive lenses. Proc Natl Acad Sci 77:1274–1277.

Garner WH, Spector A (1978) Racemization in human lens: Evidence of rapid insolubilization of specific polypeptides in cataract formation Proc Natl Acad Sci 75:3618–3620.

Garner WH, and Spector A (1979) A preliminary study of the dynamic aspects of age dependent changes in the abundance of human lens polypeptides. Doc Ophthalmol 204:1323–1326.

Garner WH, Garner MH, Spector A (1979) Comparison of the 10,000 and 43,000 dalton polypeptide population isolated from the water soluble and insoluble fractions of human cataractous lenses. Exp Eye Res 29:257–276.

Garner WH, Leff SR, Spector A (1980) Tritium incorporation into the major intrinsic membrane polypeptides of normal human lenses: 26,000 and 22,000 dalton species. In Srivastava SK (ed), "Developments in Biochemistry: Red Blood Cell and Lens Metabolism, Vol 9. New York: Elsevier, pp 367–370.

Goodenough DA, Paul DL, Culbert KE (1978) Correlative gap junction ultrastructure. Birth Defects XIV:83–97.

Kabasawa I, Tsunematsu Y, Barber GW, Kinoshita JH (1977) Low molecular weight proteins of the bovine lenses. Exp Eye Res 24:437–448.

Kuwabara T (1975) The maturation of the lens cell: A morphological study. Exp Eye Res 20:427–443.

Masters PM, Bada JI, Zigler JS Jr, (1977) Aspartic acid racemisation in the human lens during ageing and in cataract formation. Nature 268:71–73.

Mapson LW (1945) Influence of halides on the oxidation of ascorbic acid. Biochem J 39:228–236.

Ohrloff C (1978) Age changes of enzyme properties in crystalline lens. In von Hahn HP (Ed) "Interdisciplinary Topics in Gerontology." 12:158–179. Karger Basel 1978.

Ohrloff C, Ulrich T, Hockwin O (1979) Post synthetic alteration of bovine lens enzymes demonstrated by heat lability. Doc Ophthalmol 18:205–217.

Roy D, Spector A (1976a) High molecular weight protein from human lenses. Exp Eye Res 22:273–279.

Roy D, and Spector A (1976b) The absence of low molecular weight alpha crystallin in the nuclear region of old human lenses. PNAS 73:3484–3487.

Roy D, Spector A (1976c) Human alpha crystallin: Characterization of the protein isolated from the periphery of cataractous lenses. Biochemistry 15:1180–1188.

Roy D, Spector A, Farnsworth P (1979) Human lens membrane: Comparison of major intrinsic polypeptides from young and old lenses isolated by a new methodology. Exp Eye Res 28:353–358.

Satoh K, Bando M, Nakajima A (1973) Fluorescence in human lens. Exp Eye Res 16:167–172.

Sigelman J, Trokel SL, Spector A (1974) Quantitative biomicroscopy of lens light back scatter in aging and opacification. Arch Ophthalmol 92:437–442.

Spector A (1972) Aggregation of alpha crystallin and its possible relationship to cataract formation. Isr J Med Sci 8:1577–1582.

Spector A, and Garner WH (1981) H_2O_2 and Human Cataract. 33:673–681.

Spector A, and Katz E (1965) The deaggregation of bovine lens alpha-crystallin J Biol Chem 240:1979–1985.

Spector A, Li S, Sigelman J (1974) Age dependent changes of human lens proteins and their relationship to light scatter. Invest Ophthalmol 13:795–798.

Spector A, Roy D, and Stauffer J (1975) Isolation and characterization of an age-dependent polypeptide from human lens with non-tryptophan fluorescence. Exp Eye Res 21:9–24.

Spector A, Stauffer J, Roy D, Li L-K (1976) Human alpha-crystallin. I. The isolation and characterization of newly synthesized alpha-crystallin. Invest Ophthalmol 15:288–296.

Spector A, Garner MH, Garner WH, Roy D, Farnsworth P, Shyne S (1979) An extrinsic membrane polypeptide associated with high molecular weight protein aggregates in human cataract. Science 204:1323–1326.

Stauffer J, Rothschild C, Wandel T, Spector A (1974) Transformation of alpha-crystallin polypeptide chains with aging. Invest Ophthalmol 13:135–146.

von Heyningen (1961) In Davson H (Ed) "The Eye," Vol. 1. New York: Academic, p 214.

Wannemacher CF, Spector A (1968) Protein synthesis in the core of calf lens. Exp Eye Res 7:623–625.

Aging and Human Visual Function, pages 45-57

Aging Changes in the Vitreus*

Endre A. Balazs and Janet L. Denlinger

The sequence of changes that occurs during aging of human vitreus is very different from that in most animals, and it is this particular chain of events that often leads to pathological conditions typical for the human eye. In order to understand these changes, one must review briefly the fundamental vitreous architecture at the microscopic and molecular levels. Figure 1 shows a schematic drawing of the vitreus at various ages. This picture is based on the intensity of the scattering of the incident light by various regions of the vitreus. The structures responsible for the light scattering are the thin (10–20 nm thick) but uniform unbranched collagen fibrils. The presence and absence of the fibrils and their orientation and distribution determine the image obtained in the biomicroscope. The dark areas, where the scattering is weakest, represent regions where the collagen fibrils are absent or very widely spaced in a random fashion. There are channels, lacunae, and pools of liquid vitreus [Eisner, 1975, 1976; Tolentino et al, 1976]. The opaque, somewhat homogenous areas where the scattering is stronger represent regions of the gel vitreus. The collagen fibrils are more or less randomly distributed in these regions. Depending on the interfibrillar distance—that is, the denseness of the packing of the fibrils—the gel formed by the fibrils is more or less rigid. In the periphery of the vitreus, close to the retina, ciliary body, and lens, the gel is denser than in the central region.

The third elements represent accumulation and orientation of the collagen fibrils in two dimensional systems that scatter the light strongly. These structures have been called fibers, tracts (tractus vitrealis), and membranes, indicating the orientation and condensation of the fibrils. These fibers, tracts, and membranes do not contain any structural elements other than the regular, thin (10–20 nm) collagen fibrils. In other words, all the evidence available today indicates that

---

*In this paper, the authors will use "vitreus" as a noun, designating the connective tissue surrounded by the lens, ciliary body, and retina. Thus vitreus will replace vitreous humor, vitreous body, and vitreous. The two rheological states of the vitreus will be designated as "gel vitreus" and "liquid vitreus." "Vitreous" will be used, as an adjective, in the following manner: vitreous anomalies, vitreous strands, vitreous implants, etc.

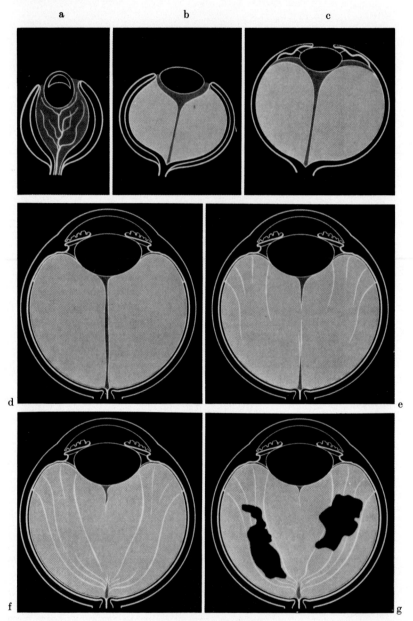

Fig. 1. Schematic representations of prenatal (a) and postnatal (b,c,d) development and aging (e,f,g) of human vitreus [Eisner, 1975]. (a) The hyaloid arteriole in the center of the vitreus. b) and (c) Light gray area: gel vitreus; dark grey area: hyaloid arteriole. (d) Young child—light gray area: gel vitreus; dark gray area: Cloquet's canal. (e) Young adult—white lines represent vitreal tracts. (f) Old adult—extensive vitreal tracts. (g) Old adult—vitreus with liquid pockets.

in the normal human vitreus of all ages, the different picture obtained with the biomicroscope originates from a variation in the distribution and orientation of the collagen fibrils.

There are two other structural elements in the normal human vitreus that complicate this picture. In the cortical or outer layer of the gel vitreus are embedded the vitreous cells or hyalocytes. These cells are differentiated and highly specialized mononuclear phagocytes localized in the collagen network of the gel vitreus from the area of the optic nerve head to the ciliary processes. The hyalocytes do not touch each other or other cells of the neighboring tissues. They are set apart from each other by 2 to 3 cell diameters, and their concentration varies with age and topography [Szirmai and Balazs, 1958; Bloom and Balazs, 1965]. They are not present behind the zonules or behind the lens. All available evidence indicates that these cells are responsible for the synthesis of hyaluronic acid in the vitreus [Österlin and Jacobson, 1968; Freeman et al, 1979].

Another structural element in the vitreus of all ages is Cloquet's canal. This is the remnant of an embryonic arteriole that enters the vitreus at the optic disc and runs across to the posterior pole of the lens, where it forms many branches and provides the blood supply for the rapidly growing tissue. It is called the hyaloid artery but actually has the typical fine structure of an arteriole embedded in loose connective tissue. The fine structure of this arteriole and its remnant, the Cloquet's canal, have been described in detail by Bloom et al [1980]. Its most characteristic features, the multilayered, fenestrated sheets, are typical for basal laminae produced by smooth muscle cells surrounding an arteriole. After birth, when the blood circulation in the arteriole ceases, the cellular elements rapidly disappear. The Cloquet's canal during the rest of life remains as an acellular skeleton of the arteriole made up of multilayered fenestrated sheets and collagen fibrils. These structures are visible in the biomicroscope and present a picture that varies with age, but they are always fairly easily distinguishable from the three vitreous structures described above. In the young human eye, the Cloquet's canal is dense and well defined. In adult eyes the canal has a relatively well-delineated superior and inferior "plicated membrane" consisting of the remnants of the basal lamina and the collapsed collagen filament structure of the arteriole wall. The membranes show some dislocation (ascension phenomenon) following the movement of the eyeball. With aging, the canal becomes less distinguishable, especially in the center of the vitreus, in the midst of the increasing fibrous and laminar structures.

One very important structural element of the vitreus is not detectable with biomicroscopy. This is the Na-hyaluronate (Na-HA) molecular network, which fills the entire space between the collagen fibrils. This molecular network consists of spheroidal Na-HA molecules having a molecular weight of 2×10^6 to 4×10^6 and a diameter about 10 times larger (200–300 nm) than that of the collagen fibrils. The spheroidal domain of a single Na-HA molecule is made up of a long random coil of a thin (1–2 nm) polysaccharide chain, and the space in between the coils is filled with water. Because of the large hydrated specific volume of this polyanion ($\overline{V}_o \simeq 2000$) and its random distribution and relatively low concentration, the scattering of light it causes is not sufficient to be observable with the biomicroscope.

Biomicroscopic studies on the human vitreus have been carried out for nearly a century. Since 1911, when Gullstrand described the modern biomicroscope—the slit lamp—many authors have studied the developing and aging human vitreus with this instrument. In general the aging of the human vitreus is characterized by the appearance of lacunae, pockets, and pools of liquid vitreus. Since biomicroscopical examination of the vitreus in very young individuals (< 5 years) does not reveal the presence of liquid channels or pockets, it has been assumed that liquefaction of the gel occurs at a later age (after 40–45 years). In a comprehensive study, Eisner [1975] described this process in its stages. Each stage represents an increase in the liquid content and a parallel increase of the tracts and fibers in the gel vitreus. In the last stage, the central liquid pocket occupies slightly more than half the volume of the vitreus.

Liquid vitreus appears in the human eye usually after the age of 4 years. After this age all postmortem human eyes examined contained a small amount (15%) of liquid vitreus. By the time the eyeball reaches its final size (14–18 years of age), approximately 20% of the total vitreous space is filled with liquid vitreus [Flood and Balazs 1977]. Biomicroscopy of the living eye, however, revealed liquid vitreus in only 9% of individuals under 20 years of age [Eisner, 1975]; at this age the liquid vitreus is distributed mostly in narrow channels in the gel, and these channels are too small to be detected with the relatively low magnification (< × 50) of the slit lamp. After the age of 40 years, however, the liquid vitreus volume increases and the channels fuse into larger pockets that are easily visible in the slit lamp. Between the ages of 40 and 84 years, 92% of all eyes examined with the slit lamp show pockets or large pools of liquid vitreus [Eisner, 1975]. Studies carried out in more than 1,000 postmortem human eyes of individuals between the ages of 20 and 97 years showed that the liquid vitreus volume steadily increases after the age of 40 years, and every eye examined had liquid vitreus (Fig. 2). By the age of 80–90 years, more than half of the total vitreus volume is liquid [Flood and Balazs, 1977]. During development the amount of gel vitreus also increases, reaching a plateau at about 10 years of age. At age 40, the same time when the second phase of increase in liquid vitreus volume begins, the gel vitreus volume begins to decrease, and this steady decrease in volume is evident for the remainder of life.

How are these rheological changes related to biochemical events during development and aging? The collagen concentration of the human gel vitreus decreases after birth, reaching its lowest level at the time when the eyeball is

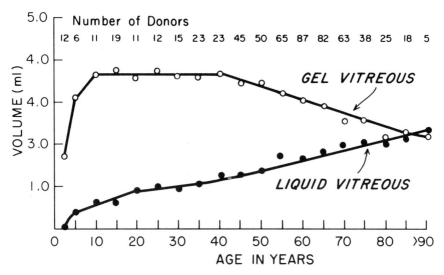

Fig. 2. Volume of gel and liquid vitreus in human eyes [Flood and Balazs, 1977]. Each point represents the mean value obtained from various numbers of donor eyes (shown at top of graph).

fully developed (Fig. 3). During this time the total amount of collagen in the gel vitreus does not change significantly. The concentration decreases because of the increase in the total gel vitreus volume. This means that during the growth of the eyeball and the parallel increase of the vitreous volume, there is no collagen fibril synthesis. The collagen fibrillar network laid down during prenatal life is expanded by the increasing water content. This means that the collagen content of the vitreus remains the same during lifetime. The increasing separation of the collagen fibrils—in other words, the decreasing concentration of collagen fibrils—means less rigidity. Therefore, the gel vitreus will be less rigid during postnatal development. During aging (after 50 years of age) the gel volume decreases (see Fig. 2). Since the total amount of collagen in the gel vitreus does not change, one must conclude that there is no loss of collagen fibrils during aging. Over 50 years of age, the collagen concentration in the gel vitreus increases (see Fig. 3). Thus, the decrease in gel volume must be due to the collapse of the fibrillar network with a consequent increases in the volume of the liquid vitreus.

The vitreus is one of the few connective tissue compartments containing only one major structural polysaccharide, Na-hyaluronate (Na-HA). There are only three other tissues that are similar in this respect—the subcutaneous connective tissue of the umbilical cord and of the rooster comb, and the synovial membrane

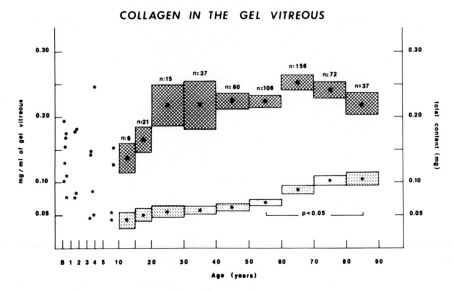

Fig. 3. Collagen concentration (mg/ml) of human gel vitreus [Flood and Balazs, 1977]. The collagen concentration (mg/ml) of gel vitreus is represented by asterisks (individual samples) or by lightly hatched boxes with asterisks representing the means. The collagen content of the gel vitreus (mg) is represented by solid dots (individual samples) and by darkly hatched boxes with asterisks representing the means. The vertical sides of the boxes indicate the standard error of the means; the horizontal, the age range of individual cases included in the group. The number of samples in each group is indicated by "n." There is a significant increase in collagen concentration of the gel vitreus between the 50–60-year-old group and the groups of the next decades. The level of significance is $p < 0.05$.

around the joint space. In all these tissues the space between the collagen fibrillar network is filled with the large Na-HA molecules that serve as stabilizers of the network. The Na-HA produced by the hyalocytes embedded in the cortical gel vitreus diffuses forward through the anterior face of the vitreus to the posterior chamber. From there it is washed by the aqueous humor to the anterior chamber, and leaves the eye through the trabecular meshwork to Schlemm's canal. Thus Na-HA is present in the liquid and gel vitreus, and, at a much lower concentration, in the aqueous humor.

The concentration of Na-HA in the gel vitreus (Fig. 4) is very low at birth but increases during the growth of the vitreus. At the time of the first appearance of the liquid vitreus, the Na-HA concentration is about the same in the liquid and the gel vitreus. The concentration of Na-HA in the liquid vitreus (Fig. 5) gradually increases and reaches adult levels by age 20. From 20 to 70 years of age, the Na-HA concentration remains the same in both gel and liquid vitreus.

CONCENTRATION OF Na HYALURONATE IN THE GEL VITREOUS

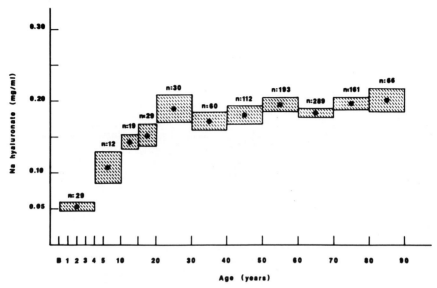

Fig. 4. Concentration of Na-hyaluronate in the human gel vitreus [Flood and Balazs, 1977]. For detailed explanation, see Figure 3.

Interestingly, after 70 years of age there is a dramatic increase in the concentration of Na-HA in the liquid vitreus (see Fig. 5) but not in the gel vitreus. There is no explanation for this phenomenon. The molecular size of the Na-HA is the same in old and young eyes, as well as in the liquid and gel vitreus [Balazs and Flood, 1978].

Another morphological change with age in the vitreus is related to the basal laminae that form the boundaries of the cortical gel vitreus adjacent to the retina, ciliary body, and lens. In general the basal lamina (basement membrane) of the retina separating the glial cells (Müller cells) from the vitreus becomes thicker during the aging of the human eye [Gärtner, 1970a; Rentsch and van der Zypen, 1971]. This thickening occurs through the entire retinal-vitreus border. The thickening of the basal lamina with age, however, is not unique to the vitreus. It was observed in skin capillaries of old rats [Gersh and Catchpole, 1949] and in glomeruli [Caulfield, 1964]. The basal lamina bordering the vitreus toward the ciliary body undergoes a more unusual developmental and aging change. In the young human, the basal lamina over the nonpigmented epithelium of the ciliary body is a 40–50-nm-thick single layer. Later in life the membrane becomes

CONCENTRATION OF Na HYALURONATE IN THE LIQUID VITREOUS

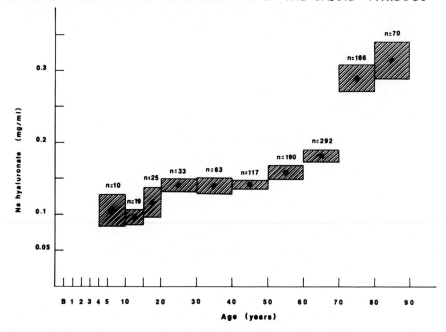

Fig. 5.   Concentration of Na-hyaluronate in the human liquid vitreus [Flood and Balazs, 1977]. Data for the first 4 years are missing because liquid vitreus does not exist at this time. For detailed explanation, see Figure 3.

multilayered, forming a system of fenestrated sheets (reticular membranous structures) extending several micrometers inside the vitreus. The vitreous fibrils are pushed back from the surface of the epithelium by this extensive membranous network. At what age these multilayered membranes first appear is not clear from the relatively few eyes studied thus far. Unquestionably, by the time the gel vitreus starts to shrink (40–50 years of age), an extensive network of basal laminae covers the entire area of the ciliary processes, and this network later extends over the pars plana as well [Rentsch and van der Zypen, 1971]. The thickness of this membranous structure over the nonpigmented ciliary epithelium can be 4000–5000 nm after the age of 60 years (Gärtner, 1970a). This tenfold increase of the basal lamina in the region of the ciliary body during aging is a uniquely human phenomenon.

With slit lamp examination of the living human eye, another aging change can be observed, called posterior vitreus detachment [Pischel, 1953; Goldmann, 1962]. It is assumed to be the separation of the cortical vitreus gel from the basal lamina. It is also possible that a thin layer of cortical gel remains attached to the basal lamina, and the break in the vitreus then occurs within the gel, creating a vitreoschisis [Balazs, 1973]. Slit lamp examination cannot differentiate between these two pathological events. The posterior vitreous detachment can be complete or incomplete depending on how large an area of the vitreus becomes separated from the retina. In one clinical investigation, posterior vitreous detachment was observed between the ages of 54 and 63 years with a frequency of 20% and between 63 and 89 years with a frequency of 49% of the cases [Eisner, 1975]. Other clinical studies reported somewhat higher (50%–65%) incidence in the population over 50 years of age [Pischel, 1953; Favre and Goldmann, 1956]. It is possible that the thickening of the basal lamina of the posterior retina is a prerequisite of some types of posterior vitreous detachment. Since this change in the rheology of the vitreus occurs in a very large number of the aging population and usually does not lead to any serious pathological change or impairment of vision, it is regarded as a normal aging change. This is further supported by the observation that 94% of the individuals with senile nuclear opacities of the lens have posterior vitreous detachment [Rosen, 1962]. Posterior vitreous detachment, however, can occur at any age as a result of chronic intraocular inflammation, severe trauma or perforating injury to the eye, and after degenerative processes in the choriocapillary-pigment epithelial system (chorioretinal degeneration). It occurs also in aphakic or highly myopic young individuals. Thus posterior vitreous detachment is a symptom that can occur only after the vitreus undergoes some fundamental structural changes. These changes encompass the entire process characteristic for the aging of the human vitreus: (1) a thickening of the basal lamina of the retina, (2) the increase in the liquid vitreous volume, (3) the collapse of the gel, and (4) the aggregation of the collagen fibrils into large fibers. These changes occur in all human eyes during aging, yet posterior detachment of the vitreus is not a universal phenomenon. The clinical observation is that posterior vitreous detachment occurs in most cases suddenly and spontaneously, often after a sudden shaking up of the eye by a fall or hit on the head. The subjective symptoms are photopsia, metamorphopsia, blurred vision, and moving opacities in the vitreus (floaters). All these symptoms emerge rapidly and can be explained by the sudden collapse of the vitreus gel made possible by the separation between the vitreous fibrillar network and the posterior basal lamina, or a schisis in the weaker precortical vitreus gel. It is important to remember that posterior vitreous detachment at its onset is seldom complete, and several connections remain, especially in the macular and optic nerve area. The fibers of the contracting gel vitreus are still attached to the basal lamina of the retina and exert a mechanical pull.

Photopsia, the spontaneous light flashes observed by the individual, is believed to be caused by this mechanical stimulus on the nerve fiber layer. This could explain why ocular movements in these cases trigger photopsia. The photopsia may last weeks or even years after its onset [Nebel, 1957]. Its duration is believed to depend on the persistence of the remaining attachments and the pull of the vitreous fibers on the basal lamina of the retina [Tolentino et al, 1976]. Photopsia is an important diagnostic symptom that should be taken seriously, because it can signal not only the onset of posterior vitreous detachment but also rheg-matogenous retinal detachment, circulatory damage to the retina or choroidal capillary system (embolus or spasm), or early warning for circulatory damage in the brain.

Metamorphosia, the distortion of the visual image, and blurred vision can also occur with posterior vitreous detachment, and they are believed to be caused by macular edema. Macular edema is a clinical syndrome probably caused by vascular damage resulting in capillary leakage, accumulation of fluid in the intercellular space of the neural retina, and swelling of the basal lamina over the macular area. It was postulated that tractions on the macula caused by the fibers of the contracting vitreous gel can cause this syndrome [Irvine, 1953; Tolentino and Schepens, 1965].

The "floaters" of the vitreus are the most common and persistent symptom after posterior vitreous detachment. They are shadows cast on the central visual area of the retina by the collapsed structures of the gel vitreus. Floaters may be the collagen fibrils aggregated into fibers or into an amorphous mass, or the membranes of the Cloquet's canal. These structures could be present but un-noticed prior to the posterior vitreous detachment. The collapsing and contracting vitreous gel, however, can bring the floaters into an area of the vitreus where they will be noticed. The visual disturbance caused by the floaters depends on how mobile they are and how their location changes with time. If they are stationary with eye movements or if they move out from a central and premacular position, the visual disturbance can completely disappear.

Posterior vitreous detachment, as is the case with other aging phenomena, can become a pathogenic factor in the development of more serious conditions in the eye. It can be followed by hemorrhage and cystoid degeneration of the macula and by retinal tears leading to retinal detachment. In addition, the age-related typical posterior vitreous detachment can trigger serious complications in eyes with diabetic retinopathy or with rhegmatogenous retinal detachment.

Posterior vitreous detachment as an aging phenomenon has not been found in any animal other than man. The rhesus monkey (Macaca mulatta) vitreus is the only one described thus far that shows developmental and aging changes very similar to humans [Denlinger et al, 1980]. Changes observed during development and aging with biomicroscopic, rheological, and biochemical inves-tigations show a striking parallelism between this primate and the human. Pos-terior vitreus detachment, however, could not be observed in animals up to 21 years of age. Since macaques are known to live more than 30 years, it is possible that posterior vitreous detachment will be observed in the future in animals older than 21 years. But it is also possible that the living conditions and diet of these animals are sufficiently different from those of humans to prevent the development of posterior vitreous detachment. It is also conceivable that, given the similar molecular structure of the rhesus monkey and human vitreus, more than 45 years of wear-and-tear or metabolic and light exposure are needed to develop this aging phenomenon.

Posterior vitreous detachment represents the culmination of the aging of the human vitreus. As we have seen, it can cause serious visual disturbances basically by two mechanisms: first, by asserting traction on the retina that in turn causes functional and structural changes in this tissue, and second, by creating optical inhomogeneities in the vitreus that interfere with clear image formation. A third quite hypothetical mechanism should be mentioned. The transformation of the single layer of basal lamina of the ciliary epithelium into a thick, multilayered network during aging occurs at the same area where the zonular fibers, the suspensory system of the lens, insert into the basal lamina. Gärtner [1970b] suggested that the "tensile strain" produced by accommodation is the cause of the development of the thickened basal laminar network. He pointed out that this transformation occurs only at the region where the zonular fibers insert. In rats, which are unable to accommodate, the multilayered basal lamina does not develop [Gärtner, 1970b]. The same is true for rabbits [Holmberg, 1959], another animal having no accommodative power. However, the thickened basal lamina does not develop in owl monkeys, and this primate is able to accommodate. Therefore it is difficult to assume that accommodation causes the development of the multilayered membrane. On the other hand, we would like to suggest that the development of this multilayered membranous network with aging is one factors contributing to the decline of accommodation in human after 40–45 years of age (presbyopia).

The morphological and rheological changes in the vitreus leading to posterior vitreous detachment are clearly understood. There is a fundamental change in the arrangement of the collagen fibrils suspended in the viscoelastic Na-HA solution, which is caused by the dislocation of the fibrils separated by the large Na-HA molecules. What causes this disturbance of the fine equilibrium on the molecular level is not known. It has been speculated that the Na-HA molecules are degraded and that their topographic distribution changes with aging. Careful studies on the aging human vitreus [Balazs and Flood, 1978] clearly showed that this is not the case. It has also been suggested that chemical changes in the collagen fibrils during aging cause contraction of the network. No experimental evidence has been presented yet to support this assumption. Until disproved, the most likely explanation is that in the young (< 5 years of age) human vitreus, a delicate balance exists between the noncrosslinked collagen fibrils and the Na-HA molecules separating them. At this stage, the collagen network is fairly uniformly distributed in the nonviscous (low Na-HA concentration) medium. As the vitreous volume increases with the growth of the eyeball, the distance between the fibrils must increase because new fibrils are not formed. At this time Na-HA is pumped into the gel to provide stability for the increasingly loose and therefore more labile fibril network. By the time the eye is fully grown, the volume of the gel reaches its maximum, as does the concentration of the Na-HA between the network-forming fibrils. This is already a precarious equilibrium, which creates small channels of liquid vitreus representing 20% of the total vitreous volume.

During aging, the movements of the eyeball and the body and mechanical impacts on the head and on the eyeball itself cause small but recurrent dislocations of the network, resulting in a decrease in volume of the gel and the formation of larger and larger liquid pools. Vascular changes in the retina and ciliary body may be responsible for the thickening of the basal laminae with aging. When the liquid vitreus reaches a certain volume and the attachments between the collapsed gel vitreus and the cortical gel or to the posterior basal lamina are sufficiently weakened, a relatively small and often unnoticed mechanical insult to the eyeball can trigger a sudden posterior vitreus detachment—the end point of the normal aging of the vitreus. The stage is then set for a relatively uneventful continuation of the aging process or, in the case of the presence of pathological changes in the neighboring tissue, for major impairment of vision due to the aging of the vitreus.

ACKNOWLEDGMENTS

This study was supported by Grant EY01747, awarded by the National Eye Institute, Bethesda, Md.

REFERENCES

Balazs EA (1973) The vitreous. Int Ophthalmol Clin 13:169–187.
Balazs EA, Flood MT (1978) Age-related changes in the physical and chemical structure of human vitreous. Presented at the Third International Congress of Eye Research, Osaka, Japan.
Bloom GD, Balazs EA (1965) An electron microscopic study of hyalocytes. Exp Eye Res 4:249–255.
Bloom GD, Balazs EA, Ozanics V (1980) The fine structure of the hyaloid arteriole in bovine vitreous. Exp Eye Res 31:129–145.
Caulfield JB (1964) Medical progress application of the electron microscope to renal diseases. N Engl J Med 270:183–194.
Denlinger JL, Eisner G, Balazs EA (1980) Age-related changes in the vitreus and lens of rhesus monkeys (Macaca mulatta). Exp Eye Res 31:67–79.
Eisner G (1975) Zur Anatomie des Glaskörpers. Albrecht Von Graefes Arch Klin Exp Ophthalmol 193:33–56.
Eisner G (1976) The anatomy and biomicroscopy of the vitreous body (new developments in ophthalmology, Nijmegen, 13–16 October 1975). Doc Ophthalmol   :87–104.
Favre M, Goldmann H (1956) Zur Genese der hinteren Glaskörperabhebung. Ophthalmologica 132:87–97.

Freeman MI, Jacobson B, Balazs EA (1979) The chemical composition of vitreous hyalocyte granules. Exp Eye Res 29:479–484.

Flood MT, Balazs EA (1977) Hyaluronic acid content in the developing and aging human liquid and gel vitreous. Annual meeting of the Association for Research in Vision and Ophthalmology (ARVO). Invest Ophthalmol Supp.

Gärtner J (1970a) Electron microscopic observations on the cilio-zonular border area of the human eye with particular reference to the aging changes. Z Anat Ent Ges 131:263–273.

Gärtner J (1970b) The fine structure of the zonular fibre of the rat. Development and aging changes. Z Anat Ent Ges 130:129–152.

Gersh I, Catchpole HR (1949) The organization of ground substance and basement membrane and its significance in tissue injury, disease and growth. A J Anat 85:457–522.

Goldmann H (1962) Senecenz des Glaskörpers. Ophthalmologica 143:253–279.

Gullstrand A (1911) Demonstration der Nernstspaltlampe. Ber Zusammenkunft Dtsch Ophthalmol Ges 37:347.

Holmberg A (1959) Differences in untrastructure of normal human and rabbit ciliary epithelium. Arch Ophthalmol 62:952–955, 1037–1046.

Irvine SR (1953) A newly defined vitreous syndrome following cataract surgery, interpreted according to recent concepts of the structure of the vitreous. Am J Ophthalmol 36:599–619.

Nebel B (1957) The phosphene of quick eye motion. Arch Ophthalmol 58:235–243.

Österlin SE, Jacobson B (1968) The synthesis of hyaluronic acid in vitreous I. Soluble and particulate transferases in hyalocytes. Exp Eye Res 7:497–510.

Pischel DK (1953) Detachment of the vitreous as seen with slit-lamp examination. Am J Ophthalmol 36:1497–1507.

Rentsch FJ, van der Zypen E (1971) Altersbedingte Veränderungen der sog. Membrana limitans interna des Ziliarkörpers im menschlichen Auge. In Bredt H and Rohen JW (eds) "Altern und Entwicklung." Stuttgart: Schattaurer Verlag, pp 70–94.

Rosen E (1962) Vitreous detachment. Associated nuclear sclerosis. A J Ophthalmol 54:837–841.

Szirmai JA, Balazs EA (1958) Studies on the structure of the vitreous body. III. Cells in the cortical layer. Arch Ophthalmol 59:34–48.

Tolentino FI, Schepens CL (1965) Edema of posterior pole after cataract extraction: A biomicroscopic study. Arch Ophthalmol 74:781–786.

Tolentino FI, Schepens CL, Freeman HM (1976) "Vitreoretinal Disorders, Diagnosis and Management." Philadelphia: Saunders.

Aging and Human Visual Function, pages 59–78
© 1982 Alan R. Liss, Inc., 150 Fifth Avenue, New York, NY 10011

Aging and the Retina

Michael F. Marmor

The retina is a complex and highly vascular tissue that is critically dependent for physiologic support upon adjacent structures such as the vitreous, pigment epithelium, and choroid. Thus, the problem of aging cannot be restricted to a discussion of cellular processes "in" the retina but must consider the interaction of cells and physiologic systems both intrinsic and extrinsic to the retina proper. To accomplish this, one must analyze aging from several vantage points (Table I). One can view the retina anatomically, noting the effects of age on each of the primary retinal cell types and on the various extraretinal tissues supporting retinal function. One can look at the retina physiologically, making the distinction between observable anatomic changes and changes in functional processes that may involve many cell types working together. Finally, one can view the aging process teleologically, and distinguish "normal" aging from pathology that disturbs visual function and merits the designation "disease."

None of these three classifications are mutually exclusive, nor can the effects of aging be appreciated without an awareness of all three. To look at the aging of individual cells is instructive but does not tell us whether the photoreceptor loss is actually secondary to pigment epithelial damage, or whether vision—the ultimate bottom line—has been affected at all. On the other hand, to document a failure in image processing without examining the physical changes in retinal neurons is to miss the opportunity to understand cellular mechanisms that might be amenable to therapy. The question of what is "normal" aging looms over any discussion of anatomic or physiologic changes. Which of the changes that occur with age are inevitable, and which are conditioned by environmental factors that might in some way be understood and modified? Where does normal aging end and pathology begin? How much aging is still compatible with good visual function?

This brief survey is not intended as either a comprehensive review of the literature or as an atlas of histopathology. My purpose is simply to provide a view as to how aging can affect the retina and how retinal aging can affect vision. The references are mostly general and will serve to lead the reader further into any topics of personal interest.

TABLE I.   Analysis of Aging

I.   Anatomic Classification
A.   Primary Tissues
1.   Photoreceptors
2.   Integrative cells
3.   Ganglion cells
B.   Supportive Tissues
1.   Retinal pigment epithelium
2.   Vasculature—retina, choroidal
3.   Glia
4.   Vitreous
II.   Physiologic Classification
A.   Anatomic Changes
1.   Cellular damage
2.   Tissue damage
B.   Functional Changes
1.   Photoreceptors and transduction
2.   Neural integration
3.   Signal transmission
4.   "Vision"
III.   Teleologic Classification
A.   "Normal" Changes
1.   Intrinsic (cellular) damage
2.   Induced (environmental) damage
B.   Pathologic Changes
1.   Extensions of the aging process
2.   Diseases to which the retina is predisposed by age

STRUCTURE AND FUNCTION OF THE RETINA

Before tackling the problems of aging, it may be well to review some normal retinal anatomy and physiology [see Hamming and Apple, 1980; Marmor, 1980]. The retina is embryologically a part of the brain, developing from a small bulge in the primal neural tube. As the embryo develops, this bulge extends out along a long stalk (to become the optic nerve) and eventually differentiates into both neurosensory retina and pigment epithelium. The central nervous system origin of the retina has important implications: As part of the brain, damaged cells in the retina and optic nerve will not regenerate, and transplantation is not feasible. The retina also shares the brain's special relation to the vasculature (called the blood-brain barrier) that limits the access of most large molecules to the extracellular space.

In cross section (Fig. 1) the retina is a multilayered structure that appears to be functionally inverted: The photosensitive cells (photoreceptors) are deepest

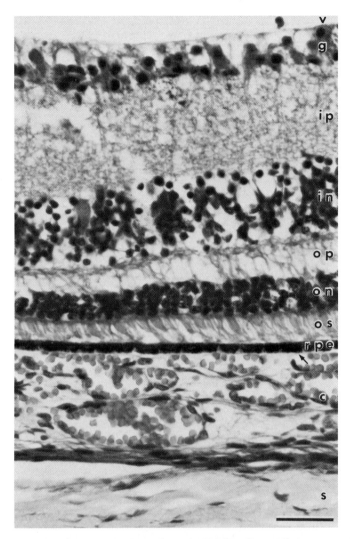

Fig. 1. Cross section of normal retina from a 3-month-old infant. The cellular layers are as follows: v, vitreous; g, ganglion cell layer; ip, inner plexiform layer; in, inner nuclear layer (horizontal, bipolar, and amacrine cells); op, outer plexiform layer; on, outer nuclear layer (photoreceptor nuclei); os, outer segments; rpe, retinal pigment epithelium; c, choroid; and s, sclera. The arrow points to Bruch's membrane. Light passes through the retina from the vitreous toward the outer segments. (H & E stain; magnification bar, 50 μ.)

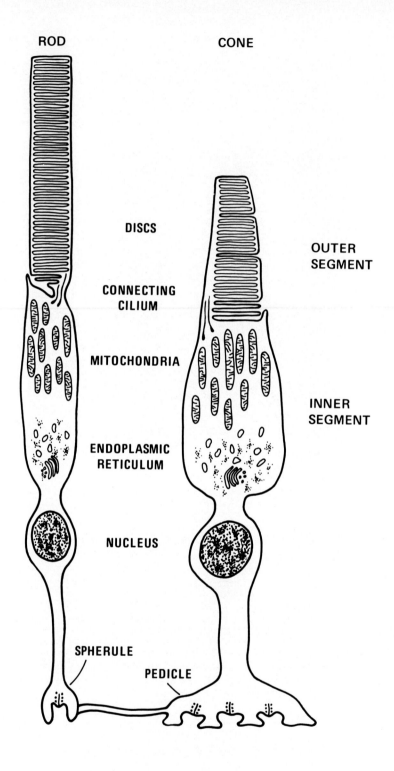

ROD

CONE

DISCS

OUTER
SEGMENT

CONNECTING
CILIUM

MITOCHONDRIA

INNER
SEGMENT

ENDOPLASMIC
RETICULUM

NUCLEUS

SPHERULE

PEDICLE

within the eye, and light must pass through the other retinal layers to reach them. Midway are the integrative elements—horizontal cells, bipolar cells, amacrine cells—that process and analyze visual information. Innermost are the ganglion cells, whose axons form the optic nerve. On the other side of the photoreceptors is a layer of cells called the retinal pigment epithelium (RPE) that helps control the local metabolic environment. The RPE is separated by a thin layer of collagenous tissue called Bruch's membrane from the choroid or vascular coat of the eye. There is a dual vasculature for the retina. The inner (integrative) retinal cells are supplied by the intrinsic retinal circulation, but the photoreceptors, which have one of the highest metabolic rates in the body, are supplied by a rich network of capillaries in the choroid. The intrinsic retinal vessels have tight walls to preserve the blood-retinal barrier; the choroidal vessels are leaky, and the blood-retinal barrier is maintained by tight membrane junctions sealing the boundaries between the cells of the RPE.

The initial retinal process of vision is the transformation (transduction) of light to a neural signal, which occurs in the highly specialized outer segment of the photoreceptors (Fig. 2). The outer segment consists of a dense stack of lipid membranes studded with molecules of visual pigment. There are two basic types of photoreceptors: Rods, which contain the pigment rhodopsin, are very light-sensitive, and provide colorless night vision; and cones, which contain one of three pigments and are responsible for color vision and sharp acuity. When light is absorbed by a visual pigment, the molecule undergoes a series of conformational changes that lead to an electrical response in the photoreceptor membrane. The bleached visual pigment is then reconstituted slowly through the combined metabolic activity of the photoreceptors and RPE.

The retina is not only complex in its radial organization but in its topographic layout within the eye. The rods and cones are concentrated selectively in specific regions, to subserve central and peripheral vision. Cones predominate in the central region, called the macula, which provides our good visual acuity (Fig. 3). The center of the macula is a small depression called the fovea, part of which contains only cones. The zone of highest rod density is 15–20° away from the fovea and is our most light-sensitive area at night.

The photoreceptors and RPE also interact through a cycle of membrane synthesis and phagocytosis. Keep in mind that the photoreceptors, like the skin, absorb a great deal of radiant energy over the years. No self-respecting piece of skin would attempt to last a lifetime—in fact our skin is growing and sloughing continually—and the photoreceptors also possess a system for self-renewal [Young, 1976]. New outer-segment membranes are synthesized all the time (Fig.

Fig. 2.   Diagram of a rod and cone. [From Marmor, 1980.]

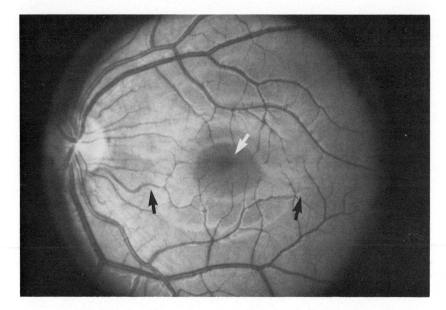

Fig. 3. Ocular fundus of a normal 12-year-old eye. A white arrow points to the fovea; black arrows span the macula. [From Marmor, 1981.]

4), and at certain intervals during the day tips are ingested (phagocytized) by the cells of the RPE. The phagocytized material is digested by enzymes within the RPE so that essential chemicals may be retained and recycled within the eye.

ANATOMIC CHANGES IN THE RETINA AND SUPPORTIVE STRUCTURES

At a clinical level, the retina and RPE show distinct changes with age, and looking in the eye, the ophthalmologist has no trouble distinguishing the most vigorous septagenarian from a teenager. In old age (Fig. 5), the ocular vessels appear narrower and more sclerotic than in youth, the RPE has less pigment and allows the choroidal pattern to show through, and the macula and fovea have lost their glistening light reflexes. Drusen (small focal yellow lesions) are often seen in the macula (Fig. 6), and the peripheral retina shows a variety of degenerative changes such as reticula pigmentation, cobblestone chorioretinal atrophy, and lattice degeneration [Kansky, 1975]. These gross anatomic changes may be seen without any obvious loss of function, but by the same token, functional loss may be present without any more obvious ophthalmoscopic changes. To

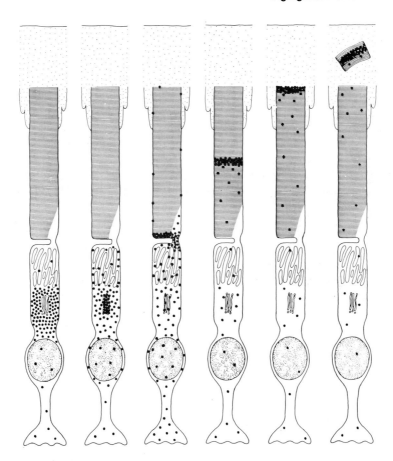

Fig. 4. Outer segment renewal in rods, revealed by autoradiography. The black dots represent radioactive amino acids, which are a marker for the newly synthesized protein. For primates, this diagram would span 9–13 days. Protein is concentrated in new membranous discs formed at the base of the outer segments and then migrates slowly outward as other discs are formed; eventually the protein reaches the end of the outer segment and is phagocytized by the RPE. [From Young, 1976.]

understand this dichotomy, we must look deeper and examine aging at the cellular and subcellular levels.

As noted earlier, the retina is actually part of the brain, and it loses cells with age as does the brain. A recent survey calculated that nearly 50% of the neurons in the visual cortex drop out by age 70 [Devaney and Johnson, 1980]. The loss of retinal neurons has not been accurately determined but unquestionably occurs [Gartner and Henkind, 1981], and the overall thickness of the retina decreases

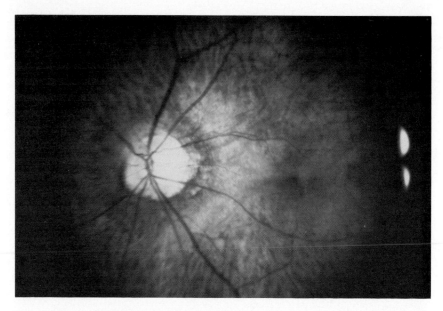

Fig. 5. Fundus of an elderly individual with arteriosclerosis. The vessels are narrow, and the choroidal vascular pattern shows through a thinned RPE. [From Marmor, 1981.]

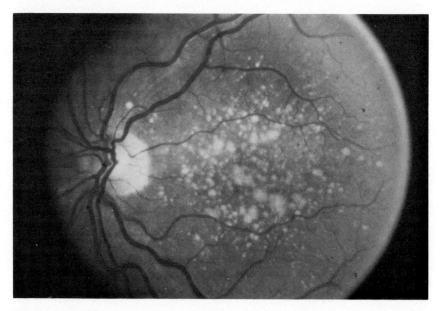

Fig. 6. Fundus of a middle-aged individual showing extensive macular drusen. [From Marmor, 1981.]

significantly with age. The thinning is particularly marked in the retinal periphery, where neuronal elements virtually disappear from sizable patches of retina and a variety of atrophic or cystic changes are seen. We don't know whether this cellular loss is an intrinsic property of retinal neurons, or occurs secondarily from vascular insufficiency. Vessels in the retina and choroid [Friedman et al, 1963] are subject to the same processes of aging and sclerosis that effect vessels elsewhere in the body, and capillary dropout is particularly striking in the thinned peripheral retina of the older eye. There is also, throughout the retina, a gradual loss of capillary endothelial cells with age, which may alter the ability of the vasculature to maintain a special metabolic environment [Kuwabara et al, 1961]. One conclusion we can draw from these data is that our retinas are composed rather fortunately of more cells than we need critically for visual function.

The retinal cells that remain show a variety of alterations with age. Most of the neurons—and especially the cells of the RPE, as discussed further below—accumulate a degenerative aging pigment called lipofuscin. Photoreceptor outer segments may show various levels of disorganization in the arrangement of the internal discs [Marshall et al, 1979] and displacement of nuclei into the outer plexiform layer [Gartner and Henkind, 1981]. The RPE cells become more irregular in size and shape [Friedman and T'so, 1968].

These photoreceptor changes may in part represent intrinsic aging or the effects of vascular insufficiency, but they are also remarkably similar to changes observed in experimental studies where animals are exposed to excessive or prolonged light stress. There is a growing body of evidence that light can be physically damaging to the retina [Lanum, 1978; Sykes et al, 1981]. Energy that is very intense or focused, as from the sun or a laser, will create heat and burn the tissue, but lower degrees of energy from either the visible or ultraviolet spectrum can also cause permanent damage. For example, animals exposed to prolonged periods of fluorescent lighting show degenerative changes in the outer segments, and eventually a dropout of cells. Recovery may be possible if the damage is not too severe, suggesting that our eyes can cope satisfactorily with the minor degrees of damage that probably occur when we spend a sunny day outdoors. However, the toll over a lifetime is unknown, and cumulative "photic" injury to the retina may well be a significant factor in causing the decrease in photoreceptors that occurs with age.

A lifetime of exposure to light may also contribute to aging by stimulating the formation of oxygen-free radicals that oxidize and denature organic lipids [Feeney and Berman, 1976]. The photoreceptor outer segments, being composed largely of lipid membrane, are particularly susceptible to this kind of damage. The cycle of photoreceptor membrane renewal (see above), by which outdated tips of the outer segments are phagocytized by the pigment epithelium, is efficient only as long as the phagocytized material is easily digestible—but oxidized lipids are poorly digested and can cause bits of molecular debris to remain in the cell

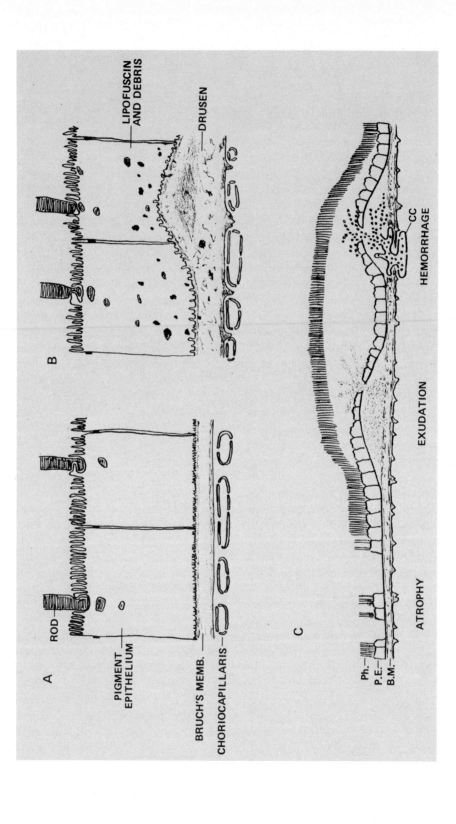

A

ROD

PIGMENT
EPITHELIUM

BRUCH'S MEMB.

CHORIOCAPILLARIS

B

LIPOFUSCIN
AND DEBRIS

DRUSEN

C

Ph.

P.E.

B.M.

ATROPHY

EXUDATION

HEMORRHAGE

CC

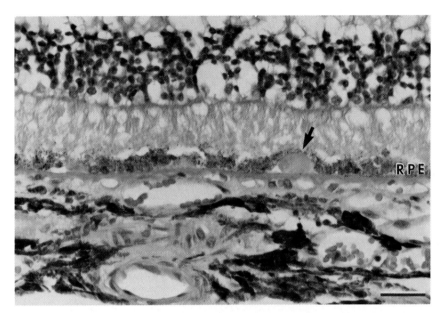

Fig. 8. Cross section of the outer retina and choroid from an aged eye. The RPE has irregular pigmentation, Bruch's membrane is thickened and contains several drusen (arrow), and choroidal vessels show arteriosclerosis. (H & E stain, magnification bar 50 μ.)

(Fig. 7, A and B). Such debris is thought to be a major component of the yellowish fluorescent lipofuscin that becomes particularly dense in the aged RPE [Feeney-Burns et al, 1980]. The RPE cells can in fact become so clogged with lipofuscin that melanin begins to degrade and decrease in concentration, accounting for the depigmentation seen clinically in the fundus of older eyes.

Another feature of the aging RPE are "drusen," which appear clinically as discrete yellowish spots most concentrated in the macula (see Fig. 6). Microscopically, drusen are thick excrescences on Bruch's membrane that are visible because the overlying RPE becomes thin and transparent (Figs. 7B and 8). The substance of drusen is thought to derive from the RPE, possibly from waste

Fig. 7. The pigment epithelium and senile macular degeneration (SMD). (A) Youthful RPE phagocytizes and digests outer segment debris. Bruch's membrane is compact and homogeneous. (B) In aged RPE, membrane debris accumulates and coalesces into lipofuscin. Bruch's membrane is thicker, contains fragments of debris, and may show focal thickenings (drusen). (C) Pathologic SMD. The atrophic form shows thinning and degeneration of RPE and photoreceptors. In the exudative form, protein-rich fluid from the choriocapillaris elevates the RPE and may break through into the subretinal space. In hemorrhagic (disciform) SMD new vessels grow through Bruch's membrane and bleed under the RPE or retina. [From Marmor, 1977.]

material extruded by the cells, since fragments of lipid membrane are sometimes found amidst a hyalin core. Bruch's membrane undergoes diffuse degenerative changes with age [Grindle and Marshall, 1978] and in some eyes may calcify and crack, causing gaps that can serve as a conduit for vascular invasion from the choroid (Fig. 7C), an ominous sign in senile macular degeneration. Keep in mind that we have no evidence that drusen or lipofuscin cause any specific dysfunction of the RPE. However, it seems likely that cells jammed with lipofuscin or stretched mercilessly over a druse are not faring very well—and when the RPE fares poorly, so does the overlying retina.

FUNCTIONAL CHANGES IN THE RETINA WITH AGE

It is well and good to outline the *anatomic* changes that occur in the retina with age, but our ultimate concern is with *function*, ie, how well the retina works. Unfortunately there is a problem in analyzing functional changes: Although there is no doubt that retinal function is critical to many of the visual processes, such as acuity, contrast sensitivity, and temporal resolution, that are considered elsewhere in this book, the actual retinal location of such complex perceptions has not been established and may well be multicentric. For example, contrast sensitivity probably depends on a combination of photoreceptor sensitivity, center-surround ("on-off") organization of the bipolar and other integrative cells within the retina, and possibly on extraretinal cortical processes as well.

In the preceding section, anatomic changes were described with little reference to their functional impact. Obviously, the loss of too many photoreceptors will be incompatible with good vision, but we noted that a large number of photoreceptors and other neurons can in fact be lost without incurring much visual disability. On the other hand, given that the aging eye invariably shows at least a degree of perceptual loss, what are the anatomic and physiologic changes accounting for that perceptual loss? The example of contrast sensitivity points out that many aspects of aging may not be easily definable in terms of damage to a single cell type [Weale, 1975]. Rather, they may represent cumulative mild effects of aging in a number of cells, or possibly a failure in the transmission of information from cell to cell. This distinction may become important, especially in clinical applications: Cumulative aging loss or "senility" is likely to be untreatable because of the multisystem involvement, but more specific types of senile disease in which a particular target tissue is affected might be amenable to therapy.

NORMAL VERSUS PATHOLOGIC AGING

Most of the changes discussed so far could be termed "normal" aging, insofar as they do not affect visual function to the point of noticeable disability. It is appropriate nonetheless, to ask whether even this mild degree of aging is inevitable or "normal." Are cells in the retina and supportive tissues preprogrammed to self-destruct after 70 years, or are the changes that occur conditioned by the environment? For example, the "normal" accumulation of lipofuscin might be prevented or reduced if free radical formation and lipid oxidation could be minimized by the use of sunglasses outdoors and ultraviolet filters indoors to lower the flux radiant energy on the photoreceptors, and by enhancing the natural defenses against oxidative damage through supplementation of antioxidants such as vitamin E or cofactors such as selenium. I caution that this is a hypothetical example, and there is at present no evidence whatsoever that ordinary lighting is harmful or that normal antioxidant defenses require or would benefit from supplementation to slow down the aging process. The point here is simply that the process of lipofuscin accumulation is on theoretical grounds preventable. If cellular damage within the eye can in fact be minimized, this would reduce significantly the amount of visual loss that occurs when "normal" aging begins to creep over into pathology.

This latter event, the transition of "normal" aging to pathology, is not easily defined. At what point does an old-appearing macula start to exhibit pathologic "macular degeneration"? The best definition probably is a functional one: Aging becomes disease when reasonable activities are interfered with. We do not expect to run a 100-yard dash in 10 sec flat at age 80, and this loss of speed is hardly "disease." On the other hand, if we cannot walk or read a book, the designation "disease" becomes appropriate. Disease in the elderly eye falls roughly into two categories: disorders that represent an unwanted extension of the aging process, and disorders that are predisposed to by age.

The most prevalent and serious disease of the aging retina, from a public health standpoint, is senile macular degeneration (SMD). It falls into the first category of aging pathology in that most of the damage evolves (see Fig. 7) out of the "normal" processes of aging [Sarks, 1976; Kornzweig, 1977]. In its mildest form, SMD is simply a cumulation of changes we have already described—loss of photoreceptors, loss of reflexes, drusen, pigment epithelial damage, generalized ischemia, etc.—that has reached a point where visual function is beginning to fail (Fig. 9A). This "dry" or "atrophic" SMD typically reduces acuity to the range of 20/50 to 20/100, at which reading becomes difficult but is still feasible with strong glasses or a magnifier. Because the changes characteristically are limited to the macula only, side vision and general mobility are unimpaired. Occasionally, the damage and atrophy become so extensive that foveal architecture is lost completely, and in those cases acuity may fall below 20/200 and reading vision will be lost altogether. There are no good statistics on the incidence of SMD, but it is probable that somewhere between 15% and 25% of the elderly population has vision of 20/50 or worse and a good percentage of this loss is a result of SMD [Kahn et al, 1977; Marmor, 1981].

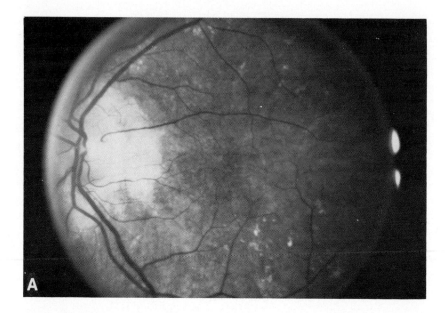

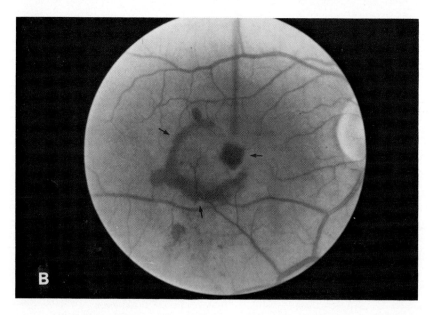

Fig. 9. Senile macular degeneration. (A) Dry atrophy, with nonspecific pigmentary changes and drusen. (B) Fresh hemorrhage (arrows) in disciform degeneration. (The vertical line is the shadow of a fixation target.) (C) Extensive scarring, a late sequela to exudative and hemorrhagic maculopathy.

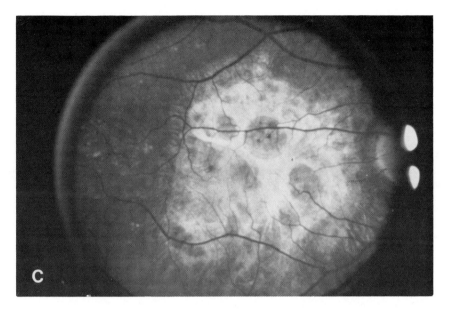

Fig. 9C

A small percentage of eyes with SMD proceed to a much more serious condition called hemorrhagic or disciform SMD (Figs. 7C and 9B), in which damage to Bruch's membrane and the RPE allows capillaries from the choroid to escape their confinement and grow up through the RPE under the retina [Gass, 1973; Friedman et al, 1980]. In this new location the vessels proliferate, leak protein, and bleed, causing localized detachments and irreversible damage to the photoreceptors. Eventually the macular neurons are replaced by scar tissue (Figs. 9C and 10). If the new vessels are discovered early and are away from the fovea, laser treatment may seal them and prevent hemorrhage. However, most of the *neovascularization* of SMD is central and cannot be treated satisfactorily. Disciform SMD is very disabling because central vision is always severely damaged and with it, the ability to read and drive. It is particularly difficult for older individuals to adjust to such a sudden loss of function, but patients may gain some small consolation from knowing that SMD does not extend beyond the macula, so they will never go totally blind.

Ischemic vascular disease is another cause of visual loss in the elderly that represents an extension of the aging process. Gradual narrowing of the vessels contributes to the thinning of the outer retina and to the atrophy of dry SMD. There may also be acute occlusion of arteries or veins within the eye, resulting from generalized vascular disease (Fig. 11A). Vein occlusions are associated with hypertension and generalized arteriosclerosis. Arterial occlusions can occur

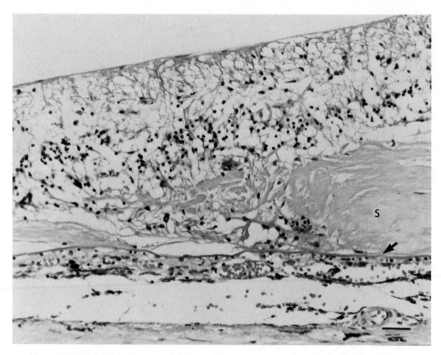

Fig. 10.   Cross section of retina from an elderly individual with disciform macular degeneration. The photoreceptors have been replaced by a thick layer of scar tissue (S); the arrow points to Bruch's membrane. (H & E stain, magnification bar 10 μ.)

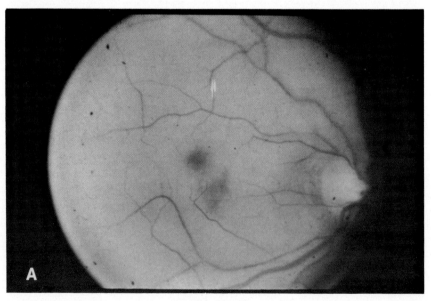

Fig. 11A.

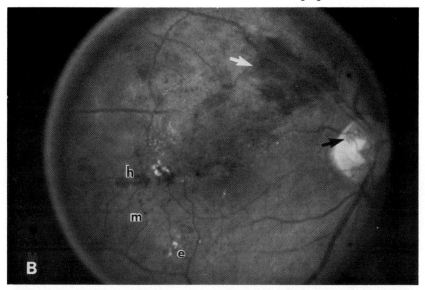

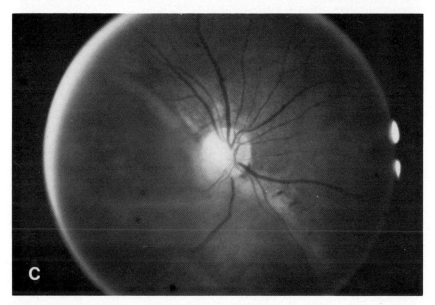

Fig. 11.   Fundus diseases of the elderly. (A) Occlusion of the central retinal artery. The retina has become whitish and opaque from ischemia; only the fovea shows through as a reddish spot. (B) Diabetic retinopathy and branch vein occlusion. Small hemorrhages (h), microaneurisms (m), and hard exudates (e) are visible in the posterior pole. A cluster of lacy new vessels (neovascularization) is growing from the optic disc (black arrow). A small branch vein occlusion with multiple flame-shaped hemorrhages is present above the disc (white arrow). (C) Retinal detachment. The infero-temporal retina is ballooned up within the eye. [From Marmor, 1981.]

from the formation of thrombi, but are more frequently a result of embolism from the carotid or heart.

Other diseases that afflict the elderly retina are less clearly extensions of intrinsic retinal aging. Diabetes is prevalent in our older population and can lead to severe retinal vascular complications (Fig. 11B), but the pathogenesis of the disease has not been established. Retinal detachment (Fig. 11C) is far more prevalent in older than younger eyes and becomes an especially serious risk after cataract surgery. A variety of factors interact to produce this state of affairs, of which vitreous traction upon the retina is probably the most important. Adhesion of the retina to the wall of the eye depends in part on metabolic activity of the RPE [Weale, 1963; Marmor et al, 1980], and thinning of the RPE with age may contribute to the incidence of detachments. Although it is beyond the scope of this paper to discuss general management of the older eye [see Marmor, 1981], we should keep in mind that the aging eye cannot be separated entirely from the aging body. Older individuals are subject to a wide variety of ocular and systemic diseases that can have manifestations in the retina.

SUMMARY AND CONCLUSIONS

Retinal aging involves an interaction of changes within the retinal substance and within supporting structures such as the vasculature and the RPE. Photo-receptors and other retinal neurons decrease in number with age, but it is not clear how much of this loss represents an intrinsic aging process and how much represents damage secondary to aging of the vasculature or the RPE. Cellular changes such as the accumulation of lipofuscin in neurons and RPE are considered a part of "normal" aging, but in fact may be conditioned by the environment. Many of the anatomic changes seen with age are hard to relate to functional loss. Conversely, some of the visual loss in elderly people may result from a cu-mulation of senile changes in many tissues, none of which is severely affected by itself. Retinal disease in the elderly may be an extension of "normal" aging; an example is senile macular degeneration, which is the most prevalent retinal problem of the aged. Other diseases, such as diabetes, vascular insufficiency, or retinal detachment, may also afflict the aged retina.

I hope that this brief review will focus attention on several areas that are particularly worthy of research effort in the future. The greatest public health problem involving the aged retina is senile macular degeneration. Pathogenesis of this disorder is probably a combination of intrinsic aging of the photoreceptors and RPE, vascular ischemia, and oxidative damage that may be conditioned by exposure to light. Research is needed on the nature of light damage and oxidative metabolism in the retina and their potential modification pharmacologically. A major question, yet unanswered, is why the macula as opposed to the periphery of the retina is so peculiarly susceptible to aging. Research is also needed on retinal detachment, which may be more effectively managed if the normal mechanisms of retinal adhesion can be better understood, and on systemic vascular disease, which obviously has a considerable effect within the eye. It is unlikely that we can ever freeze time and preserve all our youth, nor would that necessarily be desirable. However, it is within the realm of possibility to limit some of the more significant influences that cause our retinas to wear out, and if this can be done, the prospects are good for better vision in old age.

ACKNOWLEDGMENTS

Supported in part by National Eye Institute Grant EY01678 and by the Medical Research Section of the Veterans Administration.

REFERENCES

Devaney KO, Johnson HA (1980) Neuron loss in the aging visual cortex of man. J Gerontol 15:836–841.

Feeney L, Berman ER (1976) Oxygen toxicity: Membrane damage by free radicals. Invest Ophthalmol 15(10):789–792.

Feeney-Burns L, Berman ER, and Rothman H (1980) Lipofuscin of human retinal pigment epithelium. Am J Ophthalmol 90(6):783–791.

Friedman AH, Pokorny KS, Suhan JP, Kornzweig AL (1980) Senile macular degeneration: Clinical, histopathological and ultrasound studies. Mt Sinai J Med 47:227–245.

Friedman E, Ts'o MOM (1968) The retinal pigment epithelium. II. Histologic changes associated with age. Arch Ophthalmol 79:315–320.

Friedman E, Smith TR, Kuwabara T (1963) Senile choroidal vascular patterns and drusen. Arch Ophthalmol 69:220–230.

Gartner S, Henkind P (1981) Aging and degeneration of the human macula. 1. Outer nuclear layer and photoreceptors. Br J Ophthalmol 65:23–28.

Gass JDM (1973) Drusen and disciform macular detachment and degeneration. Arch Ophthalmol 90(3):206–217.

Grindle CFJ, Marshall J (1978) Ageing changes in Bruch's membrane and their functional implications. Trans Ophthalmol Soc UK 98:172–175.

Hamming NA, Apple D (1980) Anatomy and embryology of the eye. In Peyman GA, Sanders DR, Goldberg MF (Eds) "Principles and Practice of Ophthalmology," Vol 1. Philadelphia: Saunders, pp 3–68.

Kahn HA, Leibowitz HM, Ganley JP, Kini MM, Colton T, Nickerson RS, Dawber TR (1977) The Framingham Eye Study. 1. Outline and major prevalence findings. Am J Epidemiol 106:17–41.

Kanski JJ (1975) Peripheral retinal degenerations. Trans Ophthalmol Soc UK 95:173–179.

Kornzweig AL (1977) Changes in the choriocapillaries associated with senile macular degeneration. Ann Ophthalmol 9:753–764.

Kuwabara T, Carroll JM, Cogan DG (1961) Retinal vascular patterns. Arch Ophthalmol 65:708–716.

Lanum J (1978) The damaging effects of light on the retina. Empirical findings, theoretical and practical implications. Surv Ophthalmol 22:221–249.

Marmor MF (1977) The eye and vision in the elderly. Geriatrics 32:63–67.

Marmor MF (1980) Clinical physiology of the retina. In Peyman GA, Sanders DR, Goldberg MF (Eds) "Principles and Practice of Ophthalmology," Vol II. Philadelphia: Saunders, pp 823–856.

Marmor MF (1981) Management of elderly patients with impaired vision. In Ebaugh FG Jr (Ed) "Management of Common Problems in Geriatric Medicine." Menlo Park: Addison-Wesley, pp 17–44.

Marmor MF, Abdul-Rahim AS, Cohen DS (1980) The effect of metabolic inhibitors on retinal adhesion and subretinal fluid resorption. Invest Ophthalmol Vis Sci 19(8):893–903.

Marshall J, Grindle J, Ansell PL, Borwein B (1979) Convolution in human rods: An ageing process. Br J Ophthalmol 63:181–187.

Sarks SH (1976) Ageing and degeneration in the macular region: A clinico-pathological study. Br J Ophthalmol 60:324–341.

Sykes SM, Robison WG Jr, Waxler M, Kuwabara T (1981) Damage to the monkey retina by broad-spectrum fluorescent light. Invest Ophthalmol Vis Sci 20(4):425–434.

Weale RA (1963) "The Aging Eye." New York: Harper.

Weale RA (1975) Senile changes in visual acuity. Trans Ophthalmol Soc UK 95:36–38.

Young RW (1976) Visual cells and the concept of renewal. Invest Ophthalmol 15(9):700–725.

Aging and Human Visual Function, pages 79-114

Cellular Alterations in Visual Pathways and the Limbic System: Implications for Vision and Short-Term Memory

J. Mark Ordy, Kenneth R. Brizzee, and Horton A. Johnson

RATIONALE FOR RELATING AGE DIFFERENCES IN VISION TO SHORT-TERM MEMORY AND CELLULAR ALTERATIONS IN VISUAL AND LIMBIC SYSTEMS

The visual system is one of the more extensively studied and better understood components of the mammalian brain [Berkley, 1978; Kaneko, 1979; Van Essen, 1979]. The hippocampus of the limbic system has also received considerable attention in short-term or "working" memory [Olton et al, 1979] and as a cognitive spatial map, in neuroendocrine regulation of endocrine and autonomic functions, and in behavioral arousal [O'Keefe and Nadel, 1978]. Until recently, only a small number of studies have dealt with vision and aging [see reviews by Fozard et al, 1977; Ordy and Brizzee, 1979]. Current reviews of memory impairments and aging have included increasing emphases on decrements in sensory processes or iconic [Walsh and Prasse, 1980] and echoic sensory memory [Crowder, 1980] and on divided attention and depth of information processing within an encoding–storage–retrieval continuum [Craik and Simon, 1980]. Due to unique function-structure specificity of the visual system, attempts have been made to correlate age differences in visual functions with concomitant cellular alterations in the retino-geniculo-striate pathway [Ordy and Brizzee, 1979]. It has been suggested that focal and/or diffuse loss of neurons from the cerebral cortex and limbic system with age may produce decreased selective attention and result in memory impairments of the elderly [Kinsbourne, 1980]. More specifically, age decrements in convergent multisensory integration and short-term memory have been related to cell loss and age pigment or lipofuscin accumulation in specific sensory pathways and in multisensory integrative and stimulus–reward-coupling neural circuits of the limbic system (Ordy et al, 1980a).

Within an encoding, storage, and retrieval framework of memory, sensory registration, attention, learning, memory, and motor performance are all intimately related [Craik, 1979]. However, experimental studies of sensory functions in the elderly are generally restricted to a single sensory modality. They also focus on peripheral sense organs without reference to afferent pathways, learning, memory, or stimulus–reward coupling neural circuits of the brain. It is still widely assumed that the sensory systems, including the visual pathways, "terminate" in the primary projection areas of the cerebral cortex. Cerebral cortex areas not designated as primary sensory or motor are defined as so-called "association" cortex. In this view, visual sensations result in more complex perception, culminating in learning and memory, which presumably consist of "associations" between stimuli and responses in the occipital cortex. The retino-geniculo-striate pathway is critical for acuity, color vision, and stereopsis [Van Essen, 1979]. More recent studies have extended visual discrimination learning and memory to extrastriate visual areas and the inferotemporal cortex [Wilson, 1978]. Vision has been included in convergent multisensory neural circuits [Van Hoesen et al, 1972], in attention, motivation, memory and stimulus–reward coupling, and by neuropeptides and hormones in the limbic system [deWied, 1977; Ordy, 1981; Rigter and Van Riezen, 1981]. Visual-sensory, or iconic, memory has been considered to be modality specific [Walsh and Prasse, 1980]. Attention and short-term memory are believed to occur across sensory modalities [Ordy et al, 1980a]. The limbic system appears critical not only in homeostatic regulation of the internal environment, but also in convergent multisensory integration, attention, arousal, and memory consolidation through neuroendocrine modulation of reward properties of environmental stimuli. In addition to the well-studied retino-geniculo-striate pathway and current emphasis on visual input to memory circuits in the limbic system, other retinal connections to the limbic system include an input to the suprachiasmatic nuclei for visual synchronization of circadian rhythms [Moore, 1979]. Hemisphere specialization for visual-spatial, and auditory semantic memory has also been reported [Moscovitch, 1979].

Short-term memory may represent only a small segment of information processing, but it may be crucial for encoding, storage, and retrieval of all new information. It may represent a basic control process for all thinking, remembering, and consciousness [Atkinson and Shiffrin, 1971]. According to some views of short-term memory as a brief organizing process, its decline with age may occur independently of decrements in sensory process, learning, motivation, and motor performance. Its loss may be negligible if sensory information is adequately registered, or provided that the elderly are not required to divide their attention among sensory inputs, or are not asked to reorganize the material [Craik, 1977, 1979]. However, if short-term memory is conceptualized as a time-dependent, convergent multisensory, stimulus–reward coupling process in specific neural circuits rather than simply as a "brief organizing process," it can provide a challenging rationale for relating age differences in vision to short-term memory and cellular alterations in the visual and limbic systems. The specific aims of this chapter are (1) to examine age differences in visual functions and relate them to physiological, chemical, and morphological alterations in the visual system and (2) to evaluate the effects of aging on short-term or "working" memory in relation to cellular alteration in the hippocampus as a major convergent multisensory and stimulus–reward coupling center involving entorhinal, septal, thalamic, and frontal neural circuits of the cerebral cortex and limbic system. Primary emphasis is on reported age differences in vision and short-term memory of man; however, reference is also made to recent direct correlational studies of vision, short-term memory, and cell loss in the brain of nonhuman primates. Neuroanatomical pathways can provide important clues concerning the rationale for relating age differences in vision to short-term memory and cellular alterations in the visual and limbic systems. Figure 1 illustrates major cellular features of the primate visual pathway. Figure 2 illustrates vision as part of convergent multisensory, stimulus–reward coupling circuits in the cerebral cortex and limbic system.

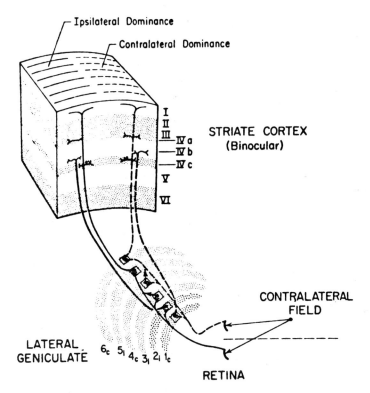

Fig. 1.   Vision as a modality-specific process: diagrammatic illustration of the structural-functional organization of the afferent retino-geniculo-striate pathway of the primate visual system. Roman nos., striate cortex laminae; Arabic nos., LGB layers. [Snodderly, 1974].

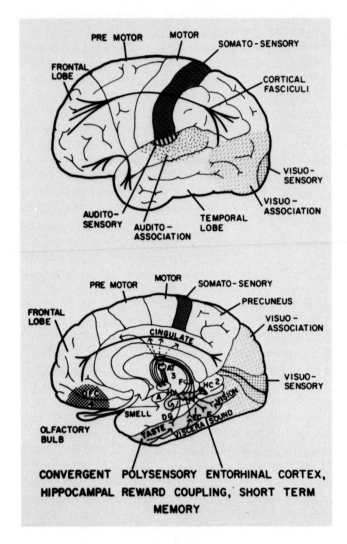

Fig. 2. Vision as part of broader information-processing framework: anatomical circuits for convergent polysensory information-processing within multimodal regions of cerebral cortex and limbic system involved in coupling of sensory and short-term memory. (1) Visual pathway, (2) auditory pathway, (3) somatosensory pathway, and (4) olfactory pathway, smell. Top-lateral view, bottom-medial view of brain. [Ordy et al, 1980a].

AGE DIFFERENCES IN VISUAL FUNCTIONS AND IN NEURAL TRANSMISSION OF INFORMATION OVER MULTISYNAPTIC PATHWAYS IN THE RETINO-GENICULO-STRIATE SYSTEM

A previous review summarized earlier findings of significant declines with age in human acuity, color vision, and depth perception [Ordy and Brizzee, 1979]. (More recent reviews are included in other chapters of this volume). These age differences in visual functions have been attributed mainly to peripheral changes in the eye [Corso, 1975; Fozard et al, 1977]. A more balanced peripheral-central approach has emphasized the relation of age differences in these psychophysical visual functions and age-related differences in visually evoked (VEP) and event-related (ERP) potentials, cerebral blood flow, glucose metabolism, loss of neurons, spines, synapses, transmitter and hormone receptors, and accumulation of lipofuscin (age pigment) in the visual system [Beck et al, 1979; Ordy and Brizzee, 1979; Ordy et al, 1980a; Hansch et al, 1980]. Multidisciplinary approaches have greatly increased prospects of correlating age differences in visual functions with specific cellular alterations in the visual system. Reviews have been published of age changes in electroencephalographic (EEG) activity in relation to sensory reaction time, cognitive function, cerebral blood flow, regional metabolism, and clinical status from maturity to old age [Thompson and Marsh, 1973; Obrist and Busse, 1975; Storrie and Eisdorfer, 1978; Hansch et al, 1980]. Normative values for visual, auditory, and somatosensory evoked potentials (EP) have been recorded from early childhood through 85 years. Major age changes in visual, auditory, and somatosensory EPs include diminished amplitude and increased latency. Figure 3 illustrates a comparison of visual (VER), auditory (AER) and somatosensory (SER) evoked responses during maturation and aging in human subjects. This figure also illustrates age declines in multisensory information from peripheral sense organs to the primary sensory projection areas. Since the visual, auditory and somatosensory evoked potentials were recorded from the same subject, they illustrate concurrent impairment in multisensory information processing, possibly a very important issue for short-term memory impairments in the elderly (Ordy et al, 1980a).

Event Related Potentials (ERP) have been used for evaluating sensory information processing, short-term memory, and cognitive activity in the elderly [Klorman et al, 1978; Ford et al, 1980]. Late positive components of the ERP presumably reflect sensory information and decision processing, or cognitive activity. The ERP components are recorded at latencies of 300–800 milliseconds after the stimulus, and they may or may not reflect modality specific activity depending on type of stimuli, and location of recording. Psychophysical correlates of P300 have been designated as information processing, orientation, selective attention, short-term memory and decision making. Several studies have reported significant age differences in P300 components of ERP during

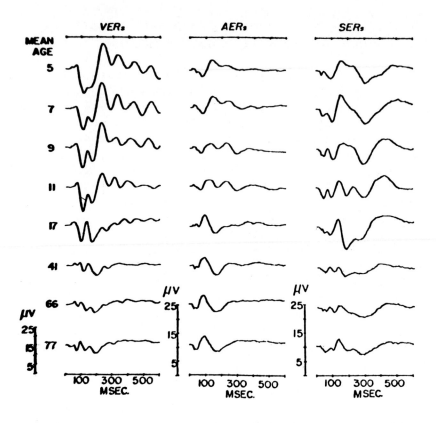

Fig. 3. Age differences in neural transmission of visual information over multisynaptic pathways. Multisensory and concurrent declines in sensory information processing as reflected in visual evoked responses (VER), auditory evoked responses (AER), and somatosensory evoked responses (SER) in man [Beck et al, 1975, 1979].

memory retrieval tasks in the elderly [Ford et al, 1980]. Significant alterations in latency and possibly in amplitude of P300 of ERP have been reported as part of normal aging in man [Klorman, et al, 1978; Hansch et al, 1980]. Also, with increasing age, significant alterations have been reported in sensory semantic, and "depth" of information processing, as reflected in ERP [Simon, 1979].

Regarding the occurrence and locus of visually evoked potentials (VEP) in relation to the retino-geniculo-striate pathway, the reported increases in latency and decreases in amplitude in the elderly may reflect significant age-differences in neural transmission of visual information processing over multi-synaptic pathways. Other evidence on neural transmission includes age declines in temporal resolution of different rates of intermittent light stimulation, generally defined as the psychophysical critical flicker fusion (CFF) threshold. In photic driving, the light evoked responses become time-locked to, or "following" the flash, presented at increasing frequency, resulting in the critical frequency of photic driving (CFPD) threshold. In one study, it was reported that the CFPD threshold of 72 flashes per second at age 30, declined significantly to 60 flashes per second after 60 [Celesia and Daly, 1977]. Spatial and temporal characteristics of visually evoked responses have been associated with x and y channels in the retino-geniculo-striate system [Van Essen, 1979]. High CFF thresholds have generally been associated with cones and photopic vision, whereas lower CFF thresholds involve rods and scotopic vision. The findings of this study may be interpreted to reflect decreasing conduction velocity, or impaired neural transmission due to loss of photoreceptors, neurons, dendritic spines, synapses, and accumulation of lipofuscin in the visual system [Ordy and Brizzee, 1979; Dustman et al, 1981].

More direct evidence on age differences in neural transmission of visual information has been reported in man as alterations in neurotransmitters and their enzymes in the geniculates and striate cortex. Physiologically, normal vision depends on a complex balance between excitatory and inhibitory neurotransmitters in the retino-geniculo-striate pathway. According to recent neurochemical studies, there is a significant decline with age in the gamma-aminobutyric acid (GABA) transmitter enzyme glutamic acid decarboxylase (GAD) in the LGN of man and in other thalamic sensory nuclei. The declining sensory information-processing capacity of man has been attributed in part to the significant age decline in GAD enzyme activity of the thalamus since it is considered to be the major relay station of sensory pathways [McGeer and McGeer, 1976]. GABA has generally been assigned an inhibitory role in the CNS. Neurochemical evidence of a selective cell loss and/or difference in the functional state of remaining neurons in the cerebral cortex of man has also been obtained not only in cases of senile dementia but also in older accident victims. Choline acetyltransferase (CAT) and GAD have been used as markers of cholinergic and GABA-containing neurons, respectively. Significant age decrements in both CAT and GAD activity have been reported to occur in visual areas 18 and 19, from 20 to 60 years of age in man [McGeer and McGeer, 1976].

AGING AND VISUAL FUNCTIONS: OPTICAL, RETINAL, AND GENICULOSTRIATE SOURCES

Basically, such major visual functions as acuity, color vision, and stereopsis depend upon optical, retinal, and geniculostriate mechanisms.

Visual Acuity

Major effects of optical factors in acuity include brightness and contrast gradients of the image focused on the retina. Since the pupil, lens, and ocular media determine retinal illuminance, age-dependent changes in visual thresholds have generally been attributed to decreased pupillary diameter or senile miosis, and opacification or cataract formation in the lens [Weale, 1973]. Part of the age changes in visual functions have been attributed to decreased pupillary diameter and changes in optical properties of the lens and ocular media [Gunkel and Gouras, 1963; Grover and Zigman, 1972]. From ages 30 to 60, a linear decline occurs in the amount of light reaching the retina, whether the eye is light- or dark-adapted [Weale, 1963]. With a standard white light source, only approximately one-third of the light that reaches the retina of a 20-year-old will reach the retina of a 60-year-old. With a blue light source, the decrease is much more pronounced and has been estimated to reach a factor of eight or nine [Weale, 1963]. Age changes in the cornea, lens, and ocular media can result in light scatter and blurring of the retinal image and in reduced acuity, particularly for targets of low luminance and spatial contrast and high frequency [Weale, 1973, 1978]. However, the maximum age decline in acuity attributable to optical changes may amount to 20%, with 80% attributable to suspected cell loss in the retino-geniculo-striate pathway from 40 to 90 years [Weale, 1975]. The rate of aging in scotopic vision may be greater than in photopic vision. But loss of rods should be less critical for acuity since spatial summation of rods is much greater than that of cones. Critical cell loss for central acuity must include foveal cones since the direct signal pathway from cones to bipolar and ganglion cells may be isolated, with little lateral inhibition or cross-talk in the central acuity channel [Kaneko, 1979]. More recent attempts to account for the age decline in acuity have included a "random-cell-loss" hypothesis, extending from loss of foveal cones to loss of neurons from the geniculostriate system [Weale, 1975, 1978]. Cell loss in the retino-geniculo-striate system will be considered in greater detail in subsequent sections.

Color Vision

As in visual acuity of the elderly, part of the decline in color vision may be associated with alterations in dioptrical mechanisms of the eye. Considerably less information is available on age-dependent changes in cones, rods, and bipolar and ganglion cells of the retina as possible major sources of age differences in color vision or spectral sensitivity. It is now widely accepted that the cone pigments of the human retina have maximum absorption at 590 (red), 540 (green), and 440 (blue) nm. Based on absorption spectra and perimetry studies of color zones in the retina, it is generally accepted that blue and yellow responses have more extensive retinal fields than red and green, which are more restricted to the cones of the fovea and macula [Rodiek, 1979]. It seems likely that the age-dependent declines in red–green discrimination after age 60 may be related to loss of foveal cones, retinal bipolar and ganglion cells, and loss of neurons from the geniculostriate system [Weale, 1978].

Microelectrode studies of single unit responses to different wavelengths have markedly increased knowledge on spectrally opponent neural mechanisms of color vision in the retino-geniculo-striate pathway of primates [DeValois and Jacobs, 1968; Berkley, 1978]. Basically, spectrally opponent cells in the geniculates receive information about color or wavelength from the photoreceptors of the retina and then transmit this information to the striate cortex. Information concerning intensity or brightness of light is transmitted in channels with non-opponent cells, and concerning color or wavelength, in channels with spectrally opponent cells. In lesion studies with primates, it has been shown that rhesus monkeys with total ablation of the striate cortex cannot discriminate colors [LePore et al, 1975]. Although, it seems likely that the age-related impairments of color vision in the elderly for hues of blue and green are in part associated with changes in dioptrical mechanisms of the eye, and with loss of photoreceptors of the retina, cell loss from the geniculostriate pathway must also play an important role, since primates with duplex retinae lose color vision after total ablation of the striate cortex [Berkley, 1978].

Depth Perception and Stereopsis

There is now considerable evidence that one of the more important functions of the striate cortex may be to analyze the disparity of retinal images from the two eyes, and to provide for binocular fusion, or stereoscopic depth perception [Van Essen, 1979]. Random dot stereograms have been used to demonstrate stereopsis in the rhesus monkey [Bough, 1970]. Using the Howard-Dolman depth perception apparatus, rhesus monkeys have been reported to have stereoacuity that is essentially identical to that of man [Sarmiento, 1975]. Earlier, cells with sensitivity to binocular depth discrimination were identified in area 18 of the macaque cortex [Hubel and Wiesel, 1970]. More recently, sharp binocular disparity tuning has been reported for many neurons in the foveal striate cortex of the unanesthetized, behaviorally alert rhesus monkey [Poggio and Fischer, 1977]. Whereas extrastriate visual areas appear quite important for stereopsis, it seems evident that the geniculostriate pathway is critical at least for the first stage of stereopsis or depth perception, based on detection of binocular disparity [Van Essen, 1979]. Although cell loss in the retino-geniculo-striate system may be of considerable importance for acuity and color vision declines in the elderly, cell loss in the striate and extrastriate visual areas must be of greater significance for impairments in stereopsis, or depth perception.

SPECIFIC CELLULAR ALTERATIONS IN THE RETINO-GENICULO-STRIATE PATHWAY OF MAN AND NONHUMAN PRIMATES WITH AGE

There is now developing considerable evidence that in lower mammals and possibly even in primates, the visual system can be modified by environmental influences [Pettigrew and Spinelli, 1974]. Whether this plasticity remains during aging has yet to be determined. After maturity, age differences in acuity, color vision, and stereopsis may be associated not only with loss of neurons but with alterations in the remaining neurons, or more likely with both possibilities. Even without the loss of neurons, gradual accumulation of lipofuscin and loss of neuronal connectivity resulting from loss of dendritic spines and synaptic contacts could result in the apparent linear decreases in neuronal network functional capacity from 30 to 60 years that have been reported in the previously cited psychophysical and electrophysiological studies. If it can be demonstrated that the rate of loss of cells is exponential at any level of the retino-geniculo-striate afferent pathway from age 60 to 90, this could provide the more compelling quantitative evidence on the specific cellular correlates for the exponential declines in these visual functions during senescence. Earlier reviews of age differences in vision attributed the major age declines primarily to alterations in pupillary diameter and the image-focusing optical mechanisms of the eye [Fozard et al, 1977]. However, on the basis of a more careful review of even the earlier evidence, it was concluded in a recent authoritative review that while these declines must play a role, they are probably not responsible for the exponential decline of visual acuity, and possibly other functions, from 60 to 90 years in man. It was concluded that cellular loss, due to some "random-cell-loss" process in the retino-geniculo-striate pathway with age must somehow represent a major source of the exponential decline of visual capacity [Weale, 1975, 1978]. Information on cellular alterations in the visual system of man is fragmentary, but several studies have reported significant age-related changes in the retina, LGB, and striate cortex.

Aging in Human Retina

There is considerable knowledge on the basic outlines of neuronal circuitry of the retina [Kaneko, 1979] and the receptive field organization for encoding spatial contrast, frequency, and orientation in acuity at different levels and possibly in different channels of the retino-geniculo-striate system [Maffei, 1978; Rodiek, 1979]. Age-related declines in human acuity and in the Stiles-Crawford function have been correlated in senile macular degeneration with age differences in funduscopic appearance, particularly in macular and foveal regions, and with reduced directional sensitivity, orientation, or alignment of photoreceptors [Fitzgerald et al, 1979]. Earlier studies have noted correlations among reduced acuity, macular degeneration, and alterations in the retinal pigment epithelium (RPE) with age [Gass, 1973]. We have yet to determine which changes in RPE and in receptors represent normal aging, or at what stage of outer segment alterations there may occur receptor cell loss, and whether this process may be characterized as macular degeneration. Until very recently, the RPE has been considered the neglected tissue of the eye [Zinn and Marmor, 1979]. Significant increase in research of RPE has been attributed to clarification of rod and cone outer segment renewal, which takes place in close metabolic and structural association with the RPE [Steinberg and Wood, 1979]. Paradoxically, progress in understanding RPE-mediated receptor outer segment renewal suggested that, due to dynamic renewal, visual cells may "grow old without aging" [Young, 1976]. However, considerable evidence can be cited in support of specific cellular changes in the macula during normal aging, particularly in the metabolic and structural relationship between the RPE and photoreceptors. These changes may affect spatial resolution since acuity and foveal cone orientation and density are intimately related in encoding of a detailed spatial visuotopic map. This hypothesis of "cone loss" is new, since most earlier studies of age decline in visual acuity attributed the decline to pupillary and optical changes in the eye [Weale, 1973, 1975]. Absolute visual thresholds and rate of dark adaptation are known to increase with age [Domey et al, 1969]. Increasing age differences in the slopes of rod and cone adaptation curves have suggested that the scotopic system may age at a more rapid rate than the photopic system [Weale, 1975]. However, due to differences in spatial and temporal summating properties of rods and cones, areal factors in the periphery of the retina may not be as important as the absolute number of cones in the foveola. Foveal cone loss must reduce central acuity as a function of luminance, contrast, frequency, and orientation [Weale, 1975, 1978; Blackwell, 1979; Ordy and Brizzee, 1979]. Prominent cellular age changes reported to occur in the human retina include (1) significant increases in lipofuscin pigment in RPE, (2) possible loss of foveal cones and peripheral rods, and (3) degeneration of bipolar and ganglion cells. In funduscopic evaluations of the elderly coupled with fluorescein angiography, a loss of the foveal reflex, granularity of RPE, increased disturbance of choroidal vessels, and progressive manifestation of drusen have been reported [Kornzweig, 1979]. Histological evaluations of age-related changes in RPE, Bruch's membrane, and choriocapillaries have indicated alterations in the RPE, particularly "basal lamina deposits" as consistent manifestations in normal aging and in senile macular degeneration [Sarks, 1976]. Specific sequences in the formation of lipofuscin and melanin pigment have been identified in the human RPE, extending from birth to age 80 [Feeney, 1978]. In a study of lipofuscin accumulation in the RPE from birth to age 88, lipofuscin was reported to increase significantly from dispersed to congregated form, with increased concentration in the posterior pole and a notable attenuation in the fovea [Wing et al, 1978]. The rate of increase in lipofuscin, from ages 30 to 60, was gradual. The rate of accumulation increased from 60 to 80 years. A close temporal association between lipofuscin accumulation and cell loss from the brain has been suspected [Brizzee et al, 1975]. The more convincing evidence on specific molecular and temporal sequences appears in the RPE, with an apparent loss of adjacent cones from the human retina. Morphological studies have indicated that the RPE is involved in phagocytosis of cone outer components in man [Steinberg et al, 1977]. A small and linear loss of cones from the human retina has been reported, from 20 to 40 years, followed by a greater rate of loss above age 40 [Weale, 1978]. Loss of cones and rods as well as other retinal degeneration has been reported in man after the fourth decade [Marshall, 1978; Gartner and Henkind, 1981].

Changes in rod outer segment length, disorganization of membrane discs, and loss of rods have also been reported [Marshall et al, 1979]. Corpora amylacea, a form of neuronal degeneration, has been observed in the bipolar layer [Avendano et al, 1980]. Ganglion cell degeneration has also been reported in the elderly [Vrabec, 1965]. A critical source of normal aging and macular degeneration in the retina may be the RPE. One major function of RPE is renewal and phagocytosis, by lysosomes, of shed rod and cone outer segments [Anderson et al, 1978]. The early onset of acuity decline at low luminance and contrast in man at age 30 may coincide not only with optical but with pigment changes in RPE [Hogan, 1972]. A role for RPE in the resolution of images appears plausible [Zinn and Benjamin-Henkind, 1979]. The life-long process of RPE metabolic interaction with receptor outer segments in response to light, oxygen, and formation of free radicals may inevitably affect RPE lipofuscin and melanin, RPE metabolic rate of receptor outer segment disc turnover [Feeney-Burns et al, 1980; Young, 1980]. Reduced RPE lysosomal recycling of outer segments may eventually result in outer segment disorganization and loss of receptors [Armstrong et al, 1979]. RPE lysosomal enzyme activity is highest in the macula of man [Shiono et al, 1980].

The use of nonhuman primates has provided great insight into neural mechanisms of acuity. Neural factors in acuity include foveal cone and ganglion cell density, their ratio and eccentricity from the fovea, a geniculostriate magnification factor, and ultimately neurons with receptive field properties that are smallest at the foveal projection area of the striate cortex in terms of fine tuning to stimuli of specific orientation and frequency [Rolls and Cowey, 1970; Van Essen, 1979]. In a recent study, direct correlations were made among visual acuity, foveal cone density, and lipofuscin in RPE of the retina in young (5 years), middle-aged (12 years), and old (22 years) rhesus monkeys [Ordy et al, 1980b]. The acuity of the young group was 0.83, that of the middle age group was 0.86, and that of the old group was significantly poorer at 2.0 min of visual angle. According to morphometric evaluations, foveal cone density decreased from 44.16 cone inner segments (CIS) in the middle-aged group to 39.00 CIS per 100 μm along the horizontal meridian of the 1° × 1° pure cone foveola.

Lipofuscin pigment in RPE increased dramatically from the young to the middle-aged group and particularly to the old-age group. Since the visual system is characterized by intrinsic afferent or "input" directionality, the molecular and temporal sequences in accumulation of lipofuscin in RPE, reduced outer segment disc renewal, and cell loss indicate intrinsic metabolic events in RPE, followed by transneuronal degeneration and deafferentation as major sources of cell loss and cellular aging in the retino-geniculo-striate system [Armstrong et al, 1979]. Figure 4 illustrates in a micrograph the fovea in which morphometric measurements were made of age differences in foveal cone density in the rhesus monkey.

Aging in Human Lateral Geniculate Nucleus (LGB)

Most if not all of the retinal ganglion cells extend their axons as part of the optic nerve to synapse in the lateral geniculate nucleus (LGB) of the thalamus. Studies of receptive field properties of retinal ganglion cells have designated cells with sustained responses to light as X cells and those with transient responses as Y cells. A greater proportion of X cells has been reported for central as opposed to peripheral vision in the cat [Fukuda and Stone, 1975]. Considerably less is known about the functional and structural characteristics of primate retinal bipolar and ganglion cells [Boycott and Dowling, 1969]. However, morphometric evaluations have been reported of rhesus monkey X and Y ganglion cells as part of a study involving tracing axonal projections to the different layers of the macaque LGB [Bunt et al, 1975, 1977]. More recent physiological studies have demonstrated spatial frequency and temporal resolution of X and Y cells in the macaque [Dreher et al, 1976; Schiller and Malpeli, 1978]. In man and other diurnal primates, there are two magnocellular layers, 1 and 2, with large cells, and four parvocellular layers 3, 4, 5 and 6, with small cells in LGB [Berkley, 1978]. In LGB, layers 1, 4, and 6 receive input from the contralateral eye, and layers 2, 3, and 5 from the ipsilateral eye (see Fig. 1). Receptive field properties of LGB cells appear similar to those of retinal ganglion cells. Also, similar to the topographic magnification ratio in the striate cortex for foveal vision, a proportionately larger number of LGB cells appears to be allocated to central than to peripheral vision. However, binocular interactions do not take place in LGB cells [Berkley, 1978; Van Essen, 1979].

There are very few studies of age differences in the human LGB. As cited earlier in this review, neurochemical studies have reported declines with age in GABA transmitter enzymes in LGB of man [McGeer and McGeer, 1976]. Since the optic nerves from the left and right eye terminate in six alternate layers of LGN, it has been reported that the three layers from each eye contain approximately an equal accumulation of lipofuscin and DNP-diaphorase oxidative enzyme activity in old age. In two cases where eye removal was necessitated in childhood, it was reported that neuronal atrophy with reduced lipofuscin accumulation and lower oxidative enzyme activity, including the neuropil, occurred

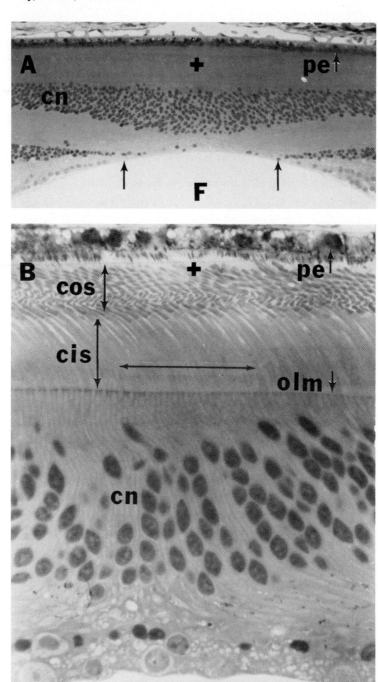

in the three associated alternate layers of LGN [Friede, 1962]. However, increases in intraneuronal lipofuscin of the three alternate LGN layers with terminal degeneration and transsynaptic atrophy have also been reported after eye enucleation in the rhesus monkey [Hasan and Glees, 1973]. Due to conflicting findings, it seems apparent that no causal relation has been established among functional activity, lipofuscin accumulation, and cell loss or degeneration in LGN. However, since the striate cortex appears to receive spatial and temporal information over anatomically and physiologically distinct x and y channels from retinal ganglion cells projecting to LGB, cell loss in the x and y channels with increasing age should be of considerable importance for declines in spatial and temporal aspects of visual information-processing in the retino-geniculo-striate pathways.

Aging in Human Striate Cortex

In man and other diurnal primates, axons of LGB cells project primarily to lamina IV, or the so-called line of Gennari, in the striate cortex, or area 17. There are significant differences among mammalian species, including diurnal primates, as to the cortical areas to which the axons of LGB cells project [Van Essen, 1979]. In man, the extensive development of the temporal and parietal lobes has restricted the representation of the central fovea and macula backward into the calcarine sulcus of the occipital pole. In even "higher" diurnal primates, such as the rhesus and squirrel monkey, the projection of the fovea and macula appears restricted to the dorsolateral surface of the striate cortex [Cowey and Ellis, 1969; Hubel and Wiesel, 1977]. Similar to the cellular magnification ratio in LGB, a proportionally greater topographic area in the striate cortex is allocated to central than to peripheral vision [Rolls and Cowey, 1970]. In studies of age differences in vision of even diurnal primate models, it seems important to recognize the significant differences in the location of the foveal projection to the striate cortex of these diurnal primates that are of the same taxonomic order as man [Ordy and Brizzee, 1979].

In one of the earlier and most widely cited studies of cell loss with age in the cerebral cortex of man, a significant loss of cells was reported from the striate cortex from age 20 to 80 in healthy normal human subjects [Brody, 1955]. Since

---

Fig. 4. (A) Horizontal sections through fovea of middle-aged macaque retina, with cone nuclei (cn), foveola (between arrows), retina pigment epithelium (pe), and cross (+) as topographic marker for center of foveola. Epon section 4 μm thick, toluidine blue stain, 150 ×. (B) Higher power (900 ×), oil immersion micrograph of foveal cone outer segments (cos), cone inner segments (cis), outer limiting membrane (olm), pigment epithelium (pe), cone nuclei (cn), and cross (+) as marker for center of foveola, (F). Epon 4 μm section, toluidine blue stain, 900 × [Ordy et al, 1980b].

cell counts were made on histologically prepared tissue, the dramatic early "cell loss" from birth to age 20 was attributed to decreases in cell packing density due to increase in cortical depth, resulting from increased neuropil density. Since cortical depth increases during development due to increased cell size and neuropil density, some of the postnatal "cell loss" reported in that study may be attributed to tissue volume increases, or decreased "cell packing density" in the striate cortex from birth to age 20. Consequently, the histological procedures may have masked and overestimated "cell loss" during development from birth to 20 years of age. However, true cell loss during aging, from 20 to 80 years, may have been underestimated, since striate cortical depth decreased from 2400 at age 20 to 1600 μm by age 80 [Brody, 1955].

In a recent study, some of the problems in histological cell-counting approaches involving age differences in cell packing density and tissue volume changes with age were reduced considerably, since counts of neuron populations in the macular projection area of man were performed with a cell dispersion technique, in which appropriate control procedures were taken for possible artifacts in evaluating age differences in cell counts due to increased membrane fragility of older cells, when subjected to mechanical dispersion. In this study, it was reported that the neuron population of the macular projection area of 23 human subjects, aged 20 to 87 years, decreased significantly from about 46 million cells per gram of tissue at age 20, to approximately 24 million by age 87. This cell loss represents an estimated loss of 54% of the neurons from age 20 to 87 in the macular projection area of the striate cortex in man [Devaney and Johnson, 1980]. Since there was also a significant decline in brain weight with age in these subjects, from approximately 1500 to 1000 grams from age 20 to 87, the significant age decrease in neuron density should reflect an absolute loss of neurons at least equivalent to the 54% loss estimated by the cell-dispersion approach to cell counting in specific regions of the visual system. The age differences in neuronal population in the macular projection area of the striate cortex for man, as reported in this study, are presented in Figure 5.

Although current knowledge on the laminar and columnar organization of the striate cortex in man is rather limited, the striate cortex regions of the cat, squirrel, and rhesus monkey are probably the most thoroughly understood areas of the cerebral cortex [Van Essen, 1979]. The limited knowledge on the cytoarchitectural organization of the human striate cortex is due largely to the inaccessibility of the human brain to application of single unit and microanatomical techniques that have been so extremely productive with the cat and nonhuman primates. However, it seems interesting to note that recently, Golgi impregnations of large motor cortex Betz cells [Scheibel and Scheibel, 1975] and of striate cortex Meynert cells [Purpura, 1975] have been used to study the effects of development and aging on highly specialized pyramidal neurons, which are very large in size, relatively small in absolute number, and also highly

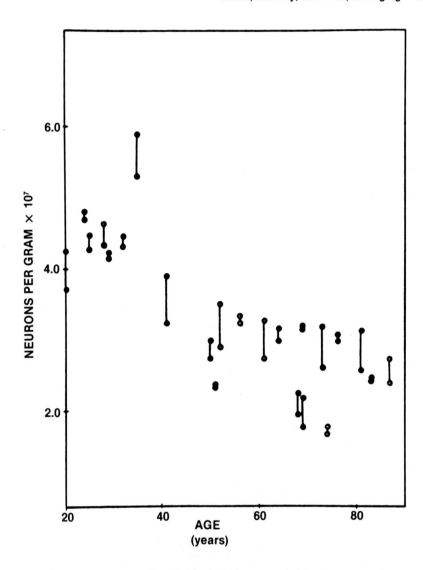

Fig. 5.   Neuron population densities in macular projection area of 23 human subjects, 20–87 years of age, in duplicate determinations. Neuron density decreased 54% from approximately 46 million neurons per gram of tissue at age 20, to approximately 24 million neurons per gram of tissue by 80 years. Open-closed circles are replication values. [Devaney and Johnson, 1980].

restricted to critical loci in primary sensory and motor areas of the cerebral cortex of man and other diurnal primates [Palay, 1978]. It has also been proposed that the cytoarchitectural organization of the human cerebral cortex and limbic system can be characterized more accurately in terms of age by distinguishing neuronal lipofuscin distribution patterns than by neuronal appearance or cell loss in Nissl preparations [Braak, 1977]. A comparison of the appearance of age differences in the human striate cortex in Nissl preparations is illustrated for a 13-year-old and for a 83-year-old human subject in Figure 6. The Nissl preparation comparisons of age differences in Figure 6 are from the same human striate cortex from which a 54% loss of neurons has been reported in the macular region from

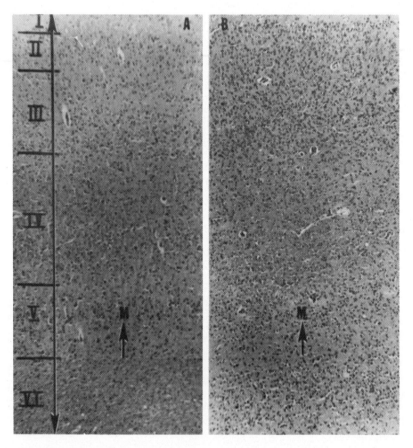

Fig. 6. Histological comparison of the appearance of age differences in the human striate cortex in Nissl preparations. (A) Striate cortex of 13-year-old human, (B) Striate cortex of 83-year-old human. 200×, 10 μm sections, Nissl stain. (I-VI laminae).

20 to 87 years (see Fig. 5). A comparison of the apparent lack of age differences in the cortex in Nissl preparations makes it quite apparent that morphometric methods have become critical for evaluating cell loss in the brain during aging.

In contrast to the relatively uniform appearance of the cytoarchitectural organization, without obvious appearance of age differences in cell loss in the striate cortex based on Nissl preparations (Fig. 6), unstained fluorescent preparations for lipofuscin accumulation with age of the same tissue invariably illustrate significant increases in pigment accumulation in small stellate and the larger pyramidal neuron populations. The significant increases in intraneuronal lipofuscin in the large pyramidal neurons (Meynert cells, lamina V) of the human striate cortex, from age 13 to 83 years, are illustrated in fluorescent preparations in Figure 7A and B. Figure 7C also illustrates in a Golgi preparation the large solitary Meynert (M) cells, which may serve as interlaminar integrators of binocular macular cone inputs in diurnal primates, with their axonal output leading to cortical and subcortical visual areas [Palay, 1978]. As yet, loss of Meynert cells from the human striate cortex has not been reported. Loss of dendritic spines has been reported from neurons in the striate cortex of old rats [Feldman, 1976].

The next level of intercortical visual information-processing extending from the striate cortex to areas 18 and 19 and beyond the occipital cortex includes information transfer mediated by pathways leading to the temporal, parietal, and frontal lobes [Wilson, 1978; Van Essen, 1979]. There are also highly organized projections to subcortical targets from visual cortical areas, such as to LGB, pulvinar, and superior colliculus [Van Essen, 1979]. Information on possible age differences in these cortical and subcortical areas of the brain in man is quite sparse and is restricted mainly to clinical cases involving both aging and neuropathology [Friede, 1965; Ordy and Brizzee, 1979].

VISION AS PART OF CONVERGENT MULTISENSORY, STIMULUS–REWARD COUPLING PROCESS IN LIMBIC SYSTEM

One of the more widely accepted views on the effects of age on the brain is that recent or short-term memory becomes impaired, whereas long-term memory for remote events remains relatively unimpaired [Bahrick et al, 1975]. In contrast to this widespread view, recent authoritative reviews of short-term memory impairment in the elderly have concluded that short-term or primary memory (PM) is of less concern than long-term or secondary memory (SM) to the elderly, unless memory, or information-processing, is conceptualized as flowing from PM to SM (or even sensory memory to PM to SM) [Botwinik, 1975, 1976]. In another authoritative review of age differences in human memory, it was proposed that age differences in PM are negligible unless the primary memory task involves divided "attention or reorganization of the material" [Craik, 1977].

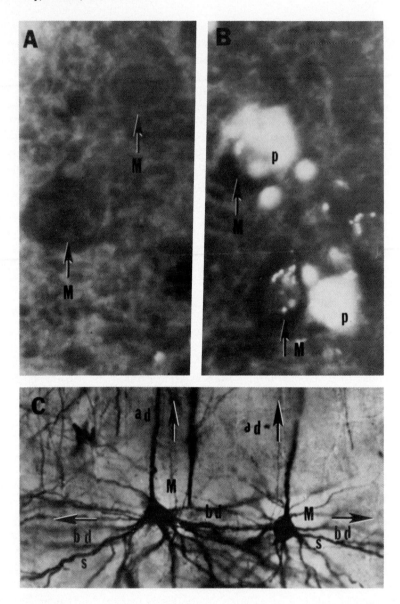

Fig. 7. Histological comparison of age difference in lipofuscin pigment in pyramidal neurons, lamina V of human striate cortex. Unstained fluorescent preparation. (A) 13-year-old human. (B) 83-year-old human. (C) Meynert cells (M) in foveal striate cortex of diurnal squirrel monkey, lamina V. (A) and (B) 900 × 6 μm sections, unstained fluorescence. (C) 400 × 1 μm section, stained with rapid Golgi impregnation.

Although short-term memory has been considered as an organizing process within an information processing framework, it is only recently that it has been conceptualized in neurobiology as part of a convergent multisensory, time-dependent, stimulus-reward coupling process involving the cerebral cortex and the limbic system [Swanson, 1979; Ordy et al, 1980a].

Even though generally not concerned with neuronal networks of short-term memory, the experimental literature on the effects of age on human memory has been interpreted increasingly within a three-stage information-processing framework. Information is received and transduced by modality-specific sensory systems, passed on to short-term or primary memory (STM-PM), which represents a limited-capacity store comprising items of sensory images or features, followed by transfer of information to long-term or secondary memory (LTM-SM), which is based on rehearsal of stimuli and possibly on reinforcement [Craik, 1977, 1979]. Short-term memory in this three-stage framework represents only a very small segment of learning, memory, or information-processing. However, short-term memory may be of critical importance for the encoding, storage, and retrieval of all new information. Consequently, short-term memory may represent the basic control process for all thinking, remembering, and consciousness [Atkinson and Shiffrin, 1971]. Despite the recognition that memory or information-processing includes a convergent multimodal sensory input into short-term memory, it has been proposed that the only useful distinction within human memory functioning consists of that between short-term and long-term memory [Craik, 1977]. Similarly, after recognition that significant age differences have been reported in iconic and echoic sensory memory, it has been concluded that short-term memory may not be impaired in the elderly if the sensory information is adequately perceived and registered, and provided that elderly subjects are not required to divide their attention between two sensory inputs or to reorganize the material [Craik, 1977]. Since the learning–performance distinction has been a pervasive issue with respect to the interpretation of age differences in learning and memory, numerous studies have also attempted to demonstrate that short-term memory impairment may somehow occur independently of declines in sensory processes, learning, motivation, emotion, and motor capacity [Marcer, 1974; Walsh, 1975; Craik, 1977, 1979]. There is considerable experimental evidence for the negligible effects of age on human short-term or primary memory in some tasks [Craik, 1977], and the significant effects of age on short-term memory, independent of sensory function, learning, and performance, particularly in animal studies [Ordy et al, 1978]. However, more recently, it has also been recognized that age declines in short-term memory, increased susceptibility to sensory interference, and decreased capacity to modify previously learned behavior may represent some of the more prominent characteristics of aged human and nonhuman primates [Bartus, 1979]. Although theoretical views concerning the interpretation of short-term memory as a brief organizing process, or as a time-dependent, convergent multisensory, stimulus-reward coupling process, may vary, there is increasing evidence that in the elderly there may be a decreasing capacity to register, encode, store, and retrieve information over brief periods of time. This has been demonstrated for visual short-term memory [Adamowicz, 1976], auditory short-term memory [Clark and Knowles, 1973], and particularly when visual and auditory stimuli are presented in combination [Craik, 1977, 1979]. Consequently, it has been proposed that age declines in modality-specific memory and particularly in convergent multisensory information-processing in multimodal sensory integration centers within the cerebral cortex and limbic system must play an important role in short-term memory impairment during aging [Ordy et al, 1980a]. According to earlier views of short-term memory, the emphasis has been on a "brief organizing process" rather than on the sequence and duration of retention intervals [Waugh and Norman, 1965]. However, according to current neurobiology models of memory, drug effects on memory are most readily observable within three distinct "time dependent" stages of acquisition, consolidation, and retrieval of specific information [Alpern and Jackson, 1978]. Consequently, age differences in short-term memory may also be most readily demonstrable in the rate of forgetting during the time span from 250 msec to 2 sec for sensory memory, or 2 to 30 sec for convergent multisensory short-term memory [Ordy et al, 1980a]. There is considerable evidence in neurobiology in support of this time-dependent interpretation of convergent multisensory, stimulus–reward coupling of short-term memory.

It is widely recognized that sensory information-processing, learning, memory, and complex motor performance are intimately related. Learning and memory depend first on a sensory information input, registration, or acquisition stage. Sensory memory (SM) is considered modality-specific, its duration is presumed to be milliseconds, or at most a few seconds, and it appears to decay rapidly with the passage of time [Crowder, 1978]. Short-term memory, or so-called primary memory, is believed to occur across sensory modalities. Its duration is presumed to be from 2 to 30 sec and it may also decay promptly. However, this may be due to interference, lack of reinforced practice, or both [Marcer, 1974; Deutsch and Deutsch, 1975]. The most clear and widely cited example of the coupling of sensory and short-term memory is looking up, dialing, and then forgetting a telephone number. Depending on reinforced practice and interference, only some small portion of the labile short-term memory may go into so-called secondary or permanent memory [Norman, 1969; Thompson, 1975]. Figure 8 illustrates schematically a so-called three-stage neurobiology memory model based on a time-dependent, convergent multisensory, stimulus–reward coupling process in the cerebral cortex and limbic system.

There is not only considerable behavioral but also electrophysiological, neurochemical, and neuropharmacological evidence that is consistent with the pro-

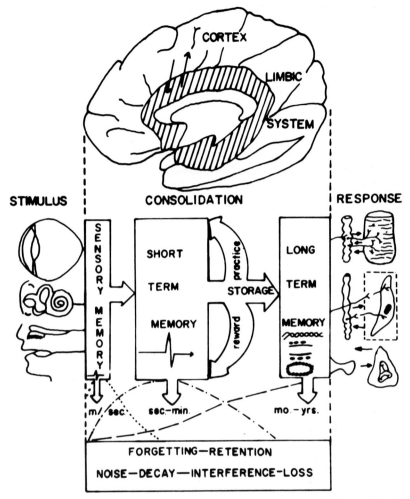

Fig. 8. Three-stage neurobiology memory model. (1) Sensory memory: modality-specific, milliseconds to seconds; (2) short-term memory: labile, polysensory memory, sensory imagery-sematic coding, second to minutes; (3) long-term memory: chemical storage, months to years [Ordy et al, 1980a].

posed three-stage time-dependent, convergent multisensory, stimulus–reward coupling, neurobiology model of short-term memory [Atkinson and Schiffrin, 1971; Marcer, 1974; Alpern and Jackson, 1978; Gibbs, 1979]. Some of the more important aspects of the three-stage neurobiology model of memory include (1) sensory encoding of information by images, symbolic, or semantic forms; (2)

convergence of modality-specific into convergent multisensory integration; (3) consolidation of modality specific and/or convergent multisensory information processing by rehearsal, reinforced practice, or stimulus–reward coupling; (4) demonstrated susceptibility of short-term memory consolidation to disruption by interference or so-called divided attention; and perhaps most importantly (5) recognized or suspected anatomical convergent multisensory, and stimulus–reward coupling networks within the cerebral cortex and limbic system. According to microanatomical studies with primates, visual, auditory, and somatosensory inputs from the respective primary projection sensory cortical areas relay information to the entorhinal area, the hippocampus, the medial dorsal thalamus, and the principal sulcus of the frontal lobe [Jones and Powell, 1970; Van Hoesen et al, 1972; Chavis and Pandya, 1974; Jones, 1974; Rosene and Van Hoesen, 1977]. Ablation studies of the medial prefrontal cortex have shown fiber degeneration extending over cingulate and uncinate routes to the hippocampus [Leichnetz and Astuc, 1975]. Neuroendocrine studies have shown hormone receptors in hippocampal circuits that may provide the coupling of convergent multisensory information and reward properties of stimuli [McEwen et al, 1974; DeWied, 1976; Deadwyler et al, 1979]. Distinct firing patterns have been reported from single neurons of the human hippocampus during performance of visual short-term memory tasks [Halgreen et al, 1978]. Combined, these studies have provided some provocative evidence for an essential role of the hippocampus in convergent multisensory integration, and stimulus–reward coupling within the limbic system (see Figs. 2 and 9). Figure 9 illustrates diagramatically and with Golgi impregnation the possible hippocampal convergent extero-intero information-processing, and stimulus–reward coupling by neuropeptides and hormones, by a CA1 pyramidal neuron model.

The hippocampus has been implicated in convergent multisensory integration, stimulus–reward coupling, short-term memory, and in neuroendocrine regulation of endocrine and autonomic function. It has received considerable attention in human and animal studies of memory and aging in the limbic system. Animal studies have established significant correlations among memory impairment, changes in adrenocorticoids, and hippocampal aging [Landfield et al, 1978; Roth, 1979]. In studies with human subjects, a 30% decline in cell packing density of neurons has been reported from the hippocampus, from ages 47 to 91 years in normal, healthy individuals [Ball, 1977]. Neurofibrillary tangles and granulovacuolar degeneration have been reported in the hippocampus with increased age, particularly in senile dementia. Other studies have also reported loss of neurons, as well as cellular degeneration in various zones of the hippocampus with increasing age, in normal subjects as well as in dementia [Tomlinson and Henderson, 1976], particularly in Alzheimer's disease [Hooper and Vogel, 1970].

In a series of recent studies, old rhesus monkeys were used to study the effects

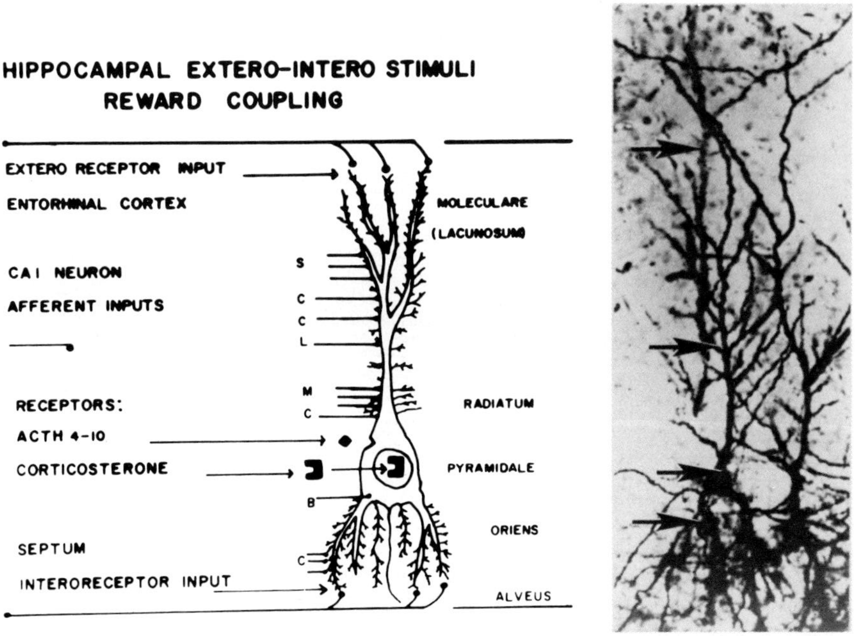

Fig. 9. Diagrammatic illustration and Golgi impregnation of hippocampal pyramidal neuron, with convergent extero-intero input, and stimulus–reward coupling circuit in CA1, CA2, and CA3 zones.

of age on short-term memory in relation to cellular alterations in the hippocampus and principal sulcus of the prefrontal cortex, representing two of the synaptically related areas involved in convergent multisensory information-processing and in stimulus–reward coupling in short-term memory. In behavioral studies, significant short-term memory impairments, susceptibility to sensory interference, and decreased ability to modify previously learned tasks were observed in old rhesus monkeys [Bartus, 1979]. In subsequent morphometric studies, significant topographic and cellular alterations were observed in the CA1, CA2 and CA3 zones of the hippocampus as well as in the cross-sectional areas bordering the principal sulcus of the prefrontal cortex [Brizzee et al, 1980]. Figure 10 illustrates in a transverse section of the hippocampus the CA1, CA2, and CA3 zones of the rhesus monkey in which the significant topographic alterations and cell loss have been reported in aged compared with young monkeys.

Direct correlational studies of age differences in sensory function, learning, and memory in relation to cell loss and lipofuscin accumulation in the striate cortex and hippocampus of man are not feasible. Such direct correlational analyses have been reported of age differences in learning, short-term memory, and

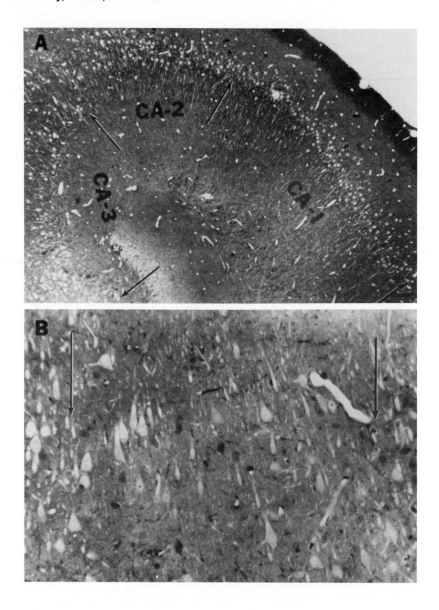

Fig. 10. (A) Transverse section of hippocampus in rhesus monkey with pyramidal cell layer, CA1, CA2, and CA3 zones with appearance of pyramidal neuron density in young adult, 12-year-old monkey. (B) Transverse section of CA1 zone near prosubiculum showing significant loss of neurons between arrows in aged, 23-year-old monkey. Semithin sections (4 μm), Toluidine Blue, 100× [Brizzee et al, 1980].

behavioral arousal in relation to cell loss and lipofuscin increase in the hippo-campus CA1 zone and in visual striate area 17 of the Fisher 344 rat. Significant age differences in 2- and 6-hour passive-avoidance retention or short-term memory between mature and old rats were related to nonsignificant age differences in days to criterion learning, starting latencies, running distance, and in time of original approach learning. The significant age differences in 2- and 6-hour retention of old, compared with mature rats were correlated significantly with loss of neurons, and very significantly with increases in lipofuscin in the hippocampus CA1 zone and in the visual striate cortex [Ordy et al, 1978; Brizzee and Ordy, 1979].

In contrast to a hypothesis relying on simple neuronal drop-out in specific circuits as the cause of sensory, attention, and memory deficits in the elderly, considerable pharmacological evidence has suggested that deficits in central cholinergic transmitters without cell loss may be involved in the short-term memory deficits of the elderly [Drachman, 1977; Drachman et al, 1980]. These drug effects on short-term memory have been proposed to have their effects on neurotransmitters in the hippocampus [Mohs et al, 1980]. The effects during development and aging of neuropeptides on attention, memory, and neurotrans-mitters have attracted great research interest [Scott and Sladek, 1980; Rigter and Van Riezen, 1981]. Although putative effects on sensory function, attention, learning, and memory remain to be established convincingly, neuropeptides and drugs that influence neurotransmitters and their interactions and receptors, or prevent lipofuscin accumulation and cell loss in specific circuits during aging provide new approaches for influencing learning and memory, and they also enhance the prospects for drug intervention in cognitive impairments of the elderly.

THEORETICAL INTERPRETATIONS OF FUNCTIONAL AND STRUCTURAL ALTERATIONS WITH AGE IN THE VISUAL AND LIMBIC SYSTEMS

Declines in sensory function with age may be related to changes in peripheral sense organs, loss of neurons, their connectivity, lipofuscin accumulation, and alterations of remaining neurons in synaptically related neuronal networks. However, it is much more difficult to formulate more specific hypotheses concerning the effects of age on short-term memory since the only currently accepted views of the neuronal basis of learning are based on neurotransmitters, neuropeptides, or hormone modulation, particularly in such specific neuroanatomical circuits as the hippocampus [Olton et al, 1979; Zornetzer, 1978; Rigter and Van Riezen, 1981]. In sensory processes, the threshold sensitivities of all special senses, including vision, appear to undergo an exponential decline with age when the intensities of the threshold stimuli are plotted in terms of psychological magnitude scales [Hinchcliffe, 1962]. Regarding age differences in the visual system, the major initial step undertaken in the present article was to identify the possible physiological, chemical, and structural correlates in the retino-geniculo-striate pathway that may be involved in the linear and/or exponential declines with age in acuity, color vision, and stereopsis. The problem of cell loss from the brain has been one of the major issues in the neurobiology of aging. However, the implications of cell loss for functional capacity have remained a formidable challenge. Cellular redundancy in the afferent geometry of neuronal network capacity in the primate visual cortex has only recently received more detailed attention [Schwartz, 1977]. Whereas cellular redundancy poses formidable problems, redundancy in cell connectivity involving dendritic spines and synaptic contacts as neuronal couplers poses even greater challenges for single-unit and network studies of aging. However, the highly specific point-to-point visuotopic mapping of central visual fields is associated with a remarkable specificity in anatomical connections in the visual system. If the assumption of a one-to-one cellular relation from the fovea to LGB and striate cortex is made, or if exact specification of convergence and/or magnification ratios for cells is provided in the central fields of the retino-geniculo-striate system, neuronal drop-out should have direct functional consequences for acuity, color vision, and stereopsis. Increasingly accurate interpretations of age differences in specific functions will become possible in terms of correlated cellular alterations in synaptically related neurons of the retino-geniculo-striate system [Creutzfeld et al, 1975].

Regarding the identity of limbic components that may be involved in short-term memory, there is increasing evidence on the afferent and efferent connections of synaptically related components, including functional and structural "plasticity" in the hippocampus during conditioning and learning [Deadwyler et al, 1978; Swanson, 1979]. In contrast to the assumed great redundancy of interneurons in the cerebral cortex, the pyramidal and granule cells of the hippocampus represent a highly convergent system, in which age-related cell loss may reduce synaptic plasticity, which may provide the neural basis for impairment of learning and memory during aging [Brizzee and Ordy, 1979]. In terms of possible functional consequences due to cell loss from the cerebral cortex and limbic system, increasing attention has been devoted to such highly specialized neurons as Betz cells in the motor cortex [Scheibel, 1979], Meynert cells in the striate cortex (this review), CA1 neurons in the hippocampus [Brizzee and Ordy, 1979; Brizzee et al, 1980], and Purkinje cells in the cerebellum [Rogers et al, 1980]. These cells are extremely large in size and few in absolute number, and most importantly from a functional standpoint, they provide primary integration and/or output of convergent information-processing in sensory, learning, and motor functions [Creutzfeld et al, 1975].

SUMMARY
Age Differences in Vision as Modality-Specific Process

Classically, vision has been regarded as a modality-specific process, localized in the afferent retino-geniculo-striate pathway "terminating" in the occipital lobe. One of the major aims of this article was to examine age differences in visual functions in relation to concomitant physiological, neurochemical, and morphological alterations in the central macular field projections of the retino-geniculo-striate pathway and in the occipital lobe of man. According to cross-sectional studies, significant age differences occur in acuity, color vision, and stereopsis with increasing age in man. The rates of decline in these central visual field functions appear linear from 20 to 60 years, and possibly exponential from 60 to 90 years. Significant age differences have been reported in psychophysical responses of the elderly in dichoptic masking and stimulus persistence tests, involving brief tachistoscopic exposures to targets, letters, or numbers, with the perceptual responses designated as visual image persistence, trace, icon, or sensory memory (see Walsh, and Kline and Scheiber, this volume). In electrophysiological studies, significant age differences have been reported in latency, amplitude, and late wave components of visual evoked potentials (VEP) recorded been the human scalp. Age differences in VEP have been interpreted as decrements in neural transmission of visual information over multisynaptic pathways in the visual system. Significant age differences have also been reported in event related potentials (ERP) and in concurrent tasks involving visual-sensory memory retrieval tasks by the elderly. Neurochemical studies have reported significant age differences in neurotransmitters and their enzymes in the geniculostriate pathway of man. Specific cellular alterations in the retino-geniculo-striate pathway of man with age include (1) increased lipofuscin in retinal pigment epithelium, (2) loss of photoreceptors, (3) degeneration of retinal ganglion cells, and (4) an estimated 54% loss of neurons in the macular striate cortex area, from 20 to 87 years. Since the visual system is characterized by intrinsic afferent or "input" directionality, the molecular and temporal sequences in the accumulation of lipofuscin in the pigment epithelium, which is involved in rod and cone outer segment renewal, suggest possible transneuronal degeneration, deafferentation, and intrinsic metabolic events of postmitotic neurons of the retina as major sources of cellular aging in the retino-geniculo-striate system.

Age Differences in Vision as Part of Convergent Multisensory, Stimulus–Reward Coupling Process in Cerebral Cortex and Limbic System

Although short-term memory may represent only a very small component of information-processing, it may represent the basic control process for all cognitive activity, including learning and consciousness. There is considerable evidence that in the elderly, there may be a declining capacity to register, encode, and retrieve information over very brief periods. Age declines in short-term memory may be based on a time-dependent, convergent multisensory, stimulus–reward coupling process involving the cerebral cortex and limbic system. According to microanatomical studies, visual, auditory, and somatosensory inputs from respective sensory cortical areas relay convergent multisensory information to the entorhinal area, the hippocampus, medial dorsal thalamus, and principal sulcus of the frontal lobe. Neuroendocrine studies have identified neuropeptide and hormone receptors in hippocampal circuits which may provide for the coupling of convergent sensory information and reward properties of stimuli. Since the hippocampus has been implicated in convergent sensory integration, stimulus–reward coupling, spatial orientation, short-term memory, and in neuroendocrine regulation of endocrine and autonomic function, it has received considerable attention in aging. In human subjects, a 30% decline in neuron packing density has been reported from the hippocampus, from 40 to 90 years. In animal studies, short-term memory impairments, susceptibility to sensory interference, and decreased flexibility in reversal learning have been correlated with cellular alterations in the hippocampus and principal sulcus of the prefrontal cortex. Some current studies of aging and visual function have been extended to include evaluation of age differences in (1) visual synchronization of sleep-wake cycles, or circadian rhythm in relation to cellular alterations of the suprachiasmatic nucleus of the hypothalamus, and (2) visual information processing, in relation to age-related differences in hemisphere specialization for spatial visual and semantic memory [Dustman et al, 1981].

REFERENCES

Adamowicz JK (1976) Visual short-term memory and aging. J Gerontol 31:39–46.

Alpern HP, Jackson SJ (1978) Stimulants and depressants: Drug effects on memory. In Lipgon MA, Killam KF, DiMascio A (Eds) "Psychopharmacology: A Generation of Progress." New York: Raven, pp 663–675.

Anderson DH, Fisher SK, Steinberg RH (1978) Mammalian cones: Disc shedding phagocytosis, and renewal. Invest Ophthalmol 17(2):117–133.

Armstrong D, Siakotos A, and Koppang N (1979) Biochemical studies on the retina and pigment epithelium in the normal and diseased canine eye. In Ordy JM, KR Brizzee (Eds) "Aging" Vol 10: "Sensory Systems and Communication in the Elderly." New York: Raven, pp 115–152.

Atkinson RC, Schiffrin RM (1971) The control of short-term memory. Sci Am 224:82–90.

Avendano J, Rodrigues M, Hackett J, Gaskins R (1980) Degenerative changes in the human retina. Invest Ophthalmol Vis Sci 19:550–555.

Bahrick HP, Bahrick PO, Wittlinger RP (1975) Fifty years of memory for names and faces: A cross-sectional approach. J Exp Psychol [Gen] 104:54–75.

Ball MJ (1977) Neuronal loss, neurofibrillary tangles and granuovacuolar degeneration in the hippocampus with ageing and dementia. Acta Neuropathol (Berl) 37:111–118.

Bartus RT (1979) Effects of aging on visual memory, sensory processing, and discrimination learning in a nonhuman primate. In Ordy JM, Brizzee KR (Eds) "Aging" Vol 10: "Sensory Systems and Communication in the Elderly." New York; Raven, pp 85–114.

Beck EC, Dustman RE, Schenkenberg T (1975) Life span changes in the electrical activity of the human brain as reflected in the cerebral evoked response. In Ordy JM, Brizzee KR (Eds) "Neurobiology of Aging." New York: Plenum, pp 175–192.

Beck EC, Dustman RE, Blusewicz MJ, Cannon WG (1979) Cerebral evoked potentials and correlated neuropsychological changes in the human brain during aging: A comparison of alcoholism and aging. In Ordy JM, Brizzee KR (Eds) "Aging" Vol 10: "Sensory Systems and Communication in the Elderly." New York: Raven, pp 203–226.

Berkley M (1978) Vision: Geniculocortical system. In Masterton RB (Ed) "Handbook of Behavioral Neurobiology" Vol I "Sensory Integration." New York: Plenum, pp 165–208.

Blackwell HR (1979) Human visual functions. Technical Commission Report, C.I.E.

Botwinick J (1975) Behavioral processes. In Gershon S, Raskin A (Eds) "Aging," Vol 2. New York: Raven, pp 1–18.

Botwinick J (1976) "Aging and Behavior: A Comprehensive Integration of Research Findings, 2nd Ed. New York: Springer, pp 311–322.

Bough EW (1970) Stereoscopic vision in the macaque monkey: A behavioral demonstration. Nature 225:42–44.

Boycott BB, Dowling JE (1969) Organization of the primate retina: Light microscopy; a second type of midget bipolar cell in the primate retina. Philos Trans R Soc Lond [Biol] 255:109–184.

Braak H (1977) The pigment architecture of the human occipital lobe. Anat Embryol 150(2):229–250.

Brizzee KR, Ordy JM (1979) Age pigments, cell loss, and hippocampal function. Mech Ageing Dev 9:143–162.

Brizzee KR, Kaack B, Klara P (1975) Lipofuscin: intra- and extra-neuronal accumulation and regional distribution. In Ordy JM, Brizzee KR (eds) "Neurobiology of Aging." New York: Plenum, pp 463–484.

Brizzee, KR, Ordy JM, Bartus RT (1980) Localization of cellular changes within multimodal sensory regions in aged monkey brain: Possible implications for age-related cognitive loss. Neurobiol Aging 1(1):45–52.

Brody H (1955) Organization of the cerebral cortex. III. A study of aging in human cerebral cortex. J Comp Neurol 102:511–556.

Bunt AH, Hendrickson AE, Lund JS, Lund RD, Fuchs AF (1975) Monkey retinal ganglion cells: Morphometric analysis and tracing of axonal projections with a consideration of the peroxidase technique. J Comp Neurol 164(3):265–286.

Bunt AH, Minckler DS, Johanson GW (1977) Demonstration of bilateral projection of the central retina of the monkey with horseradish peroxidase neuronography. J Comp Neurol 171(4):619–630.

Celesia CG, Daly RF (1977) Effects of aging on visual evoked responses. Arch Neurol 34:403–407.

Chavis D, Pandya DN (1974) Frontal lobe projections of the cortical sensory association areas of the rhesus monkey. Trans Am Neurol Assoc 99:192–195.

Clark LE, Knowles JB (1973) Age differences in dichotic listening performance. J Gerontol 28:173–178.

Corso JF (1975) Sensory processes and age effects in normal adults. J Gerontol 26:90–105.

Cowey A, Ellis CM (1969) The cortical representation of the retina in the squirrel and rhesus monkey and its relation to visual acuity. Exp Neurol 24:374–385.

Craik FIM (1977) Age differences in human memory. In Birren JE, Schaie KW (Eds) "Handbook of the Psychology of Aging." New York: Van Nostrand, pp 384–420.

Craik FIM (1979) Human memory. In Rosenzweig MR, Porter LW (Eds) "Annual Review of

Psychology." Palo Alto, Calif: Ann Revs, pp 63–102.

Craik FIM, Simon E (1980) Age differences in memory: The roles of attention and depth of processing. In Poon LW, Fozard JL, Cermak LS, Arenberg D, Thompson LW (Eds) "New Direction In Memory And Aging." New Jersey: Erlbaum, pp 95–112.

Creutzfeldt O, Innocenti GM, Brooks D (1975) Neurophysiological experiments on afferent and intrinsic connections in the visual cortex (area 17). In Santini M (Ed) "Golgi Centennial Symposium: Perspectives in Neurobiology." New York: Raven, pp 319–337.

Crowder RG (1978) Sensory memory systems. In Carterette EC, Friedman MP (Eds) "Handbook of Perception." New York: Academic.

Crowder RG (1980) Echoic Memory and the Study of Aging Memory Systems. In Poon LW, Fozard JL, Cermak LS, Arenberg D, Thompson LW (Eds) "New Directions In Memory and Aging." New Jersey: Erlbaum, pp 181–204.

Deadwyler SA, Dunwiddie T, Lynch G (1978) Short-lasting changes in hippocampal neuronal excitability following repetitive synaptic activation. Brain Res 147(2):384–389.

Deadwyler SA, West M, Lynch G (1979) Synaptically identified hippocampal slow potentials during behavior. Brain Res 161:211–225.

Deutsch D, Deutsch JA (1975) "Short-Term Memory." New York: Academic.

DeValois RL, Jacobs GH (1968) Primate color vision. Science 162:533–540.

Devaney KO, Johnson HA (1980) Neuron loss in the aging visual cortex of man. J Gerontol 35:836–841.

DeWied D (1976) Hormonal influences on motivation, learning and memory processes. Hosp Practice Jan:123–131.

DeWied D (1977) Behavioral effects of neuropeptides related to ACTH, MSH, and BLPH. Ann NY Acad Sci 297:263–274.

Domey RG, McFarland RH, Chadwick E (1969) Dark adaptation as function of age and time. II. A derivation. J Gerontol 15:267–279.

Drachman DA (1977) Memory and cognitive function in man: Does the cholinergic system have a specific role? Neurology 27(8):783–790.

Drachman DA, Noffsinger D, Sahakian BJ, Kurdziel S, and Fleming P (1980) Aging, memory, and the cholinergic system: A study of dichotic listening. Neurobiol Aging 1(1):39–43.

Dreher B, Fukada Y, Rodieck RW (1976) Identification, classification and anatomical segregation of cells with x-like and y-like properties in the lateral geniculate nucleus of old-world primates. J Physiol 258:433–452.

Dustman RE, Snyder EW, Schlehuber CJ (1981) Life-span alterations in visually evoked potentials and inhibitory function. Neurobiol Aging 2:187–192.

Feeney L (1978) Lipofuscin and melanin of human retinal pigment epithelium. Invest Ophthalmol Vis Sci 17:583–600.

Feeney-Burns L, Berman ER, Rothman H (1980) Lipofuscin of human retinal pigment epithelium. Am J Ophthalmol 90:783–791.

Feldman ML (1976) Aging changes in morphology of cortical dendrites. In Terry R, Gershon S (Eds) "Aging: Neurobiology of Aging." New York: Raven, pp 211–228.

Fitzgerald CR, Enoch JM, Campos ED, and Bedell HE (1979) Comparison of visual function studies in two cases of senile macular degeneration. Graefes Arch Klin Exp Ophthalmol 210(2):79–91.

Ford JM, Roth WT, Mohs RC, Hopkins WF, Koppel BS (1980) The effects of age on event related potentials in a memory retrieval task. Electroencephalogr Clin Neurophysiol 47(4):450–459.

Fozard JL, Wolf E, Bell B, McFarland RA, Podolsky S (1977) Visual perception and communication. In Birren JE, Schaie KW (Eds) "Handbook of the Psychology of Aging." New York: Van Nostrand, pp 497–534.

Friede RL (1962) The relation of the formation of lipofuscin to the distribution of oxidative enzymes in the human brain. Acta Neuropathol 2:113–125.

Friede RL (1965) "Topographic Brain Chemistry." New York: Academic.

Fukuda Y, Stone J (1975) Direct identification of the cell bodies of Y-, X-, and W-cells in the cat's retina. Vision Res 15:1034–1036.

Gartner S, Henkind P (1981) Aging and Degeneration of the Human Macula. 1. Outer Nuclear Layer and Photoreceptors. Br J Ophthalmol 65(1):23–28.

Gass JD (1973) Drusen and disciform macular detachment and degeneration. Arch Ophthalmol 90 (Sept):206–217.

Gibbs M (1979) The molecular mechanisms of memory. New Scientist 25:261–263.

Grover D, Zigman S (1972) Coloration of human lenses by near ultraviolet photo-oxidized tryptophan. Exp Eye Res 13(Jan):70–76.

Gunkel RD, Gouras P (1963) Changes in scotopic visibility thresholds with age. Arch Ophthalmol 69:4–9.

Halgreen E, Babb TL, Crandall PH (1978) Activity of human hippocampal formation and amygdala neurons during memory testing. Electroencephalogr Clin Neurophysiol 45(Mar):585–601.

Hansch EC, Syndulko K, Porozzolo FJ, Cohen SN, Tourtellotte WW, Potvin AR (1980) Electrophysiological measurement in aging and dementia. In Pirozzolo FJ, Maletta GJ (Eds) "Advances in Neurogerontology," Vol I "The Aging Nervous System." New York: Praeger, pp 187–210.

Hasan R, Glees P (1973) Lipofuscin in lateral geniculate body of rhesus monkey. Acta Anat 84:85–95.

Hinchcliff R (1962) Aging and sensory thresholds. J Gerontol 17:45–50.

Hogan MJ (1972) Role of the retinal pigment epithelium in macular disease. Trans Am Acad Ophthalmol Otolaryngol 76:64–80.

Hooper MW, Vogel FS (1970) The limbic system in Alzheimer disease. Am J Pathol 85:1–20.

Hubel DH, Wiesel TN (1970) Cells sensitive to binocular depth in area 18 of the macaque monkey cortex. Nature 225:41–42.

Hubel DH, Wiesel TN (1977) Functional architecture of macaque monkey visual cortex. Proc R Soc London [Biol] 198:1–59.

Jones EG (1974) The anatomy of extrastriate visual mechanisms. In Schmitt FO, Worden FG (Eds) "Third Neuroscience Study Program." Cambridge Mass MIT Press, pp 215–228.

Jones EG, Powell TPS (1970) An anatomical study of converging sensory pathways within the cerebral cortex of the monkey. Brain 93:793–820.

Kaneko A (1979) Physiology of the retina. Am Rev Neurosci 2:169–191.

Kinsbourne M (1980) Attentional Dysfunctions and the Elderly: Theoretical Models and Research Perspectives. In Poon LW, Fozard JL, Cermak LS, Arenberg D, Thompson LW (Eds) "New Directions In Memory And Aging." New Jersey: Erlbaum, pp 113–130.

Klorman R, Thompson LW, Ellingson RJ (1978) Event-related brain potentials across the life span. In Callanay E, Teuting R, Koslow SH (Eds) "Event Related Brain Potentials in Man." New York: Academic, pp 511–570.

Kornzweig AL (1979) Aging of the retinal pigment epithelium. In Zinn KM, Marmor MF (Eds) "The Retinal Pigment Epithelium." Cambridge Mass Harvard University Press, pp 478–496.

Landfield PW, McGough JL, Lynch G (1978) Impaired synaptic potentiation processes in hippocampus of aged, memory-deficient rats. Brain Res 105:85–101.

Leichnetz GR, Astuc J (1975) Preliminary evidence for a direct projection of the prefrontal cortex to the hippocampus of the squirrel monkey. Brain Behav Evol 11:355–364.

LePore GC, Cardu B, Rassmussen T (1975) Rod and cone sensitivity in destriate monkeys. Brain Res 93(2):203–221.

Maffei L (1978) Spatial frequency channels: Neural mechanisms In Autrum H, Jung R, Loewenstein WR, MacKay DM, Teuber H.-L (Eds) "Handbook of Sensory Physiology," Vol VIII: "Perception." Berlin: Springer-Verlag, pp 39–66.

Marcer D (1974) Ageing and memory loss-role of experimental psychology. Gerontol Clin 16:118–125.

Marshall J (1978) Ageing changes in human cones. In the Twenty-third International Congress on Ophthalmology, Kyoto, Japan. Excerpta Medica Abstract. (See Weale, RA, 1978.)

Marshall J, Grindle J, Ansell P, Borwein B (1979) Convolution in human rods. Br J Ophthalmol 63:181–187.

McEwen BS, Denef CJ, Gerlach JL, Plapmiger L (1974) Chemical studies of the brain as a steroid hormone target tissue. In Schmitt FO, FG Worden (Eds) "Third Neuroscience Study Program." Cambridge Mass MIT Press, pp 599–620.

McGeer E, McGeer P (1976) Neurotransmitter metabolisms in the aging brain In Terry RD, Gershon S (Eds) "Aging," Vol 3: "Neurobiology of Aging." New York: Raven, pp 389–403.

Mohs RC, Davis KL, Darley C (1980) Cholinergic drugs and memory: Implications for the treatment of dementia in the elderly. In Poon LW (Ed) "Aging in the 1980's: Selected Contemporary Issues in the Psychology of Aging. Washington, D.C.: American Psychological Assoc. (in press).

Moore RY (1979) The anatomy of central neural mechanisms regulating endocrine rhythms. In Krieger DT (Ed) "Endocrine Rhythms." New York: Raven, pp 63–88.

Moscovitch M (1979) Information processing and the cerebral hemispheres. In Gazzaniga MS (ed) "Handbook of Behavioral Neurobiology," Vol II: "Neuropsychology." New York: Plenum, pp 379–446.

Norman D (1969) "Memory and Attention." New York: Wiley.

Obrist WD, Busse EW (1975) The electroencephalogram in old age. In Wilson WP (Ed) "Application of Electroencephalography in Psychiatry." Durham NC Duke University Press, pp 185–205.

O'Keefe J, Nadel L (1978) "The Hippocampus As A Cognitive Map." Oxford: Clarendon.

Olton DS, Becker JT, Handelmann GE (1979) Hippocampus, Space, and Memory. Behav Brain Sci 2:313–365.

Ordy JM (1981) Neurochemical aspects of aging in humans. In van Praag HM, Lader MH, Rafaelsen OJ, Sachar EJ (Eds) "Handbook of Biological Psychiatry," Part IV: "Brain Mechanisms And Abnormal Behavior." New York: Dekker, pp 355–416.

Ordy JM, Brizzee KR (1979) Functional and structural age differences in the visual system of man and nonhuman primate models. In Ordy JM, Brizzee KR (Eds) "Aging," Vol 10: "Sensory Systems and Communication in the Elderly." New York: Raven, pp 13–50.

Ordy JM, Brizzee KR, Kaach B, Hansche JW (1978) Age differences in short-term memory and cell loss in the cortex of the rat. Gerontology 24:276–285.

Ordy JM, Brizzee KR, and Beavus TL (1980a) Sensory function and short-term memory in aging. In Maletta GJ, FJ Pirozzolo (Eds) "Advances in Neurogerontology," Vol I: "The Aging Nervous System." New York: Praeger, pp 40–78.

Ordy JM, Brizzee KR, Hansche J (1980b) Visual acuity and foveal cone density in the retina of the aged rhesus monkey. Neurobiol Aging 1:133–140.

Palay S (1978) The Meynert Cell, an unusual cortical pyramidal cell. In Brazier MAE, Petache H (Eds) "Architectonics of the Cerebral Cortex," Vol 3. New York: Raven, pp 31–42.

Pettigrew JD, Spinelli DN (1974) Effects of early sensory experience on brain and behavior. In Rozenzweik M (Ed) "Neural Mechanisms in Learning and Memory." New York: Academic, pp 320–342.

Poggio, GF, Fischer B (1977) Binocular interaction and depth sensitivity in striate and prestriate cortex of behaving rhesus monkey. J Neurophysiol 40:1392–1405.

Purpura DP (1975) Morphogenesis of visual cortex in the preterm infant. In Brazier MAE (Ed) "Growth and Development of the Brain." New York: Raven, pp 33–49.

Rigter H, van Riezen H (1981) Modulation of behavior by neuropeptides: Modes of action and clinical prospects. In van Praag HM, Lader MH, Rafaelsen OJ, Sachar EJ (Eds) "Handbook of Biological Psychiatry," Part IV: "Brain Mechanisms And Abnormal Behavior." New York: Dekker, pp 469–510.

Rodiek RM (1979) Visual pathways. In Cowan WM, Hall ZW, Kandel ER (Eds) "Annual Review of Neuroscience," Vol II. Palo Alto, Calif.: Annual Review, pp 193–226.

Rogers J, Silver MA, Shoemaker WJ, Bloom FE (1980) Senescent changes in a neurobiological model system: Cerebellar Purkinje cell electrophysiology and correlative anatomy. Neurobiol Aging 1(1):3–12.

Rolls ET, Cowey A (1970) Topography of the retina and striate cortex and its relationship to visual acuity in rhesus and squirrel monkeys. Exp Brain Res 10:298–310.

Rosene DL, and Van Hoesen GW (1977) Hippocampal efferents reach widespread area of cerebral cortex and amygdala of rhesus monkey. Science 198:315–317.

Roth GW (1979) Hormone action during aging: Alterations and mechanisms. Mech Ageing Dev 9:497–514.

Sarks S (1976) Ageing and degeneration in the macular region: A clinico-pathological study. Br J Ophthalmol 84:810–819.

Sarmiento RF (1975) The stereoacuity of macaque monkey. Vision Res 15:493–498.

Scheibel AB (1979) Aging in human motor control systems. In Ordy JM, Brizzee KR (Eds) "Sensory Systems and Communication in the Elderly." New York: Raven, pp 297–310.

Scheibel ME, Scheibel A (1975) Structural changes in the aging brain. In Brody H, Harman D, Ordy JM (Eds) "Aging," Vol 1: "Clinical, Morphological and Neurochemical Aspects in the Aging Central Nervous System." New York: Raven, pp 410–422.

Schiller PH, Malpeli JG (1978) Functional specificity of lateral geniculate nucleus laminae of the rhesus monkey. J Neurophysiol 41(3):788–797.

Schwartz EL (1977) Afferent geometry in the primate visual cortex and the generation of neuronal trigger features. Biol Cybern 28:1–14.

Scott DE, Sladek JR Jr (1980) Brain–Endocrine Interaction Symposium. IV. Neuropeptides, Development and Aging. New York: Ankho International.

Shiono T, Hayasaka S, Hara S, Mizuno K (1980) Topographic distribution of lysosomal enzymes in human ocular fundus. Abstract, p 186 in Assoc Res Vis Ophthalmol (Vol 12).

Simon E (1979) Depth and elaboration of processing in relation to age. J Exp Psychol 5:115–124.

Snodderly DM (1974) Outline of a primate visual system. In Chirelli AB (Ed) "Perspectives in Primate Biology." New York: Plenum, pp 93–149.

Steinberg RH, Wood I (1979) The relationship of the retinal pigment epithelium to photoreceptor outer segments in human retina. In Zinn KM, Marmon MF (Eds) "The Retinal Pigment Epithelium." Cambridge Mass Harvard University Press, pp 32–44.

Steinberg RH, Wood I, Hogan MJ (1977) Pigment epithelial ensheathment and phagocytosis of extrafoveal cones in human retina. Philos Trans R Soc Lond [Biol] 277(958):459–474.

Storrie MC, and Eisdorfer C (1978) Psychophysiological studies in aging: A ten year review. In Lipton MA, DiMascio A, Killam KF (Eds) "Psychopharmacology: A Generation of Progress." New York: Raven, 1489–1497.

Swanson LW (1979) The hippocampus—new anatomical insights, submitted in grant. TINS, Vol 2 (1) pp 1–4.

Thompson LW, and Marsh GR (1973) Psychophysiological studies of aging. In Eisdorfer C, MP Lawton (Eds) "The Psychology of Adult Development and Aging." Washington, D.C.: American Psychological Assoc., pp 112–150.

Thompson RF (1975) "Introduction to Physiological Psychology." New York: Harper.

Tomlinson BE, Henderson G (1976) Some quantitative cerebral findings in normal and demented old people. In Terry RD, Gershon S (Eds) "Aging," Vol 3: "Neurobiology of Aging." New York: Raven, pp 183–204.

Van Essen, DC (1979) Visual areas of the mammalian cerebral cortex. In Cowan WM, Hall ZW, Kandel ER (Eds) "Annual Review of Neuroscience," Vol II. Palo Alto, Calif.: Annual Reviews, pp 227–263.

Van Hoesen GW, Pandya DN, Butters M (1972) Cortical afferents of the entorhinal cortex of the rhesus monkey. Science 175:471–473.

Vrabec F (1965) Senile changes in ganglion cells of human retina. Br J Ophthalmol 49:561–570.

Walsh DA (1975) Age differences in learning and memory. In Woodruff D, Bierren JE (Eds) "Aging: Scientific Perspectives and Social Issues." New York: Van Nostrand, pp 252–280.

Walsh DA, Prasse MJ (1980) Iconic memory and attentional processes in the aged. In Poon LW, Fozard JL, Cermak LS, Arenberg D, Thompson LW (Eds) "New Directions In Memory And Aging." New Jersey: Erlbaum, pp 153–180.

Waugh NC, Norman DA (1965) Primary memory. Psychol Rev 72(Mar):89–104.

Weale RA (1963) "The Aging Eye." London: Lewis.

Weale RA (1973) The effects of the ageing lens on vision. Ciba Found Symp 19:5–24.

Weale RA (1975) Senile changes in visual acuity. Trans Ophthalmol Soc UK 95:36–38.

Weale RA (1978) The eye and aging. Interdiscipl Topics Gerontol 13:1–13.

Wilson M (1978) Visual system: Pulvinar-extrastriate cortex. In Masterton RB (Ed) "Handbook of Behavioral Neurobiology," Vol I: "Sensory Integration." New York: Plenum, pp 209–248.

Wing GL, Blanchard GC, Weiter JJ (1978) The topography and age relationship of lipofuscin concentration in the retinal pigment epithelium. Invest Ophthalmol Vis Sci 17:601–617.

Young RW (1976) Visual cells and the concept of renewal. Invest Ophthalmol 15:700–726.

Young RW (1980) The participation of visible radiation and molecular renewal in the pathogenesis of macular disease. Abstract p 258 in Assoc Res Vis Ophthalmol (Vol 12).

Zinn KM, Benjamin-Henkind JV (1979) Anatomy of the human retinal pigment epithelium. In Zinn KM, Marmor MF (Eds) "The Retinal Pigment Epithelium." Cambridge Mass.: Harvard University Press, pp 3–31.

Zinn KM, Marmor MF (1979) Toxicology of the human retinal pigment epithelium. In Zinn KM, Marmors MF (Eds) "The Retinal Pigment Epithelium." Cambridge Mass Harvard University Press, pp 395–412.

Zornetzer SF (1978) Neurotransmitter modulation and memory: A new neuropharmacological phrenology? In Lipton MA, DiMascio A, Killam KF (Eds) "Psychopharmacology: A Generation of Progress." New York: Raven, pp 637–650.

III. CHANGES IN BASIC VISUAL FUNCTIONS

Aging and Human Visual Function, pages 117–120
© **1982 Alan R. Liss, Inc., 150 Fifth Avenue, New York, NY 10011**

Introduction

Consideration of age-related change in any basic visual function eventually focuses on the crystalline lens. One reason is that basic visual functions change with the increased optical density of the lens in older eyes. One fascinating fact about the aging of the lens is that there are substantial differences among people in the rate at which their lenses seem to age. Moreover, a number of studies suggest that the lenses of various groups may age at different rates. For example, some evidence (cited in Carter, this volume) indicates onset of presbyopia varies with geographic location of the populations being studied. Although a number of other factors may contribute, it is worth noting that environmental variables may influence changes in the lens and other ocular tissues. Particularly interesting are differences between aging lenses from equatorial and nonequatorial regions. For example, might the density of the crystalline lens be accelerated by environmental conditions, notably exposure to ultraviolet light? At least one set of investigators [Girgus et al, 1977] has attempted to evaluate this hypothesis using noninvasive, in vivo estimates of lenticular density. Girgus et al failed to find a correlation between estimated lens density and self reports of the amount of time spent in the ultraviolet rich outdoor light environment. Confirmation of their findings using more direct methods is desirable. This kind of study is just one example of concern with interaction between ocular processes associated with aging and environmental stimulation. There is every reason to expect that future work on aging and changes in basic visual functions will focus not only on passage of time as an independent variable but also upon the environmental and dietary stresses to which the aging eye may be particularly vulnerable. Young [1982] has provided a useful integrative treatment of such interactions as they relate to the retina.

Although not mentioned during the symposium, the Stiles-Crawford Effect [Stiles and Crawford, 1933] ought not to be overlooked in a discussion of vision and aging. This eponym designates the finding that light is more effective when its path is normal to the retina than when it strikes the retina obliquely. Directional selectivity of the retina is usually attributed to the photoreceptors themselves.

An important consequence of the Stiles-Crawford Effect is that it diminishes the visual effectiveness of stray or scattered light. Such light would most likely strike the retina in directions that would minimize the response of the photoreceptors. We now know that the Stiles-Crawford Effect depends on the orientation of the photoreceptors toward the entrance pupil of the eye. In fact, human photoreceptors are phototropic. When an eye is patched, the photoreceptors lose their sense of direction and become randomly, or more nearly randomly, oriented [Enoch et al, 1979]. The consequence is reduced direction selectivity of response to light, ie, the Stiles-Crawford Effect is diminished. Recent, unpublished studies suggest that the Stiles-Crawford Effect may be reduced in the eyes of healthy older people [Pokorny and Smith, personal communication]. The reduced directional selectivity of the older retinas may mean that they are more sensitive to stray light. Since the Stiles-Crawford Effect is primarily, though not exclusively, associated with cones, increased sensitivity to stray light is particularly serious for tasks requiring resolution of spatial details by the older eye.

The Photostress Test [Wolkstein & Carr, 1979] was mentioned several times during the symposium and is a useful, though not common, clinical tool. We should point out that this test does not measure dark adaptation per se. Because the Photostress Test measures the recovery time for resolution of fine details (typically the lowest line of an acuity chart that a patient can read), it gauges primarily recovery of the visual mechanisms mediating spatial resolution, presumably foveal cones. This is why the Photostress Test is particularly useful in assessing macula status.

Although it is typically reported that visual fields constrict with advancing age, there is good reason to believe that most if not all of this constriction is explicable with reference to reduced retinal illuminance associated with increased lenticular density and senile miosis. Generally, tests of visual fields with older observers have tended to be lacking in rigor.

A number of key relationships in the area of vision aging are completely unexplored. In fact, even the most cursory examination of the literature reveals many key questions on which we have no data. For example, the ability of the retina to transduce light and mediate visual sensations depends on a proper supply of blood. It is remarkable that we have no well-controlled studies correlating the status of the retinal vasculature with visual function in individual nonclinical observers. The possible relation among age, blood supply, and vision is something that many investigators have considered. More generally, we know virtually nothing about the relation between the microstructure of the aging retina and its visual function. For example, drusen are a common feature of the aging fundus, but we have no studies that quantify the relationship between the presence and character of drusen and the visual function of those areas of the retina within which they occur. Such studies would require the ability to present localized targets on known areas of the retina under highly controlled conditions. Such studies would be difficult and time consuming but most worthwhile.

It is almost commonplace to observe that acuity may be as good in the disease-free older eyes as in the eyes of 20-year-olds. In the absence of cataract, senile macular degeneration, and other diseases afflicting the aging eye, the eyes of 70- or 80-year-olds may support acuity as fine as that found in disease-free eyes of 20-year-olds. It is reassuring to learn that acuity need not deteriorate with age. But there is one caveat that needs to be considered before such claims are accepted at face value: One must insure that acuity of the younger groups, against which the older are compared, has been measured in a way that allows their best possible acuity to be expressed. In particular, most charts or devices used to measure acuity tend to produce an artificial ceiling on the highest acuities that can be measured. Typically, acuity charts fail to have an adequate number of lines below the 20/20 (or equivalent) line. When these limitations are removed, the acuities found in healthy younger eyes tend to be considerably higher than those found in healthy older eyes [Frisen and Frisen, 1981].

This problem with acuity measurements is endemic to the use of acuity in clinical investigations. More generally, acuity is not treated with sufficient respect as a complex measurement requiring considerable care and thought. Since it is so easy to measure acuity—all one has to do is present a chart—many investigators have been fooled into producing estimates of acuity that are woefully in error. In addition, the interexaminer variability in acuity measurements [Gibson and Sanderson, 1980] further complicates the picture. Interexaminer variability in measurements of acuity is likely to be even more exaggerated when older patients or subjects are involved. It is well known that some older people require considerable coaxing in order for them to be willing to "guess" letters on an eye chart. Thus, the inexperienced or impatient tester may well produce spuriously low estimates of visual acuity in certain older people. As Sloan [1980] and others have argued, a good deal more attention needs to be paid to the manner in which this basic measurement in clinical investigations is made.

The discussion of cell loss offered by Weale (this volume) highlights the fact that we lack anatomical data on the changes in the retina with age. His comments on the possibility, from psychophysical observations, that extrafoveal cones may age at a different rate than rods is in intriguing. But the absence of relevant anatomical measurements [cf Marshall et al, 1979], including detailed cell counts of receptors at various eccentricities and counts of retinal ganglion cells, prevents clear relations from being established. Although their work comes from a somewhat different domain, the paper by Marc and Sperling [1977] can give the reader some idea of the power and understanding of visual function that is to be gained by appropriate, detailed anatomical work on the retina. We are very far, in the area of aging and vision, from work that can compare.

REFERENCES

Enoch J, Birch DG, Birch EE (1979) Monocular light exclusion for a period of days reduces directional sensitivity of the human retina. Science 206:705–707.

Frisen L, Frisen M (1981) How good is normal visual acuity? A study of letter acuity thresholds as a function of age. Albrecht Von Graefes Arch Klin Exp Ophthalmol 215:149–157.

Gibson RA, Sanderson HF (1980) Observer variation in ophthalmology. Br J Ophthalmol 64:457–460.

Girgus J, Coren S, Porac C (1977) Independence of in vivo human lens pigmentation from UV light exposure Vis Res 17:749–750.

Marc R & Sperling HG (1977) Chromatic organization of primate cones. Science 196:454–456.

Sloan L (1980) Needs for precise measures of acuity. Arch Ophthalmol 98:286–290.

Stiles WS, Crawford BH (1933) The luminous efficiency of rays entering the pupil at different points. Proc R Soc Lond [Biol] 112:428–250.

Wolkstein M, Carr R (1979) Macula function tests. In Yannuzzi Gitter & Schatz (eds) "The Macula, A Comprehensive Test and Atlas." Baltimore: Williams & Wilkins, 14–24.

Young R (1981) A theory of central retinal disease. In Sears (ed) "Future Directions in Ophthalmic Research." New Haven: Yale Univ Press, 237–270.

Aging and Human Visual Function, pages 121-130

The Effects of Aging on Selected Visual Functions: Color Vision, Glare Sensitivity, Field of Vision, and Accommodation

John H. Carter

INTRODUCTION

Aging affects visual function in two ways. Biochemical, structural, and other physical concomitants of aging affect the level and character of visual performance. Certain diseases, whose prevalence tends to increase with age, produce statistically significant changes in visual function. The discussion that follows is directed toward visual changes that attend uncomplicated aging. However, the distinction between the effects of normal aging and those of disease is not always as clear as one might wish.

EFFECTS OF AGING ON COLOR VISION STATUS

There are systematic changes in color vision that appear as a normal consequence of aging. These resemble somewhat the effect of a younger person looking through a yellow filter. Blue light is attenuated more than light of longer wavelengths, resulting in a shift in the appearance of white toward yellow. There is a relative darkening of blue-colored objects and a general bias of colors away from the blues toward colors of longer wavelength. There may also be slight reduction in the ability to discriminate among hues associated with lights of closely related dominant wavelengths, particularly so at low photopic light levels. Verriest et al [1962] reported on age changes in hue discrimination, measured using the Munsell-Farnsworth Hundred Hue Test. These effects result predominantly, perhaps entirely, from changes in transmittance of the optical media of the eye, in particular of the crystalline lens. The crystalline lens is known to yellow progressively with age, a fact accounted for in part by pigmentary absorption and in part by scattering [Said and Weale, 1959].

Senile miosis, common among the elderly, accentuates the color distortion produced by a yellowed lens and results in greater reduction in retinal illuminance than would be predicted on the basis of relative pupillary area. Why is retinal illuminance not simply attenuated in proportion to the reduction in pupillary area? Mellerio [1971] and Coren and Girgus [1972] showed that, for certain purposes, it is legitimate to regard the lens as an optical filter having uniform extinction per unit pathlength. Under this model, it becomes apparent that pupillary miosis must increase light loss due to extinction by limiting light entering the eye to only those rays which pass very close to the center (the thickest part) of the lens.

The effects of senile miosis and lenticular absorption and scatter combine to elevate detection thresholds and to impair color recognition. These effects become especially significant when ambient luminance falls to lower photopic or upper mesopic levels. This is because hue discrimination and acuity tend to deteriorate as the retina approaches and enters the mesopic range, wherein occurs the transition from cone to rod function. Mesopia is approached at significantly higher ambient luminances in the aged due to diminished media transmission. In fact, Weale [1963, pp 168–169] reports that due to senile miosis and lenticular yellowing, only about a third of the light available to the retina of the 20-year-old is available to the retina at age 60. Under such conditions, special hazards may attend activities such as the operation of motor vehicles by the elderly [Allen and Carter, 1964].

EFFECTS OF AGING ON GLARE

Glare represents the effect of light that impairs visual efficiency. Glare may be due principally to optical factors (too much light or adventitious light) or it can depend significantly upon such retinal factors as may impact neural and/or photochemical mechanisms. Glare can be classified in a number of ways. One system of classification is that of Bell et al [1922]. These authors have classified glare as dazzling, veiling, and scotomatic. Aberrations, scattering, and optical imperfections result in numerous rays falling outside the geometric image on the retina. Only under conditions of high brightness, however, does the intensity on the retina in areas illuminated by these aberrant rays become sufficiently great to impair visual resolution to significant degree. It is possible that retinal interaction effects too may contribute to dazzling glare. We observe the effects of dazzling glare when we attempt to make out the detail of a hot filament in an unfrosted incandescent lamp. In "veiling glare," stray light is more or less uniformly distributed across the retinal image of interest, thus resulting in reduced brightness contrast between the image and its background. The effect of light from within an automobile being reflected by the windshield into the eye of its driver provides an example of veiling glare. In "scotomatic glare," light overloads the retinal photoreceptors and produces functional neural and/or photochemical changes that culminate in significantly reduced retinal sensitivity. The presence of an afterimage that prevents good vision immediately after one has been exposed to a bright flash of light, such as that produced by a photographic flash bulb, provides an example of scotomatic glare.

A variety of optical factors can contribute to glare effects. Light may enter the eye other than through the pupil to serve thereby as a source of veiling glare (transillumination). Stray light can result from multiple intraocular reflections, such as between refracting surfaces (flare). According to Boynton and Clarke [1964], stray light within the eye results from light scattered by the optical media, principally by the crystalline lens but to a lesser extent by the cornea. Intraocular stray light can derive from multiple reflections between areas on the ocular fundus and/or between various other surfaces within the eye (intraocular reflection). Light can be back-reflected from the choroid and/or sclera to strike the retina a second time (halation). And, under certain circumstances, intraocular stray light can result from fluorescence of ocular structures. Both the cornea and the crystalline lens fluoresce, thereby producing visible light in response to the absorption of (selected wavelengths of) ultraviolet and/or visible radiation. While corneal fluorescence is of low magnitude and increases only slightly with age, Satoh [1973] has shown that lens fluorescence consists of at least two components and that, while the level of the "purple" fluorescence component (activation about 290 nm, emission 325–340 nm) is relatively greater, it is the "blue" fluorescence component (activation about 345 nm, emission about 420 nm) that increases markedly with age. It seems likely that, in the aged motorist, the fluorescence of the cystalline lens and lenticular light scatter combine to produce the marked visual difficulty associated with seeing poorly illuminated, low-contrast objects in the presence of the bright postsunset sky. Why should this be true? The fact that older motorists frequently complain of visual difficulties at dusk probably results from the relatively large solid angle subtended in the pupillary plane by the sky. An additional factor may be that the post sunset sky tends to be relatively rich in the shorter wavelengths. Both these factors would tend to increase intraocular stray light. Allen and Carter [1964] showed significant acuity improvement in young subjects when the twilight sky was effectively removed as a glare source. Although not tested empirically, even greater effects would be expected among the aged where lenticular scatter and fluorescence play relatively far greater roles.

Scotomatic glare commonly is experienced by the aged. This becomes quite conspicuous to the older individual at night as he approaches the headlights of an oncoming automobile. Reading [1968] has shown that the visual impact of scotomatic glare is worsened by the effects of a small pupil and lenticular yellowing. As we have seen, pupillary miosis and lenticular extinction combine to lower the brightness of the retinal image. Under conditions of scotomatic glare, relative insensitivity of the retina compounds the visual loss otherwise resulting from inadequate retinal illumination. While scotomatic glare can occur in any eye if light intensity is extremely high, it commonly is present in aged eyes at intensities unlikely to produce significant visual loss among the young. Wolf [1960] has presented data that show an abrupt increase in sensitivity to glare at about age 40.

Retinal factors presumably play a dominant role in scotomatic glare. Macular disease is common among the elderly and "photostress" tests have been advocated by Severin et al [1967a and b] for its detection. Here, the retina is exposed to a measured flash of light and the time required for functional recovery to a specified level of visual acuity is measured. Visual recovery following exposure to a bright flash is reported to be delayed significantly among those over 40, even when ocular disease has carefully been excluded.

THE EFFECTS OF AGING ON THE FIELD OF VISION

The total (relative) field of vision of an eye is the area over which the eye can see when it gazes straight ahead. The eye is not uniformly sensitive, however, and it is useful to regard field of vision in terms of the "acuity" or "sensitivity" of various zones. The term "acuity" perhaps is preferable for perimetry conducted with test objects of graded sizes, since acuity is the reciprocal of an extensive threshold. (The term "acuity" as used in this context should not, however, be equated with minimum separable or with Snellen acuity.) The term "sensitivity" is perhaps more appropriate for perimetry when test object size is held constant and contrast is varied, for the term "sensitivity" implies a reciprocal of an intensive threshold. In any event, the relative acuity or sensitivity of various zones of the retina varies with state of adaptation. While it is impractical to attempt to hold mean retinal illuminance constant, flux density in the plane of the pupil can be controlled. Conventional field testing is performed at an adaptation level that for most eyes falls in the lower photopic or extreme upper mesopic region. Then, acuity is quite high at the foveal center but falls, at first rapidly and then more slowly, toward the periphery. In the extreme retinal periphery, acuity once more declines rapidly.

Static methods of field testing assess differential thresholds at each of a series of locations within the field. Kinetic methods, on the other hand, determine loci of points with equal "minimum visible" acuity. These loci are known as isopters. Knowledge of the characteristics of the individual field of vision is useful both in the detection/diagnosis of disease and in the practical evaluation of a subject's ability to detect eccentrically placed stimuli. This latter capability might be of interest, for example, as a factor to consider in granting licenses to operate a motor vehicles.

The integrity of the clinically recorded field of vision depends on the effectiveness of the eye's dioptric system, the clarity of its media, and upon proper functioning of the retina, nervous pathways, and associated cortical centers. Clinical perimetry ordinarily is performed near the lower end of the range through which Weber's fraction is reasonably constant. Gross reduction in amount of light entering the eye, such as may be realized under conditions of senile miosis combined with marked yellowing of the crystalline lens and perhaps some loss of nuclear transparency, can drop the retinal illuminance to middle or low mesopic levels. Then, the pattern of retinal sensitivity changes. Its profile becomes quite "flat," with central retinal sensitivity only marginally above that of the periphery [Potts, 1972]. Artifacts that may affect visual fields recorded among the aged include those caused by nose and/or brow limitations associated with relative enophthalmos.

Concerned principally with functional properties of the field of vision and using 4-mm white targets in the AO screening perimeter, Burg [1968] found the total lateral field of vision to be maximum to about age 35, and thereafter to decline with age. He also found a very slight sex difference, females tending to have slightly larger total fields.

Drance et al [1967] were concerned about changes in the field of vision with age because normal changes in field are of significance when one wishes to monitor the efficacy of treatment of a chronic disease such as open angle glaucoma. They used the Goldmann perimeter with I_2 and I_4 targets (the approximate equivalents of 1/1000 and 5/1000 white) and a controlled pupil, and found decreasing sizes for both isopters beginning in youth and continuing through senescence. This relationship was approximately linear when area was plotted as a function of age. They also found a slight increase in blindspot size with age. Perhaps most important was their finding that the I_2 isopter can pass outside, through, or within the blindspot, thereby creating a potential for a short-lived "baring of the blindspot" among disease-free elderly eyes. These authors also found the extent of the superior field to decline most rapidly with age, compared with field loss in other cardinal meridians. They attributed this to interference by the upper eyelid. Wolf and Nadroski [1971] found only gradual changes in the visual field to age 60, with rapid changes thereafter. They felt that this senescent shift may be due in significant measure to retinal factors and demonstrated similar field changes among the young under conditions of hypoxia. Pointing to an empirical relationship between chronic pulmonary disease and retinal diseases such as retinal breaks and lattice degeneration, they speculated that insufficient retinal oxygenation may play a significant role in field loss among the elderly.

EFFECTS OF AGING ON ACCOMMODATION AND RELATED FUNCTIONS

Accommodation is the process responsible for maintaining a clear retinal image in the presence of varying vergence of light entering the eye. Accordingly, it allows clear vision over a range of distances and additionally can enable the hyperope to compensate his error of refraction to obtain improved vision. In man, accommodation involves altering ocular refracting power through change in crystalline lens curvature. Contraction of the ciliary muscle *permits* the lens to become increasingly convex in near vision by relaxing tension on the zonular fibers. Clinical convention dictates that accommodative amount is regarded as zero when the ciliary muscle is relaxed and the eye's dioptric power is minimum.

Refracting power ordinarily is expressed in terms of the diopter. For a thin lens, refracting power in diopters is the reciprocal of the principal focal distance in meters. When the eye accommodates, its power changes, but the principal plane to which optical power customarily is referred also moves slightly. Thus, there is no completely "natural" plane to which ocular accommodation may be referred. In laboratory studies, accommodation often is referred to the center of the eye's entrance pupil since this is easily located, fixed in position, and near the eye's principal planes. Clinicians prefer to refer accommodation to the spectacle plane where refractive power measurements ordinarily are obtained. Choice of reference plane is relevant to the following discussion because amplitude of accommodation invariably diminishes with age and because its rate of decline increases with forward position of the plane of reference preferred by the clinician.

When subjective methods involving blur recognition are used to assess accommodative amplitude, its measured value is augmented by the depth of focus of the eye. Depth of focus defines the limit on defocus in advance of blur detection. Since the pupil constricts when the eye looks at near objects and accommodates, depth of focus tends to be very large near the accommodative amplitude limit. Thus, clinical methods like Donders' push-up technique generally yield appreciably higher amplitude estimates than do laboratory methods that ordinarily are free from depth-of-field contamination. When Donders' method is used, the minimum amplitude measurement obtained is not zero but a finite nominal limit dictated by depth of field.

According to Hamasaki et al [1956], the average value of the true accommodative amplitude declines steadily from some early age until it reaches zero between the ages of 50 and 52. It generally is agreed that this age reduction in amplitude is due almost entirely to lenticular factors. The lens fails to increase in convexity as the zonule relaxes during ciliary muscle contraction. The changes in the lens that give rise to this effect are complex and not fully understood.

Nonlenticular factors potentially contributing to this age reduction in accommodative amplitude have been cited, but evidence that these actually play a significant role is limited. The equatorial diameter of the crystalline lens is known to increase with age and this should loosen the zonule by reducing the circumlental space [Weale, 1963 pp 115–116]. However, the expected change in ocular farpoint does not occur and Farnsworth and Shyne [1979] have shown that, with age, the zonule tends to move onto the anterior lens face, so loss of tension due to diminishing circumlental space probably is not realized.

There are dramatic changes in the ciliary body with age that include significant alterations in the ciliary muscle itself. The ciliary processes enlarge and there is vascular sclerosis, loss of elastic tissue, and replacement of atrophic muscle fibers by connective tissue. Weale [1963, pp 60–62] cites the work of Stieve, who showed that, with age, the ciliary muscle shortens posteriorly and becomes more triangular in form due to enlargement of its so-called circular bundle. However, as Weale suggests, these changes may well be concomitants of accommodative loss rather than its cause.

The first large-scale study of how accommodative amplitude varies with age was conducted by Donders [1864]. Duane [1909, 1912] criticized Donders' methodology and presented the results of his own investigations. Hofstetter [1944, 1950] referred Duane's and Donders' data to a common spectacle plane location, noted their modest curvatures to be in opposing directions, observed that their composite was approximately a straight line, and derived a formula for the line of best fit.

In the resulting formula—$D = 18.5 - 0.3 A$—D is the amplitude of accommodation in diopters and A is age in years. Noting the linearity of these composite data and that cross-sectional data often have described the age-accommodation relationship as nonlinear, Hofstetter speculated that perhaps a nonlinear result may be the consequence of a sample population wherein participants have both differing initial amplitudes and differing rates of accommodative decline. He therefore conducted a longitudinal investigation of two subjects and this demonstrated accommodative decline with age to be linear [Hofstetter, 1965].

Presbyopia is not synonymous with age-dependent accommodative decline, but depends upon the inadequacy of available accommodation to sustain clear vision at the customary near working distance. While we have seen that accommodative decline proceeds slowly, most persons becoming presbyopic perceive their affliction to be both of sudden onset and rapidly progressive. This impression occurs for two reasons. Loss of focusing ability in excess of that actually needed is moot but, as accommodation becomes insufficient to meet actual need, further amplitude loss becomes all too apparent. And, while accommodation declines almost linearly in dioptric measure, recession of the nearpoint of accommodation with age takes place at an accelerating rate since it involves a reciprocal function of dioptric change.

Presbyopia has been reported to begin at an earlier age in females than in males [Lebensohn, 1966]. Perhaps this is due principally to their smaller stature and consequent use of shorter near working distances, although Lebensohn [1966] attributes it to the onset of menopause. Presbyopia also has been reported to begin earlier near the earth's equator, a fact that could result from any of a number of causes [Weale, 1963, p 111; see also Borish, 1975].

Changes in accommodative speed with age are of interest, both because some presbyopes complain of accommodative inertia (slowness of accommodative change) and because such changes in accommodative speed affect the development and testing of theoretical models of presbyopia. Allen [1956] presented data that, he felt, showed a marked increase in action time for positive accommodation among older subjects. Action time for accommodative relaxation, on the other hand, increased only slightly among older subjects. He explained these data on the basis of a model describing presumed physical changes within the crystalline lens. Weale [1963, pp 120–123] presented an alternative interpretation of Allen's data. Most of the time expended by older subjects during accommodation for near objects is utilized close to the amplitude limit. If accommodation is considered in terms of percentage of total amplitude, then older subjects can be shown to *begin* to accommodate significantly faster than the young. Weale suggested that this is consistent with an increased strength of the circular fibers of the ciliary muscle at the onset of presbyopia, perhaps the result of work hypertrophy.

When fusion is suspended, accommodation is attended by a change in vergence. The amount of vergence change that accompanies a unit of accommodative change is known as the ACA ratio. And, when focus-accommodation is inhibited, such as by placing a pinhole aperture before each eye, then convergence is attended by a corresponding change in accommodation. The amount of accommodative change that attends a unit change in convergence is known as the CAC ratio. The CAC ratio, far less stable generally than the ACA, declines with age as one would expect if presbyopia were the result of a progressive lack of responsiveness of the crystalline lens to neuromuscular effort.

The issue of whether or not the ACA ratio changes with age is particularly significant inasmuch as it affects models of presbyopia causation. If the same amount of ciliary effort were required to produce a unit of accommodation at any age, then the ACA ratio would be expected to be age independent. If, on the other hand, increasing ciliary effort were required to produce a unit of accommodation with ascending age, then an ACA ratio increase with age would be expected. Unfortunately, experimental results that bear upon this issue have tended to be ambiguous. Cross-sectional studies [Morgan and Peters 1951, Davis and Jobe 1957] have tended consistently to fail to show any significant ACA increase with age. Such studies have, however, (for sound practical reasons) used a quasi-ACA, known as the "stimulus" ACA. The "stimulus" and "response" ACA ratios would be expected to be identical only if a unit change in accommodative stimulus would, on the average, be expected to result in a unit change in accommodative response. We know this not to be the case. Fry [1959] conducted a long-term longitudinal study of his own ("response") ACA ratio and found this to have increased sharply with the onset of presbyopia. While a definitive answer is not yet at hand to explain the discrepancy between cross-sectional and longitudinal data concerning age change in ACA, it nevertheless is interesting to speculate concerning possible reasons why these may differ. While several interpretations are possible, it seems most likely that the majority of persons, upon finding accommodation difficult at the onset of presbyopia, allow response to lag progressively further behind stimulus. This yields the result that heterophoria fails to shift in an eso direction with age, as would be expected if accommodative lag were to remain constant while the amount of ciliary effort required to produce a unit of accommodation steadily increased.

SUMMARY AND CONCLUSION

In this segment, we have dealt with the effects of aging upon each of four different visual functions, these having been selected more or less arbitrarily from among a broader group. Specifically, we looked at the impact of aging on color vision, on glare sensitivity, on the field of vision, and on accommodation. While, as we have seen, the impact of age on visual function involves numerous factors, it nevertheless is interesting to consider whether any single ocular component might change with age in such a way as to affect strongly each of these rather diverse functions. The answer is affirmative. The responsible element for an array of significant visual changes with age is the crystalline lens.

Systematic shifts in the spectral transmission of the crystalline lens and the associated decrement in its overall light transmission account for observed changes in color discrimination among the healthy. Increase in lenticular light scatter is a key factor in the rather considerable increase in glare sensitivity encountered among the aged. Clinical field tests are conducted near the extreme lower end of the photopic range. While retinal factors too are likely to be involved, decrements in retinal illuminance, which are due largely to increases in crystalline lens extinction and actually may bring the retina well into the mesopic range, play a highly significant role in bringing about those age-related decrements in extent of the visual field that are encountered among the healthy. Finally, it generally is acknowledged that changes in the physical properties of the crystalline lens and its capsule are chiefly responsible for the systematic decline in amplitude of accommodation that occurs with age and hence causes the clinical condition known as presbyopia.

REFERENCES

Allen MJ (1956) The influence of age on the speed of accommodation. Am J Optom Arch Am Acad Optom 33(4):201–208.

Allen MJ, Carter JH (1964) Visual problems associated with motor vehicle driving at dusk. J Am Optom Assn 35(1):25–30.

Bell L, Troland LT, Verhoeff FH (1922) Report of the subcommittee on glare of the research committee. Tr Illum Engin Soc 17:743 ff.

Borish IM (1975) "Clinical Refraction," 3rd Ed, Vol I. Chicago: Professional Press, pp 168–169.

Boynton RM, Clarke FJ (1964) Sources of entoptic scatter in the human eye, J Opt Soc Am, 54(1):110–119.

Burg Albert (1968) Lateral visual field as related to age and sex. J App Psychol 52(1):10–15.

Coren S, Girgus JS (1972) Density of human lens pigmentation In vivo measures over an extended age range (Letter to the Editor) Vis Res 12:343 ff.

Davis CJ, Jobe FW (1957) Further studies on AC/A ratio as measured on the ortho-rater. Am J Optom Arch Am Acad Optom 34(1):16–25.

Donders FC (1864) "On the Anomalies of Accommodation and Refraction of the Eye." Trans Moore WD, London: New Sydenham Society.

Drance SM, Berry V, Hughes A (1967) Studies on the effects of age on the central and peripheral isopters of the visual field in normal subjects. Am J Ophth 63(6):1667–1672.

Duane Alexander (1909) The accommodation and Donders' curve and the need of revising our ideas regarding them. JAMA 52:1992–1996.

Duane, Alexander (1912) Normal values of the accommodation at all ages. JAMA Part 2, 59:1010–1013.

Farnsworth PN, Shyne SE (1979) Anterior zonular shifts with age. Exp Eye Res 28:291–297.

Fry Glenn A (1959) The effect of age on the AC/A ratio. Am J Optom Arch Am Acad Optom 36(6):299–303.

Hamasaki D, Ong J, Marg E (1956) The amplitude of accommodation in presbyopia. Am J Optom Arch Am Acad Optom 33(1):3–14.

Hofstetter HW (1944) A comparison of Duane's and Donders' Tables of the amplitude of accommodation. Am J Optom Arch Am Acadm Optom 21(9):345–363.

Hofstetter HW (1950) Useful age-amplitude formula. Optom World 38:42–45.

Hofstetter HW (1965) A longitudinal study of amplitude changes in presbyopia. Am J Optom Arch Am Acad Optom 42(1):3–8.

Lebensohn JE (1966) Changes in the aging eye. Postgrad Med 40(6):746–751.

Mellerio J (1971) Light absorption and scatter in the human lens. Vis Res 11:129–141.

Morgan MW, Peters HB (1951) Accommodative Convergence in Presbyopia, Am J Optom Arch Am Acad Optom 28(1):3–10.

Potts Albert M (ed) (1972) "The Assessment of Visual Function." St. Louis: Mosby, pp 39–41.

Reading Veronica M (1968) Disability glare and age. Vis Res 8:207–214.

Said FS, Weale RA (1959) The variation with age of the spectral transmissivity of the living human crystalline lens. Gerontologica 3:213–231.

Satoh Kenshi (1973) Fluorescence in human lens. Exp Eye Res 16:167–172.

Severin Sanford L, Tour RL, Kershaw RH (1967a) Macular function and the photostress test 1. Arch Ophthamol 77:2–7.

Severin SL, Tour RL, Kershaw RH (1967b) Macular function and the photostress test 2. Arch Ophthalmol 77:163–167.

Verriest G, Valdevyvere R, Vanderdonck R (1962) Variations de la descrimination chromatique. Rev Opt (Theor Instrum) 41:499–509.

Weale RA (1963) "The Aging Eye." New York: Harper.

Wolfe Ernst (1960) Glare and age. Arch Ophthalmol 64:54/502–66/514.

Wolf E, Nadroski AS (1971) Extent of the visual field-changes with age and oxygen tension. Arch Ophth 86:637–642.

Aging and Human Visual Function, pages 131–159
© 1982 Alan R. Liss, Inc., 150 Fifth Avenue, New York, NY 10011

The Effects of Aging on Selected Visual Functions: Dark Adaptation, Visual Acuity, Stereopsis, and Brightness Contrast

Donald G. Pitts

INTRODUCTION

Aging affects many aspects of visual function but the changes are primarily physiological and anatomical. The physiological changes may involve biochemical changes or observable physical changes, such as the increase in lenticular opacification, as an almost normal progression of events. The anatomical changes may be to the musculature, the neural system, the visual receptor, or the visual cortex. In any of these changes there is a loss of sensory function that results in a decrement in performance as a person ages. In this section of the volume, the challenge is to look at the data on dark adaptation, visual acuity, stereopsis, and brightness contrast in an attempt to define those changes that result in a change in visual function. In dark adaptation, the data of Weale has been heavily relied on but the approach in analysis is different even though the conclusions are almost identical. The dark adaptation portion is essentially an updating of a paper written and presented but not published in 1961. It is hoped that the data on the sensory functions covered in this review may serve as an impetus for further research into geriatric vision and its associated problems.

DARK ADAPTATION AS RELATED TO THE AGING PROCESS

The human eye is capable of automatically adjusting to extremely wide limits of light intensities by a process known as adaptation. Light adaptation occurs when the eye changes from a dark to a light environment. Dark adaptation occurs when the eye is exposed to a dark environment after previous exposure to light. Light adaptation is rapid and difficult to measure but dark adaptation is a slower process and, consequently, more easily measured. Research on the effects of aging on adaptation has been almost exclusively limited to the dark adaptation

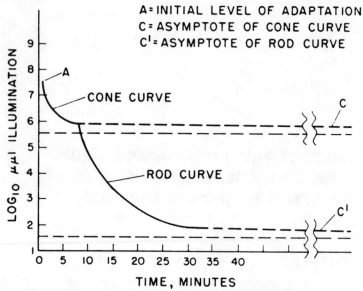

Fig. 1. A typical dark adaption curve. A represents the initial level of adaptation and C represents the final level of adaptation for the cones while C¹ is the final threshold for the rods. The two phases of the curve represent the total dark adaptation curve for the rod and cone receptors, respectively [after McFarland et al, 1960].

process. It is the dark adaptation process and its effects on the aging eye that are the subjects of this section.

The word "adaptation" has an interesting history in vision research. LeGrand [1957] and Duke-Elder [1939] attribute the origin of the term "adaptation" to H. Aubert in 1865; therefore, "adaptation" was introduced to physiological optics or visual science after the writings of Helmholtz. LeGrand has suggested that Mathey was the first to conduct research on the reduction of visual threshold with time in the dark and associate the reduction with the adaptation process. He stated that Mathey reported on 54 emmetropes aged 11 to 59. Homatropine was used to dilate the pupils and a blue test light was used as the stimulus. Dark adaptation has been shown to vary with the duration and intensity of pre-exposure, size of the test stimulus, length of exposure of the test light, retinal position, color, pupillary size, and the test subjects themselves. Therefore, it becomes necessary to fully specify the test conditions under which the dark adaptation was determined for the data to be meaningful. Dark adaptation data are usually presented in graphic form with the abscissa giving the duration in the dark in minutes and the ordinate presenting the log of the threshold luminance, as in Figure 1. The initial phase of the curve is attributed to cone (photopic) adaptation

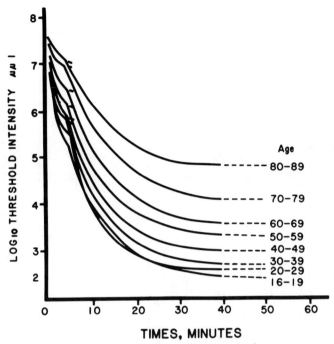

Fig. 2. Dark adaptation as a function of age [after McFarland et al, 1960].

and reaches as asymptote after about 8 min in the dark. The final phase of the curve represents rod (scotopic) adaptation and continues for up to 8 hr; however, for practical considerations scotopic adaptation is complete after 40 min. The transition area between the two curves is shown by the upper dotted lines and is attributed to mesopic adaptation. The shape of the dark adaptation curve changes if a colored stimulus is used. A test stimulus that is red produces only the first phase or the cone portion of the curve. Stimuli that are blue or violet emphasize the scotopic portion of the curve. Stimuli that are yellow or green demonstrate the two phases of the adaptation process almost as well as a white stimulus.

The relationship between dark adaptation and the aging process has been studied by Birren and Shock [1950], Birren et al [1948], Robertson and Yudkin [1944], Steven [1946], Luria [1960] and others, but the most extensive research and analysis to date has been accomplished by McFarland and co-workers [McFarland and Fisher, 1955; McFarland and Domey, 1958; McFarland et al, 1958, 1960] and Domey and co-workers [Domey et al, 1960a, 1960b; Domey and McFarland, 1961; Domey, 1964]. (Fig. 2). All of their research has shown

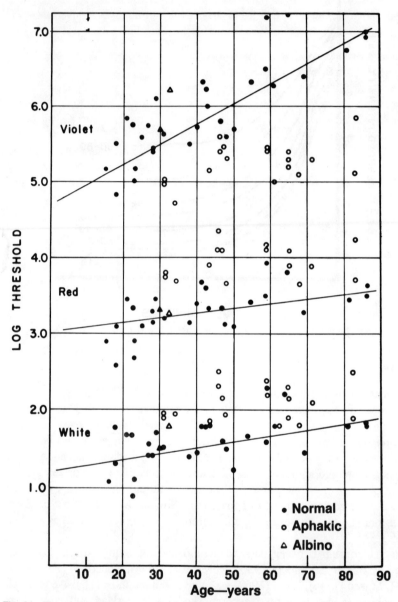

Fig. 3. The relationship between the visual thresholds for stimuli of violet, white, and red hues and age for normal, aphakic, and albino subject [after Gunkel and Gouras, 1963].

a significant decline in the final threshold as age increases with the decline most marked above the age of 60. McFarland et al, through extensive statistical analysis of the data, have shown:

1. The transition point for the mean data occurred between the fifth and sixth minutes after adaptation and was independent of age.
2. The threshold for dark adaptation at different time intervals after the test was begun correlated with both threshold level and time. This means that the dark adaptation curve can be predicted reliably if the initial point is established.
3. The cone and rod thresholds were correlated.
4. The rate of change of dark adaptation with age was 0.3 log units for every 13 years. This change corresponds to a factor of 2 and indicates that the target luminance must be doubled every 13 years just to be seen by the dark-adapted eye. It also means that the 80-year final calculated threshold would be elevated approximately 1.8 log units when compared with age 20. It should be noted that the experimental difference was about 2.2 log units.

What happens to change the process of adaptation with age? In an attempt to answer this question, we shall take a look at the wavelength of the stimulus, ocular transmittance, pupillary miosis, and other factors to examine their effects on dark adaptation.

In an attempt to resolve the questions of the stimulus wavelength, Gunkel and Gouras [1963] used a 10° test object and a ½-sec flash to study the effects of spectral stimuli on scotopic visibility for subjects ranging in age from 16 to 86 years (Fig. 3). The slope for normal subjects' threshold to the violet stimulus (408 nm) versus age was 0.011 log units per year. At the age of 80 there was a 1.0 log unit difference in the thresholds of normal and aphakic subjects. According to Gunkel and Gouras, the data show that the changes in transmittance of the aging lens were the predominant factor in elevating the threshold. They also state that the increase in threshold for the long wavelength (red) test light was the result of pupillary or neural changes, because aphakic patients showed similar dark adaptation curves with slightly elevated thresholds for the red and white stimuli. It was suggested that the pupillary effects could be isolated by the use of artical pupils of the proper diameters or by using a Maxwellian view. The remaining effect would be due to neural changes with increases in age. It should be noted that the pupillary and neural effects combined are about 0.3 log unit. Gunkel and Gouras state that a mydriatic did not "measurably lower the thresholds for older subjects" (p 7); therefore, it appears that the pupillary effects in their data were minimal. If this was the case, the differences in thresholds measured with red stimuli were most probably neural changes.

It is well known that the pupil becomes gradually smaller as a person ages (Fig. 4). The miosis of the pupil with age has been attributed to several factors including atrophy of the dilator muscle fibers, deposition of a hyaline substance

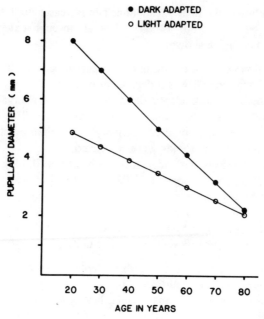

Fig. 4. Diameter of the pupil as related to age for both the dark-adapted and light-adapted eye [after Kornzweig, 1954].

below the sphincter muscle of the iris [Kornzweig, 1954], and loss of the retinal receptors responsible for the pupillary neural pathways. Weale [1961b] has calculated the retinal illuminance to age 60 and found that retinal illuminance corresponds to about one-third of the value at 20. The pupil is important for dark adaptation studies because the young pupil would ordinarily dilate after preadaption but the dilation found in the young eye does not occur for the aged eye. The effects of the pupil do not seem to be great; however, it appears that when corrections for pupillary variations were made, the threshold values would be lowered 0.4 log units at 40–49 years, 0.5 log units at 50–59 years, and 0.6 log units at 70–79 years.

Since dark adaptation depends on the transmittance of the ocular media, it would be appropriate to determine if the changes in the lens density with age were sufficient to affect the ability to see under conditions of darkness. Said and Weale [1959] have related density changes of the lens to age and wavelength. Their data show that the 63-year-old lens is about one log unit greater in density than the 45-year-old lens, and that these differences are greater at shorter wavelengths than at longer wavelengths (Fig. 5). The change was approximately 0.05

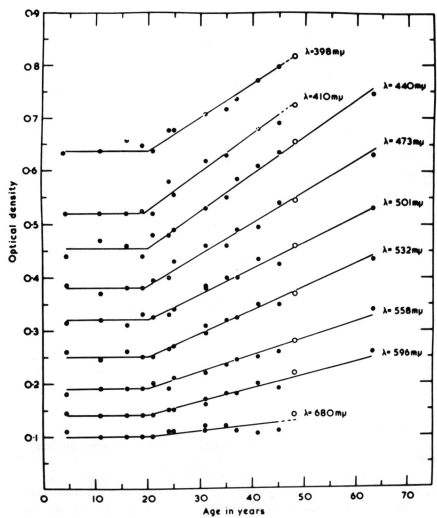

Fig. 5. Variation in optical density of the lens for different wavelengths and ages [after Said and Weale, 1959].

log units increase in density for each 10 years of increase in age. A density change of 0.05 corresponds to 9% per year.

Weale [1961a] (Fig. 6) selected data from five investigators in considering the variation of the absolute threshold with age. By chance, those authors who controlled pupillary size used a blue target stimulus and those who employed a natural pupil used a white target stimulus. In both portions of the graph, the

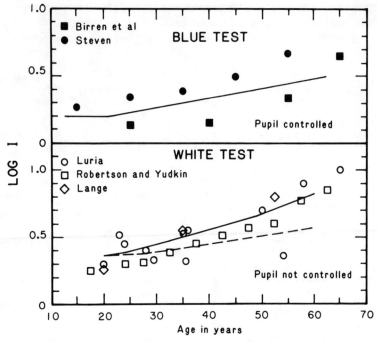

Fig. 6. Threshold levels for the blue stimulus with pupils controlled and white stimulus without pupils controlled for subjects of different ages [after Said and Weale, 1959]. (See text for further explanation.)

solid line shows the threshold as calculated from lenticular transmittance for variation with age. Correction for the age variation of the pupil size has been included and is seen as the dotted line at the bottom portion of the graph. The data of Birren and co-workers [Birren et al, 1950b] and of Steven [1946] show a 0.3-log-unit rise in calculated threshold while the data of Luria [1960] and Robertson and Yudkin [1944] show a 1.0-log-unit rise in calculated threshold. Thus, good agreement is found between the measured thresholds and the calculated thresholds. The data of McFarland and Fisher [1955] were obtained with a stimulus at 405 nm and represent transmittance losses of 80% (density of 0.7) at 40–49 years, 84% (density of 0.80) at 50–59 years, and 90% (density of 0.90) at 70–79 years.

Correction for transmittance losses and pupillary size would lower the dark adaptation final threshold by about 1.5 log units for the 70-year age level; therefore, the corrected data indicate that there is a threshold rise of about 0.5 log units that may be due to interference in the metabolism and to changes in the neural system. McFarland and co-workers [1960] have shown a rise in the visual threshold when there is a decrease in blood sugar (hypoglycemia) and an "oxygen want" (hypoxia). Research indicates that there are changes in cerebral circulation and subsequent retinal circulation with age. Therefore, McFarland et al [1955] postulated that the underlying mechanism for the increase in threshold was related to an interference in the normal metabolic processes within an individual's nerve cells in the brain and retina that may be due to a "reduced rate of transference of the essential substances" (p 428) (sugar and O_2) because of a reduced supply, reduced circulatory delivery, or slower diffusion rates. However, the data demonstrate overwhelmingly that losses in ocular transmittance and pupillary miosis resulting from the aging process are sufficient to account for most of the loss in adaptation, and that only a small portion of the total effect can be attributed to other causes.

These data may better explain some of the visual difficulties experienced by persons 55–60 years of age. The reduction in ocular transmittance as a person ages is accompanied by an increase in scatter. Scatter in the lens is increased further at shorter wavelengths; therefore, if the illuminance is increased in an attempt to aid older people, the increase should be preferably in the longer visual spectrum wavelengths. The increased scatter could result in veiling glare and reduce the contrast of any visual task. Thus, the increased scatter and resultant reduction in contrast may partially account for the reduction of visual acuity with age that is reported in the literature and that will be discussed in the next section.

VISUAL ACUITY AS A FUNCTION OF AGE

The study of visual acuity appears to be a rather simple task because acuity refers to the ability of the eye to see the shapes of objects in the world; however, the acuity becomes very involved when all of the variables or parameters are considered. The test for visual acuity commonly involves symbols or letters on a chart, which a person states that he can perceive. Measurement of the letters or symbols is usually expressed as the reciprocal of the "just resolvable visual angle" in minutes of arc and is an expression of the resolution of the retina. Measurement may also be given as a Snellen fraction, using the distance that a letter or object subtends in 5 min of arc as the numerator and the distance the letter can be seen distinctly as the denominator. The fact that there is no absolute criterion for visual acuity only allows one to compare the results of one test to another.

There are certain characteristics inherent in visual acuity scales that make the evaluation of acuity difficult. The Snellen fraction is the most commonly used designation, but data must usually undergo some modification when average acuity must be represented on a graph. For example, if 50 people aged 10 to 19 were evaluated, their acuity might vary from 20/10 to 20/100, with the majority

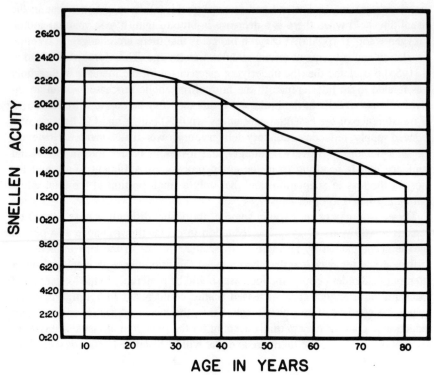

Fig. 7. Changes in Snellen visual acuity association with age as reported by Donders in 1864.

showing acuity close to 20/20. How can an average value be graphed that represents the acuity of the group? Additionally, those familiar with acuity are aware that the steps between acuity values do not represent equal differences in visual acuity because it is well recognized that a visual acuity of 20/20 is not twice as good as 20/40. Visual acuity has been shown to vary with the type of target used, contrast, level of illuminance, duration of exposure of the target, distance from the stimulus, size of the test target, and method used to measure acuity performance. To further complicate the problem, there are several characteristics of the eye that influence visual acuity and these include retinal adaptation, region of the retina stimulated, pupillary size, and individual differences under various brightness levels. The complex interactions of the target parameters and the characteristics of the eye independently and combined insure that the measurement of acuity is anything but simple.

Certain difficulties are encountered when attempting to compare the data of various authors. The selection of the method used to obtain visual acuity varies:

the printed chart may have excellent contrast but poorly controlled luminance, and projection charts and optical instruments may induce proximal accommodation. Some studies combine the data of men and women into a single category while other studies separate male and female data. The age group intervals of the subject vary from 5 years to 70 years and at odd year intervals. Visual acuity values vary from a single designation such as 20/20 to a range of Snellen values such as 20/20 to 20/70. Most data fail to cover a full range of ages and consequently, the differences between the young eye and the aged eye have to be judged from limited age ranges. Data is also reported for the better eye, uncorrected or corrected, and for binocular acuity both corrected or uncorrected. In the following review of the literature, we have attempted to select data that may be compared in spite of these difficulties. There was some difficulty in determining what constituted the normal eye. Are all subjects with disease processes to be eliminated from the data? What conditions constitute the normal aging process? Finally, nearly all studies showed a steadily declining number of subjects at the higher age levels.

The initial effort to relate changes in visual acuity to age was reported by Donders [1864]. He stated that his student, de Haan, used the recently developed Snellen optotypes as a letter chart. Patients were instructed to walk toward the chart until the letter could just be discriminated. It is evident that both Donders and de Haan recognized the importance of the illuminance and took care to insure that it was reasonably constant. The letters on the chart were assigned numbers that represented the distance D at which the letter subtended a visual angle of 5 min of arc. Visual acuity was measured by determining the distance that the letter was seen distinctly (d) and the "sharpness or accuracy" of vision was calculated:

$$\text{Visual acuity} = d/D$$

Figure 7 presents the data of de Haan, which will be compared with other data.

Collins and Britten [1924] present a study of 4,862 white youths aged 6 to 16 years and 6,479 male white workers aged 20 to 60 years and over. The number of persons with 20/20 or better in both eyes increased from 6 years to about 20 years, with a moderate decrease to the age of 45 years, when the rate of decrease in acuity is accelerated. Their data are divided into three classes of vision: normal vision with 20/20 or better, moderately defective vision with 20/30 to 20/40 in the better eye, and markedly defective vision with 20/50 or less in the better eye. Acuity tests were made with the Snellen chart at a distance of 6 m (20 ft) and, apparently, without correction. Unfortunately, this division of the data into broad categories of acuity does not lend itself to direct comparison with many studies.

Geldard and Crockett [1930] used the Landolt C to check the acuity of 204 subjects ranging from 6 to 71 years of age. The data are reported in minutes of arc and show that visual acuity varies as a function of age, declining steadily with the older years. They calculated an index of the relative difference in acuity between the two eyes (relative acuity) and found little difference with age. In other words, the absolute acuity varies with age but it varies approximately equally between the two eyes.

Feree et al [1934] determined visual acuity for presbyopic and nonpresbyopic subjects with the illuminance varied between 5.4 and 108 lm/m^2 [Lux]. They showed that there was an increase in acuity for increases in intensity of the illuminance when both eyes were used. The acuity increased more rapidly for the presbyopic group. There was also a difference in acuities between the non-presbyopic and presbyopic groups at the low levels of light intensity.

Chapanis [1950] studied the visual acuity of 574 subjects in the 5- to 80-year age range using Snellen optotype charts. He found a curvilinear relationship, with acuity increasing up to the age of 15–20, reaching a peak at the 25- to 45-year age range, and steadily declining above the age of 45. Kornzweig et al [1957] measured the visual acuity of 1,068 residents in a home for the aged in the 65- to 90-year age range and found poor vision to no light perception in 13.9%, but good to adequate vision in 16.1%. The prevalence of good to adequate vision decreased to about 10% above the age of 80 and poor vision increased proportionately. They suggest that cataracts, glacuoma, and macular degeneration accounted for the majority of those losses of visual acuity.

Burg [1966] studied both static and dynamic visual acuity for 17,500 subjects in the age range from 16 to 92 years. Visual acuity was measured with the orthorater using a checkerboard target. The data showed a progressive decline in acuity with age and revealed that visual acuity for the moving target (DVA) was poorer than acuity for a stationary target. Carlson and Tassone [1963] found that acuity and stereopsis were lowered for older subjects, which was emphasized when the older subjects were not allowed to wear their spectacles. Burg [1966] and Farrimond [1967] studied the dynamic visual acuity (DVA) in subjects from 16 to 80 years and demonstrated a decline in DVA with age. Farrimond presented evidence to show that the decline in DVA with age may be due to changes in the visual processes. Burg argues that nonacuity factors play an important role in determining DVA, the DVA was poorer than static acuity, and that DVA became worse as the velocity of the moving target increased. Burg showed a high correlation between DVA and static acuity—first time that such correlation has been found.

Richards [1966, 1972] studied visual acuity and contrast sensitivity for 141 individuals in the 16- to 90-year age range and reported that his selected population had normal vision to the age of 70, above which it began to decline rather rapidly. It should be noted that in later years, neural changes, metabolic changes, and other factors begin to combine with the earlier aging processes to become much more noticeable to the individual.

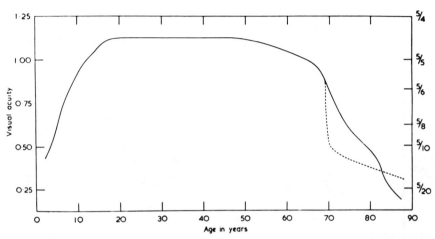

Fig. 8. Visual acuity of a patient population selected randomly. Acuity remains normal to about the age of 60 and then steadily declines to the age of 80. The dotted line shows the losses of acuity for patients with cataracts.

Weymouth [1960] presented the data of Hirsch for a group of 16,675 subjects in the 40- to 80-year range. This cross-sectional data probably represents the most reliable population sample to date, since the subjects were randomly selected patients from Hirsch's practice. The data shows a rather steady normal acuity up to the age of 60 and then a decline in acuity (Fig. 8). For the vast majority of the patients, visual acuity at 20/20 and above was found to the age of 65. In an attempt to explain the losses in acuity, Weymouth checked the records of each patient whose acuity decreased below 20/25 and found the distribution of conditions shown in Table 1. The loss of acuity from unknown conditions is almost as prevalent as for all other conditions combined, with the exception of cataracts.

Figure 9 is a composite of the visual acuity data from eight authors. It was often necessary to modify the data for comparison purposes; however, age was taken as the middle of the age range used by each of the authors. To compare acuities, Snellen decimal acuity was used to calculate a weighted mean acuity for each age category. It is evident from Figure 9 that visual acuity shows a slight improvement from the younger ages up to the 20- to 30-year age group, remains rather constant to 40–50 years of age, and then steadily declines to the age of 80, when the average acuity becomes approximately that of the younger age groups. Figure 9 also demonstrates that acuity measured with the orthorator is slightly poorer below the age of 25 and becomes steadily better in each ensuing decade of life. These differences are probably due to proximal accommodation

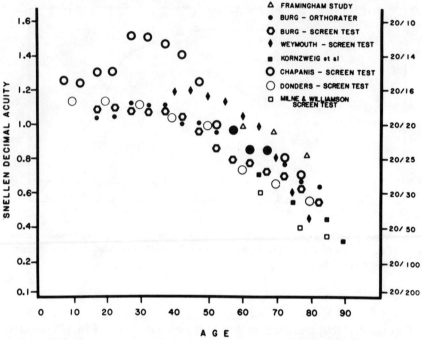

Fig. 9. The composite of visual acuity as it changes with age, from eight authors. Acuity was the best corrected for either eye changed to decimal form, with the mean weighted, and the age was taken as the middle age range for each set of data. The text should be read to understand the problems encountered in comparing visual acuity data from various authors.

or instrument myopia induced at the younger ages but lost as sclerosis of the crystalline lens reduces accommodation in the later years of life. The data also demonstrate a greater variation in acuity for the older ages beginning at about 40 years of age. The superior acuity shown for the ages of 25–40 years found in the Chapanis data cannot be explained.

The causes for the loss in acuity associated with the aging process are, in order of importance: cataract, senile macular degeneration, retinal pathology including diabetic retinopathy, open angle glaucoma and other unknown causes in the retina, vascular system, and metabolism. The Framingham study [Kahn et al, 1977] shows that these conditions increase dramatically above the age of 70 until 98% of all acuity losses can be accounted for with the four major conditions (Table II). It is encouraging that the most common condition, cataracts, can be alleviated by surgery and acuity can be restored to normal when corrective spectacles, contact lenses, or other optical appliances are used.

TABLE I. Conditions Found for Acuities of 20/25 or Less

	Data of Hirsch[a]		Framingham Study, %[b]		
			52 to 64	65 to 74	75 to 85
Condition	Number	%			
Cataract	165	36.3	5	18	46
Mascular degeneration	65	14.3	2	11	28
Retinal Pathology	42	9.2	2	3	7
Glaucoma	24	5.3	1.4	5.1	7.2
Amblyopia	13	2.9			
Post-surgical	12	2.6			
Injury	11	2.4			
Vitreous	9	2.0			
Corneal diseases	6	1.3			
Congenital malformations	4	0.9			
Unknown	104	22.8			
Totals	455	100.0			

[a]Weymouth, 1960.
[b]Kahn et al, 1977.

TABLE II. Distribution of Best Corrected Visual Acuity in Better Eye by Age and Sex*

Age (years) and sex	No. screened[a]	Percent Distribution					Log Visual Angle[b]	
		20/10 to 20/25	20/30 to 20/40	20/50 to 20/70	20/80 to 20/100	20/200 and worse	Mean	SD
Total	2471	91.7	5.1	2.0	0.4	0.9	0.15	0.50
Men	1043	93.9	3.4	1.8	0.4	0.6	0.13	0.49
Women	1428	90.1	6.4	2.1	0.4	1.1	0.17	0.50
Age 52–64	1293	98.4	0.9	0.5	0.1	0.1	0.05	0.26
Men	573	98.1	0.9	0.9		0.2	0.06	0.35
Women	720	98.6	1.0	0.3	0.1		0.05	0.15
Age 65–74	786	91.9	5.6	1.4	0.1	1.0	0.18	0.55
Men	318	95.3	3.1	0.6	0.3	0.6	0.13	0.48
Women	468	89.5	7.3	1.9		0.13	0.21	0.60
Age 75–85	392	69.1	17.9	7.9	1.8	3.3	0.44	0.79
Men	152	75.0	13.2	7.9	2.0	2.0	0.38	0.78
Women	240	65.4	20.8	7.9	1.7	4.2	0.47	0.79

*Framingham Eye Study [Kahn et al, 1977].
[a]Excludes six with best visual acuity unknown (five age 75 + and one age 65–74, all women, and all examined outside the clinic).
[b]Values assigned as follows: count fingers at 20 ft (6.1 m): 3.22; count fingers at 1 ft (30.5 cm): 6.22; hand motion: 6.40; light perception and projection: 6.55; light perception: 6.68; and no light perception: 7.40.

The Framingham study may provide useful information relative to visual acuity and aging, but the data are not readily converted to a form that can be compared with data from other studies. The best corrected visual acuity for the better eye in percent distribution for three age ranges and sex are shown in Table II. These acuities are slightly better than acuities reported in the other studies (see Fig. 9). The improved vision found in the Framingham study can probably be accounted for by the differences in the sample selection for the various studies.

The U.S. National Health Survey of 1968 (refraction status and motility defects of persons 4–74 years, 1971–1972) and the Duke longitudinal study [Anderson and Palmore, 1974] have not been incorporated into this review because the volume of the data, differences in visual acuity intervals, differences in age intervals, and lack of consistency in data collection make comparison most difficult. These reports should be studied by those interested in change in visual acuity with age.

There are several apparent deficiencies when the subjects of visual acuity and its relation to aging are evaluated. Foremost, there is a need for a standardized visual acuity test and for a standardized measurement procedure. The age span needs to be selected to cover the total population. The discrete age intervals within the population should be manipulable so that the data can be compared with other studies. Care should be taken to randomize the selection of subjects and to insure that a sufficiently large age population is tested. Finally, adequate statistical analysis of visual acuity data is needed. The lack of rigorous research and statistics is probably due to the fact that visual acuity is obtained in discrete steps that do not express equal losses of vision, and description of the results is difficult.

Sloan has published two papers stressing the need for precise measures of visual acuity and for the metric expression of acuity [Sloan, 1978, 1980]. Sloan argues that severe impairments in acuity (20/100 to 20/200) are measured with less precision and reproducibility than are the lower acuities and describes both the equipment and the methodology to overcome these deficiences. Practitioners and vision researchers should become aware of and incorporate standardized charts and procedures into their work.

While contrast sensitivity is not the equivalent of visual acuity, the two methodologies may be related by using the measured letter acuity and comparing it to the extrapolated high-frequency spatial contrast. Several studies have compared contrast sensitivity obtained from the elderly with certain pathological conditions to the contrast sensitivity functions of younger subjects. It may be appropriate to cover this work here.

Hess and Woo [1978] compared contrast sensitivity thresholds and Snellen acuity for 10 subjects who had uniocular senile cortical or nuclear type cataracts. The results showed two different types of abnormalities. The first abnormality was a loss of high spatial frequencies while the second involved a loss of all spatial frequencies. Neither abnormality correlated with the type of cataract. It appears that the loss of high frequencies may be modeled after dioptric defocus but the loss of the low frequency contrast was not correlated with the degree of high frequency loss. Thus, these two spatial frequency losses may result from changes in at least two different processes of vision.

Several factors contribute to the loss of vision for the aging eye. The section on dark adaptation has shown that the changes in light sensitivity related to aging can be attributed principally to miosis and ocular media changes. The section on brightness contrast demonstrates that increases in contrast of the visual media may be used to compensate for losses in vision. In addition, disability glare shows an increase as the intraocular media changes cause greater scattering of light [Wolf, 1960; Fisher and Christie, 1965]. Finally, the level of illuminance required for a particular visual task may partially compensate for the losses in visual performance as the subject ages. We shall attempt to discuss each of these factors briefly in an attempt to arrive at some suggestion to solve the problem.

Ferree et al [1934] determined the visual acuities for subjects aged 25–27 and 42–62 years over an illuminance range from 5.4 to 108 lm/m^2 [Lux]. Their data demonstrate that the older observers required higher illuminances than did the younger observers and that the increase in acuity with increases in illuminance was greater for the old eyes than for the young eyes. Weale [1961b] calculated that the light sensitivity losses from miosis and media changes indicate the need for an increase in illuminance by a factor of 3.0 to compensate for the aging process when the 60-year-old eye was compared with the 20-year-old eye. Blackwell and Blackwell (1971) suggested that an increase in contrast by a factor of 3.03 was required to maintain the visual performance of the 60-year-old eye to that of the 20-year-old eye for 70% of the population.

We have ignored the effects of refractive error on visual acuity. The studies cited above were accomplished using observers with fully corrected visual acuities for all age groups; however, it is well known that as the eye ages, there is a reduction usually in distance vision and a concomitant but larger decrease in visual acuity at near ranges. Ogle [1961a and b] and Cole [1974] have demonstrated that ametropia reduces contrast sensitivity. They have shown that a 1.0-diopter defocus requires a two to three times increase in illuminance to be seen at mesopic levels and 2.0 diopters of defocus requires a five to six times increase in illuminance to be seen.

Weston [1948] measured the visual performance of 12 subjects aged 12 to 48 by establishing the rate of determining the orientation of Landolt rings in a near task using an illuminance range of 5.4 to 5380 lm/ft^2 [Lux]. The visual task was varied in size to establish visual angles of 1.5, 3.0, and 4.5 min of arc, with the contrast held constant. The data showed a decline in visual performance of about 7% annually. The increase in illuminance by a factor of 3 did not fully compensate for the loss in performance for the older observers, but the older observers gave relatively larger increases in visual performance for the same increases in illuminance. Guth [1957] used visibility to determine the illuminance required to maintain equal visibility for observers from 17 to 65 years and found that twice the level of illuminance was needed for the 60- to 65-year age group. Thus, the data indicate that an increase of 2 to 3 is required to maintain vision when the older person is compared with the young person if high contrast targets are used.

These studies demonstrate that there are several parameters that may be considered in maintaining the older person's vision and visual performance. Foremost is the fact that uncorrected refractive errors contribute immeasurably to the loss of contrast sensitivity. Low contrast objects require at least a 2.5 times increase in illuminance to be seen at the same performance level as the younger person. Optical correction of refractive errors provide an immediate method of effectively reducing increased contrasts and illuminance needs. For those who are corrected, light sensitivity losses, brightness contrast changes, and illuminance requirements can be met by increasing the level of illuminance by a factor of 2 to 3 times as a person increases in age from presbyopia to above 60 years.

STEREOPSIS AS A FUNCTION OF AGE

It has been assumed if an individual possesses excellent stereopsis, he must also possess excellent abilities to judge distance although stereopsis is but one of about 20 factors contributing to distance judgments. Unfortunately, all of the papers relating depth perception to age are based on stereoscopic tests even though stereopsis may not be the most important process in depth perception.

Stereoscopic perception requires the existence of different images of the same object on the two retinas, ie, disparate retinal images. The threshold of stereopsis ranges from 1.6 sec to 24 sec and is effective only to a distance of 450 to 650 m. Stereopsis increases by a factor of four as exposure duration increases from 4 msec to 100 msec, and the improvement in stereopsis with increased viewing duration implies that the neural processes involved require a certain duration to operate optimally. In studying the basis for stereopsis, it has been found that stereopsis will occur when stimuli are correlated but out of spatial phase with respect to the reference system.

Tiffin [1942] reported that there was a trend for the loss of stereopsis with an increase in age, but later [1952] suggested that stereoscopic losses were irregular in nature and not great. Piaget and Lamercier [1956] reported that there was an improvement in the ability to judge distance up to 7–8 years followed by a small decline to the age of 12 and a further improvement to adulthood. Wallace [1956] showed that depth perception abilities decreased in older persons. Hoffman et al [1959] compared stereopsis obtained with the Howard-Dohlman apparatus for young subjects (mean age, 32.5 years) with normal 60- to 69-year-

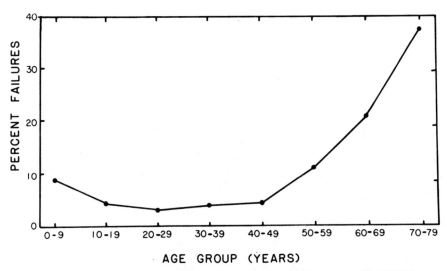

Fig. 10.   Relation between stereopis failure and age using the diastereo test [Jani 1966].

old (64.0-year mean) subjects and concluded that depth perception was significantly reduced at higher ages.

Jani [1966] used the diastereo test [Hofstetter, 1968] to examine the stereopsis of 1,207 observers from 0–9 to 70–79 years of age. Jani considered only subjects with 20/40 visual acuity in the better eye and eliminated all visual anomalies in order to insure that the population was "visually normal." A total of 65 subjects failed the disastereo test. When the data are plotted as age versus percentage of failures, Jani found a slight increase in stereoacuity up to the age of 10, a rather constant stereopsis to the age of 40–49, and a steady decline in stereoacuity at the age levels about 50 years (Fig. 10). Jani attributed the stereoacuity loss to increased blurredness as age increased above 50 years.

Bell et al [1972] used the Verhoeff stereopter to study the relationship between aging and stereopsis in 164 normal subjects from 25 to 75 years of age. Their data indicate that stereopsis remained relatively constant until the age of 40 years, at which point it began to decline and continued to decline steadily to the age of 70 (Fig. 11). They indicate that these stereopsic changes coincide with the age at which losses of accommodation, the increase in sensitivity to glare, and ocular media transmittance changes are evident, but concluded that stereopsis losses were not related to the age of onset of visual field losses, dark adaptation losses, or critical fusion frequency changes. They concluded that the loss of stereopsis was related to changes in the anterior ocular structures that begin at

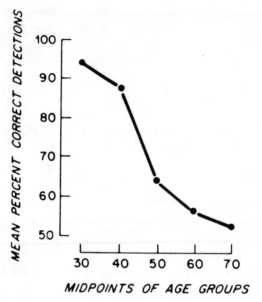

Fig. 11. Mean percentage of correct responses for stereopsis in different age groups using a modified Verhoeff test [after Bell et al, 1972].

a younger age (age 40 to 50 years) rather than the later changes (ages above 60 years), which may result from neural and metabolic alterations.

More recently, Hofstetter and Bertsch [1976] used the diastereo test to examine 242 subjects whose ages ranged from 8 to 46 years. All subjects were screened to eliminate pathology and to insure that they possessed a monocular and binocular visual acuity of 20/20 or better. The mean stereopsis value was 5.6 sec of arc with an error of $+3$ to -2.1 seconds of arc. The results showed no trend with age and no differences between the sexes, and it was concluded that stereopsis did not change with age.

The limited age range of the Hofstetter and Bertsch study does not allow definitive decisions relating age and stereopsis although the study did demonstrate that the results depend on the criteria used to select subjects. The Hofstetter and Bertsch data also show that normal adults up to the age of 46 are capable of normal stereopsic responses. These results are not surprising since 47 years is the lower age level at which anterior ocular changes might be serious. The total number of subjects in the age 50–80 groups for all studies are insufficient for conclusions to be made relating age and stereopsis. We suspect that if one were to test stereopsis on a randomly selected population without using pretest selection criteria, stereopsis would be found to decline with age beginning at about 50 years. However, if the proper pretest selection process were used, normal stereopsis could be found in the extremely aged groups. It must be emphasized that the previous statements are speculation based on the knowledge of the tremendous variability of individuals at all age levels. Well-designed research studies are needed to settle those questions and, indeed, to determine if stereopsis and age are related.

THE DIFFERENTIAL OR BRIGHTNESS CONTRAST THRESHOLD RELATED TO AGE

The ability of the eye to detect differences in the brightness of an object and its background has been called the differential or brightness contrast threshold. The test object may be brighter than the background (positive contrast) or dimmer than the background (negative contrast). The ability of the eye to detect these differences may be determined by measuring the difference between the background luminance and the target luminance that can just be distinguished by the eye. This measure is expressed as a fraction of the background and the stimulus differences:

$$C = B_S - B_B/B_S + B_B$$

where B is the contrast threshold, B_S is the luminance of the stimulus, and B_B is the luminance of the background. Contrast sensitivity is the reciprocal of the differential or contrast threshold value.

The contrast threshold value varies with stimulus size, shape of the stimulus, region of the retina, area, hue, and exposure duration. If all other stimulus factors are held constant, the brightness contrast threshold varies as the luminance of the background is changed from dark to extreme light (Fig. 12). Very few data relating brightness contrast sensitivity to age can be found in the literature; hence, the following discussion will be brief.

Bouma [1936] studied the differential sensitivity for subjects from age 20 to age 45 with a constant background luminance and both with and without a glare source. His data are illustrated in Figure 13a and b and are compared with the data of Cane and Gregory [1957]. Without the glare source, the retinal sensitivity was found to increase to a maximum at about the age of 30 and then decrease steadily to age 45. With the glare source, the retinal sensitivity shows a maximum at age 20 which steadily declines to age 45. Weale [1961] explains these differences as the result of scatter of the glare source by the optical media of the eye.

Wolf [1960] measured the differential thresholds for 20-year-old and 70-year-old subjects. Figure 14 presents Wolf's data as modified by Weale [1961] to illustrate the increase in differential threshold with an increase in background

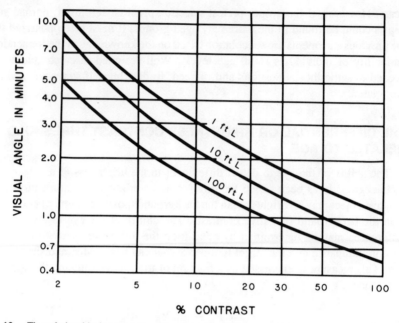

Fig. 12. The relationship between the size of the target, contrast of the target, and background luminance. Visual acuity improves as both the contrast and the background luminance increase; therefore, there should be an ideal contrast at a given luminance for maximum acuity that changes with age.

luminance and the differences between the two age groups. Consistent with previous studies, Wolf's data shows that more luminance is needed by the 70-year-old person at all background levels than for the 20-year-old. Weale showed that the greater difference at younger ages is an artifact of senile miosis and diminishes when corrected for miosis (see Figs. 4 and 6).

Blackwell and Blackwell [1971] have related the contrast functions of Blackwell and Taylor [1970] obtained by the forced-choice method from 35 subjects in the 20- to 30-year age group to the brightness contrast data obtained from 68 subjects in the 40- to 70-year age range obtained by the method of adjustment. In spite of the differences between the research methodologies, the data can be related by contrast multiplicative factors for the data up to the age 60–70 group. Figures 15 and 16 give the contrast multiplier data of Blackwell and Blackwell for 156 persons from age 25 to age 65. The contrast multiplier provides the amount that the contrast must be increased for the object to be just seen. The data show several factors that relate contrast and age:

1. Observer variability increases as age increases.

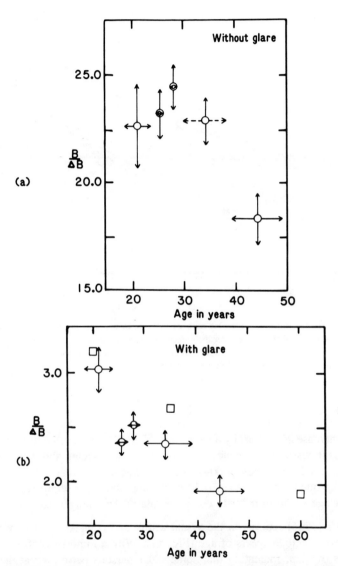

Fig. 13. The differential sensitivity for observers from age 20 to age 45 for a constant background luminance and both without (a) and with (b) a glare source. For comparison, the data of Cane and Gregory [1957] are shown as the open squares in the bottom graph. The data show that contrast sensitivity undergoes a steady decline as a person ages and especially when a glare source is introduced into the field of vision [after Bouma, 1936].

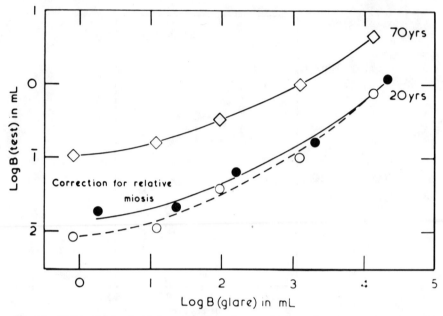

Fig. 14. Differential thresholds increase with an increase in age and an increase in background luminance. The data indicate that greater differences are seen at the lower background luminances but Weale's calculation, shown as the filled circles, demonstrates that it was an artifact of senile miosis rather than a true experimental finding [after Wolf, 1960].

2. An increase in contrast by a factor of 1.17 to 2.51 is required to compensate for the loss in visual performance or to maintain equal seeing ability as a person increases from 20–30 years to 60–70 years of age.

3. Background luminances of 0.34 cd/m² and above are required for the 60- to 70-year age group in order to compare data to the younger age levels.

Richards [1966] reports on the visual acuity and contrast sensitivity of 141 subjects from 16 to 90 years of age (Fig. 17). With a luminance of 3.4 cd/m², the curves overlap, indicating that some older persons performed at the same level as the younger persons but all young persons performed as well as or better than the older persons at all levels of background luminance. As the luminance level is reduced to 0.34 cd/m² and 0.034 cd/m², the performance of younger subjects greatly exceeded that of the older age subjects. As the contrast of the test letters decreased below 30% to 40%, vision decreased rapidly and the 60-year-old subjects required a 25% increase in contrast to see the same target as the 20-year-old subject.

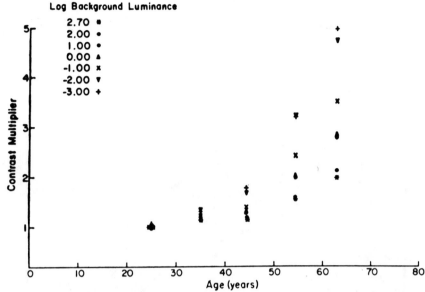

Fig. 15. Contrast threshold functions for 156 normal observers aged 25 to 65 years. The contrast multiplier indicates the amount that contrast must be increased for the target to be just seen. Beginning at age 40, there is a large increase in data variability as age increases [after Blackwell and Blackwell, 1971].

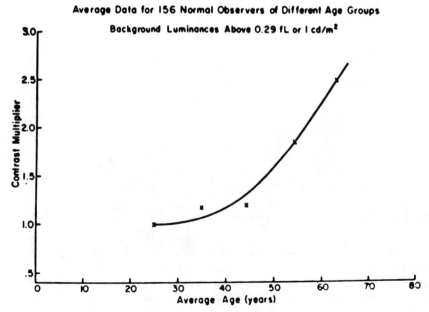

Fig. 16. The average contrast multiplier needed for normal observers of different age groups when the background luminance was above 0.29 ft.L. or 1.0cd/m² [after Blackwell and Blackwell, 1971].

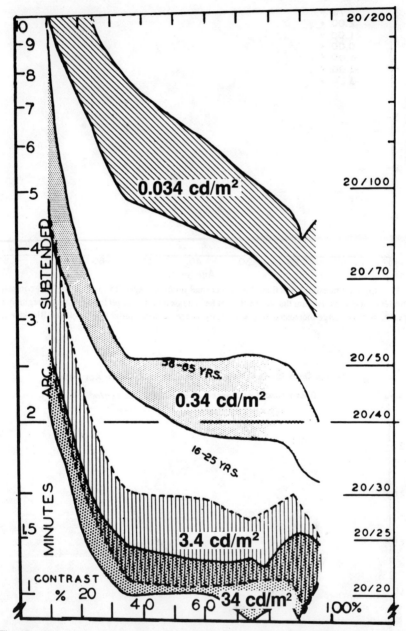

Fig. 17. The visual acuity and contrast sensitivity of 141 subjects from 16 to 90 years of age. At the higher background luminanes, the data for the different ages overlaps but the younger subjects performed better at all levels of background luminance than the older subjects.

The brightness contrast studies clearly demonstrate that not enough older subjects were included to allow a definitive statement relating the changes with age and contrast sensitivity.

REFERENCES

Anderson B, Palmore E (1974) Longitudinal evaluation of ocular function. In Palmore E (Ed) "Normal Aging." Durham, North Carolina: Duke University Press.

Bell B, Wolf E, Bernholtz CD (1972) Depth perception as a function of age. Aging Hum Dev 3:77–81.

Birren JE, Bick MW, Fox C (1948) Age changes in the light threshold of the dark adapted eye. J Gerontol 3:267–271.

Birren JE, Bick MW, Yiengst M (1950a) The relation of structural changes of the eye and vitamin A to elevation of the light threshold in later life. J Exp Psych 40:260–266.

Birren JE, Shock NW (1950b) Age changes in rate and level of visual dark adaptation J Appl Physiol 2:407–411.

Birren JE, Casperson RC, Botwinick J (1950b) Age changes in pupil size. J Gerontol 5:267–271.

Blackwell HR, Taylor JH (1970) A consolidated set of foveal contrast thresholds for normal human binocular vision, Ohio State University and University of California, San Diego Report.

Blackwell OM, Blackwell HR (1971) Visual performance data for 156 normal observers of various ages. J Illum Eng Soc 1:3–13.

Bouma PJ (1936) The problem of glare in highway lighting. Phillips Tech Rev 1:225–229.

Burg A (1966) Visual acuity as measured by dynamic and static tests. J Appl Psych 50:460–466.

Cane V, Gregory RL (1957) Noise and the visual threshold. Nature 180:1403–1405.

Carlson VR, Tassone EP (1963) Size-constance and visual acuity. Percept Motor Skills 16:223–228.

Chapanis, A (1950) Relationships between age, visual acuity and color vision. Human Biol 22:1–33.

Cole, BL (1974) Prescribing light for the aging patient. Aust J Optom 57:207–214.

Collins SD, Britten RH (1924) Variation in eyesight at different ages as determined by the Snellen test. Public Health Reports 39:3189–3195.

Corso JF (1971) Sensory processes and age effects in normal adults. J Gerontol 26:90–105.

Dieterle P, Gordon E (1956) Standard curve and physiological limits of dark adaptations by means of the Goldman-Weekers adaptometer. Br J Ophthalmol 40:652–655.

Domey RG (1964) Statistical properties of foveal CFF as function of age, light/dark ratio, and surroundings. J Opt Soc Am 54:394–398.

Domey RG McFarland RA (1961) Dark adaptation as a function of age: Individual prediction. Am J Ophthalmol 51:1262–1268.

Domey RG, McFarland RA, Chadwick E (1960b) Threshold and rate of dark adaptation as functions of age and time. Human Factors 2:109–119.

Donders FC (1864) On the anomalies of accommodation and refraction of the eye. With a preliminary essay on physiological optics. New Sydenham Society, London, pp 188–204.

Duke-Elder Sir W (1939) Textbook of Ophthalmology Vol 1. St. Louis pp 995.

Fankhauser F, Schmidt T (1957) Die Untersuchung der Funktionen des dunkeladaptierten Auges mit dem Adoptometer Goldman-Weekers. Ophthalmologica 133:264–272.

Farrimond T (1967) Visual and auditory performance variations with age: Some implications. Austral J Psych 19:193–201.

Feree CE, Rand G, Lewis EF (1934) The effect of increase of intensity of light on the visual acuity of presbyopic and non-presbyopic eyes. Trans Ill Eng Soc 29:296–313.

Fisher AJ, Christie AW (1965) A note on disability glare. Vis Res 5:565–571.

Geldard FA, Crockett WB (1930) The binocular acuity relation as a function of age. J Genetic Psych 37:139–145.

Gibson JJ (1950) "The perception of the Visual World." Boston: Houghton Miffin.

Gregory RL, Cane V (1955) A statistical information theory of visual thresholds. Nature 176:1272.

Gunkel RD, Gouras P (1963) Changes in scotopic visibility thresholds with age. Arch Ophthalmol 69:4–9.

Guth SK (1957) Effects of age on visibility. Amer J Optom Arch Amer Acad Optom 47:463–477.

Hecht S, Mandelbaum J (1939) The relation between vitamin A and dark adaptation. JAMA 112:1910–1916.

Hess R, Woo G (1978) Vision through cataracts. Invest Ophthal Vis Sci 17:428–435.

Hoffman Carl S, Cooper Price A, Garrett ES, Rothstein W (1959) Effect of age and brain damage on depth perception. Percep Motor Skills 9:283–286.

Hofstetter HW, Bertsch JD (1976) Does stereopsis change with age? Am J Optom and Physiol Optics 53:644–667.

Hofstetter HW (1967) Absolute threshold measurements with the diastero test. Dublin International Optical Congress Transactions, 1965, Dublin, Dakota, Ltd, pp 5–10. Reprinted (1968) in Arch Sociodad Am Oftalmol Optom 6:327–342.

Jani SN (1966) The age factor in stereopsis screening. Amer J Optom Arch Amer Acad Optom 43:653–657.

Kahn HA et al (1977) The Framingham Eye Study, 1. Outline and major prevalence findings. AJ Epidem 106:17–41.

Kornzweig AL (1954) Physiological effects of age on the visual process. Sight Saving Review 24:138.

Kornzweig AL, Feldstein M, Schneider J (1957) The eye in old age: IV. Ocular survey of over one thousand aged persons with special reference to normal and disturbed visual functions. AJ Ophthal 44:29–37.

LeGrand, Y (1957) "Light, Colour and Vision." London: Chapman and Hall. pp 233–235.

Levis EM Jr (1972) Interaction of age and alcohol on dark adaptation time. (Report No. ICRL-CR-709). Department of Health, Education and Welfare, Injury Control Research Laboratory.

Luria SM (1960) Absolute visual threshold and age. J Opt Soc Am 50:86–67.

McFarland RA, Domey RC, Warren AB, Ward DC (1960) Dark adaptation as a function of age. I. A statistical analysis. J Gerontol 15:149–154.

McFarland RA, Domey RG (1958) Experimental studies of night vision as a function of age and changes in illumination. Highway Research Board Bulletin 191:17–32.

McFarland RA, Warren AB, Karis C (1958) Alternations in critical flicker frequency as a function of age and light: Dark ratio. J Exp Psych 56:529–538.

McFarland RA, Fisher MB (1955) Alternations in dark adaptation as a function of age. J Gerontol 10:424–428.

Milne JS, Williamson J (1972) Visual acuity in older people. Gerontol Clin 4:249–256.

Ogle KN (1961a) Foveal contrast thresholds with blurring of the retinal image and increasing size of test stimulus. J Opt Soc AM 51:862–869.

Ogle, KN (1961b) Peripheral contrast thresholds and blurring of the retinal image for a point light source. J Opt Soc Am 51:1265–1268.

Peckham, RH, Hart WM (1959) Retinal sensitivity and night visibility. Highway Research Board Bulletin No. 226:1–6.

Piaget J, Lamercier M (1956) Recherches sur le development des perceptions, XXIX, Grandeurs projectives et grandeurs reeies avec etalon eloinge. Arch. Psychol 35:256–280.

Richards OW (1966) Vision at levels of night road illumination: XII. Changes of acuity and contrast sensitivity with age. A J Optom Arch A Acad Optom 43:313–319.

Richards OW (1972) Some seeing problems: Spectacles, color driving and decline from age and poor lighting. A J Optom Arch A Acad Optom 49:539–546.

Roberts J (1978) Refraction status and motility defects of persons 4–74 years, 1971–1972, Vital and Health Statistics, Series 11, Data from the National Health Survey No. 206.

Robertson GW, Yudkin J (1944) Effect of age upon dark adaptation. J Physiol 103:1–8.

Said FS, Weale RA (1959) The variation with age of the spectral transmissivity of the living human crystalline lens. Gerontologia 3:213–231.

Sloan LL (1980) Needs for precise measures of acuity. Arch Ophthal 98:286–290.

Sloan LL (1978) Considerations related to "going metric." Arch Ophthal 96:1567.

Steven DM (1946) Relation between dark adaptation and age. Nature 157:376–377.

Tiffin Joseph (1942) "Industrial Psychology," 1st ed. New York: Prentice-Hall, pp 134–135.

Tiffin Joseph (1952) "Industrial Psychology," 3rd ed. New York: Prentice-Hall, pp 231–232.

Vital and Health Statistics, Data from the National Health Survey, Monocular-Binocular Visual Acuity of Adults, United States 1960–1962, National Center for Health Statistics Series 11, No. 30, PHS Publication No. 1000, Series, 11, Nov. 30, 1968.

Wallace JG (1956) Some studies of perception in relation to age. Brit J Psychol 67:283–297.

Weale RA (1961a) Notes on the photometric significance of the human crystalline. Vis Res 1/2:183–191.

Weale RA (1961b) Retinal illumination and age. Trans Illum Eng Soc 26:95–100.

Weale RA (1962) Presbyopia Br J Ophthalmol 46:660–668.

Weale RA (1963) "The aging eye." London: Lewis.

Weale RA (1965) On the eye. In Welford AT, Birren JE (Eds) "Behavior, Aging, and the Nervous System." Springfield, Ill: Charles C Thomas, 307–325.

Weale RA (1971) "The aging eye." The Scientific Basis of Medicine Annual Reviews. British Postgraduate Medical Federation. Atlantic Highlands: Athlone Press, London 244–260.

Weale RA (1975) Senile changes in visual acuity. Trans Ophthal Soc UK 95:36–38.

Weale RA (1973) The effect of the aging lens on vision. CIBA Found Symp 19:5–24.

Weale RA (1978) The eye and aging. In Hockivin O (Ed) "Interdisciplinary Topics in Gerontology," Vol 13. Gerontological Aspects of Eye Research." Basel: Karger, 1–13.

Weymouth FW (1960) Effects of age on visual acuity. In Hirsch MJ, Wick RE (Eds) "Vision of the Aging Patient." Philadelphia: Chilton Book Co, pp 37–60.

Wolf E (1960) Glare and age. Arch Ophthal 64:502–514.

Aging and Human Visual Function, pages 161–171

Senile Ocular Changes, Cell Death, and Vision

R. A. Weale

INTRODUCTION

The rate at which theories of aging are being put forward at present is almost as great as the rate of human aging itself. Not surprisingly, the emphasis is on cell rather than on system, even though not even the cell qua senescent entity is too ready to be analyzed.

A consideration of the senescence of vision may therefore seem not only premature but indeed the height of folly. Not only does vision involve a variety of cellular assemblies in some of the components of the visual pathway, but, and this is one of the nubs of the problem, it depends on the interdigitation of a variety of systems that demonstrably age at different rates.

Two simple examples will suffice to illustrate this point. The pupil of the dark-adapted eye reaches its maximum diameter in our early teens and progressively diminishes thereafter, thereby reducing the amount of light it transmits to the retina. By contrast, the crystalline lens, which also acts like a filter, begins to reduce its transmissivity only during the fourth or fifth decade.

In spite of these discouraging auguries, the study of senescent vision deserves unremitting support. The reason is that it is by the analysis of function that the significance of senescent systems components may come to be assessed. Are preretinal factors the only ones to matter? Does the type of cell deatb reported for the cerebellum and the cortex extend throughout the whole of the CNS and therefore to the retina? Is the regular geometric organization of the rods and cones a device that decelerates aging effects or is it irrelevant to them? Are they masked or accentuated by phototoxic phenomena?

As life expectancy approaches what appears to be its theoretical limit, the answer to these questions will involve vast economic considerations. Yet most eye experts are content to concern themselves mainly with presbyopia.

Presbyopia is of course not the only visual disability to accompany increased age. A number of authors have shown, for example, that after the age of 40, visual acuity drops slowly but systematically [cf Weale, 1975]; visual thresholds appear to rise from an early age, if not from birth [Gunkel and Gouras, 1963; Birren et al, 1948; Robertson and Yudkin, 1944; Steven, 1946]. Carter and Pitts describe in this volume changes in accommodation, acuity, field of vision, and color vision.

Until relatively recently, it was assumed that these decrements are due just to neural loss or to vegetative or vascular deficits, leading perhaps to oxygen deficiency, and hence to malfunction and ultimate failure. With one or two exceptions, no attempt has been made to support these interesting hypotheses quantitatively, and this paper is intended as a very tentative step to remedy this state of affairs.

THRESHOLDS

When a threshold is expressed in terms of the stimulus energy impinging on, and thus measured outside, the eye, losses occurring before it reaches the retina have to be compensated. The two principal relevant factors to vary with age are senile miosis and lenticular yellowing [cf Weale, 1963]. As some of the above authors have shown, these corrections significantly affect the measured decrements: in other words, at the retinal and more central levels, the system deteriorates more slowly than uncorrected sensory measurements can lead one to believe.

The exhaustive work on dark adaptation by McFarland et al [1960] is one of the most instructive studies in this context. Using Hecht's original apparatus with a violet test field, they determined visual thresholds during 40 min of dark adaptation following a 3-min exposure to a white stimulus of 1600 mL. As Wright [1946] has shown, the whiteness so-called of the stimulus also varies with age. The study by McFarland et al covered an age spectrum of 16 to 89 years. The averaged experimental curves for each decade rose systematically on the log energy threshold scale, and the authors concluded that this manifested a progressively accentuated oxygen shortage. The reason is that, when dark adaptation is measured, for example in a decompression chamber, a rise in threshold is also observed in hypobaric conditions.

These data are not subject to a correction for senile miosis as Hecht's apparatus contained an artificial pupil. However, a crystalline lens correction is indispensable in view of the short wavelength of the test radiation and the strong light absorption of the lens in this spectral range. Figure 1 gives an indication of the senile variation of lenticular absorbance at 460nm [Weale, 1981]. While very gradual during the first four decades, its rise accelerates smartly thereafter, owing to a variety of causes. It follows that at about 430nm, the approximate wavelength of Hecht's test stimulus, the rise in retinal threshold is increased by almost one logarithmic unit across the experimental age range. Its effect is shown in Figure

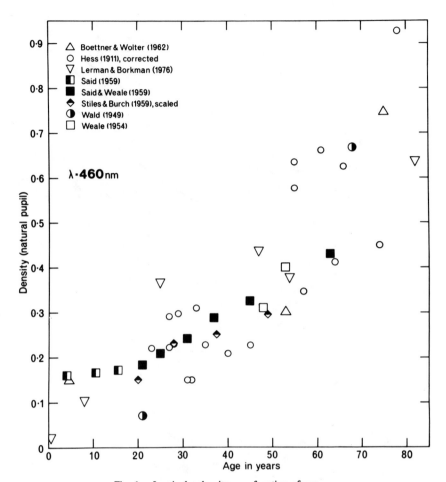

Fig. 1. Lenticular density as a function of age.

2. This gives the threshold plotted against age, with the time of dark-adaptation as a parameter (a), and the same values corrected for lenticular absorbance (b): details of the transformation have been given earlier [Weale, 1978].

The slopes of the curves in (b) are evidently much smaller than those in (a), and those corresponding to the early (cone-mechanism) section are approximately half in magnitude of those for the later (rod mechanism) section. Attention has already been drawn to the peculiar drop in threshold as revealed by the higher age groups during the early part of dark-adaptation, and the implications which lens fluorescence may have for this have been considered [Weale, 1981].

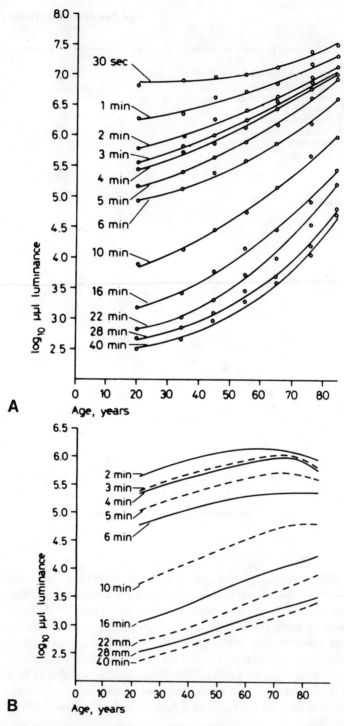

Fig. 2. (A) Threshold luminance as a function of age (McFarland et al, 1960). (B) The functions from A corrected for lenticular absorbance [Weale, 1978].

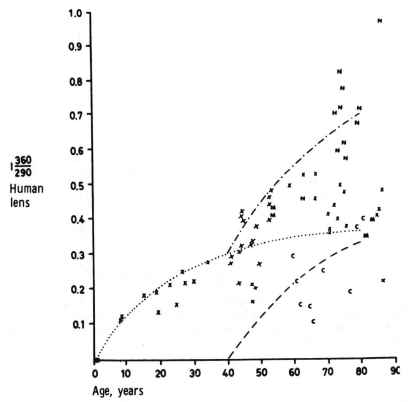

Fig. 3. Lenticular fluorescence. I (360/290-5) ratios represent the intensity of fluorescence at 440 nm (ie, an excitation at 360 nm) divided by the fluorescence of tryptophan at 332 nm (corresponding to an excitation at 290-5 nm). X represents normal aging human lenses; N, brown nuclear cataracts; C, cortical cataracts; and M, mixtures. The dotted curve is an exponential with a time constant of 60 years, the dashed curve is one with a time constant of 83 years, and the dash-dot is the sum of the two [Lerman and Borkman, 1976; Weale, 1982].

Lerman and Borkman (1976) have provided evidence for the senile variation of the fluorescence of the human crystalline lens, and shown that one of the two fluorogens so far detected begins accumulating from early life while the other starts its manifestation during the fifth decade (Fig. 3). The emission of fluorescent radiation is presumably detected by the cones and results from the inevitably high stimulus levels used by McFarland et al. If one assumes that the apparent decrease in threshold (Fig. 2b) is due to fluorescent light contributing to the stimulation of the retina, an estimate of its age of onset can be made as follows. In the absence of fluorescence—this can be tested in aphakic eyes—the rise in threshold would probably progress as shown in Fig. 4A. Let I(T) be the

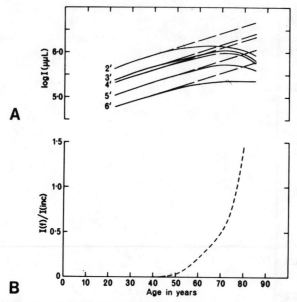

Fig. 4. (A) The top part of Fig. 3B extrapolated rectilinearly suggests that the apparent reduction in threshold may be due to the type of fluorescence shown by the dot-dash curve in Fig. 4. (B) The difference between the continuous and dashed functions in Fig. 4B plotted as a function of age is in qualitative agreement with Fig. 3.

true threshold, I(F) the intensity of fluorescence striking the retina in the test area, and I(M) the measured threshold, ie, the light directed onto the retina. Then

$$I(F)/I(M) = I(T)/I(M) - 1$$

which is plotted in Fig. 4B, and seen to rise above zero at much the same age that the later fluorogen starts accumulating (see Fig. 3). This coincidence may be accidental. It is nevertheless remarkable that the effects of fluorescence on measurements of retinal function have been ignored in spite of this phenomenon having been known to ophthalmology for some 70 years or more. The short wavelength end of the spectrum has always caused problems [Mollon and Polden, 1977], and it will be interesting to discover whether some of them at least may not be relatively easy to account for by a consideration of fluorescence levels and action spectra, even when the observers under test are less than 40 years of age.

VISUAL RESOLVING POWER

This faculty decreases with age, no matter whether measured with conventional test types [cf Weale, 1975; Pitts, this volume) or with contrast thresholds [Arundale, 1978; Skalka, 1980]. Insofar as contrast thresholds are diffraction limited [Campbell and Green, 1965], senile miosis would be expected to lead to a curtailment of the cut-off frequency as the effective pupil diameter drops below 3 mm.

However, the senile drop in visual acuity is hard to account for just in terms of optics [Weale, 1975]. Although lenticular irregularities are also often mentioned in this context, not only the analysis of Zuckerman et al [1973] but also clinical experience lead to the view that these irregularities have to be very severe to interfere seriously with image formation. Accordingly, the suggestion was made [Weale, 1975, 1978] that cell death may play a decisive role if no repair process occurs [Reading, personal communication]. If just under 0.3% of nerve cells atrophy per annum so that some 2.5% are lost per decade [Hall et al, 1975] randomly throughout the visual system, and the latter contains n independent stages between the site of light absorption and the locus of visual decision making, then it can be shown that visual acuity (VA) in decade A after the age of 40 is given by

$$\log_e VA(A) = \log_e VA(40) - 0.4343 \, pnA$$

Since p has been fixed at 0.025 per decade, an estimate is obtained for n. The experimental data (Fig. 5) are contained within a small bracket of n (4–7). It is, of course, possible to postulate variants of this concept. Note that the implicit hierarchy relates specifically to central vision with the classical assumption of a one-to-one relation between peripheral and central neurons, and the consequent indifference as to the stage where a knock-out lesion occurs [Weale, 1975].

FURTHER IMPLICATIONS OF CELL LOSS

The senile rise in threshold can, of course, be caused by a number of circumstances, eg, the available pigment density may gradually diminish owing to a misprogrammed reduction in concentration and/or a change in pathlength. Metabolic changes in the pigment epithelium may intervene. Changes may occur owing to cell loss, as mentioned above, and neurotransmission and/or synaptic organization may alter (Ordy et al, this volume). Subtle modifications may take place at a central (decision-making) level.

More especially, it is undecided to what extent an abnormal or moribund cell is actually defunct rather than simply needing enhanced stimulation to respond. There is no interpretational problem of similar weight when cells are lost, al-

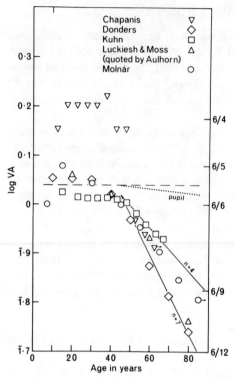

Fig. 5. The logarithms of visual acuity as a function of age. n is defined as the number of independent stages between the locus of light absorption and the decision-making center. The reduction in VA on optical grounds is indicated by the dotted line [Weale, 1978].

though substitution processes may slow down the rate of decline. But photoreceptors showing disrupted laminae may still absorb light, and, particularly if the disruption is distal, be capable of initiating a visual response. If so, head counts on the basis of damage are unlikely to prove instructive.

The analyses in the preceding sections can nevertheless be taken further. We ask ourselves what is the change in retinal threshold per decade, when corrections for physical changes have been made. This is shown in Table I, separately for rod and nonfoveal cone mechanisms. The rates for cone mechanisms are clearly only about one-third to one-half those for rod mechanisms. Because there is no a priori reason for central neurons subserving photopic and scotopic vision respectively to age at different rates, let us examine a simpler hypothesis, namely that the two photoreceptor types may age at different rates (Fig. 6).

The above observations may be placed in the following framework. Cones are more resistant to fixatives than are rods [Weale, 1971] but less resistant than

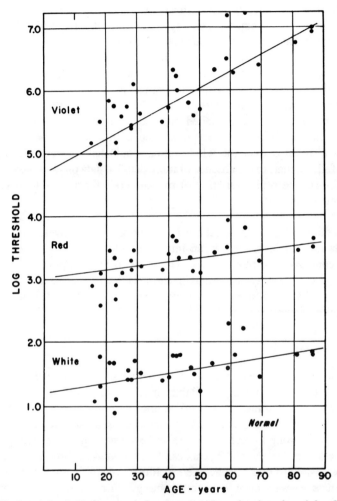

Fig. 6. Nonfoveal thresholds for normal observers plotted as a function of age [after Gunkel and Gouras, 1963].

TABLE I. Rates of Threshold Rise per Decade

Mechanism	log I	Reference
Cone	0.05	Gunkel and Gouras, 1963
	0.08	McFarland et al, 1960
Rod	0.15	Gunkel and Gouras, 1963
	0.16	McFarland et al, 1960

rods to heat. This suggests a difference in membrane permeability. Second, cones appear to survive better in some type of retinopathy [cf Bird, 1975]. There are indications that older normal cones have a better morphological appearance in the fovea than in the periphery [Marshall, personal communication].

No one appears to have published a systematic study of the senile variation of foveal thresholds, the data in Table I referring to nonfoveal ones. It is also to be noted that there is an inverse relation between threshold and the number of receptors stimulated. In a limited area, the loss of a ganglion cell may be equivalent to one of 50–100 receptors. The corresponding loss of receptors randomly distributed over the whole retina would have a very much smaller effect. It follows that, in the absence of more detailed data on possible phototoxic effects in man, the senile variation of rod and cone function will have to wait for its accurate interpretation.

It is, however, noteworthy that the stamina of normal foveal visual acuity (see preceding section) and the relatively rapid rise of long wavelength nonfoveal thresholds (see Table I) provide an interesting gloss on the idea that the two types of cone age at different rates. This adds to the complications of distinguishing between senility and cumulative effects due to phototoxicity, and raises the question of whether foveal cones may not perhaps be afforded some protection by the yellow macular pigment.

CONCLUSION

It is rather curious that no data on the senile variation of the foveal visual threshold appear to be readily available. It is idle to speculate whether such a change, if any, would have a spectral component other than that discernible in peripheral (rod) data. But it is clearly of interest to establish whether the tentative hypothesis purporting to account for the senile variation of visual acuity in terms of cell death after the age of 40 years can be supported by threshold data. These problems are not just of academic interest. If there is any significant phototoxicity in man, these answers have to be forthcoming, otherwise photic environmental control measures would be hard to justify.

REFERENCES

Arundale K (1978) An investigation into the variation of human contrast sensitivity with age and ocular pathology. Br J Ophthalmol 62:213–215.

Bird AC (1975) X-linked retinitis pigmentosa. Br J Ophthalmol 59:177–199.

Birren JE, Bick MW, Fox C (1948) Age changes in the light threshold of the dark-adapted eye. J Gerontol 3:267–271.

Campbell, FW, Green DG (1965) Optical and retinal factors affecting visual resolution. J Physiol 181:576–593.

Gunkel RD, Gouras P (1963) Changes in the scotopic visibility threshold with age. Arch Ophthalmol 69:4–9.

Hall TC, Miller AKH, Corsellis JAN (1975) Variations in the human Purkinje cell population according to age and sex. Neuropath Appl Neurobiol 1:267–292.

Lerman S, Borkman R (1976) Spectroscopic evaluation and classification of the normal, aging, and cataractous lens. Ophthal Res 8:335–353.

McFarland RA, Domey RG, Warren AB, Ward DC (1960) Dark-adaptation as a function of age: I. A statistical analysis. J Gerontol 15:149–154.

Mollon JD, Polden PG (1977) An anomaly in the response of the eye to light of short wavelengths. Trans Roy Soc London Biol 278:207–240.

Robertson GW, Yudkin J (1944) Effect of age upon dark adaptation. J Physiol 103:1–8.

Skalka HW (1980) Effect of age on Arden grading acuity. Br J Ophthalmol 64:21–23.

Steven DM (1946) Relation between dark-adaptation and age. Nature 157:376–377.

Weale RA (1963) "The Aging Eye." London: Lewis.

Weale RA (1971) On the birefringence of rods and cones. Pflügers Arch gesammt Physiol 329:244–257.

Weale RA (1975) Senile changes in visual acuity. Trans Ophthalmol Soc UK 95:36–38.

Weale RA (1978) The eye and aging. Interdisc Topics Gerontol 13:1–13.

Weale RA (1981) Physical changes due to age and cataract. In Duncan G (Ed) "Mechanisms of Cataract Formation in the Human Lens." New York: Academic Press.

Wright WD (1946) "Researches in Normal and Defective Colour Vision." London: Henry Kimpton.

Zuckerman JL, Miles D, Dyes W, Kepper M (1973) Degradation of vision through a simulated cataract. Invest Ophthal 12:213–224.

Aging and Human Visual Function, pages 173-180

The Impoverishment of Ocular Motility in the Elderly

R. John Leigh

INTRODUCTION

In order to maintain a panoramic survey of the environment, it behooves many organisms, the human species included, to look around. This we can apparently do quite adequately with head movements, so why do the eyes need to move at all? Study of the comparative anatomy and physiology of ocular motility led G.L. Walls [1942] to postulate that early in evolution the eyes, although mobile, could not be independently aimed at objects. This is the case, for example, in many fish and in the rabbit. However, for any species to maintain clear vision requires that the eyes be held steady, despite pertubation of the head due to bodily movement or transmitted pulsation from the heart. This ocular gyroscopic function is carried out by the vestibulo-ocular reflex [Wilson and Melvill Jones, 1979]. If this reflex is not working adequately, images of the seen world are not held steady on the retina and visual acuity falls. This function may therefore become critical in old age when changes in the eye or visual pathways threaten vision. The reflex depends upon the labyrinth of the inner ear, which contains sensitive acceleration detectors transducing every transient head movement so that the brain can reflexively enact prompt compensatory eye movements. Visual systems are, by comparison, much slower in operation and could not enable the rapid correction called for by most natural head movements. This is because of the relatively slow processing of neural signals within the retina. Vision may be used, however, to stabilize the eyes during sustained rotation of the body, the so-called optokinetic responses [Ter Braak, 1936; Robinson, 1977]. With the evolution of the fovea and the frontal position of the eyes has come the need to voluntarily redirect our best vision toward objects situated to one side or another. Dodge [1903] was among the first to point out that our voluntary eye movements are of several types. To visually refixate targets located in the periphery of vision, we make rapid eye movements or saccades. To continuously follow moving objects, we make smooth pursuit movements. Vergence eye movements enable binocular vision of close objects.

Such a teleological approach to eye movements offers certain advantages in interpreting any deficits of ocular motility such as those encountered in the elderly. It enables a realization of what functional disability will be imposed and, because we now have some knowledge of the neuroanatomy and neurophysiology underlying each type of eye movement, it is possible to direct our research efforts at the most pertinent areas of brain function.

Studies of ocular motility to determine the nature of the changes that accompany advancing age are few, save for those circumstances where specific disease process has produced clear disruption of the way that the brain controls the eyes' movements. Thus the effects of stroke and certain degenerative conditions such as Parkinson's disease—and these effects are common in the elderly—have been studied in some detail. However, it is those changes in ocular motility that seem to be consequent simply upon the aging process itself that will be principally discussed here.

My comments are based on the cited studies of others and my own observation of the residents of a local nursing home and the inpatients seen consecutively on the neurological consultation service of our hospital. These personal observations comprise 50 patients, all of whom were over 60 years of age (mean age, 74 years).

THE REFLEX CONTROL OF EYE MOVEMENTS

Several studies of vestibular function in elderly populations have been reported [see Van der Laan and Oosterveld, 1974; and Bruner and Norris, 1971, for reviews]. Most investigators have preferred to use caloric tests to assess vestibular function. Although these tests are indeed very valuable in identifying disease located within the vestibular end organ, they are less valuable in answering the question "Is the vestibulo-ocular reflex still adequate to maintain clear vision during natural head movements?" A better way to answer this question is to measure the gain of the vestibulo-ocular reflex (that is the ratio of eye movements to head movements) during head rotation. This, of course, should be −1 (conventionally expressed as 1), if our eyes are to be held steady in space. This test can be done in the laboratory but also can be performed at the bedside by a simple but sensitive ophthalmoscopic method [Zee, 1978]. The optic nerve is observed with the ophthalmoscope while the subject rotates the head from side to side at a frequency of 2 cycles per second or greater. If the vestibulo-ocular reflex gain is 1, the optic disc does not seem to move, for eye movements and head movements are perfectly matched. Using this technique, I found that almost all elderly subjects studied had normal vestibulo-ocular responses. Clinicians are well aware that vertigo, the symptom of vestibular disturbance, is common in the elderly but this is usually due to specific pathologies: vascular disease or degenerative conditions of the vestibular labyrinth. Indeed, if the gain of the vestibulo-ocular reflex were commonly less than 1, as some studies have suggested, then the result would be oscillopsia and this is not a complaint of the healthy elderly person. How is the integrity of the vestibulo-ocular reflex preserved so well through life? The answer probably lies in the ability of the brain to shore up any vestibular imbalance due to disease. The neural plasticity of the vestibulo-ocular reflex has been the subject of great interest to neurophysiologists in recent years. Gonshor and Melvill Jones [1976] have shown that subjects who chronically wear as spectacles reversing prisms that invert their visual world show an eventual reversal of the gain of the vestibulo-ocular reflex so that the eye movements are once again compensatory. Robinson [1976] has studied this phenomenon in cats and presented evidence to suggest that the cerebellum or its inputs are necessary for these modulations in the gain of the vestibulo-ocular reflex.

Optokinetic and optic stabilization reflexes have yet to be systematically studied in aging populations. Proper study of these responses requires laboratory evaluation.

THE VOLUNTARY CONTROL OF EYE MOVEMENTS

In contrast to the normal vestibulo-ocular reflex, the voluntary control of eye movements often becomes progressively compromised as life runs its course. It is as if those oculomotor skills that have evolved most recently are the most tenuously held and are the first to leave us.

Smooth pursuit movements are impaired in most healthy elderly individuals. Sharpe and Sylvester [1978] measured pursuit gain (that is the ratio of eye velocity to target velocity) in a group of elderly subjects and in a young control population. Young subjects could keep pace with targets moving as fast as 30°/sec, but elderly subjects (mean age 72 years) had difficulty in accurately pursuing targets going as slow as 10°/sec. In my own studies, I noted that smooth pursuit tracking was impaired regardless of whether this was done with the head still or with a combined movement of head and eye. This latter observation implies that the deficient pursuit command could not be used to adequately cancel or suppress the vestibulo-ocular reflex during tracking movements of the head. If an individual can no longer use smooth pursuit to follow moving objects, then saccadic tracking must be resorted to with inevitable impairment of visual performance. Normal smooth ocular pursuit is dependent on the integrity of several sites within the nervous system. First, disease of the cerebral hemispheres, particularly the parietal lobes, may cause deficient pursuit. The vestibulocerebellum has also been shown to be important for this function. Both cerebral and cerebellar hemispheres have been shown pathologically to progressively lose nerve cells with age [Critchley, 1931; Brody, 1955; Hall et al, 1975].

In bedside evaluation a significant number of the currently studied series of patients had difficulty with accommodative *vergence eye movements*. Clearly some of these difficulties may be secondary to the problem elderly patients have with accommodation [see Carter, this volume].

Saccadic eye movements, extensively investigated in healthy young subjects, have not been so well studied in the elderly. Clinical observations suggest that particularly in senility there is an increased latency before a saccade is initiated to command. This may sometimes represent a defect in attention. When saccades are executed, it appears from simple observation that their velocity seems appropriate for their size. There is clearly need for comparison of the peak velocity-to-amplitude relationship that has been so well defined for younger subjects [Bahill and Stark, 1979].

It is of interest to note that elderly subjects will often show an excess of small saccades while trying to *fixate* a target [Chu et al, 1979]. These "micro square wave jerks" are easily seen with an ophthalmoscope. Their pathogenesis remains uncertain though they are quite characteristic of certain degenerative conditions of the brain that occur in late life. It is possible that such an instability of fixation will interfere with the visual performance of the aged individual.

What is most evident in all types of voluntary eye movements is that with advancement of age comes *limitation of range of movement,* particularly on attempting upward gaze. This restriction is often less when the subject is given a specific target to look at or when a slowly moving object is followed with the eyes. Chamberlain [1971] has studied the range of upward movement of the eyes in a large group of subjects and found progressive deterioration of this ability with advancing age. Personal observations suggest that less frequently, mild restriction of voluntary eye movements to either side may also be present but seldom is there any difficulty in looking down.

What could be the cause of this restriction of upward eye movements? Based on the finding of preserved upward gaze in elderly patients with kyphosis, Chamberlain made the intriguing suggestion that progressive failure of upward gaze was the result of disuse of this movement with advancing age. There can be little doubt that affected patients are making a full effort to look up as is evidenced by the retracted lids and elevated eye brows. Could this be a mechanical restriction imposed by stiffening of the ocular muscles? Miller [1975] has demonstrated histological changes in the muscles of aged monkeys, and similar changes have been seen in man [Ringel et al, 1978]. However this seems unlikely to be an important factor. Chamberlain [1971] performed forced upward ductions on the anesthetized eyes of some of his affected patients. Although he made no measurement of the forces required to raise the eye, he felt that there was no mechanical restriction. In my personal studies, reflex movements of the eyes produced by head rotation often increased the range of movement beyond that induced by will, though sometimes a full upward excursion of the eyes was prevented by firm resistance of the neck muscles to flexion or by a downward rapid eye movement. More likely, then, is the possibility that the command signals from the brain are deficient. Could this be due to a loss of neurons within the ocular motor nuclei? Vijayashankar and Brody [1977a, 1977b] have performed careful cell counts in the fourth and sixth nerve nuclei from brains of patients ranging from infancy to old age. No significant loss of neurons was noted. Although it is the third nerve nucleus that is responsible for upward gaze, it seems unlikely that there is a local loss of neurons within this nucleus. The relative preservation of the vestibulo-ocular reflexes supports this view. We must therefore look to the prenuclear inputs that enable voluntary eye movements. Though there is much for us yet to discover in this area of ocular motor control, it is now generally accepted that the cerebral hemispheres do not project directly to the ocular motor nuclei but rather to a hierarchy of cell stations that eventually organize the various drives to the eyes. Acknowledging this fact, can we still find it likely that loss of neurons from cerebral cortex is the basis for failure of upward gaze? In my own studies, I was impressed that limitation of upward gaze did not seem to correlate with preservation of intellect and initiative. It is possible that the fault lies not in the cerebral hemispheres but in the brain stem mechanisms that control gaze. Here the neurons that control eye movements are not discretely organized anatomically, lying within the brain stem reticulum.

POSSIBLE DIRECTIONS FOR FUTURE RESEARCH

New techniques are allowing us to understand both the roles of the cerebral hemispheres and of the brain stem reticular formation in the voluntary control of eye movements. Study of the effects of certain human diseases also presents opportunities. Disorders of the cerebral hemispheres seldom produce failure of upward gaze but brain stem afflictions may do so and here one such condition is described in detail, to attempt a correlation between the site of pathological disturbance and the consequent clinical disability.

Progressive supranuclear palsy is a degenerative condition of later life first fully described by Steele, Richardson, and Olszewski in 1964. The progressive neurological deficits of this condition consist of disturbances in tone and posture, difficulty with swallowing, dementia, and impairment of voluntary eye movements. Often the first ocular motor manifestation of this condition is slowing of vertical saccades, often first in the downward direction. With time, voluntary gaze is severely affected in the vertical plane and only a few degrees of movement may be possible when the patient attempts to track a smoothly moving object. By contrast, vestibular stimuli, ie, passive head rotation, usually result in a full range of vertical movement. Horizontal versional and vergence eye movements are also affected. There is an instability of fixation of gaze with "micro square wave jerks," impaired smooth pursuit, and slowed, hypometric saccades. Horizontal vestibular responses, however, are usually well preserved [Troost and Daroff, 1977]. With time the condition progresses to affect all eye movements so that in the terminal stages the eyes may be immobile. Pathological changes consist of loss of nerve cells, granulovacular degeneration, and development of neurofibrillary tangles that, by electronmicroscopy, have been found to have a characteristic "straight tubule" appearance [Powell et al, 1974]. These findings are not present in the cerebral hemispheres but occur in subcortical, brain stem nuclei, and, in particular, those structures surrounding the aqueduct of Sylvius. This last site includes several important structures known to be important in the brain stem control of eye movements.

In presenting a description of this disorder, I do not wish to imply that the ocular motor deficits of old age are due to such a process; indeed the pathological findings in this disorder are quite unique. However, studying conditions such as progressive supranuclear palsy may enable us to understand which areas of the brain are failing when the eyes no longer move adequately. Until recently our methods for recording human vertical eye movements have not been satisfactory. We are now however in a position to accurately delineate these abnormalities using methods such as Robinson's search coil [Robinson, 1963].

Experimentally we stand to learn a lot from the technique of *recording single unit activity* in alert primates who are trained to make specific eye movements. In this manner, we are beginning to probe strategies used by the cerebral cortex and subcortical centers in the voluntary control of eye movements [see for example Goldberg and Robinson, 1977]. Another tack is to *experimentally produce models of disease*. Conventionally the brain has been lesioned electrolytically and when large fiber tracks are the target, the result have often been most revealing. For example, Pasik, Pasik, and Bender [1969] have lesioned the posterior commissure of monkeys and produced paralysis of upward gaze. However electrolytic lesions are of less value where nerve cells and fibers of passage are located together; in such circumstances, the interpretation of results may be difficult. A recent technical advance has been the discovery of substances such as kainic acid, a glutamate agonist that when injected in minute quantities into the brain will produce local death of neurons with minimal disturbances of adjacent cell processes [Herndon and Coyle, 1977]. Using such techniques it may be possible to determine, in combination with anatomical evidence, which cell bodies project through the posterior commissure to enable voluntary upward gaze.

If indeed the impoverishment of ocular motility found in the elderly is due to a degeneration of the nervous system then one aspect of research that inevitably must be tackled is whether this "degeneration" is due to a general loss of neurons or to atrophy of a specific subpopulation combined with *inadequacy of a specific neurotransmitter*. Examples of the latter include Parkinson's disease and possibly Alzheimer's dementia. Thus Parkinson's disease, although due to a predominant loss of dopaminergic neurons is characterized by a deficiency of neurotransmitter that can be corrected by providing the appropriate precursor, L-Dopa. Recent findings have suggested that although there is no greater loss of cortical neurons from patients with Alzheimer's dementia than from aged-matched controls, there is a relative deficiency of a subpopulation of neurons perhaps related to the acetylcholine system [Terry and Davies, 1980; Perry et al, 1978]. Because eye movements are relatively easily recorded, study of their responses to certain pharmacological agents may be easily assessed. In this way, study of the ocular motor deficits of the aged may allow convenient assessment of the effects of medications given for other aspects of the neural degenerative changes associated with aging.

ACKNOWLEDGMENTS

I am grateful to the residents and staff of the Lorien Nursing and Convalescent Home, Columbia, Maryland. This paper was supported by the National Institute on Aging, Grant #1 KO8 AG00061. I would like to thank Vendetta Matthews for editorial assistance.

REFERENCES

Bahill A T, Stark L (1979) The trajectories of saccadic eye movements. Sci Am 240:108–118.

Brody H (1955) Organization of the cerebral cortex. III. A study of aging in the human cerebral cortex. J Comp Neurol 102:295–302.

Bruner A, Norris T W (1971) Age-related changes in caloric nystagmus. Acta Otolaryngol Suppl 282.

Chamberlain W (1971) Restriction in upward gaze with advancing age. Am J Ophthalmol 71:341–346.

Chu F C, Reingold D B, Cogan D G, Williams A C (1979) The eye movement disorder of progressive supranuclear palsy. Ophthalmology 86:422–428.

Critchley M (1931) The neurology of old age. Lancet 1:1119–1126.

Dodge R (1903) Five types of eye movements in the horizontal meridian plane of the field of regard. Am J Physiol 8:307–329.

Goldberg M E, Robinson D L (1977) Visual mechanisms underlying gaze: Function of the cerebral cortex. In Baker R, Berthoz A (Eds) "Control of Gaze by Brain Stem Neurons." New York: Elsevier, pp 469–477.

Gonshor A, Melvill Jones G (1976) Extreme vestibulo-ocular adaptation induced by prolonged optical reversal of vision. J Physiol 256:381–414.

Hall T C, Miller A K H, Corsellus J A N (1975) Variations in the human Purkinje cell population according to age and sex. Neuropath Appl Neurobiol 1:267.

Herndon R, Coyle J T (1977) Selective destruction of neurons by a transmitter agonist. Science 198:71–72.

Miller J E (1975) Aging changes in extraocular muscles. In Lennerstrand G, Bach-y-Rita P (Eds) "Basic Mechanisms of Ocular Motility and their Clinical Implications." Oxford: Pergamon, pp 47–62.

Pasik P, Pasik T, Bender M B (1969) The pretectal syndrome in monkeys. Brain 92:521–534.

Perry E K, Tomlinson B E, Blessed G, Gibson P H, Perry R H (1978) Correlation of cholinergic abnormalities with senile plagues and mental test scores in senile dementia. Br Med J 2:1457–1459.

Powell H C, London G W, Lampert P W (1974) Neurofibrillary tangles in progressive supranuclear palsy. J Neuropath Exp Neurol 33:98–106.

Ringel S P, Wilson W B, Barden M T, Kaiser K K (1978) Histochemistry of human extraocular muscle. Arch Ophthalmol 95:1067–1072.

Robinson D A (1963) A method of measuring eye movement using a scleral search coil in a magnetic field. IEEE Trans Biomed Electron 10:137–145.

Robinson D A (1976) Adaptive gain control of the vestibulo-ocular reflex by the cerebellum. J Neurophysiol 39:954–969.

Robinson D A (1977) Linear addition of optokinetic and vestibular signals in the vestibular nucleus. Exp Brain Res 30:447–450.

Sharpe J A, Sylvester T O (1978) Effect of aging on horizontal smooth pursuit. Invest Ophthalmol Vis Sci 17:465–468.

Steele J C, Richardson J C, Olszewski J (1964) Progressive supranuclear palsy. Arch Neurol 10:333–359.

Ter Braak J W G (1936) Untersuchungen uber optokinetischen nystagmus. Archs neerl Physiol 21:309–376.

Terry R D, Davies P (1980) Dementia of the Alzheimer type. Annu Rev Neurosci 3:77–95.

Troost B T, Daroff R B (1977) The ocular motor defects in progressive supranuclear palsy. Ann Neurol 2:397–403.

Van der Laan F L, Oosterveld W J (1974) Age and vestibular function. Clin Aviat Aerospace Med 45:540–547.

Vijayashankar N, Brody H (1977a) A study of aging in the human abducens nucleus. J Comp Neurol 173:433–438.

Vijayashankar N, Brody H (1977b) Aging in the human brain stem. A study of the nucleus of the trochlear nerve. Acta Anatom 99:169–172.

Walls G L (1942) Eye movements and the fovea. In Walls G L "The Vertebrate Eye." Bloomfield Hills, Michigan: Cranbrook Institute of Science, Chapter 10.

Wilson V J, Melvill Jones G (1979) "Mammalian Vestibular Physiology." New York: Plenum.

Zee D S (1978) Ophthalmoscopy in examination of patients with vestibular disorders. Ann Neurol 3:373–374.

IV. CHANGES IN PERCEPTION AND INFORMATION PROCESSING

Aging and Human Visual Function, pages 183–184

Introduction

Since Galton's large-scale study in 1884, data has been steadily accumulating indicating a decline with age in the effectiveness of the sensory organs, and in particular those of vision. Much of the current information available on these changes has been presented in detail in the foregoing chapters. Only more recently has systematic research been carried out regarding age-associated changes in the central processes that transform sensory data into perceptual experience. It is now becoming increasingly clear that as we age, significant changes occur in the systems that operate upon sensory information: sorting, timing, interpreting, and organizing it. Some of the most recent findings regarding the effects of aging on these processes are the subject of the chapters in the following section.

One of the most interesting recent developments in vision research has been the recognition that the visual system is composed of multiple channels with different sets of neurons responsible for targets of different types. For example, it is now apparent that the channels responsible for our sensitivity to small targets are not the same as those that mediate the perception of larger targets. That is, different neuronal systems appear to respond optimally to targets of high spatial frequency, while others are most responsive to stimuli of lower spatial frequency. A measurement technique, the contrast sensitivity function (CSF), is now available that indicates an individual's ability to detect objects of any possible size. Only recently has this technique been applied to the spatial vision abilities of older persons by Robert Sekuler and his colleagues. The specific details of this highly promising line of research as well as its important practical ramifications are discussed by Sekuler and Owsley in their chapter.

The major assumption of an information-processing approach to perception is that perception is not an immediate outcome of stimulation but the result of a systematic sequence of processes that actively develop and transform representations of environmental stimuli over time. The most frequently used method for investigating the different stages of the processing of visual information is backward visual masking. In this technique a target stimulus of brief duration is followed closely by a masking stimulus that diminishes the visual effectiveness of the target stimulus. The stimulus onset asynchrony of the two stimuli at which the observer "escapes" the influence of the mask can be used to estimate the time required for processing of the target. Manipulation of other variables such as stimulus energy, duration, and type as well as method of presentation seem to allow for the examination of apparently separate stages of visual information processing. During the last decade, backward masking studies have been extended to include comparison of young and old adults. Much of this research has been carried out by David Walsh and his co-workers. They have evidence suggesting that there is a slowing with age that occurs independently in both the peripheral and central stages of information-processing. In his chapter, Walsh presents a detailed discussion of the methods, theory and findings of this work.

Age differences in visual masking are but one important manifestation of the more general loss of the older visual system's temporal resolving power. It has been postulated that the loss in visual temporal resolution can be attributed to the protracted effectiveness of stimuli in the older nervous system. According to this stimulus persistence hypothesis, the older nervous system is slower to recover from the effects of stimulation and thus is more susceptible to interactions between temporally contiguous stimuli. Although most of the initial support for the hypothesis was derived post hoc from existing data, Kline and his co-workers have provided increasing evidence on the usefulness of a general persistence model. The stimulus persistence model, however, has limited value as a scientific heuristic since its posits no specific mechanisms to account for the older visual system's relative inability to separate discrete visual events. In their chapter, Kline and Schieber examine the data pertaining to the decline in temporal tracking ability as well as present a "transient/sustained" shift hypothesis that attempts to account for this and a variety of other changes associated with visual aging.

Theoretical approaches to the study of visual aging can be attempted at several levels: at the level of neural processes, at the level of elementary information processes, or in terms of higher order or "executive" processes. Using a resource allocation perspective, Hoyer and Plude review and organize current research and theory in regard to age differences in the capacity and the selectivity of information-processing. They propose that with aging and age-related perceptual experience, higher order cognitive processes play an increasingly important role in the organization and processing of visual information. This is in contrast to the preceding chapters of this section, which primarily emphasize the channel or signal limitation aspects of the senescent visual system. That is, they serve to remind us of and give emphasis to the necessity for considering the role of the active perceiver in attempting to understand perceptual aging.

Aging and Human Visual Function, pages 185–202

The Spatial Vision of Older Humans

Robert Sekuler and Cynthia Owsley

INTRODUCTION

Early in this volume, Birren and Williams reminded us of the work Francis Galton began at the International Health Exhibition of 1884. During the life of his Anthropometric Laboratory, first at the Exhibition and then later at the South Kensington Museum, Galton collected anthropometric and psychometric data on more than 9,000 people of various ages. Among the visual functions measured in the Laboratory were acuity, color perception, the perception of length and orientation, and speed of response to a visual stimulus [Galton, 1885]. Although Galton's data contain much that is noteworthy, for us they are particularly significant because they suggest very low correlations between visual acuity and other visual functions [Koga and Morant, 1923].

Later in the volume, Weale also touched on this issue, noting that our visual systems probably did not evolve for the specific purpose of reading and that, in fact, we can do many significant tasks with eyes that have marginal acuity. A similar point has also been made by others [for example, Merritt et al, 1978]. Clearly, many visual spatial abilities are related weakly, if at all, to visual acuity [Leibowitz et al, 1980; Leibowitz et al, 1982].

All these observations, beginning with Galton's, acknowledge a division of labor within the visual system: The diversity of visual function in our daily lives requires the cooperation of several different subsystems. One current approach to human spatial vision takes explicit account of this division of labor, depicting the human visual system as an ensemble of multiple channels [Sekuler, 1974]. This model assigns to different sets of neurons the responsibility for perceiving different kinds of targets. For example, one set of neurons enables us to see large targets, a different one enables us to see small targets, and yet another helps us to see targets of intermediate size. Here we shall not be concerned with precisely how many different sets of neurons—channels—there may be, just with the notion that there are different sets and that their visual responsibilities vary. From this approach to vision, one can partition visual tasks according to their dependence on ability to see targets of various sizes. One such taxonomy of visual tasks can be found in Sekuler et al [1982, Appendix I].

The multiple channels approach has given rise to a large and vigorous scientific literature. But what are the practical consequences of such an approach? A particularly important consequence prescribes the proper way to assess any observer's spatial vision. If, for example, different neurons are needed to see large and small targets, it is not impossible that someone might have perfectly good acuity but still have difficulty seeing most of the objects that everyday activity requires him to see. Recall that good visual acuity simply means that a person is able to see very small objects.

Regan et al [1977] have reported just such cases: multiple sclerosis patients in whom good acuity coexisted with impaired visibility of larger objects. Presumably, the demyelinating process in multiple sclerosis can affect neurons in channels required for seeing large objects while leaving unaffected neurons in the channel that mediates acuity. Certainly, a comprehensive description of human spatial vision demands more than measures of the ability to see very small targets, visual acuity. We need measures of the ability to see targets covering the complete range of object sizes that our everyday activities require us to see.

MEASURING CONTRAST SENSITIVITY

Recently this assessment capability has become available. The *contrast sensitivity function* (CSF) characterizes an observer's ability to see targets ranging from the smallest to the largest. Such measurements are becoming an important part of the ophthalmological and optometric literatures [Michaels, 1980; Sjostrand, 1979; Bodis-Wollner and Camisa, 1980]. In fact, there have now been more than 75 clinical papers dealing with contrast sensitivity. But instead of reviewing previous work on CSF, I'll describe how we have used it at Northwestern, most recently to assess the spatial vision of older observers. The work we shall describe here was done in collaboration with Lucinda P. Hutman and Culver Boldt (Northwestern) and Dennis Siemsen (Illinois College of Optometry).

In the work we shall discuss in greatest detail, the targets were vertical sinusoidal gratings. With sinusoidal variation in luminance along the horizontal, these gratings have two parameters of particular importance: spatial frequency and contrast. "Spatial frequency" refers to the number of cycles of the sinusoidal grating per each unit of visual angle. Typically, the units of spatial frequency are cycles per degree (c/deg). A grating with many c/deg has high spatial frequency; one with few c/deg has low spatial frequency. Putting this another way, a grating with high spatial frequency has fine spatial structure; one with low spatial frequency has coarse spatial structure. Contrast is defined by a ratio; the numerator is the difference between the grating's highest and lowest luminances, and the denominator of the ratio is the sum of the grating's highest and lowest luminances. Defined in this way, contrast can assume values from 0.0 to 1.0. As contrast decreases, the structure of the grating becomes more difficult to see; for any grating one can find a contrast just low enough to wash out its spatial structure. To measure the contrast sensitivity function, one determines, for gratings of various spatial frequencies, the contrast that just permits the observer to see the grating.

To be of use clinically, a contrast sensitivity function must sample the spatial frequency continuum with sufficient density that a band-limited anomaly could be detected. Previously, it took 40 minutes or more to generate this sort of well-defined contrast sensitivity function. In addition, the psychophysical technique may have called for considerable practice before data could be collected. Altogether, the need for long sessions and sophisticated observers discourage the extensive use of contrast sensitivity measurements in clinical settings. These problems can be overcome by using a measurement technique introduced to audiometry by von Bekesy. This method gives reliable data very rapidly [Sekuler & Tynan, 1977]. Equally important, it seems to be appropriate for a wide range of inexperienced observers [Owsley et al, in preparation].

Previous Work

The literature offers a contradictory and confusing picture of how aging affects contrast sensitivity. For example, Arden and Jacobsen [1978] found no influence of age. Skalka [1980a] and McGrath and Morrison [1980] reported the opposite: Contrast sensitivity at all frequencies was affected by age. Our own, preliminary study with a small sample of older observers [Sekuler et al, 1980] found that older observers had decreased sensitivity to low and intermediate spatial frequencies. Finally Arundale [1978] and Derefeldt et al [1979] found losses of contrast sensitivity for spatial frequencies of 4 c/deg and higher.

With such disagreement over the effect of age on the CSF, we thought it useful to conduct a study that would avoid the shortcomings of the previous work in this area. Earlier studies had been flawed in a number of ways. First, observers were not always tested with best optical correction for the test distance. This is important because blur significantly affects contrast sensitivity at higher frequencies [Campbell and Green, 1965]. Second, observers were not always screened for ocular diseases characteristic of the older population (eg, cataract, macular disease, glaucoma). Several of these diseases are known to affect an observer's CSF [Hess and Woo, 1978; Atkin et al, 1979; Skalka, 1980b]. Third, sample sizes in the earlier work, especially for the older age ranges, were often quite small, making it difficult to determine how pervasive changes in contrast sensitivity actually are. Substantial individual differences in contrast sensitivity render inferences from very small samples risky [Ginsburg et al, 1981].

Observers

Our large-scale study of contrast sensitivity and aging [Owsley et al, in preparation] measured CSFs on a large sample ($N = 67$) of older individuals who were in their 60s, 70s, and 80s. One reason we were able to test such a large sample of older observers is that we carried out the testing right in a senior citizen center with portable contrast sensitivity equipment. By prescreening, we tried to eliminate potential subjects who had serious ocular disease. In addition, Dennis Siemsen, our optometric consultant, verified that nearly all observers were free from significant ocular disease. The incidence of cataracts (traces) and early senile macular degeneration will be discussed elsewhere [Owsley et al, in preparation]. All observers were carefully refracted for the test distance, 3 m.

We also measured CSFs on a group of younger adults ($N = 33$) in their 20s to 50s as a comparison group. These individuals were tested in the Vision Laboratory at Northwestern and were also free of eye diseases, as indicated by their most recent visit to their own doctor. Before testing, they too were refracted for the 3-m test distance.

Method

Contrast sensitivity was measured by an Optronix Vision Tester (Series 200), an integrated microcomputer-controlled television display system, which presented sinusoidal gratings. Mean luminance of the screen was 103 cd/square meter; the screen subtended $4.2° \times 5.5°$ at our viewing distance of 3 m. Contrast threshold was measured for static gratings of 0.5, 1, 2, 4, 8, and 16 c/deg. In addition, we measured contrast thresholds for gratings of 1 c/deg deg that moved rightward at either 1.1 or 4.3 deg/sec. Here, we shall concentrate on the results with nonmoving gratings.

Viewing was monocular, using the eye with better acuity. Best-corrected distance acuity for the eye whose CSF was measured was 1.27 minarc for observers in their 60s, 1.38 for the 70s, and 1.82 for the 80s. For our younger adults, best-corrected acuity for the eye whose CSF we measured was 0.68 minarc for observers in their 20s, 0.79 for the 30s, 0.78 for the 40s, and 1.07 for the 50s. Observers communicated with the Vision Tester by means of a handheld switch. Whenever a grating was visible on the screen, the observer depressed the switch and held it down. Sensing this, the Vision Tester decreased the grating's contrast at a slow, steady rate. Eventually, of course, the contrast got so low that the grating became invisible. The observer then released the switch, causing the Vision Tester to increase contrast, again, at the same, slow steady rate. Depressing and releasing the switch, the observer caused the grating to change from invisibility to visibility and back again. In this way, the observer kept the grating's contrast around the threshold level. For each spatial frequency, the Vision Tester averaged the contrasts at the transitions from visibility to invisibility and vice versa to determine the contrast threshold. The observer's *sensitivity* is defined as the reciprocal of this contrast threshold.

Before testing at any spatial frequency, the Vision Tester gave the subject a clearly visible preview of the grating he would be tested on. This preview reduces stimulus uncertainty, thereby aiding sensitivity [Davis and Graham, 1981]. The Vision Tester is programmed to start with a low spatial frequency grating (0.5 c/deg). After the observer has tracked his threshold, the Vision Tester pauses for 10 seconds and repeats the procedure with a grating of twice the spatial frequency. This procedure is repeated until testing is completed with 16 c/deg. This method gives us a complete contrast sensitivity function in about 6 minutes.

Advantages of Bekesy's Method

This tracking method for measuring the CSF has more to recommend it than just efficiency. Let us digress by identifying those of its advantages particularly important for work with older people. First, this tracking method captures and holds observers' attention. Observers tell us they like playing an active role— controlling the grating contrast. Second, if two observers differed in overall reaction times for detecting a grating, the tracking method would tend to equalize obtained thresholds for the two. Consider an observer who tended to be slow in responding. Approaching threshold from below, his slow reaction time would give us an artificially elevated threshold; approaching threshold from above, his slow reaction time would give us an artificially depressed threshold. These opposed systematic errors would tend to cancel one another, resulting in an average threshold that was accurate. Since reaction time does vary with age, if you wish to compare sensory function in older and younger people, a method that neurtralizes reaction time effects is certainly attractive. Finally, the tracking method we used minimizes possible effects of uncertainty: The observer knows exactly what the target is [cf Davis and Graham, 1981]. This knowledge could diminish possible effects of confusion or disorientation in some neurological patients.

Results

The mean CSFs for each decade of age are presented in Figure 1. Several features of Figure 1 are especially noteworthy. Subjects of all ages had approx- imately equal sensitivity at 0.5 and 1 c/deg, but older observers had lower sensitivity beginning at about 4 c/deg, with greater losses at older ages. Addi- tionally, beginning at about age 60, the peak of the CSF for older observers was at a lower frequency, 2 c/deg, as compared with younger adults, whose peak was at 4 c/deg. Thus with a large sample, it becomes apparent that older observers exhibit sensitivity losses predominantly at intermediate and high frequencies.

The present results also reveal another interesting and important fact about contrast sensitivity. There is only a very weak correlation between an observer's

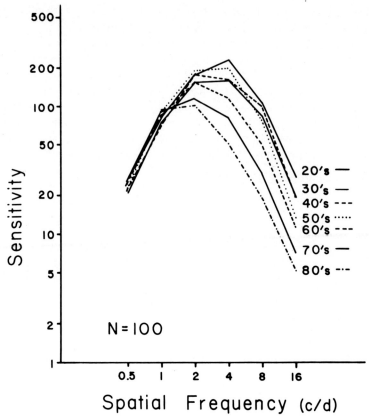

Fig. 1. Mean contrast sensitivities for well-corrected observers of various ages [after Owsley et al, in preparation].

sensitivity at a very low spatial frequency—for example, 1 c/deg—and his sensitivity at a high frequency—for example, 16 c/deg. In the sample shown in Figure 1, the correlation between sensitivities at 1 and 16 c/deg is only −0.09, which is not statistically significant. Sensitivities to highly similar spatial frequencies are well correlated, with rs ranging from +0.50 to +0.79.

The weak correlation between high and low spatial frequencies demonstrates that measuring sensitivity to high spatial frequencies (as visual acuity does) gives us very little ability to predict how well the same observer will be able to see large or intermediate size objects. This is consistent with the multiple channels approach described earlier; it is obviously *not* consistent with the traditional approach to assessing spatial vision, by means of acuity alone.

We were interested in how much of the higher frequency loss was due to the decreased retinal illuminance in the aged eye. Weale [1963] has estimated that the average 60-year-old eye transmits about one-third the amount of light transmitted by the 20-year-old eye. It is well known that lowering retinal illuminance decreases contrast sensitivity to higher frequencies while leaving lower frequencies relatively unaffected [Fiorentini and Maffei, 1973]. We remeasured contrast sensitivity in seven observers in their 20s as they viewed through a 0.5 neutral density filter, which reduced their retinal illuminance by one-third, roughly simulating the light reduction experienced by the 60-year-olds. This reduced retinal illuminance in the young observers decreased sensitivity to higher frequencies, but not to the level of the 60-year-olds. This suggested that at least part of the higher frequency loss is due to factors other than reduced retinal illuminance.

In addition, there is good reason to believe that the age-related decrease in sensitivity is not explicable by the age-related decreased acuity of our older subjects nor by an increase in intraocular scatter of light. A full discussion of these points, as well as a complete presentation of our entire study will appear elsewhere [Owsley et al, in preparation]. For the moment, we are working on the hypothesis that at least part of the decrease in contrast sensitivity we observe with advancing age is neural in origin.

MOTION SENSITIVITY

Of course, we use our eyes for seeing things other than stationary targets. In fact, some have claimed that the mammalian visual system seems to have been designed to ensure particularly good perception of moving targets. Taking the importance of visual motion seriously, we have done work comparing older and younger observers' sensitivity to visual motion. As described elsewhere [Sekuler et al, 1980], we used the method of limits to determine contrast thresholds for gratings of 1 c/deg moving at either 0.5 or 10 deg/sec. About half the observers in each age group had been tested before; the rest were new to our laboratory. The observer's task was to adjust the contrast of the moving grating so that he could just tell that the display screen was not completely uniform. In the literature on motion perception, this criterion is called a "motion criterion" because at threshold, the observer usually sees only "formless" motion; he cannot make out the grating itself. Average ages were 20.2 (N = 25) and 75 years (N = 8). The data for individual observers are shown in Figure 2. The most important finding is that with moving, low spatial frequency targets, younger observers are about three to four times more sensitive than are older observers.

Similar results have been obtained with another, larger sample of observers, aged 20–80 years [Owsley et al, in preparation]. These were the same subjects whose CSFs were presented in the preceding section. Owsley et al found that

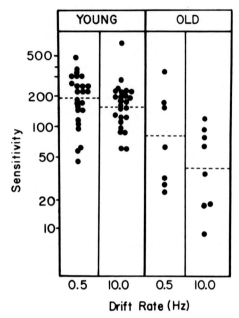

Fig. 2. Sensitivity of younger and older observers for 1 c/deg gratings drifting either at 0.5 or 10.0 deg/sec. Dotted lines indicates mean thresholds in each condition.

younger observer's sensitivity for 1-c/deg grating was enhanced over its value at no motion about fourfold when the grating moved 4.3 deg/sec; sensitivity was much less enhanced by the slower rate of movement, 1.0 deg/sec. Others had previously reported such enhancement by temporal variation of the stimulus [see Sekuler, 1974]. The novel result here is that the ability of motion to enhance sensitivity varies with age. This phenomenon is illustrated in Figure 3. Each point represents a ratio between sensitivity to a *moving* 1-c/deg grating and sensitivity to a *static* 1-c/deg grating. The upper curve represents data for movement of 4.3 deg/sec; the lower curve represents data for movement of 1.1 deg/ sec. With increasing age, the more rapid motion has diminished capacity to enhance sensitivity ($p < 0.001$). The slower motion, producing only slight enhancing power even for young subjects, showed no systematic decline in the enhancing power with observers' age ($p > .10$).

The data in Figure 3 admit of several explanations, including the possibility that the aging visual system has diminished capacity to take advantage of the potential gain in sensitivity associated with transient stimulus presentation. One possibility is that the diminished response to stimulus motion is related to the decreased response to transient stimulus presentations generally (see Kline and

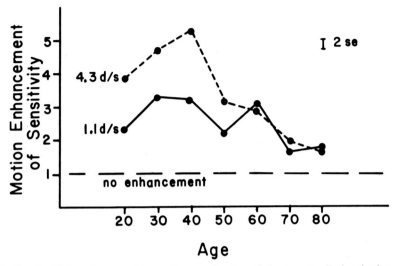

Fig. 3. Sensitivity enhancement by motion as a function of observer age. Each point is a ratio between sensitivity to a moving grating of 1 c/deg and sensitivity to the same grating presented without movement. The upper curve shows the amount of sensitivity enhancement with movement of 4.3 deg/sec; the lower curve shows the amount of sensitivity enhancement with movement of 1.1 deg/sec. The straight dashed line shows the expected value with no enhancement whatever. The short vertical bar at the upper right represents the mean value of two standard errors.

Schieber, this volume). To test this possibility, we are extending the work on detection of motion to cover a wide range of spatial frequencies, rates of movement, and perceptual tasks connected with temporal modulation.

But whatever their ultimate explanation, it is important to recognize that these measurements of response to motion are quite distinct from measurements of dynamic visual acuity. Dynamic visual acuity (DVA) is a measure of resolution ability taken with moving targets and does decrease with age [Reading, 1972]. But there are several reasons for believing that the motion detection data we have just described are unrelated to DVA. First, the gratings (1 c/deg) used to study contrast sensitivity for moving targets are orders of magnitude larger than targets used in studies of DVA; second, the grating's speeds (0.5 to 10 deg/sec) are well below those at which target motion affects acuity appreciably. Rather than reflecting changes in DVA, our results demonstrate quite a different kind of loss in response to motion.

But what is the practical significance of the age-related losses we have observed? In particular, what role do low and intermediate spatial frequencies play in our normal perceptual activities? Answering these questions may help identify circumstances and tasks that place older observers at a perceptual disadvantage.

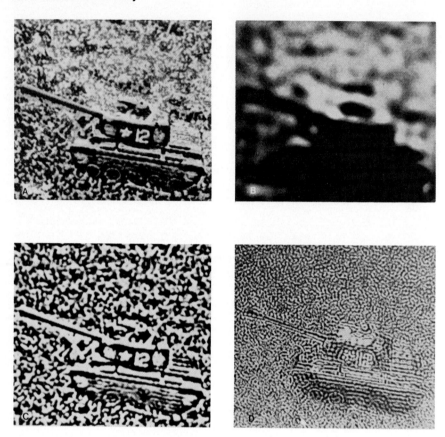

Fig. 4. Panel (a): Original image of tank; panel (b): Low-frequency components of original image; panel (c): intermediate-frequency components of original image: panel (d): high-frequency components of original.

Figure 4 helps to show the possible perceptual role of low and intermediate frequencies. The figure shows a series of computer images created by Andrews [1972]. Panel (a) shows the original, a photograph of a tank. The other three panels portray various bands of spatial frequency information present in the task. Seen from a distance of one-third mile, the tank would subtend a visual angle approximately 1° wide.

Panel (b) shows the low spatial frequency information present in the original. It has been constructed by filtering the original through a low-pass filter. Note that from the low frequency alone you can recognize that an object—of some sort—is present.

In other words, the low spatial frequency content of a scene may carry figure-ground relationships. In fact, if you had some prior knowledge of the set of alternatives to which the object belonged, you might be able to identify it as a tank (for example, if the alternatives were "a tank" and "a lamp"). You might even be able to tell in which direction the tank's gun turret pointed, a distinction of some considerable importance. In other words, from the low-frequency information alone, one can obtain a substantial amount of information about the visual objects in one's environment.

In addition, notice that nonvisual information can be of considerable supplementary help to an observer. The nonvisual information may take the form of hypotheses, things learned from previous experience with the same situation, or information from others. The potentially important interaction between visual and nonvisual information is often ignored by vision researchers. But it may be especially important in analyzing the performance of observers with sub-normal vision. The performance of some observers outside the clinic may be considerably better than the assessment of their vision would suggest. Their visual "overachievement" may result from their effective use of nonvisual information to supplement what their eyes tell them.

Let us now continue with our discussion of Figure 4. Panel (c)—produced by a bandpass filter with an intermediate frequency as its center frequency—shows that intermediate frequencies would contribute something to our ability to read the insignia on the tank and see its treads, etc. Finally, panel (d)—produced with a highpass filter—portrays only the high spatial frequency components in the original. The high-frequency information (fine details) does not seem to help very much, at least for this object.

DETECTION OF FACES

Recent work confirms that older observers actually do have diminished ability to detect relatively large targets—human faces—of low contrast. Since recognition of faces may depend heavily on spatial frequencies in the range of 2–4 c/deg [Ginsburg, 1977], one would expect the older observers, who showed a decline in the peak of the CSF, to have diminished sensitivity to the faces. Here I'll describe only one part of our work on face perception. All faces were about the same size and had neither facial hair nor eyeglasses since such details might spuriously affect performance in part of our study. Samples of these faces are shown in Figure 5.

Owsley, Sekuler, and Boldt [1981] made measurements in 14 college students and 13 older people. Average ages of the two groups were 20 and 75 years, respectively; none of the observers had been tested in any of our previous experiments. Each observer was tested in two tasks: face detection and face discrimination. In the face-detection task, targets were eight slides of unfamiliar faces presented one at a time on a rear-projection screen 115 cm in front of the

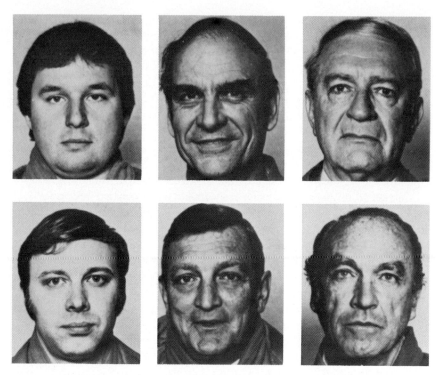

Fig. 5. Sample of faces used in face perception study. Like these, all the faces were of white, middle-aged males seen in full frontal view. See text for details.

observer. On each trial, the face was first presented at no contrast. The observer then adjusted the contrast until he could just see that something was present on the screen in front of him. At this point, the *detection* threshold, the observer could not make out much more than the vague outline of a face. In the face-discrimination task, targets were *pairs* of faces presented side by side on the screen. On half the trials, the two faces were the same; on the other half of the trials, the two faces were different. Beginning at no contrast, the observer's task was to increase contrast until he could say whether the two faces were the same or different. The datum on each trial was the contrast at which the judgement could be made—hence, the contrast threshold for *discrimination*.

In addition to measuring detection and discrimination of faces, Owsley, Sekuler, and Boldt also determined each observer's visual acuity using a standard letter chart. All measurements, thresholds, and acuity were made with each observer's best optical correction in place.

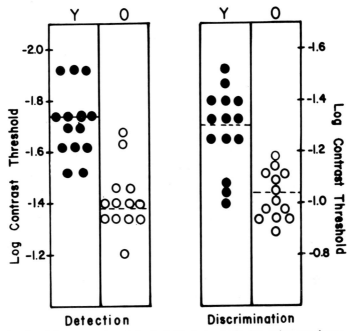

Fig. 6. Results of face perception study. Individual observer's data points are shown—younger observers' in columns headed "Y" and older observers' in columns headed "O." The left two panels show results for the detection part of experiment; the right two panels show results for discrimination. In each column the dashed horizontal line represents the average of the data in that column.

Results of face detection and discrimination are shown in Figure 6. Each point is the average threshold for one observer. Data in the left two columns are for the detection task; data in the right two columns are for discrimination. Columns labeled "Y" contain data for the younger observers; columns labeled "O" contain data for the older observers. The outcome is clear and unambiguous: Older observers required more contrast both to detect the presence of a single face and to discriminate between faces in a pair. The average older observer required about three times more contrast to perform either task. Control measurements reported elsewhere [Owsley et al, 1981] demonstrate that these age differences are the result of neither criterion differences nor of the reduced retinal illuminance associated with senile miosis. As indicated before, it is particularly important to verify, whenever possible, that criterion differences do not themselves explain obtained psychophysical differences between age groups.

Figure 7 allows us to compare the results on face perception with the acuity measurements made on the same observers. Again, each point represents the

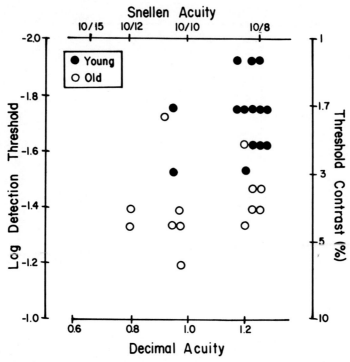

Fig. 7.   Acuities are plotted against the abscissas (Snellen values against the upper abscissa; decimal equivalents on the lower abscissa). Face detection measurements are plotted against the ordinates— log detection thresholds against the left ordinate; threshold contrasts against the right hand ordinate. Filled data points are for 14 younger observers; open data points for 13 older observers.

data of one observer. The ordinate values of any point reflect the observer's contrast threshold for detecting faces; the abscissa values reflect the observer's visual acuity. Filled data points are for older observers, open points for younger. Although the two groups do differ slightly in their mean visual acuities (abscissa values), the *overlap* between the two groups is quite striking. Considerable overlap among acuity measurements at different ages is to be expected from normative work [Frisen and Frisen, 1981]. But for contrast thresholds (ordinate values), the separation between groups is much more striking.

So, on the average, the older observers require about two times more contrast than do the younger observers in order to see faces. Of course, this is precisely what one would expect if (1) the faces were being detected on the basis of frequencies near the peak of the CSF and (2) if older and younger observers differed in peak frequency sensitivity as did other observers of comparable ages whom we had tested previously (described earlier).

Simply because someone has good visual acuity, we cannot assume he or she will function well on other visual tasks. But tests with the abstract sinsuoidal grating targets actually give us the ability to predict performance—and performance losses—with more meaningful stimuli.

The results of Figures 6 and 7 have serious implications for vision screening of potential automobile drivers. Acuity measured under high-contrast, photopic conditions, as is the custom in all states, does not have much predictive ability for an observer's vision at night [Fisher, 1979] or under conditions of reduced contrast, such as driving in rain or fog [Merritt et al, 1978]. If you need to predict someone's visual acuity under conditions of reduced contrast, it is best not to rely exclusively upon acuity measurements made at high contrast.

We need rapid, practical procedures to complement the acuity tests that are usually the only assessment of potential drivers' vision [Leibowitz et al, 1982]. We need to identify people who should be especially careful while driving at night or under low-contrast conditions. The people who should be extra careful are not just those over a certain age; individual differences in contrast sensitivity are large enough to make age-related criteria unworkable, as well as unfair [see Ginsburg et al, 1981]. Nor are people diagnosed as "night blind" by traditional, clinical criteria [Michaels, 1980] the only people who should be careful about night or twilight driving. Others with diminished contrast sensitivity may also be at risk. Although the test we need are already available in rudimentary form, a substantial effort will be required to refine and validate them against driving performance [cf Fisher, 1979]. A comparable effort has already had some success in relating the performance of military pilots to their contrast sensitivities [Ginsburg et al, 1982].

FUTURE DIRECTIONS

Let us close by considering some directions that research might take in the future. First, a comprehensive, cross-sectional study would provide a detailed description of the rates at which different visual functions change with age. Presumably, not all visual functions change at the same rate with age. For theoretical as well as practical reasons, it will be useful to know which functions form clusters, changing at the same rate, and which do not. A more extensive cross-sectional study would also provide information about individual differences in various visual functions. Individual differences are important for two reasons: First, they keep us from overgeneralizing about people at particular ages; and second, individual differences in visual function may ultimately correlate with the physiological status of an individual, with the environmental conditions to which he has been exposed, or with that individual's genetic makeup [Young, 1981].

There is another direction to be explored. A complete description of spatial vision cannot emerge from studies restricted, as ours have been, to daylight (photopic) conditions. In fact, we need tests that challenge or provoke spatial vision to operate at its limits. I think of such tests as related to the provocative tests used in medicine. For example, if narrow-angle glaucoma is suspected, a patient may be asked to drink two pints of water immediately upon waking, maximizing the chances of dramatic elevation in intraocular pressure. We need to develop analogous tests that provoke visual function.

There are many conditions in everyday life in which the only information that our visual systems *could* use is information contained in low or intermediate spatial frequencies. For example, twilight (mesopic) or night (scotopic) conditions diminish the visual system's sensitivity to high and even intermediate spatial frequencies or eliminate that sensitivity entirely [Fiorentini and Maffei, 1973; DeValois et al, 1974]. Tests under conditions of low contrast or low luminance provoke the visual system, placing an extra burden on observers who have impaired sensitivity to low and intermediate frequencies. In addition, this form of provocative test measures performance under conditions that are important everyday [see Sivak et al, 1981].

Taking a different tack, psychophysical work on vision and aging should be supplemented by carefully coordinated anatomical and physiological studies. For example, although we know that the number of photoreceptors decreases with age [Rosen, 1979], we do not know how the decrease distributes itself across the retina. The loss of photoreceptors in the periphery may or may not be at the same rate. For example, static perimetry [Verriest and Israels, 1965] shows that with age, sensitivity may decline more rapidly in the periphery than in the center of vision. But of course the locus of such effects is difficult to determine without additional research.

Perhaps our work at Northwestern will stimulate anatomical study of non-clinical material from aging visual systems. This would be a particularly beneficial development since normal changes in visual structures with aging may be qualitatively similar to many pathological changes [Young, 1981]. Ultimately, studies of visual anatomy in normal, aging eyes could increase our understanding of pathological changes and vice versa.

CONCLUSIONS

Galton's work almost a century ago suggested that visual acuity has limited perdictive value for telling us how well someone acutally *sees*. Acuity measurements are not without value, but they are certainly not the alpha and omega of vision testing. To the previous demonstrations that supplementary measures are needed, the work described here represents a modest addition. Moreover, it appears that the standard way of assessing spatial vision is especially prone to underestimate the potential handicaps under which older people in our society operate. Fortunately, we have the techniques that could help us rectify this failing. If used properly, these techniques might finally give us an accurate description of spatial vision in humans of all ages.

ACKNOWLEDGMENTS

This paper was supported by National Institute of Aging Grant AG-02151.

REFERENCES

Andrews HC (1972) Digital computers and image processing. Endeavour 31:88–94.

Arden GB, J Jacobson (1978) A simple grating test for contrast sensitivity: Preliminary results indicate value for screening in glaucoma. Invest Ophthalmol Vis Sci 17:23–32.

Arundale K (1978) An investigation into the variation of human contrast sensitivity with age and ocular pathology. Br J Ophthalmol 62:213–215.

Atkin A, Bodis-Wollner I, Wolkstein M, Moss A, Podos S (1979) Abnormalities of central vision in glaucoma. Am J Ophthalmol 89:205–211.

Bodis-Wollner I, J Camisa (1980) Contrast sensitivity measurement in clinical diagnosis. In Lessell S, Van Dalen JTW (Eds) "Neuro-ophthalmology." Amsterdam: Excerpta Medica, 373–401.

Campbell, FW, Green, DG (1965) Optical and retinal factors affecting visual resolution. J Physiol, 181: 576–593.

Davis ET, Graham N (1981) Spatial frequency uncertainty effects in the detection of sinusoidal gratings. Vis Res 21:705–712.

Derefeldt G, G Lennerstrand, B Lundh (1979) Age variations in normal human contrast sensitivity. Acta Ophthalmol 57:679–690.

DeValois RL, Morgan H, Snodderly DM (1974) Psychophysical studies of monkey vision. III. Spatial luminance contrast sensitivity tests of macaque and human observers. Vis Res 14:75–81.

Fiorentini A, Maffei L (1973) Contrast in night vision. Vis Res 13:73–80.

Fisher JH (1979) Comparison of young and old drivers reading road signs at night. Paper presented to the Annual Meeting of the Human Factors Society.

Frisen L, Frisen M (1981) How good is normal visual acuity? A study of letter acuity thresholds as a function of age. A Von Graefes Archiv Klin Ophthalmol 215:149–157.

Galton F (1885) On the anthropometric laboratory at the late International Health Exhibition. J Anthropol Inst 14:205–221.

Ginsburg AP (1978) Visual information processing based upon spatial filters constrained by biological data. Aerospace Med Res Lab Rep AMRL-TR-78-129, Vols. 1 and 2.

Ginsburg A, Cannon M, Sekuler R, Evans D, Owsley C, Mulvanny P (1981) Large-population spatiotemporal contrast sensitivity functions. Paper presented at Annual Meetings of the Optical Society of America, Orlando, Florida.

Ginsburg A, Evans D, Sekuler R, Harp S (1982) Contrast sensitivity predicts pilots' performance in aircraft simulators. Am J Optom Physiol Optics, 59:105–109.

Hess R, G Woo (1978) Vision through cataracts. Invest Ophthalmol Vis Sci 17:428–435.

Hutman LP, Sekuler R (1980) Spatial vision and aging. II. Criterion effects. J Gerontol 35:700–706.

Koga Y, Morant GM (1923) On the degree of association between reaction times in the case of different senses. Biometrika 15:346–372.

Leibowitz HW, Owen DA (1977) Nighttime driving accidents and selective visual degradation. Science 197:422–423.

Leibowitz HW, Post R, Ginsburg A (1980) The role of fine detail in visually controlled behavior. Invest Ophthalmol Vis Sci 19:846–848.

Leibowitz HW, Post R, Brandt T, Dichgans E (1982) Implications of recent developments in dynamic spatial orientation and visual resolution for vehicle guidance. In Wertheim A, Wagenaar W, Leibowitz HW (Eds) "Tutorials in Motion Perception." London: Plenum.

Ludvigh E (1941) Effect of reduced contrast in visual acuity as measured with Snellen test letters. Arch Ophthalmol 25:469–474.

McGrath C, JD Morrison (1980) Age-related changes in spatial frequency perception. J Physiol 310:52P.

Merritt JO, Newton RE, Sanderson GA, Seltzer ML (1978) Driver visibility quality: An electro-optical meter for invehicle measurement of modulation transfer (MTF). Report prepared for Department of Transportation (DOT HS 804 105).

Michaels DD (1980) Visual Optics and Refraction: A Clinical Approach, Second Ed. St Louis: C.V. Mosby.

Owsley C, Sekuler R, Boldt C (1981) Aging and low-contrast vision: Face perception. Invest Ophthalmol Vis Sci 21:362–365.

Owsley C, Sekuler R, Siemsen D Contrast sensitivity throughout the lifespan, in preparation.

Reading VM (1972) Visual resolution as measured by dynamic and static tests. Pflügers Archiv 333:17–26.

Regan D, Silver R, Murray TJ (1977) Visual acuity and contrast sensitivity in multiple sclerosis—Hidden visual loss. Brain 100:563–579.

Rosen ES (1979) Involutional macular degeneration. In Yannuzzi LA, Gitter KA, Schatz H (Eds) "The Macula: A Comprehensive Text and Atlas" Baltimore: Williams and Wilkins.

Sekuler R (1974) Spatial vision. Annu Rev Psychol 25:195–232.

Sekuler R, and Tynan P (1977) Rapid measurement of contrast-sensitivity functions. Am J Optom Physiol Optics 54:573–575.

Sekuler R, Hutman LP, Owsley C (1980) Human aging and vision. Science, 209:1255–1256.

Sekuler R, Kline D, Dismukes K (Eds) (1982) Vision and Aging Naval Pilots. Report of Working Group 55, National Academy of Sciences, National Research Council.

Sivak M, Olson PL, Pastalan LA (1981) Effect of driver's age on nighttime legibility of highway signs. Hum Factors, 23:59–64.

Sjostrand J (1979) Contrast sensitivity in macular disease using a small-field and a large-field TV-system. Acta Ophthalmol 57:832–846.

Skalka HW (1980a) Effect of age on Arden grating acuity. Br J Ophthalmol 64:21–23.

Skalka HW (1980b) Comparison of Snellen acuity, VER acuity, and Arden grating scores in macular and optic nerve disease. Br J Ophthalmol 64:24–29.

Verriest G, Israels A (1965) Application du perimetre statique de Goldmann au rélève topografique des seuils differentiels de luminances pour de petits objects colorés projetés sur un fond blanc. Vis Res 5:151–174.

Weale, RA (1963) "The Aged Eye." London: H.K. Lewis.

Wolkstein MA, Carr RE (1979) Macular function tests. In Yannuzzi LA, Gitter KA, Schatz H (Eds) "The Macula: A Comprehensive Text and Atlas." Baltimore: Williams and Wilkins.

Young RW (1981) A theory of central retinal disease. In Sears ML (Ed) "Future Directions in Ophthalmic Research." New Haven: Yale University Press.

Aging and Human Visual Function, pages 203–230
© 1982 Alan R. Liss, Inc., 150 Fifth Avenue, New York, NY 10011

The Development of Visual Information Processes in Adulthood and Old Age

David A. Walsh

The human world is a visual world. Our ability to see was important to our evolutionary past and will be important to our evolutionary future. Locating prey and escaping predators may be less important in the industrial societies of the twentieth century than they were in our past, but other visual tasks have become more important. Adults in the modern world must deal with visual tasks never imagined by even our recent ancestors. The development of high-speed transportation systems allows us to travel rapidly through a diversity of environments. These developments have created heavy visual monitoring demands for drivers, pedestrians, pilots, and air traffic controllers. They have increased the demands for acquiring spatial layout information and using the visual information that supports moving about in an urban environment. The industrial world has broadened the need for education and educational materials. While adults in modern society may spend little time tracking animals across fields, they spend ever-increasing amounts of time tracking words across printed pages.

The importance of visual functioning has motivated research interest in examining changes in these processes across the adult years. Researchers have examined topics ranging from structural changes in the eye [Weale, 1965] to differences in the ability to acquire spatial layout information for urban environments [Walsh et al, 1981]. One line of investigation has examined age differences in visual functioning from the viewpoint of contemporary models of visual information-processing drawn from the field of experimental-psychology. These investigations will be the focus of this paper.

In general, investigations of age-related differences in visual information-processing have tried to provide an empirical data base that has clear theoretical interpretations. In the pages that follow, a model of visual information-processing that has directed my own research in this area will be presented. The research paradigms used to investigate questions of aging will be described and the growing data base we have collected will be reported. Special attention will be given to a recent investigation that allows us to examine relationships between what we believe to be separate stages of visual information-processing.

A VISUAL INFORMATION-PROCESSING MODEL

Turvey [1973] identified separate peripheral and central processes underlying visual perception by observing the types of stimuli that are successful masks and the form of the resulting masking functions in a backward masking paradigm. Backward masking occurs when the perception of a leading stimulus (target stimulus) is impaired by a rapidly following stimulus (masking stimulus). Turvey used letters as targets and both visual noise and patterned stimuli as masks. Figure 1 shows examples of the target and visual noise masks that were used in these investigations. When visual noise was presented monoptically (same eye receiving target and mask), an energy-sensitive peripheral masking phenomenon was found. Three characteristics define peripheral masking:

(1) Peripheral masking is an energy-dependent phenomenon: In order for masking to occur, the energy of the mask must exceed the energy of the target.

(2) Target energy is related by a power function to the interstimulus interval necessary to escape masking (ISI_c). Specifically, target energy $(TE)^b \times ISI_c$ is equal to a constant for masking that arises peripherally.

(3) The figural characteristics of the mask are noncritical in peripheral masking. Turvey found that visual noise or a homogeneous flash were effective masks only with monoptic and binocular presentations, those conditions of presentation that permit peripheral interference in all parts of the visual pathway.

Turvey's [1973] model of peripheral processes assumes that the visual pathway anatomically includes the retina, lateral geniculate nucleus, and terminal connections at the striate cortex. Conceptually, he characterizes the peripheral pathway as a set of independent neural nets specifically attuned to figural characteristics of visual stimulation, but sharing many receptor and intermediate neurons [Thomas, 1970]. The processing of the target by the neural nets is assumed to be hierarchically organized, and its speed of processing is believed to be directly related to the energy of the target—the greater the target energy, the faster peripheral processing is completed.

Masking that arises centrally is described by a completely different set of characteristics. Whereas the energy relationship between target and mask is critical in peripheral masking, it is unimportant in masking that arises centrally. The critical variable in central masking is the degree of similarity between target and mask features. Furthermore, escape from central masking is determined by the time separating the onset of the target and mask (the stimulus onset asynchrony, SOA). In contrast to peripheral masking, (1) a target may be masked by a stimulus of lower energy, (2) an additive relation—target duration (TD) + ISI_c = a constant = SOA—describes escape from masking that arises cen-

PATTERN MASK   VISUAL NOISE   TARGET STIMULUS

Fig. 1.   Examples of masking and target stimuli.

trally, and (3) central masking is dependent on similarity of figural characteristics between the target and mask.

The additive relationship showing SOA to be the critical variable in central masking is explained by the operating time requirements of central, sequential, decision processes. Turvey's model proposes that these sequential decision nets operate on both stored outputs from peripheral nets and the output of prior decision processes. Later decision nets must await outputs from all sequentially prior nets. Central masking occurs when the stored peripheral output of a target is replaced by mask output before sequentially later decision processes have completed their operation.

With this summary of Turvey's [1973] distinction between peripheral and central perceptual processes as a base, we can now outline a more general model of visual information-processing that has directed the research reported below. Figure 2 presents a diagrammatic representation of the model. Light incident on the eye initiates processing by sets of peripheral nets attuned to specific visual features. These nets are assumed to operate in parallel, with the operating speed of each net determined by the visual features to which it is sensitive and the amount of energy incident on the retinal receptors. Concurrent with the operation of the peripheral nets, central decision nets begin to process the output of the peripheral stage. It is assumed that the operation of the central stage is contingent on output from the peripheral stage. Thus, as long as the energy of a visual stimulus is high, and peripheral processes are completed before contingent stages of central processing are ready for that output, then peripheral and central processes can be assumed to operate concurrently. The function of central processing stages, as conceptualized by Turvey [1973] is the synthesis of context-dependent features of the visual input. It is important to understand that the output of the central stage is *not* assumed to be an identification of the visual input. Rather, this central stage is assumed to yield higher-level sets of visual features that provide the material on which subsequent pattern-recognition processes operate.

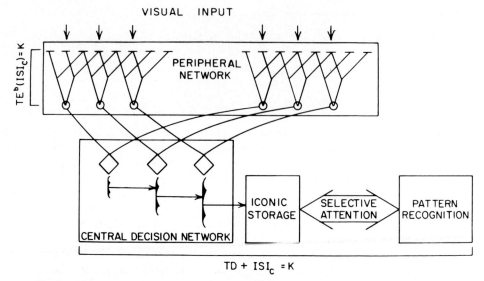

Fig. 2. Diagrammatic representation of a visual information-processing model of human performance. Included are peripheral and central decision networks, iconic storage, selective attention, and pattern-recognition stages.

The central processing stage output, as proposed by the model, is stored in a brief visual sensory memory such as those described by Sperling [1960] and Averbach and Coriell [1961] and labeled "iconic memory" by Neisser [1967]. Iconic memory provides a temporary storage for "to-be-identified" context-dependent visual features. This early store in the flow of visual information is assumed to be visual, of large capacity, and susceptible to irreversible decay that is complete in about 250 msec following stimulus onset.

The "to-be-identified" features stored in iconic memory are selectively attended to and identified by processes subsequent to the central perceptual processes outlined by Turvey [1973]. Our conceptualization of these processes has been heavily influenced by Neisser's [1967] concepts of selective and focal attention. His analysis suggests that subareas of the large informational capacity of iconic memory can be selectively attended to, and that the processing resources available for pattern recognition can be focused on separate areas in order to identify clusters of context-dependent features. An important implication of the work by Averbach and Coriell [1961] is the demonstration that the processes of selective and focal attention, which Neisser proposes as support systems for pattern-recognition processes, take real and measurable amounts of processing time. The latter two stages of Figure 2 represent the selective attention and pattern-recognition stages of visual information-processing.

DEVELOPMENTAL QUESTIONS

Investigations of the adult development of visual functioning using information-processing models have made considerable progress in describing age differences in some of the stages of visual information-processing outlined above. Many data document age differences in the speed of peripheral and central perceptual processes [Hertzog et al, 1976; Till, 1978; Walsh, 1976; Walsh et al, 1978; Walsh et al, 1979]. The results that show older adults require longer processing times than young adults to complete both peripheral and central processes can be interpreted as evidence for a general slowing associated with aging [Birren, 1965]. However, none of the investigations cited above collected measures of peripheral and central processing speed on the same subject sample. Clearer support for the idea that aging is associated with a general slowing in many stages of information-processing could be provided by examining the intercorrelation of subjects' speed of information processing at separate stages. The present paper addresses this question with data from a recent investigation conducted in our laboratory.

The examination of intertask correlations as evidence for or against the hypothesis of a general slowing in the speed of information-processing with age is not a simple undertaking. Birren, Riegle, and Morrison [1962] suggest that evidence for a general slowing hypothesis should include increased correlation between individuals' speeds of performance on various tasks in addition to increases in mean performance times as they age. The large variability in speed of processing typically found in old age groups is one factor that could produce higher intertask correlations for old than young subjects. Furthermore, if the increased variability results from individual differences in the magnitude of age-related slowing, which affects the speed of some individuals' performances on all tasks, then additional increases in intertask correlations could be expected. Although the above factors may produce larger intertask correlations for old than for young subjects, other patterns of intertask correlation could also provide support for the general slowing hypothesis. For example, if aging is associated with a 20-msec increase in task performance for each decade lived, and this 20-msec constant is added to all tasks for all subjects, then no change in intertask correlations would be expected with age. (Adding a constant to each pair of scores for all observations in a sample has no effect on the correlation among the scores.) While the situation described in this example would have no effect on the within-age-group correlations, it would produce an intertask correlation computed across all age groups that was substantially larger than the intertask correlations within any separate age group.

On the other hand, if aging is not associated with a general increase in processing time, then a different pattern of overall intertask correlations might be observed. For example, if aging is associated with slowing in different stages of information-processing for different individuals, then we should not expect to find intertask correlations computed over all subjects that are larger than those found for separate age groups. The possible patterns of correlation outlined above represent clear evidence for or against the idea of general slowing in the rate of visual information-processing. Of course, other patterns intermediate to these extremes might be observed. The most likely cases would involve some reliable but modest relationships among the speeds of processing in separate stages. It is important to recognize that no completely objective criteria are available for assessing the amount of support for the hypothesis of general slowing provided by correlations of different magnitudes. Rather, it will be necessary to consider both the amount of explained and unexplained variance in one task provided by knowledge of performance on another.

PERIPHERAL PERCEPTUAL PROCESSES

Investigation of age differences in peripheral perceptual processes have shown that groups of adults between 60 and 70 years of age require longer processing times than do adults between the ages of 18 and 25 to complete peripheral stages of visual information-processing. This conclusion is based on three investigations that used visual masking paradigms meeting the criteria proposed by Turvey to define masking due to interference in peripheral perceptual processes. These criteria, reviewed at length above, include monoptic or binocular presentation of target and mask in succession to the same visual pathway, the use of low target and high mask energies, and resulting data functions showing that the relationship of ISI_c to target energy is described by a power function.

Walsh, Till, and Williams [1978] examined two separate examples of young (average ages, 20 and 24 years) and old adults (average ages, 65 and 68 years) in two similar monoptic backward masking paradigms. The first investigation measured the accuracy with which subjects could report target stimuli (single letters) presented at 9.6, 19.2, and 38.4 (cd/m² × msec) energy levels. The masking stimulus was always presented at a 1,050 (cd/m² × msec) energy level and followed the target at 9 SOAs (0 to 80 msec in 10 msec steps). The second investigation employed the same target and mask energy levels, but an ascending limits procedure was used to determine the ISI required to report four consecutive target stimuli. The first investigation used a forced-choice responding procedure to control for different response criteria that might be used by the separate age groups. Figure 3 presents the results of these investigations, which show that the older adults required longer ISI_cs to escape the effects of peripheral masking. However, the relationship between energy and ISI_c for each age group was found to be described by the same power function with an exponent equal to 0.34: $TE^{.34} \times ISI_c$ = a constant. This outcome demonstrates that changes in target energy result in proportional changes in peripheral processing speed for young and old adults.

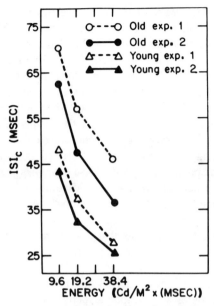

Fig. 3. Effect of target energy on interstimulus interval required to escape peripheral masking (ISI$_c$) for two different groups of young (20 and 24 years) and old (65 and 68 years) adults. [From Walsh et al, 1978].

An important question associated with the results of the Walsh, Till, and Williams [1978] and other aging investigations of peripheral perceptual processes [cf Till, 1978; Kline and Szafran, 1975] regards the mechanism responsible for the speed differences observed. It is well known that the human eye undergoes many changes with age that serve to change the amount of energy reaching the retina from a light source. For example, the pupil decreases in size and the crystalline lens yellows, factors that decrease the amount of light reaching the retina. In contrast, the response time of the pupil also increases and could operate to increase the amount of light entering the eye. While there are large individual differences in the degree to which these changes occur, in general, less energy from a light source can be expected to reach the retina of an older eye. These physical changes in the eye could have some important implications for interpreting the differences in the estimates of peripheral processing speed shown in Figure 3. The functions relating ISI$_c$ to target energy for each age group show that the former increases as the latter decreases. Thus, it is necessary to consider the possibility that the difference in peripheral processing speed between young and old adults at any given target energy is a result of less energy reaching the retina of the older eye. The Walsh et al [1978] investigation addressed this issue by careful subject selection for their first investigation. A sample of 10 older women were recruited who did not differ from the young sample in the minimum lumination required to report the unmasked target stimuli. The results of that investigation, shown in Figure 3, demonstrate that this exceptional sample of older subjects required longer processing times to escape peripheral masking effects than did a sample of young subjects even when both age groups showed similar target energy thresholds. Furthermore, the results of a second investigation using less select older subjects who had target energy thresholds higher than those of the young comparison group, resulted in similar absolute age differences in peripheral processing speed. These outcomes suggest that the large and reliable differences between young and old adults in processing times required to escape peripheral masking effects cannot be explained completely by the amount of light reaching the retina of a young and old eye. Rather, the results of these investigations suggests that a substantial proportion of the observed slowing probably results from changes in the rate of neural net operation in the peripheral system.

Other investigations have been reported that provide support for the above conclusions regarding aging and peripheral perceptual processes. Till [1978] extended the results of the Walsh et al [1978] investigation using some higher target energies. The result of Till's [1978] work replicate the findings of age differences in the speed with which peripheral perceptual processes are completed. Furthermore, they show that similar power functions relating target energy to ISI_c describe the performances of 20- and 55-year-old adults. Another investigation, by Kline and Szafran [1975], can be interpreted as further evidence for age differences in peripheral perceptual processes as defined by Turvey's model of these phenomena [cf Walsh, 1976].

Results from a recent investigation in the author's laboratory provide some confirmation of the above results and some evidence of other changes in peripheral processes in later life. This investigation, which will be an important focus for the remainder of this paper, collected measures of visual information-processing at each of the stages depicted in the model shown in Figure 2, on a sample of 24 young (average age 18.7 years, range 17–21 years), 24 middle-aged (average age 46.5, range 40–53 years), and 24 old adults (average age 70.3 years, range 67–74 years). The processing times required to report target stimuli with 70% accuracy were measured. In general, our procedure involved a measure of the ISI_c that subjects required to report four targets correctly, using the method of ascending limits, followed by a more careful determination of the processing time required to report 14 of 20 target stimuli correctly (ie, 70% correct performance). This was accomplished by examining the accuracy of report for 20 stimuli presented at the ISI_c determined with the methods of ascending limits. If performance was above or below 70% correct at ISI_c, then ISI was either

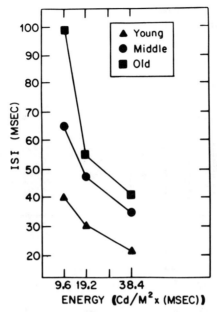

Fig. 4. Effect of target energy on the interstimulus interval required for 70% correct perceptual performance in a peripheral masking paradigm. Twenty-four adults whose average ages were 19, 47, and 70 years participated in each age group.

decreased or increased by one-fifth and another set of 20 targets was presented. This procedure continued until either the ISI producing exactly 70% performance was located, or until ISIs yielding performance above and below 70% had been determined. In the latter case, we used linear interpolation to estimate the ISI that would produce 70% performance for a subject. These procedures were used in order to assure high reliability of our measures of processing time. The high intercorrelation between repetitive measures of peripheral processing time, shown in Figure 6, demonstrate that these efforts were quite successful.

Figure 4 presents the results of the peripheral masking conditions. (The target energy levels used in this investigation are the same as those reported by Walsh et al [1978].) Figure 4 shows that older adults require longer processing times, as indexed by ISI, to avoid masking that results from interference in the peripheral processing system than do younger adults. Furthermore, the relationship between ISI and target energy is described by similar power functions for the young and middle-aged subjects. The major difference between these results and those of other investigations is the finding that the power function that relates ISI to target energy for the 70-year-old group is different from the power function that describes the data of young and middle-aged adults. The exponents of these func-

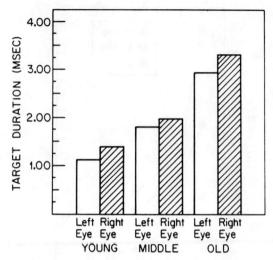

Fig. 5. Target energy thresholds of 19-, 47-, and 70-year-old adults. Luminance was held constant at 2.4 cd/m² and duration was varied (target energy = target duration × luminance).

tions were determined by transforming the power function $k = TE^b \times ISI_c$ to the logarithmic form of an equation for a straight line. A linear regression analysis was performed on the (log TE, log ISI_c) pairs to find the line of best fit. The slope of the regression line provides the best estimate of the exponent in the power function [cf Walsh et al, 1978]. These exponents were -0.46, -0.46, and -0.59 for the young, middle-aged, and old subjects, respectively ($F(2,64)$ = 6.5, $p < 0.01$). Since the subject groups tested in earlier investigations were not as old as the one studied in this investigation, these results suggest that the rate of change in peripheral processing speed as a function of changes in target energy may be different in age groups beyond 65 years.

As in our other investigations, we collected measures of the target energy required to see target stimuli on unmasked trials. Figure 5 shows that the three age groups required different amounts of light energy to achieve equivalent levels of unmasked target recognition. This result allowed us to examine the amount of variance in peripheral processing speed that can be predicted from differences in energy thresholds. This relationship is of interest since Turvey's [1973] work demonstrates that the ISI required to escape peripheral masking decreases as target energy increases. Thus individual differences in the proportion of light entering the eye might play a substantial role in determining the ISI required to escape peripheral masking effects. With less light entering the eye, the longer should be the ISI required to escape masking. While the general form of the

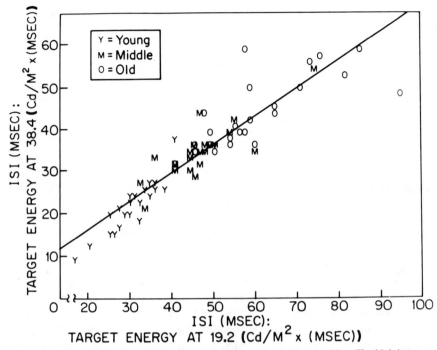

Fig. 6. Scatter plot of subjects' ISI$_c$s in two conditions of peripheral masking. The high intercorrelation reflects the high degree of reliability of the measurement procedures used in this investigation. Subjects in the young (Y), middle-aged (M), and old (O) samples are distinguished in the plot.

relationship between target energy and ISI$_c$ is exponential, a comparison of the fit of exponential and linear models to the relationship between subjects' unmasked energy thresholds and their ISI$_c$ to escape peripheral masking showed that a better fit was obtained with a linear equation. (These comparisons were made by contrasting the correlation between the log of these measures with the correlation between the untransformed values.)

Therefore, the question of the relationship between target energy threshold and peripheral processing speed was examined using linear correlation. Before discussing these correlations it is important to note that the reliability of our measures of peripheral processing speed and unmasked threshold was quite high. The average intercorrelations of the ISI$_c$s determined for subjects in the 9.6, 19.2, and 38.4 (cd/m^2 × msec) energy levels were 0.83, (range from 0.77 to 0.92), while the intercorrelation of unmasked thresholds for the two eyes was 0.74. Figure 6 presents a scatter plot of the 0.92 correlation between the ISI$_c$s required to escape peripheral masking at the 38.4 and 19.2 (cd/m^2 × msec)

TABLE I. The Correlation of Target Energy Threshold With the ISI_c Required to Escape Peripheral Masking at Three Target Energies

Target Energy[a]	Age Group			
	Young	Middle-Aged	Old	All Ages
9.6	0.21	0.37	0.40	0.63
19.2	0.25	0.38	0.67	0.76
38.4	0.25	0.30	0.69	0.73

[a]Target energies are in $(cd/m^2 \times msec)$ units.

energy levels. The intercorrelations between the unmasked energy thresholds and the ISIs to escape peripheral masking effects were examined for each of the three target energies and these correlations were computed across all 72 subjects and for each age group separately. In general, the correlations between unmasked energy threshold and the 9.6 energy level were the lowest, with the strength of the relationship for the 19.2 and 38.4 levels being about equal. Table I presents these correlations for each age group and all subjects considered together. Overall, 50% of the variance in peripheral processing speed could be accounted for by differences in unmasked target thresholds. However, the strength of this relationship was less in each age group considered separately: Only 6%, 12%, and 36% of the variance in peripheral processing speed could be accounted for by the unmasked energy thresholds for young, middle-aged, and old subjects, respectively.

Although these results show that a considerable amount of the variance in processing speed is predicted by differences in target energy threshold, there is still 50% of the variance in peripheral processing speed that cannot be predicted from target thresholds. The unexplained variance suggests that some of the differences in ISI_c probably result from age-related differences in the rate of peripheral net operations. Further support for this conclusion is provided by an analysis of covariance on the ISI_cs required to escape peripheral masking using subjects' unmasked thresholds as the covariate. This analysis showed the effect of age to be highly reliable even after peripheral masking values were adjusted for differences in unmasked energy thresholds ($F(2,62) = 14.4, p < 0.001$).

CENTRAL PERCEPTUAL PROCESSES

Investigations of age differences in central perceptual processes have shown that groups of adults between the ages of 60 and 70 years require longer processing times than adults between the ages of 18 and 25 years to complete central stages of visual information-processing. This conclusion is based on the results of three investigations that used visual masking paradigms that meet the criteria

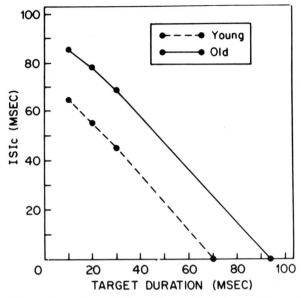

Fig. 7. Critical interstimulus interval (ISI$_c$) and target duration required to escape masking for 20- and 64-year-old adults. The linear functions fit the central rule reported by Turvey: TD + ISI = K, a constant. [From Walsh, 1976.]

Turvey proposed to define masking that results from interference in central perceptual processes. These criteria, reviewed in detail above, include dichoptic presentation of target and mask, target energies greater than mask energies, similar features composing the target and masking stimuli, and data functions that show an additive relationship between target duration and ISI$_c$ (TD + ISI$_c$ = K, a constant).

Walsh [1976] investigated the differences between young adults (18 to 23 years) and old adults (60 to 68 years) in the ISI$_c$ required to escape masking due to interference in central perceptual processes. Subjects viewed letters as targets and a random arrangement of line segments (pattern mask) as the masking stimulus. Subjects were tested with target durations of 10, 20, and 30 msec using a mask duration of 10 msec in all cases. Furthermore, the target and masking stimuli were presented dichoptically, and in a fourth condition, ISI was held at 0 msec while the target duration required to escape masking was determined. The results of this investigation, shown in Figure 7, revealed that the older subjects required 24% longer processing times than the young subjects to escape the effects of masking due to central influences. In addition, the linear functions

TABLE II. Means and Standard Deviations of ISI Across and Within Days of Testing (in msec)

Days		ISI$_1$		ISI$_2$	
		Young	Old	Young	Old
1	Mean	65.00	93.25	59.67	78.00
	SD	10.42	33.05	7.62	21.06
2	Mean	54.67	90.25	47.42	77.75
	SD	8.57	23.46	9.44	26.85
3	Mean	45.58	73.92	38.25	68.33
	SD	8.47	21.45	14.26	18.51
4	Mean	41.50	79.75	36.25	63.25
	SD	10.54	39.88	14.28	16.38
5	Mean	36.50	66.33	37.83	60.08
	SD	10.97	21.53	7.80	20.24

of Figure 7 fit the additive rule reported by Turvey [1973] to describe central masking phenomena (TD + ISI$_c$ = K).

Further support for the finding of age differences in the speed of central perceptual processes is provided by an investigation designed to examine the stability of processing speed differences across 5 days of practice [Hertzog et al, 1976]. Twelve young subjects with an average age of 19 years and 12 old subjects with an average age of 66 years participated in a central masking paradigm identical to that used in the Walsh [1976] investigation. During each of 5 consecutive days, an ISI$_c$ was determined at the beginning and end of a 1-hour experimental session. Separating the two ISI$_c$ determinations were 60 practice trials at which target and mask stimuli were presented at ISIs close to the initial measure. One-third of the practice trials were presented at the initial ISI$_c$ determination, another third at 5 msec above that value, and the remainder at 5 msec below ISI$_c$. The results of this investigation, shown in Table II, demonstrate that the absolute age difference in the processing times required to escape the effects of central masking remained stable at about 30 msec across the 5 days of practice. While both groups showed a substantial reduction in the ISI$_c$ required to escape masking, the rate of decline was best fit by linear functions that did not interact with age. The Hertzog et al investigation is also interesting in that it provides a close replication of the absolute estimates of central processing speed reported by Walsh [1976]. Walsh found average ISIs of 64 msec and 87 msec for 20- and 64-year-old adults, respectively, whereas the Hertzog et al investigation found prepractice ISIs of 65 msec and 93 msec for groups of adults

19 and 66 years of age. Thus, the Hertzog et al investigation provides some strong support for the idea that age differences in central perceptual processing speed are stable and highly replicable.

Finally, an investigation by Walsh, Williams, and Hertzog [1979] examined age differences in two subcomponents of central perceptual processes suggested by the information-processing model depicted in Figure 2. The first stage involves the operation of central decision nets involved in constructing context-dependent features of the "to-be-recognized" displays. The second stage is pattern recognition [cf Michaels and Turvey, 1979]. Interference in Stage I is believed to occur when output from peripheral nets related to both target and mask is combined into a confused set of context-dependent features on which Stage II pattern recognition processes must operate. Under these conditions, only chance identification of the targets should be expected. However, when Stage I processes separate target and mask features into successive stimuli, then interference in Stage II processes can be observed. Stage II interference is believed to result from the replacement of target features in iconic memory by mask features before pattern recognition of the target is complete. This analysis of the operation of Stage I and II processes suggests a method for examining age differences in each separately: The shortest ISI at which target identification increases above chance can be used as a measure of the time required to complete Stage I processes. The slope of the function relating target detection to ISI from chance to asymptote can be used to measure the rate of Stage II processing.

The Walsh et al [1979] investigation examined the accuracy of subjects' target identifications as a function of the SOA between target and mask onset. Two important results of that investigation can be seen in Figure 8: (1) The performance of the young subjects rises above chance at shorter SOAs than those of the old, and (2) the slope of the function relating improvement in accuracy to SOA is greater in the young than in the old sample. The statistical analysis of these results reported in the Walsh et al [1979] investigation confirms the observations pointed out in Figure 8. Furthermore, an analysis of the relative age differences showed that the older subjects required 38% longer processing times than the young to complete Stage I processes and 36% longer processing times to complete Stage II processes. It is interesting to note that the magnitude of the age difference observed in the Walsh et al investigation, about 37%, is larger than that reported earlier with comparably aged samples. The Walsh [1976] and Hertzog et al [1976] investigations reported age differences of 24% in the processing times required to complete central perceptual processes. One difference in the procedures of these investigations was an attempt in the Walsh et al [1979] investigation to control for criterion differences by using a forced-choice response procedure. The larger age differences found in that investigation seem to suggest that the young use more conservative criteria than the old, which may serve to increase our measures of young subjects' processing time, unless they are forced to respond on each trial.

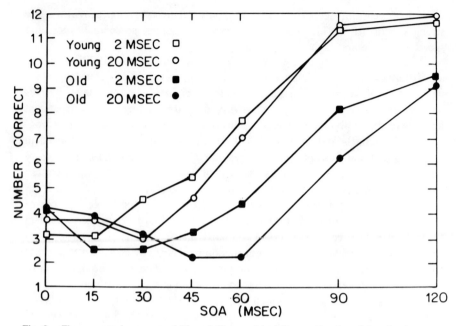

Fig. 8. The perceptual accuracy of 20- and 68-year-old adults as a function of the stimulus onset asynchrony (SOA) between target and mask. Chance responding would result in three letters being reported correctly. [From Walsh et al, 1979.]

Recent research in the author's laboratory has further examined the relationship between age and the speed of central perceptual processing. The investigations by Walsh [1976], Hertzog et al [1976], and Walsh et al [1979] have focused only on the differences between 20-year-old and 65-year-old age groups. While the results of those investigations demonstrate that older adults require longer processing times to complete central processes, they provide little information about the life-span development of this slowing. Our recent work was designed to explore the differences in processing speed among young, middle-aged, and old adults. Dichoptic masking paradigms similar to those described above were used but more careful measures of processing speed were collected; we used ascending limits procedures in combination with perceptual accuracy measures to map out carefully the ISI required for 70% performance. The result of this investigation, shown in Figure 9, is that a 46-year-old age group required processing times intermediate to those of 19-year-old and 70-year-old age groups. This result suggests that the slower processing speeds of older adults may have a gradual onset beginning in young adulthood.

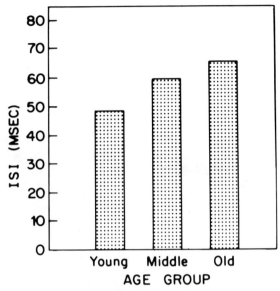

Fig. 9. The ISI_c required to escape central masking effects for three groups of 24 adults whose average ages were 19, 47, and 70 years. The processing times were measured using a dichoptic backward masking paradigm.

Other analyses of the data reported in Figure 9 correlated these measures of central processing speed with measures of peripheral processing speed collected on this same sample of subjects. These analyses were carried out in order to examine the possibility that a general slowing with age in the rate of information-processing might explain the age differences in average processing times observed for peripheral and central masking paradigms [cf Birren et al, 1962].

The model of information-processing presented in Figure 2 assumes a concurrent but contingent relationship between peripheral and central perceptual processes in the fashion proposed by Turvey [1973]. Thus, it would not be surprising to find little relationship between the speed of peripheral and central processes in young populations: As long as target energy is relatively high, as was the case in our central masking paradigms, we should expect peripheral processes to be completed before contingent central processes are ready to operate on the output from peripheral networks. The intercorrelation of our measures of peripheral and central processes support this idea: Less than 1% of the variance in the central processing speed of our young sample could be accounted for by the speed of peripheral processes. However, we did find that larger amounts of the variance in central processing speed could be explained by peripheral pro-

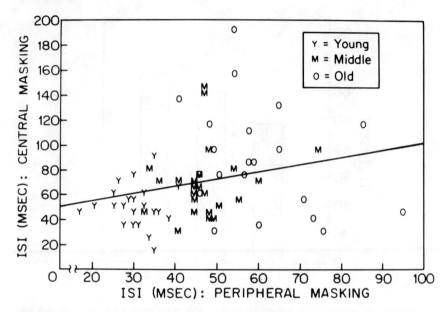

Fig. 10.   Scatter plot of subjects' ISI$_c$s required to escape peripheral and central masking effects. Subjects in the young (Y), middle-aged (M), and old (O) samples are distinguished in the plot. Estimates of peripheral processing time were collected with target energies of 19.2 (cd/m^2 × msec).

cessing speed in our middle-aged and old samples (17% and 18% of the variance, respectively). However, this outcome does not provide much support for the hypothesis that a general speed factor underlies the processing time differences between young and old adults. While it was the case that the correlations between central and peripheral processing speed were positive for the middle-aged sample, the correlations were negative in the old sample. Middle-aged adults with slower central processing speed also tended to have slower peripheral processing speed, but just the opposite relationship was found in the old population. The slope of the regression equation for the old subjects showed that each 10-msec increase in peripheral processing speed was associated with a 1.3-msec decrease in central processing speed.

The correlation between peripheral and central processing speeds computed across all ages does not provide any support for the idea that general slowing with age underlies the longer processing times required by groups of old adults to complete these stages of information-processing. Only 8% of the variance in central processing speed could be predicted from subjects' performance in peripheral processing speed. Of the three correlations that bear on this question, only one was found to be statistically reliable even though the correlations are based on 72 subjects. Figure 10 shows the scatter plot of subjects' ISL_cs required to escape peripheral and central masking effects. As can be seen in Figure 10, a substantial portion of the middle-aged and old adults evidence disproportionate slowing in one of the two stages of visual information-processing being correlated.

An examination of the interrelationship of peripheral and central processing speeds provides little support for the idea that a general mechanism operates to explain the often-replicated finding that groups of older adults are slower than groups of young adults in both peripheral and central perceptual processes. However, it is not unreasonable to suggest that a general mechanism might operate to slow the performance of older adults at a number of separate stages of central perceptual processing. The investigation by Walsh et al [1979] examined the processing time required to complete Stage I and Stage II of central perceptual processes. The results of that investigation, reviewed above, showed that groups of older adults were about 37% slower than groups of young adults in completing both stages of central processes. In the pages that follow, we will focus on age differences in the speed of completing selective attention and pattern-recognition stages of central processing as conceptualized by the model of visual information-processing shown in Figure 2. A primary aim of this discussion will be to determine if older adults show a higher degree of intercorrelation than young adults in the speed with which some separate stages of central processes are completed.

SELECTIVE ATTENTION AND PATTERN RECOGNITION

The research of Sperling [1960] and Averbach and Coriell [1961] provided much of the impetus for visual information-processing research over the last two decades. While the results of these investigations focused on characteristics of iconic memory, they also demonstrated the ability of human observers to redirect their attention and identify alphabet characters with surprising speed. These impressive attentional and pattern-recognition abilities can best be understood by considering the diagrammatic representation of the partial report procedure shown in Figure 11. Subjects in the Averbach and Coriell [1961] experiments were presented with arrays of 16 letters arranged in two parallel rows of 8 items. The letter arrays were displayed for 50-msec intervals and followed at variable intervals by a marker placed over or under the position previously occupied by one of the 16 letters. Subjects in their experiment were able (1) to locate the marker, (2) to focus their attention on the designated location, and (3) to recognize which consonant of the alphabet was located in that position in about 200 msec.

Our investigations of age differences in selective attention and pattern recognition have been heavily influenced by the conceptual analysis of the cognitive demands of the partial report task proposed by Neisser [1967]. He suggested

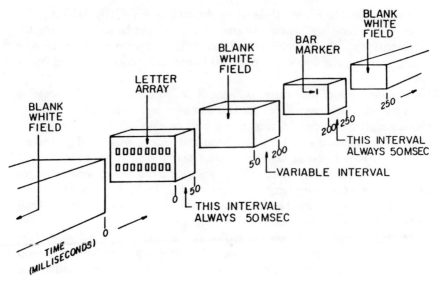

Fig. 11. A diagrammatic representation of the partial report procedure used by Averbach and Coriell [1961]. A subject's task was to report only the one letter indicated by the bar marker.

that the partial report task involves stages of selective and focal attention followed by pattern recognition. An investigation in our laboratory attempted to use a partial report task to examine age differences in iconic memory. The results of that investigation suggested that aging might be associated with some major slowing in selective attention and pattern-recognition processes. The surprising finding was that adults over 60 years of age were unable to perform a partial report task in which the marker appeared at the same time as the letter arrays. The difficulty of the old subjects was in sharp contrast to the performance of the young subjects who showed perfect perceptual performance under the identical conditions. Subsequent investigations [cf Kline and Baffa, 1976; Kline and Orme-Rogers, 1978; Walsh and Thompson, 1978] have shown that the difficulty of the older adults was unlikely to result from any substantial age-related decline in iconic memory duration.

Two approaches have been taken in our laboratory to examine the role of age differences in selective attention and the rate of pattern recognition as explanations for the poor performance of old adults in our investigations using partial report tasks. Both approaches have been careful to reduce the complexity of the visual displays so that acceptable levels of performance for adults of all ages could be obtained. The first approach has examined the amount of processing time required by different age groups to identify displays composed of one, two,

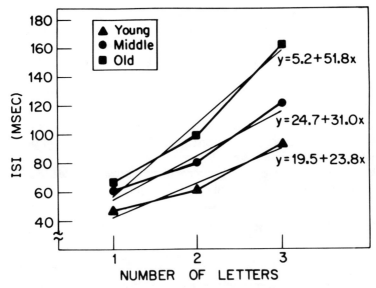

Fig. 12. The interstimulus intervals required by three groups of 25 adults, whose average ages were 19, 47, and 70 years, to identify one-, two-, and three-letter displays. The slopes of the linear functions represent the number of milliseconds required to identify a second and third letter. Processing times were measured using a dichoptic backward masking paradigm.

or three letters. The basic logic behind the selection of these conditions assumes that the readout of letters from these displays is a serial process requiring successive stages of selective attention and pattern recognition. The basic paradigm for this investigation was the central masking paradigm described above. Displays of one, two, or three letters were presented dichoptically with a pattern masked composed of straight-line segments similar in width to the contours of the target letters. Target and mask energies were relatively high (74 cd/m^2) and the stimuli were photographic positives consisting of black figures on a white background. Figure 12, which presents the results of this investigation, shows that the processing times of young, middle-aged, and old adults increased as a linear function of the number of letters in the display. In general, the relationship between the number of items in a display and the ISI$_c$ required to escape masking was linear. For the middle-aged and old subjects, the average linear correlation between these two variables was 0.95. However, the relationship between ISI$_c$ and the number of items in a display departed significantly from linearity for 6 of the young subjects. These 6 subjects were excluded from the analyses reported below. For the remaining 18 young subjects, the average linear correlation between ISI$_c$ and the number of items in a display was 0.93—a value that did not differ from the goodness of linear fit found for the other age groups, $F(2,63)$ = .61. The linear functions that have been fit to the masking results of Figure 12 show that the recognition of each additional letter required 23.8, 31.0, and 51.8 msec for the young, middle-aged, and old subjects, respectively. An examination of the 95% level confidence interval on the slope for each age group showed that both the young and middle-aged samples differed from the old sample but not from one another.

The question of a general speed factor underlying age differences in central processes was again examined by inspecting the intercorrelations of our visual information processing measures. The results of these correlational analyses provide no support for the idea that a common mechanism underlies the age differences between groups of young and old adults in the speed of separate stages of central processes. Specifically, we examined the intercorrelation of subjects' ISIs to escape central masking effects when one letter was the target with the slope of the function that describes the increase in ISI required to identify one, two, and three letters. The slope variable is believed to reflect the amount of time required by subjects to shift their attention and recognize an additional item in the multielement displays. The intercorrelations of the slope values with the ISIs for single letter identifications were −0.16, 0.04, and −0.12 for the young, middle-aged, and old adults, respectively. These correlations show that more variance in the slope values could be predicted by variance in central processing times for the young than for the old subjects. Furthermore, the direction of the relationships found for the young and old groups is opposite to that which would be expected if a single mechanism accounted for the slowing in both tasks. In other words, these results suggest that subjects who completed central processes most quickly were slower in switching their attention and recognizing alphabet characters. Furthermore, an inspection of the intertask correlations computed across all subjects did not provide support for the hypothesis of a general slowing mechanism. The overall correlation of central processing speed with the readout rate functions was not statistically reliable and only 1% of the variance in speed of one process could be predicted by speed of the other (r = 0.10, df = 71). Figure 13 shows the scatter plot of the ISI_cs subjects required to escape Stage I central processes with the rate of Stage II processes involving selective attention and pattern recognition. As Figure 13 shows, there is little association between the processing rates measured at these two stages of central processing for any age group.

A second approach to investigating age differences in the processing time required for selective attention and pattern-recognition processes has focused on an analysis of some of the component processes we believe are required by the partial report task. Reference to Figure 11 will help to clarify this analysis. The first requirement of the partial report task involves the location of a visual marker. A second component involves the "readout" or pattern recognition of the alphabet

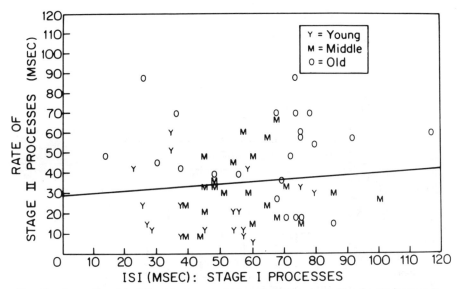

Fig. 13. Scatter plot of the ISI$_c$ subjects required to escape masking due to Stage I central processes with the rate (slope) at which Stage II processes involving selective attention and pattern recognition were completed. Subjects from the young (Y), middle-aged (M), and old (O) samples are distinguished in the plot.

character indicated by the marker. Neisser [1967] has suggested that a stage of cognition intermediate to the location of the marker and recognition of the character involves the focusing of attention on the indicated position before pattern recognition processes can begin. Three variations of a central masking paradigm that differed in the nature of the target field were used to examine age differences in these processing components. The first target field duplicated the conditions of central masking described above with the modification that target letters with small visual angles were used. (These letters could be easily identified by anyone with 20/100 vision or better.) A fixation field appeared 1.5 sec before each masking trial, clearly indicating the spatial location (center of the viewing field) where the "to-be-identified" target would appear. Thus, the ISI values required to avoid central masking effects can be thought of as the time required to recognize alphabet characters unconfounded by visual search and focal attention-processing times. The second set of target fields were designed to assess visual search time alone. Subjects were presented with rectangular viewing fields that contained a "T" in one of four possible positions (corners of the viewing field about 1.5° from fixation in each direction). The target field was preceded by a 1.5-sec fixation field and followed by a field containing four pattern masks

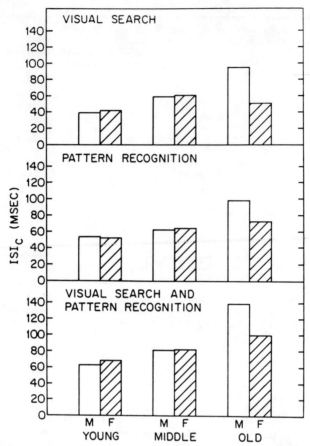

Fig. 14. Processing times (ISI$_c$) required to complete a visual-search, pattern-recognition, and combined visual-search and pattern-recognition task. Three groups of 24 adults whose average ages were 19, 47, and 70 years served as subjects. Processing times were measured using a dichoptic backward masking paradigm.

that overlapped each of the four areas where a "T" could appear. The third viewing field was designed to assess the processing time required to complete visual search, focal attention, and pattern-recognition processes in combination. Subjects viewed the same fixation and masking fields as in the second condition, but the target field was modified so that one of four letters could appear in any of the four locations previously occupied by a "T". Thus the third condition assessed the time required by subjects to locate *and* identify the target character.

The results from these conditions are shown in Figure 14. In general, subjects required longer processing times to complete pattern-recognition processes than

TABLE III. The Correlation of Visual-Search (VS), Pattern-Recognition (PR), and Combined Visual-Search and Pattern-Recognition (VS and PR) Task for Young, Middle-Aged, and Old Adults

Age Group	VS/PR	Intercorrelated Conditions VS/VS and PR	PR/VS and PR
Young	0.44	0.52	0.50
Middle-Aged	0.54	0.63	0.83
Old	0.58	0.18	0.55
All Ages	0.62	0.50	0.72

visual-search processes. The time required to complete the combined visual-search and pattern-recognition task was greater, for each age group of subjects, than either of the times required to complete the tasks separately. The pattern of age group differences is also clear in Figure 14. The old age group required longer processing times than the middle-aged and young subjects to achieve equivalent levels of perceptual performance. While this general finding holds for both the males and females tested, Figure 14 shows that the older males were substantially slower than the older females in each of the three task conditions. Although there is some tendency for the older subjects to show a disproportionate increase in the time to complete the combined visual search and pattern recognition task relative to these tasks separately, neither the age × task nor the age × sex × task interactions was statistically significant.

The intercorrelation of subjects' performances on these three processing tasks was examined to see if any support could be found for the idea that a common mechanism might explain the longer processing times required by the older adults in each of the conditions shown in Figure 14. The intercorrelations of subjects' performances on the visual-search, pattern-recognition, and combined visual-search and pattern-recognition task are shown in Table III. The intercorrelations are reasonably large but the intercorrelations within the old group were not larger than those within the young and middle-aged groups. As can be seen in Table III, the correlations between these tasks ranged from about 0.50 to 0.60, with two strong exceptions. The low correlation of visual search with the combined visual-search and pattern-recognition task within the old sample suggests that the visual-search component of this task changes substantially for the older adults when pattern-identification processes are required. The other exception was the high correlation (0.83) of the pattern-recognition task with the combined visual-search and pattern-recognition task within the middle-aged group. The strength of this relationship is consistent with the strong relationship found between these two tasks when the correlations were computed on all subjects. This outcome suggests that the pattern-recognition component is the most salient aspect of the combined visual-search and pattern-recognition task.

Table III also presents the intercorrelations between the three task conditions of Figure 14 computed across all subjects. While these correlations are large and reliable, they do not differ significantly from those computed within each separate age group. This pattern of correlations shows that a considerable relationship exists between the processing times required by all subjects to complete these three experimental tasks. However, aging does not appear to be associated with the increase in correlations among these tasks that would be expected if a single mechanism, such as slowing of central nervous system operation, were responsible for the age differences seen in group averages on each of these three tasks.

DEVELOPMENTAL IMPLICATIONS

This paper has reviewed the results of a number of investigations demonstrating that groups of older adults are slower than groups of young adults in many separate stages of visual information-processing. This generalization seems to hold for peripheral processes responsible for the transmission of visual information to the brain, and central processes involved in (1) the construction of higher level visual features, (2) visual search, and (3) pattern recognition. These findings provide some important descriptions of differences in the speed of visual information processes of adults across the life span, but they do not, by themselves, provide support for a single explanation of these widespread age differences. Although the results of separate investigations might be interpreted as evidence for a general slowing with age, the results of the research reported here provides little support for this hypothesis.

Two sources of evidence have been presented that argue against a general slowing explanation of the average age differences seen in many visual information processing tasks. First, the correlations between separate stages of visual information processing computed across subjects of all ages have not been larger than the correlations found within the separate age groups. Furthermore, the regression of processing speed at one stage on the speed of processing at another stage has not accounted for sizable amounts of the variance in processing speed. For example, the results reported above showed that only 8% of the variance in central processing speed could be predicted from peripheral processing speed and that less than 1% of the variance in central processing speed measured with single letter displays could be predicted by the rate of identifying successive items in multielement displays. Figures 10 and 13 present scatter plots for the intercorrelations of these sets of variables. An inspection of the scatter plots of all subjects' performances in these stages of information-processing provides further evidence against a general slowing hypothesis. The plots in Figures 10 and 13 show that only about half of the older adults are proportionately slow in separate stages of processing; the other subjects show disproportionate slowing in one of the two stages being correlated. The performance of this latter group of older adults is incompatible with the general slowing hypothesis. However, the results for the former group are not incompatible with some selective slowing explanations. For example, if the processing speed of different stages is affected by different experiences, such as disease or dietary factors, then we should expect to see slowing in those stages in which an individual has been exposed to the causal experience. Individuals who have experienced more of the causal factors would be expected to show slowing in more stages of processing. Conversely, individuals who have been exposed to a limited set of slowing factors would be expected to demonstrate slowing in only a few processing stages.

There are some exceptions to the conclusions stated above. For example, measures of the processing times required to complete a visual-search task and a pattern-recognition task were found to be highly correlated. However, the central masking procedures used in measuring both processing stages were quite similar and the total time required to perform each task probably includes a large and common component of context feature construction. The correlation of these measures within the three separate age groups was similar in magnitude to the correlation computed across all ages. This result provides some support for the suggestion that the high correlation found between the visual-search and pattern-recognition processing times probably results from the large amount of feature-construction time associated with each measure rather than from a general slowing in both visual-search and pattern-recognition processes.

In conclusion, the research reviewed in this paper demonstrates that groups of older adults are slower than groups of young adults in all stages of visual information-processing. However, research examining the correlation of adults' performance between separate stages of information-processing provides little support for the hypothesis that these widespread age differences are the result of a single causal factor. In contrast, the correlational analyses and their associated scatter plots show that a large proportion of the older subjects showed disproportionate slowing in separate stages of visual information-processing. These findings have been interpreted as possible support for a hypothesis of selective slowing in which experiences such as disease or nutritional factors may play a major causal role.

REFERENCES

Averbach E, Coriell AS (1961) Short-term memory in vision. Bell Syst Tech J 40:309–328.

Birren JE (1965) Age changes in speed of behavior: Its central nature and physiological correlates. In Welford AT, Birren JE (Eds) "Behavior, Aging, and the Nervous System." Springfield, Ill.: Charles C Thomas.

Birren JE, Riegle KF, Morrison DF (1962) Age differences in response speed as a function of controlled variation of stimulus conditions: Evidence of a general speed factor. Gerontologia 6:1–18.

Hertzog CK, Williams MV, Walsh DA (1976) The effect of practice on age differences in central perceptual processing. J Gerontol 31:428–433.

Kline DW, Szafran J (1975) Age differences in backward monoptic visual noise masking. J Gerontol 30:307–311.

Kline DW, Baffa G (1976) Differences in the sequential integration of form as a function of age and interstimulus interval. Exp Aging Res 2:333–343.

Kline DW, Orme-Rogers C (1978) Examination of stimulus persistence as the basis for superior visual identification performance among older adults. J Gerontol 33:76–81.

Michaels CF, Turvey MT (1979) Central sources of visual masking: Indexing structures supporting seeing at a single, brief glance. Psych Res 41:1–61.

Neisser U (1967) "Cognitive Psychology." New York: Appleton-Century Crofts.

Sperling G (1960) The information available in brief visual presentations. Psych Mon Gen Appl 74:1–28.

Thomas JP (1970) Model of the function of receptive fields in human vision. Psych Rev 77:121–134.

Till RE (1978) Age-related differences in binocular backward masking with visual noise. J Gerontol 33:702–710.

Turvey MT (1973) On peripheral and central processes in vision: Inferences from an information-processing analysis of masking with patterned stimuli. Psych Rev 80:1–52.

Walsh DA (1976) Age differences in central perceptual processing: A dichoptic backward masking investigation. J Gerontol 31:178–185.

Walsh DA, Thompson LW (1978) Age differences in visual sensory memory. J Gerontol 33:383–387.

Walsh DA, Till RE, Williams MV (1978) Age differences in peripheral perceptual processing: A monoptic backward masking investigation. J Exp Psych: [Hum Percept Perform] 4:232–243.

Walsh DA, Williams MV, Hertzog CK (1979) Age-related differences in two stages of central perceptual processes: The effects of short duration targets and criterion differences. J Gerontol 34:234–241.

Walsh DA, Krauss IK, Regnier VA (1981) Spatial ability, environmental knowledge and environmental use: The elderly. In Liben, L., Patterson, A., Newcombe, N. (Eds.), "Spatial Representation and Behavior Across the Life Span." New York: Academic Press.

Weale RA (1965) On the eye. In Welford A, Birren J. (Eds.), "Behavior, Aging and the Nervous System." Springfield, Ill.: Charles C Thomas.

Aging and Human Visual Function, pages 231–244

Visual Persistence and Temporal Resolution

Donald W. Kline and Frank J. Schieber

Of the various changes that occur with age, one of the best documented is a decline in speed of performance, a slowing seen both in the rate at which various processes are carried out and in the latency with which they are initiated. This deficit has been observed across a diverse array of experimental tasks and in different sensory modalities including vision. One aspect of this change is an apparent loss of temporal resolving power in the senescent visual system. Closely succeeding visual events that would be viewed as separate by young individuals are often seen as fused or indistinguishable by old ones. There is, for example, a well-documented decline with age in the critical flicker frequency (CFF) threshold [eg, Brozek and Keys, 1945; Coppinger, 1955; Falk and Kline, 1978; Huntington and Simonson, 1965; Misiak, 1947; Weale, 1965]. The CFF is the minimum frequency of a pulsating light source at which the light appears to be on constantly and indicates the visual system's limited ability to track temporally rapid changes in illumination. Most of the loss in temporal resolution reflected in the CFF appears attributable to neural components in the retina. A receptor is capable of following a stimulus flickering at a rate of several hundred times a second. However, at the level of primary visual cortex, depending upon the state of light adaptation, the pulses must be spaced between 10 and 100 msec apart [Haber and Hershenson, 1973].

Part of the decline with age in CFF can be attributed to changes in the optical media of the eye. With normal aging there is a yellowing and thickening of the crystalline lens as well as a significant reduction in resting pupillary diameter [Birren et al, 1950]. Weale [1961] has estimated that as a result of preretinal visual changes, the retina of the 60-year-old receives approximately one-third the light of its 20-year-old counterpart. Considering that lower luminance levels are generally associated with diminished temporal sensitivity, some decline in CFF would be expected. Perhaps half or more of the age difference in CFF may be associated with the reduction in retinal illumination. When Weekers and Roussel [1946] compared the CFFs of subjects of different ages with and without induced pupillary dilation, the mean age difference between the youngest (aged 20–30) and oldest groups (aged 61–70) was reduced from 8.6 to 4.4 Hz.

Retinal and/or central visual system changes also appear to be implicated in the age reduction in the CFF [Weale, 1965]. Semenovskaia and Verkhutina [cited in Weiss, 1959] bypassed the effects of light transmission on CFF by assessing age differences in the pulse rate of an electrical current that produced disappearance of phosphene flicker. They found that electrical phosphene critical flicker frequency was inversely related to age and paralleled the mean values reported by Weekers and Roussel [1946] for CFF with pupils dilated. McFarland, Warren, and Karis [1958] examined the interacting influences on CFF of age, illumination, and light-to-dark ratio. Eight age groups of male subjects (aged 13–89) were tested under two conditions of illumination (0.041 and 21.9 fc) and ten light/dark ratios. Generally, age differences in CFF were maximized by low percentages of light-on-time in the presentation cycle and were increased by higher ones. This light/dark ratio effect was similar under both illumination conditions for all groups and suggests that it cannot be accounted for by age differences in retinal illumination [Fozard et al, 1977].

Simonson, Anderson, and Keiper [1967] have also reported data that indicate a neural component in the age-related decrease in CFF. Movement of the stimulus across the foveal area of the retina significantly elevates the CFF in comparison with that obtained with a stationary stimulus. Presumably, this is due to the larger number of previously unexcited and thus nonrefractory retinal elements stimulated in the former case [Miller et al, 1965]. In accord with this view, comparison of age differences in CFF with a stationary and a moving target offered Simonson and his colleagues a means to assess indirectly age differences in the relative density of functional elements in the retina and visual pathways. Thresholds were determined for a young (19–24 years) and an old group (46–55) under three levels of stimulus movement (stationary, 2.16, and 4.32 degrees per second [deg/sec]). The corresponding average thresholds were 20.2, 27.0, and 39.4 Hz for the young subjects and 17.2, 21.0, and 29.2 Hz for the old. The slope of the regression line of CFF against stimulus movement was significantly steeper for the younger group (4.45 Hz per deg/sec) than the older one (2.76 Hz per deg/sec). That is, increases in the rate of stimulus movement led to greater increments in CFF in young subjects than in older ones. This finding was consistent with the authors' hypothesis that the number of excitable (nonrefractory) neural elements in the visual pathways decreased with age.

THE STIMULUS-PERSISTENCE HYPOTHESIS

One suggestion offered to account for the relative failure with age in the temporal resolution of discrete stimuli is the stimulus-persistence hypothesis put forward by Axelrod [1963] and more recently extended by Botwinick [1973, 1978]. In this view, the older nervous system is slower to recover from the effects of short-term stimulation and consequently, stimuli are more likely to "smear" or overlap when presented in close temporal contiguity. In addition to the findings from CFF studies, the data from a variety of tasks, visual and nonvisual, have been offered as post hoc support for this model [for a review see Botwinick, 1978]. For example, older subjects are more likely than young ones to report pairs of auditory clicks as a single click [Weiss, 1963] and to fuse successive presentations of mild electric shocks [Axelrod et al, 1968]. As discussed in detail in another chapter in this book, older adults also show prolonged susceptibility to the interactive effects of temporally contiguous stimulus presentations in backward visual masking tasks, apparently at both peripheral and central loci in the nervous system [Kline and Szafran, 1975; Kline and Birren, 1975; Walsh, 1976, Walsh et al, 1978]. Some physiological support for the stimulus-persistence hypothesis can also be derived from Mundy-Castle's [1953] study of age differences in EEG responses to photic stimulation. He observed that following cessation of stimulation, EEG afterdischarges "appeared far more often amongst the older group than the younger . . ." (p 21).

Eriksen, Hamlin, and Breitmeyer [1970] have presented evidence suggesting that the critical duration over which light energy is integrated does increase with age. The task of the subject was to identify the quadrant location of the gap in a Landolt-C. The size of the C yielding 75% correct forced-choice identification was individually adjusted for subjects ranging in age from 30 to 55 years. Stimuli were presented monocularly at a constant energy level (msec $\times$ ml = 13) with a 4-mm artificial pupil. (It should be noted that under the luminance conditions employed, a 4-mm artificial pupil might be somewhat too large to compensate fully for age differences in resting pupil size [Birren et al, 1950]). Compared with their performance in a preceding experiment where energy level varied with stimulus duration, the older subjects equaled the acuity performance of the younger subjects at the longer exposure durations. These results suggested that the older subjects were able to compensate for their elevated light threshold by integrating energy over a greater duration, increasing the effectiveness of the stimulus. Noting the suggestion by Kahneman, Norman, and Kubovy [1967] that time-intensity reciprocity in form perception indicates central factors, the authors speculated that their data might reflect an increase with age in the period of a central scanning process or psychological moment. Whether or not the lengthening of a hypothesized moment proves to be the best explanation, the observed age increase in integration period is consistent with the stimulus-persistence hypothesis.

STIMULUS PERSISTENCE: A PROSPECTIVE ANALYSIS

Although the data from studies specifically designed to evaluate the persistence hypothesis have provided considerable support for it, the support has not been unequivocal. Using a technique adopted from Eriksen and Collins [1967], Kline and Baffa [1976] gave young (mean age = 21.3 years) and old (mean age = 55.6 years) subjects word stimuli constructed so that they could be presented as corresponding word halves with an intervening interstimulus interval (ISI) of varied duration. The words were composed of black dots on a white background with approximately half the dots from each letter in a word half. It was hypothesized that an age-related increase in stimulus persistence would "bridge" the ISI between the word halves and lead to superior identification performance by the older subjects. Just the opposite was observed: The young subjects achieved higher word recognition scores at all levels of ISI. Further, this difference was not reduced by increases in the ISI. Although these data appeared to question the persistence model, the authors surmised that the older subjects

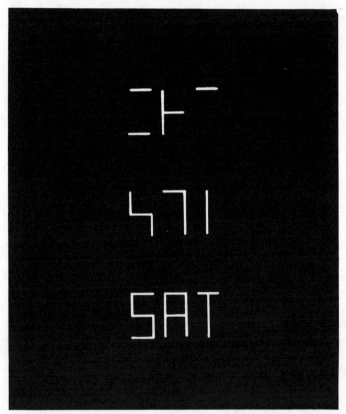

Fig. 1. Sample stimulus from Kline and Orme-Rogers [1978]. The two top patterns of straight lines, when superimposed temporally, result in the bottom stimulus from which the word *sat* can be read.

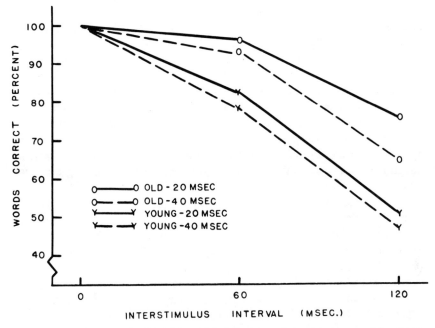

Fig. 2. Percentage of words correctly identified as a function of age and exposure duration from the Kline and Orme-Rogers [1978] sequential integration of form procedure.

may have been disadvantaged by their relative inability to achieve closure with incomplete stimuli [Basowitz and Korchin, 1957] or by greater contrast reduction from luminance summation across the illuminated backgrounds of the stimulus halves (which is itself a persistence effect).

Kline and Orme-Rogers [1978] repeated the Kline and Baffa study but eliminated the closure and luminance summation problems by constructing the stimulus halves of white straight segments on a black background (see Fig. 1). The twelve common words used as stimuli were divided into corresponding halves and presented at two durations (20 and 30 msec) with an ISI of 0, 60, or 120 msec. The old subjects identified significantly more of the words than did the young ones at both stimulus duration levels (see Fig. 2). Further, the superiority in performance of the old subjects increased as the ISI was lengthened. These results were not predictable from the general perceptual aging literature and hence were interpreted by the authors as providing strong support for the stimulus-persistence hypothesis.

Support for the stimulus-persistence idea has also been extended to the retinal level in a study of age differences in the durability of complementary afterimages.

Such afterimages are developed by fixating a colored primary stimulus for sufficient duration and then projecting the consequent afterimage onto an extended projection field (usually colorless). After a brief positive phase, the afterimage enters a longer stage in which it is close to the color complement of the primary stimulus. The duration of this stage represents the time course for physiological recovery of the retina. Kline and Nestor [1977] measured the duration of complementary afterimages in young (mean = 18.8 years) and old subjects (mean age = 62.0 years) as a function of primary stimulus exposure durations of 30, 60, and 90 sec. Consistent with the stimulus-persistence hypothesis, the older subjects showed greater afterimage persistence at all three exposure durations, although there was a reduction in the age difference with increasing exposure duration.

A study by Walsh and Thompson [1978], however, appeared to disprove the stimulus-persistence hypothesis using a "direct" measurement technique of Haber and Standing [1969]. In this procedure the subject reports the apparent continuity of a target circle when it is alternated cyclically with a blank interstimulus interval. The largest ISI at which the illusion of target continuity is maintained is used to estimate target persistence. Finding a lower ISI for their old subjects, the authors concluded that their data offered "clear disconfirmation of the stimulus-persistence hypothesis" at the "sensory memory stage" (p 386). Kline and Schieber [1980a] argued, however, that there are a number of potential shortcomings in the Haber and Standing technique, and also in Walsh and Thompson's implementation of the procedure, suggesting that this conclusion may have been premature. The switching of tachistoscopic fields required by the technique produces a luminance transient, a "flicker" in the stimulus which appears to contradict its apparent continuity. It may be more difficult for the older observer to ignore this flicker, and this in conjunction with their possibly greater cautiousness could have contributed to the low estimates obtained. Minimally, use of the technique appears to require a preliminary familiarization session to establish an appropriate judgment criterion. There is also the problem of the unestablished reliability of the Haber and Standing technique. Although the authors concluded that their data for young subjects were in line with those of Haber and Standing, when comparison is made across the most similar conditions, Walsh and Thompson's estimates are markedly lower: 289 vs 386 msec. The interpretation of their data is further complicated by a confounding of age and sex.

Kline and Schieber [1980a] considered these problems in a comparison of young and old subjects on the monoptic version of the Haber and Standing technique (target stimulus and blank ISI cycled in the same eye). Prior to the test trials, subjects received a practice session in which the circle target stimulus was presented so as to approximate progressively the test conditions. To obtain persistence measurements free of luminance summation effects, the test stimuli

TABLE I. The Persistence of a Monoptically Presented Target as a Function of Study, Age, and Contrast Condition on the Direct Measure Estimation Technique of Haber and Standing [1969] (msec)

	Young		Old	
	Mean	SD	Mean	SD
Kline and Schieber, 1980a (white on black)	183	58.7	262	55.7
Kline and Schieber, 1980a (black on white)	206	70.1	272	47.9
Walsh and Thompson, 1978	306	38.3	252	69.7
Haber and Standing, 1969	386	37	—	—

were presented in a white-on-black contrast format as well as a black-on-white one. In a marked reversal of Walsh and Thompson's findings, Kline and Schieber found that visual persistence was greater for the old subjects than for the young ones. The mean persistence estimates of the old subjects were 79 msec greater than those of the young subjects, whereas Walsh and Thompson observed an age difference of 54 msec in the opposite direction. The persistence estimates of the old subjects were quite similar in the two studies; the reversal of the age difference was based on the relative performances of the two young groups (see Table I). No evidence was found to indicate the visual persistence was reduced by luminance summation in either age group. In fact, for both age groups, the black-on-white stimulus was associated with somewhat greater persistence than was the reverse condition.

The Kline and Schieber results are consistent with those from other studies indicating the increased persistence of visual stimuli in the senescent nervous system and counter strongly Walsh and Thompson's apparent refutation of the stimulus-persistence hypothesis. The strength of support for the stimulus-persistence hypothesis is limited, however, by the inconsistency of results obtained using the Haber and Standing technique. As can be seen in Table I, the Haber and Standing, Walsh and Thompson, and Kline and Schieber studies all yielded markedly different persistence estimates for young subjects. It appears that in the Haber and Standing task, the observer employs a subjective judgment criterion that is established within the context of a single study and emphasizes different features of the stimulus display in assessing stimulus persistence.

AGE DIFFERENCES IN VISUAL PERSISTENCE: HOW MANY TYPES ARE THERE?

It has been suggested that some of the discrepancies in the visual persistence literature may result from different investigators basing their persistence measurements on qualitatively different features of the visual residual [Hawkins and

Shulman, 1979]. Dependent on the type of task, the instructions received by the subjects and even the variables manipulated by the experimenter, the subject may attend to different aspects of the sensory residual in judging its persistence. For example, some studies report that persistence is greater for stimuli of higher luminance [eg, Sakitt, 1976], while other studies report the reverse [eg, Haber and Standing, 1969]. Hawkins and Shulman [1979] have suggested that many of these problems can be resolved by differentiating between what they term Type I and Type II persistence. Type I persistence is based on the minimum interval over which a fading sensory residual yields a detectable decrement; Type II persistence represents the phenomenal duration of the stimulus (see Fig. 3). For example, they view the Haber and Standing technique as measuring Type I persistence, and Sakitt's click-indexing of visual aftereffect duration [eg, Sakitt, 1976] as a Type II measurement. Applied to aging, the lowering of CFF [Misiak, 1947] could be viewed as representing an increase in Type I persistence, and the superiority of old subjects in identifying sequentially presented word halves [Kline and Orme-Rogers, 1978] as indicating an increase in Type II persistence.

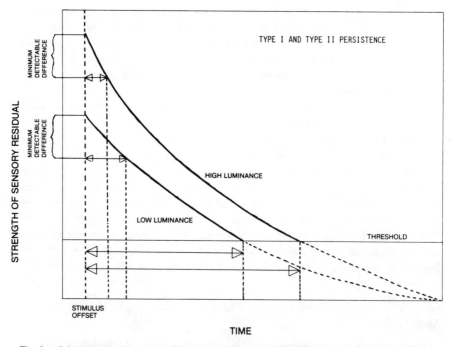

Fig. 3. Schematic representation of Hawkins and Shulman's [1979] Type I and Type II persistence. The effect of stimulus luminance on (1) the decay of the sensory residual following stimulus offset, (2) the measured duration of Type I persistence, and (3) the measured duration of Type II persistence.

It should be noted that Hawkins and Shulman consider the two forms of persistence ideal types and that in practice, persistence estimates will often reflect a mixture of both. This distinction may help to explicate the contradictory age findings of Kline and Schieber [1980a] and Walsh and Thompson [1978] in using the Haber and Standing measurement technique. The procedures and instructions employed in the two studies may have differentially emphasized Type I (eg, flicker) vs Type II (eg, stimulus continuity) features of the stimulus display, perhaps in interaction with age. In any case, it is important to recognize that there are various forms of persistence and that any discussion of age differences in visual persistence must take these different forms into account.

Long [1979], in response to Hawkins and Shulman [1979], has postulated that there are three rather than two forms of visual persistence. He suggests that Type I persistence is based on the latency of off-responses and that there are two forms of Type II persistence, one based on persistence in the cones (cone icon) and one based on persistence in the rods (rod icon). Further research will be needed to determine the extent to which age differences occur in these various types of persistence.

STIMULUS PERSISTENCE AND AGE: A POSSIBLE MECHANISM

In addition to persistence at the retinal level, recent demonstrations that visual persistence is a function of the spatial properties of stimuli suggest that mechanisms at more central neurological locations may also be implicated in the mediation of short-term visual storage. Meyer and his associates have reported that the persistence of temporally oscillating square-wave gratings was decreased by adaptation to gratings of the same color and orientation [Meyer, 1977; Meyer et al, 1975]. Relatedly, Meyer and Maguire [1977] found that the perceived duration of temporally oscillating gratings increased with increases in their spatial frequency (the number of cycles of grating per degree of visual angle) suggesting to them that the "icon is mediated by a neural mechanism that exhibits different temporal characteristics for different spatial frequencies . . ." (p 524). A possible mechanism for the explication of persistence at both peripheral and central levels may be provided by the sustained-transient channel distinction made in both the psychophysical and electrophysiological literature [Breitmeyer and Ganz, 1976; Legge, 1978]. Sustained channels show a long-latency protracted response and are activated primarily by patterned stimuli rather than by luminance fluctuations. They respond most strongly to stimuli of high spatial frequency [eg, Lupp et al, 1976]. In comparison, transient channels show immediate strong brief responses to stimulus onsets and offsets (ie, respond optimally to movement and flicker) and are stimulated most strongly by stimuli of low spatial frequency [eg, Breitmeyer and Ganz, 1976; Kulikowski and Tolhurst, 1973]. Ikeda and Wright [1974] have presented evidence that there are neurons in the visual cortex that can be classified as "sustained" or "transient" following the criteria used for retinal ganglion or lateral geniculate nucleus cells. Further, cortical cells classified as "sustained" or "transient" were different in their tuning to stimuli varied in spatial frequency.

A model has been proposed to account for the relationship between spatial frequency and visual persistence phenomena. In this view, the activity of the sustained channels is inhibited by the response of the transient channels to low spatial frequency stimuli [Breitmeyer, 1975; Singer and Bedworth, 1973]. Conversely, as stimuli of higher spatial frequency are presented, transient activity is reduced and sustained activity (persistence) disinhibited [Bowling et al, 1979; Breitmeyer and Ganz, 1976]. Certainly evidence is mounting that is consistent with this proposal. Bowling, Lovegrove, and Mapperson [1979] replicated the previously reported direct relationship between spatial frequency and visual persistence [Meyer and Maguire, 1977] and found no evidence to support an alternative contrast reduction explanation of the relationship. Further, there is evidence that the period over which luminance and duration are reciprocally related (Bloch's law) is increased by increases in spatial frequency [Breitmeyer and Ganz, 1977; Legge, 1978]. Relatedly, increasing the spatial frequency of stimuli appears to increase the period over which form stimuli can be integrated. Further, and consistent with the model, for low spatial frequency stimuli, the brief temporal summation period is followed by a pronounced inhibitory phase (ie, a transient-like response) [Watson and Nachmias, 1977]. Increasing the spatial frequency of the stimuli, however, yields summation functions consistent with a release of transient inhibition of the sustained channel response; the inhibitory phase is absent or greatly reduced [Bowling et al, 1979]. There is also evidence that the CFF threshold is lowered (ie, persistence increases) by increments in the spatial frequency of the stimulus [Kelly, 1972].

From this general model it is possible to derive a transient/sustained shift hypothesis that can explain a wide variety of age-related failures in the temporal resolution of visual stimuli. It may be that there is with increasing age a disjunctive decline in the functioning of the transient vs sustained visual channels. If indeed the persistence of stimuli in the sustained channels is inhibited by transient channel activity, then a decline in the effectiveness of these channels would produce an age increase in visual persistence and relatedly a loss in temporal resolving power of the senescent nervous system. Evidence of age differences on a variety of tasks is consistent with this hypothesis.

First, there is the evidence indicating a loss with age in the reactivity of the transient channels. For example, Kline and Schieber [1980b] had young and old subjects, matched on the Vocabulary Subtest of the WAIS, judge the order of offset two stimuli as a function of offset asynchrony. The detection scores of the old subjects were significantly lower at all but the longest offset asynchronies, where a ceiling was reached for both age groups (see Fig. 4). More directly to the point, Sekuler, Hutman and Owsley (1980) found that motion enhancement

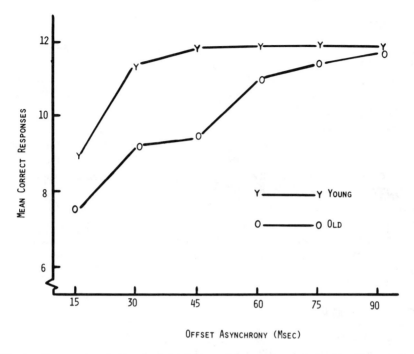

Fig. 4. Correct order-of-offset discriminations as a function of age and stimulus offset asynchrony for the Kline and Schieber [1980b] temporal resolution procedure.

of contrast sensitivity for a one-cycle-per-degree visual grating was much greater among young subjects than old ones.

Age differences in Type I and Type II persistence tasks [Hawkins and Shulman, 1979] are also consistent with the proposed age-related decline in functioning of the transient channels. Presumably, a loss in transient sensitivity would manifest itself in a direct increase in such Type I persistence measures as CFF. As already noted, this is indeed the case [eg, Misiak, 1947]. In addition, infirmity in the transient channels would "disinhibit" the sustained channels enhancing Type II persistence of the patterned stimuli to which they respond, and there is some evidence, albeit indirect, that this also occurs. Older persons appear to be better able to integrate form over long intervals [Eriksen et al, 1970; Kline and Orme-Rogers, 1978]. Further, in the Kline and Orme-Rogers study, subjects were compared on their ability to integrate stimuli presented in a black-on-white format, a contrast relationship that would presumably minimize transient stimulus activity. Consequently, the superior performance of the older persons that they observed is wholly consistent with the sustained-transient explanation of stimulus persistence being offered.

CONCLUSIONS

It is clear that there is a loss with age in the temporal resolving ability of the visual system. There is also mounting evidence that at least some of this loss can be attributed to an increase in the persistence of visual stimuli in the senescent nervous system. However, in its present form, the stimulus-persistence hypothesis has only modest value as a scientific heuristic; it is descriptive of certain differences but posits no mechanisms to explain them. Clearly, a model that specifies the mechanisms underlying the loss of the ability to discriminate contiguous visual events is needed. The "transient-sustained shift" hypothesis proposed here is one such alternative. However, the evidence offered in support of the hypothesis has been derived post hoc from the extant literature. An adequate evaluation of the utility of this or any hypothesis must occur in a test of the research hypotheses it generates. Whether or not this particular postulate can be substantiated, further research is needed to clarify the extent and causes(s) of the important loss with age in the temporal resolving power of the nervous system.

ACKNOWLEDGMENTS

Preparation of this paper was supported in part by a research grant from the National Institute on Aging (Grant No. AG01072).

REFERENCES

Axelrod S (1963) Cognitive tasks in several modalities. In Williams RH, Tibbits C, Donahue W (Eds) "Processes of Aging," Vol 1. New York: Atherton, pp 132–145.
Axelrod S, Thompson LW, Cohen LD (1968) Effects of senescence on the temporal resolution of somesthetic stimuli presented to one hand or both. J Gerontol 23:191–195.
Basowitz H, Korchin SJ (1957) Age differences in the perception of closure. J Abnorm Soc Psych 54:93–97.
Birren JE, Casperson RC, Botwinick J (1950) Age changes in pupil size. J Gerontol 5:216–221.
Botwinick J (1973) "Aging and Behavior." New York: Springer.
Botwinick J (1978) "Aging and Behavior," Second Ed. New York: Springer.
Bowling A, Lovegrove W, Mapperson B (1979) The effect of spatial-frequency and contrast on visual persistence. Perception 8:529–539.
Breitmeyer BG (1975) Predictions of U-shaped backward pattern masking from considerations of the spatio-temporal frequency response. Perception 4:297–304.
Breitmeyer BG, Ganz L (1976) Implications of sustained and transient channels for theories of visual pattern masking, saccadic suppression, and information processing. Psych Rev 83:1–36.
Breitmeyer BG, Ganz L (1977) Temporal studies with flashed gratings: Inferences about human transient and sustained channels. Vis Res 17:861–865.
Brozek J, Keys A (1945) Changes in flicker-fusion frequency with age. J Consult Psych 9:87–90.
Coppinger NW (1955) The relationship between critical flicker frequency and chronological age for varying levels of stimulus brightness. J Gerontol 10:48–52.

Eriksen CW, Collins JF (1967) Some temporal characteristics of visual pattern perception. J Exp Psych 74:476–484.

Eriksen CW, Hamlin RM, Breitmeyer BG (1970) Temporal factors in visual perception as related to aging. Percept Psychophys 7:354–356.

Falk J, Kline DW (1978) Stimulus persistence in CFF: Underactivation or overarousal? Exp Aging Res 4:109–123.

Fozard JL, Wolf E, Bell B, McFarland RA, Podolsky S (1977) Visual perception and communication. In Birren JE, Schaie KW, (Eds) "Handbook of the Psychology of Aging." New York: Van Nostrand, pp 497–534.

Haber RN, Hershenson M (1973) "The Psychology of Visual Perception." New York: Holt.

Haber RN, Standing LG (1969) Direct measures of short-term visual storage. Quart J Exp Psych 21:43–54.

Hawkins HL, Shulman GL (1979) Two definitions of persistence in visual perception. Percept Psychophys 25:348–350.

Huntington JM, Simonson E (1965) Critical flicker fusion frequency as a function of exposure time in two different age groups. J Gerontol 20:527–529.

Ikeda H, Wright MJ (1974) Evidence for "sustained" and "transient" neurons in the cat's visual cortex. Vis Res 14:133–136.

Kahneman D, Norman J, Kubovy M (1967) The critical duration for the resolution of form: Centrally or peripherally determined? J Exp Psych 73:323–327.

Kelly DH (1972) Adaptation effects on spatio-temporal sine wave thresholds. Vis Res 12:89–101.

Kline DW, Baffa G (1976) Differences in the sequential integration of form as a function of age and interstimulus interval. Exp Aging Res 2:333–343.

Kline DW, Birren JE (1975) Age differences in backward dichoptic masking. Exp Aging Res 1:17–25.

Kline DW, Nestor S (1977) Persistence of complementary afterimages as a function of age and stimulus duration. Exp Aging Res 3:191–201.

Kline DW, Orme-Rogers C (1978) Examination of stimulus persistence as a basis for superior visual identification performance among older adults. J Gerontol 33:76–81.

Kline DW, Schieber FJ (1980a) What are the age differences in visual sensory memory? J Gerontol 35:in press.

Kline DW, Schieber FJ (1980b) Age and the discrimination of visual successiveness. Exp Aging Res, in press.

Kline DW, Szafran J (1975) Age differences in backward monoptic visual noise masking. J Gerontol 30:307–311.

Kulikowski JJ, Tolhurst DJ (1973) Psychophysical evidence for sustained and transient detectors in human vision. J Physiol 232:149–162.

Legge GE (1978) Sustained and transient mechanisms in human vision: Temporal and spatial properties. Vis Res 18:69–81.

Long GM (1979) Comments on Hawkins and Shulman's Type I and Type II visual persistence. Percept Psychophys 26:412–414.

Lupp U, Hauske G, Wolf W (1976) Perceptual latency to sinusoidal gratings. Vis Res 16:969–972.

McFarland RA, Warren B, Karis C (1958) Alterations in critical flicker frequency as a function of age and light: Dark ratio. J Exp Psych 56:529–538.

Meyer GE (1977) The effects of color specific adaptation on the perceived duration of gratings. Vis Res 17:51–56.

Meyer GE, Maguire WM (1977) Spatial-frequency and the mediation of short-term visual storage. Science 198:524–525.

Meyer GE, Lawson R, Cohen W (1975) The effects of orientation-specific adaptation on the duration of short-term visual storage. Vis Res 15:569–572.

Misiak H (1947) Age and sex differences in critical flicker frequency. J Exp Psych 37:318–332.

Miller GD, Anderson A, Simonson E (1965) Foveal flicker fusion using a moving stimulus. Percept Motor Skills 21:43–51.

Mundy-Castle AC (1953) An analysis of central responses to photic stimulation in normal adults. EEG Clin Neurophysiol 5:1–22.

Sakitt B (1976) Iconic memory. Psych Rev 83:257–274.

Sekuler R, Hutman LP, Owsley C (1980) Human aging and vision. Science 209:1255–1256.

Simonson E, Anderson D, Keiper C (1967) Effect of stimulus movement on critical flicker fusion in young and older men. J Gerontol 22:353–356.

Singer W, Bedworth N (1973) Inhibitory interactions between X and Y units in the cat lateral geniculate nucleus. Brain Res 49:291–307.

Walsh DA (1976) Age differences in central perceptual processing: a dichoptic backward masking investigation. J Gerontol 31:178–185.

Walsh DA, Thompson LW (1978) Age differences in visual sensory memory. J Gerontol 33:283–297.

Walsh DA, Till RE, Williams MV (1978) Age differences in peripheral perceptual processing: A monoptic backward masking investigation. J Exp Psych [Hum Percept Perform] 4:232–243.

Watson AB, Nachmias J (1977) Patterns of temporal interaction in the detection of gratings. Vis Res 17:893–902.

Weale RA (1961) Retinal illumination and age. Trans Illum Eng Soc 26:95–100.

Weale RA (1965) On the eye. In Welford AT, Birren JE (Eds) "Aging, Behavior and the Nervous System." Springfield, Illinois: Charles C Thomas, pp 307–325.

Weekers R, Roussel F (1946) Introduction a l'etude de la frequencee de fusion en clinique. Ophthalmologica 112:305–319.

Weiss AD (1959) Sensory functions. In Birren JE (Ed) "Handbook of Aging and the Individual." Chicago: University of Chicago Press, pp 503–542.

Weiss AD (1963) Auditory perception in aging. In Birren JE, Butler RN, Greenhouse SW, Sokoloff L, Yarrow MR, (Eds) "Human Aging: A Biological and Behavioral Study." Washington, D.C.: PHS Publication No. 986, U.S. Government Printing Office, Washington, D.C., pp 111–140.

Aging and Human Visual Function, pages 245–263
© 1982 Alan R. Liss, Inc., 150 Fifth Avenue, New York, NY 10011

Aging and the Allocation of Attentional Resources in Visual Information-Processing

William J. Hoyer and Dana J. Plude

The purpose of this chapter is to organize and review current research and theory bearing on adult age differences in the capacity and selectivity of visual information-processing. The classic problem of relating basic visual functioning to complex higher-order abilities is viewed from a resource allocation perspective. Although perceptual aging research has traditionally emphasized age-related data or signal limitations, the usefulness of resource allocation and selectivity models is emphasized herein. It is proposed that with aging and age-related perceptual experience, higher-order cognitive processes play an increasingly important role in organizing and processing incoming visual information.

DATA LIMITATIONS VS PROCESSING RESOURCE LIMITATIONS

Age-related declines in visual function can be attributed to *data limitations,* to *processing resource limitations,* or to both data and resource limitations (interactively or additively). Data limitations have to do with processes and structures that serve to reduce the quality of sensory input and other aspects of the sensory signal [Norman and Bobrow, 1975]. An excellent review of the age-related data limitations in vision is provided by Fozard et al, [1977]. Carter (this volume) and Pitts (this volume) have also provided thorough reviews of the most recent research on aging changes in the eye. Reduction in the accommodative ability of the eyes with advancing age has been attributed to an increase in the size and density of the crystalline lens [Adler, 1965]. Increased accumulation of granular material and fibrillar protein [Dark et al, 1969], progressive yellowing [Said and Weale, 1959; Weale, this volume], and increased opacity of the lens [Carter, this volume; Wolf, 1960] are associated with losses in sensitivity to low levels of illumination and with losses in distinct vision with advancing age. Aging changes in the oxygen supply to the retina [McFarland, 1968], other retinal and ocular structural changes (see chapters by Spector, and Balazs and Denlinger in this volume), and cellular changes in the retino-geniculo-striate pathway and limbic system also explain part of the age-related change in sensory input [Grossberg, 1980; Ordy et al, this volume].

Age-related limitations of *processing resources* also contribute to a reduction of efficiency in human visual function. A central assumption of current resource allocation models is that the human processing system has a *finite* amount of processing resources to be allocated. These resources have been variously labeled "attention" [Posner and Boies, 1971], "capacity" [Shiffrin and Schneider, 1977], and "effort" [Kahneman, 1973]. Whether the pool of resources is fixed or plastic and whether there is a single pool of resources [Shiffrin, 1976] or multiple separate resources [Navon and Gopher, 1979], or both [Logan 1979] remains a point of controversy. Regardless, there is general agreement that performance on complex visual tasks is a positive function of the resources available for performing the task. Also, the more complex the task, the more the demand on processing resources. Task complexity has been found to interact with age such that older adults compared with younger adults are disproportionately disadvantaged by increased complexity [Craik, 1977].

Welford [1964] proposed the *complexity hypothesis* to explain adult age differences in information-processing performance. According to Welford [1964], the older adult is at a disadvantage under conditions of increased complexity because of age-related slowing in the *rate* of information-processing. An alternative hypothesis is that young and elderly adults distribute or allocate differently the resources that control visual function [Hoyer and Plude, 1980]. One purpose of this chapter is to examine adult developmental differences in the allocation of attentional and other processing resources. Research and theory bearing on the quantity, quality, and distribution of processing resources are discussed.

There are two major aspects of processing resource limitations that may account for the observed age-related decline in visual function: capacity or quantity of resources, and selectivity or distribution of resources. Before reviewing these aspects, conceptions of the role of attention in visual performance are discussed.

Attention and Visual Function

Perceptual research has been guided by a sequential, stage-wise conceptualization of information processing. A synthesized or "modal" model of processing describes the sequence of processing as follows: First, stimulus information from the environment is processed "preattentively," and it is then stored briefly in modality-specific "buffers." Much of the information in the sensory buffers is then lost or filtered with attentional processes serving the function of transferring some of this information to a limited-capacity short-term memory system. Information is maintained in short-term or working memory by rehearsal and other control processes. Only some of the contents of short-term memory is then transferred to long-term memory, which is assumed to have an unlimited storage capacity [see Atkinson and Shiffrin, 1968; Broadbent, 1977].

This modal model, while still useful for organizing texts and book chapters on cognitive psychology, is an inadequate description of how humans process information. One problem is that such a model does not take account of the richness and the active, constructive nature of perception. Erdelyi [1974], for example, has discussed research showing that perceiver expectations affect performance on some perceptual tasks. A second problem with the modal model of human information-processing has been the lack of precision in specifying the locus, functions, and structures of processing limitations. There are age-related interindividual differences in the capacity to select and extract stimulus information [see Hoyer and Plude, 1980], but the study of processing limits and of the developmental or organismic boundaries of processing capacity and selectivity has not been advanced by the modal model.

The third problem with the modal model has been the difficulty in operationalizing and distinguishing the various stages of sequential information processing. Many investigators who identify themselves with the research areas of perception, attention, and memory have used a componential approach to the study of information-processing. One criticism of the componential view is the arbitrariness of the various constructs such as perception, short-term memory, and attention. Often these terms are operationally indistinguishable and are used interchangeably. Although stage analysis paradigms have facilitated the empirical analysis of mental activities, Neisser [1976] has cautioned that such artificiality may head information-processing research toward obsolescence: "Lacking in ecological validity, indifferent to culture, even missing some of the main features of perception and memory as they occur in ordinary life [cognitive] psychology could become a narrow and uninteresting specialized field" (p 7).

Several writers [eg, Neisser, 1976; Newell, 1973; Simon, 1979] have suggested that modal models are not accurate representations of human information-processing as it occurs in reality. It is our view that when possible, we should bring the procedures and methods of basic science to bear on the study of ecologically important aspects of information-processing. Most basic visual information-processing research has been conducted with convenient subject pools such as college undergraduates. The study of age-related interindividual differences and intraindividual change in visual function is a step in a more ecologically valid direction; such research supplements our knowledge of basic visual processes.

Capacity Limitations of Attentional Resources

Capacity limitations have to do with the factors and processes that restrict the amount of information that can be processed at any given time. Perceptual processes are customarily thought of as limited-capacity systems. That is, at any one time, only some visual information is perceived and processed, only some is responded to, and only some becomes part of the individual's conscious experience. The study of attention is mainly concerned with the limits and selectivity of information-processing. What are the limiting factors? How do the limits of human information-processing change with advancing age?

There are two general observations suggesting that human *processing capacity* is limited, and one general finding suggesting that processing reserves are for the most part unbounded or "plastic." The first observation is that individuals perform less efficiently under conditions of increased information load. For example, Logan [1980] demonstrated the effects of task complexity and memory load in several types of reaction time tasks [see also Logan, 1978]. The second observation is that some individuals (eg, young adults) perform more efficiently than other individuals (eg, older adults and young children) across a wide variety of information-processing tasks, suggesting that capacity limitations are genetically and ontogenetically fixed factors [eg, Craik, 1977; Hoyer and Plude, 1980].

Capacity limitation models, regardless of whether they are formulated to explain psychometric intelligence, memory, or attention, are implicitly based on knowledge of the *genetic* or *ontogenetic* boundaries of behavior. Presumably, individuals differ from each other in intelligence, memory, or perceptual processing, primarily because of time-ordered, biologically-based, and experientially based antecedents.

Related to these general observations is the finding that processing efficiency is a direct function of general as well as task-specific experience [Hirst et al, 1980; Schneider and Shiffrin, 1977]. In one study, Spelke et al, [1976] trained young adult subjects to copy unrelated, dictated words while reading and comprehending short stories. After about 6 weeks of training, the two college students, Diane and John, were able to carry out both activities simultaneously with no decrement in reading speed or comprehension. More recently, Hirst et al, [1980] reported two experiments as further evidence for the position that attention is a skill that improves with practice. In the first study, some subjects were trained to copy words while reading highly redundant short stories while other subjects were trained with less redundant materials. When subjects were switched from the highly redundant to the less redundant information, three of the four undergraduates immediately transferred their well-practiced skill. In the second study, subjects who were trained to copy complete sentences while reading made fewer copying errors with real sentences than with random words, recalled real sentences better than random words, and integrated information from successive sentences. Hirst et al interpreted these findings as suggesting that the sentence information was *not* processed automatically. The overall conclusion of the report was that the ability to divide attention is constrained by skill level acquired through practice and not by limited processing resources. Thus capacity limitations may apply to unskilled behavior but not to well-practiced performance.

Some perceptual tasks (eg, unfamiliar ones) challenge or exceed the individual's capacity for processing, while others (eg, noncomplex or familiar tasks) may require relatively little processing effort. This distinction is exaggerated in older populations. That is, frequently, age and task complexity are found to interact such that older adults are more negatively affected by complexity than are younger adults [Cerella et al, 1980]. Even tasks that require relatively little storage of stimulus information suffer interference when active memory or attention is loaded with irrelevant or unfamiliar information. Shulman and Greenberg [1971], for example, reported that decision times were longer when subjects were required to retain a set of eight consonants in memory during a line judgment task. More recently, Logan [1980] conducted four experiments with college-aged adults to determine whether the increased reaction time associated with loading memory with irrelevant information was due to task complexity or stimulus-response (S-R) mapping conditions. The S-R mapping explanation suggests that mapping rules or strategies are held in memory and enable performance to occur. Logan's data indicated that interactions between memory load and task complexity are not standardized and fixed, but rather depend on the perceiver's strategies and S-R constructions. Further, memory load interference was *not* restricted to any particular stage of information-processing.

Logan [1980] suggested that memory load interference reflects the attentional demands of preparation rather than activation of performance. Consistent with earlier work, it was reported that attention and short-term memory are functionally equivalent in that both are fundamental to information-processing, both have information-specific capacity limitations, both can be allocated selectively as resources, and both control behavior [see also Kahneman, 1973; Newell, 1973]. One functional difference between attention and short-term memory may be that attention serves to "prepare" and "maintain" a set to respond in visual processing tasks, whereas short-term memory may serve to "activate" or "enable" cognitive performance. It has not yet been possible to differentiate which process, attention or short-term memory, shows the greater benefit of exposure to consistent stimulus information.

Two-process models of capacity limitations suggest that there is an initial parallel stage of processing in which all sensory inputs receive some degree of analysis followed by selective or serial filtering of signals relatively late in the sequence of processing [Solso, 1979]. According to this view, one locus of age decline in processing capacity would be found during the initial (ie, parallel) stages of visual processing. Alternatively, the locus of age differences could be in the later (serial) stages (of processing).

Abel [1972], as reported in Botwinick [1978], used a modified version of Sperling's [1960] partial-report technique to assess age differences in visual short-term storage. There was little decrement with age in the ability to report cued portions of a display. Elderly subjects (60–70 years), like younger adults (19–22 years), showed partial-report superiority over full report. However, the lower levels of report by elderly subjects suggested that the capacity of initial processing stages declines with advancing age.

In addition to the study by Abel [1972] and data reported in Walsh and Prasse [1980], there is other work by Walsh and his colleagues [Till, 1978; Walsh et al, 1978; Walsh et al, 1979] that shows adult age deficits in the speed of relatively early peripheral and central perceptual processes (see Walsh, this volume, for a review). Kline's [eg, Kline and Orme-Rogers, 1978] research on stimulus persistence and sequential integration also points to the importance of early processing limitations in accounting for adult age differences in perception.

Age limitations in capacity are also attributable to changes occurring later in processing, during channel selection, filtering, or response selection [Hoyer and Plude, 1980; Welford, 1977]. Using a variety of experimental paradigms, several investigators have reported age-related deficits relatively late in the information-processing sequence. Older adults compared with younger subjects are at a disadvantage on tasks requiring (1) the manipulation of the contents of active or working memory [Craik, 1977], (2) the encoding of unfamiliar stimulus information [Thomas et al, 1978; Smith, 1980], (3) the discrimination of target vs distractor information [Rabbitt, 1965, 1977; Wright and Elias, 1979], (4) the identification and categorization of stimulus materials [Plude and Hoyer, 1982; Simon and Pouraghabagher, 1978], and (5) divided attention [Kirchner, 1958].

One of the first demonstrations of an age-related deficit in divided attention was reported by Kirchner [1958]. Subjects in two adult age groups, young (18–24 years) and old (60–84 years), observed a display of 12 lights. In one phase of the experiment, subjects were required to press a switch below a light when the light came on. Pressing the switch turned off that light and turned on another light. In this phase older subjects performed at levels comparable to young subjects. When the task was made more complicated by requiring subjects to press the key corresponding to the previous light, older subjects made significantly more errors than the younger adults. These findings suggest an age-related inability to switch attention between memory for the light and response. Thus, with advancing age there is a decrease in processing capacity under conditions requiring attention to be divided (1) between two input sources (2) between stimulus input and rehearsal, and (3) between rehearsing and retrieving or responding [Craik, 1977; Craik and Simon, 1980; Kirchner, 1958].

The localization, theoretically and structurally, of capacity limitations remains a major concern of contemporary information-processing researchers [for example, see Miller, 1981; Navon, 1981]. According to Broadbent's [1958] theory, attentional limitations operate relatively early in the processing sequence (ie, before perception). Deutsch and Deutsch [1963], in contrast, proposed that all sensory information is registered, briefly stored, and perceptually analyzed. Only after all incoming stimuli are fully analyzed for meaning are the most important stimuli selected for further processing. Furthermore, Deutsch and Deutsch [1963] suggested that limitations of attentional capacity are more a problem of retrieving the results of perceptual analysis from memory than of sensory signal. Compared with Broadbent's data-driven filter theory, therefore, "late selection models" formulated since the time of Deutsch and Deutsch [1963] give more emphasis to the role of semantic factors and other top-down factors in attention.

As an alternative to the early vs late selection hypotheses, Craik and Jacoby [1979] have suggested that attentional selectivity takes place throughout the processing sequence depending on stimulus characteristics, task demands, and the subject's degree of skill. Erdelyi [1974] has also argued that "selectivity is pervasive throughout the cognitive continuum, from input to output" (p 12). Such a view raises questions not only about the usefulness of attempts to localize attentional processes, but also about whether attentional resources are fixed.

In concluding this section, it is important to mention some of the problems with fixed capacity interpretations of adult age differences in information-processing—there are at least three. First, there is not a clear understanding of the components of information-processing. Since Galton's [1869] classic chapter on "classification of men according to their natural gifts," very little solid evidence for a functional relationship between sensory functioning and mental performance has been obtained. Further, Walsh (this volume) has recently reported a lack of relationship between central and perceptual processing speeds. Such data call into question the implicit assumption that ontogenetically or genetically pro-grammed sensory capacity is prerequisite to higher-order cognitive functioning. That the efficiencies of two or more perceptual processes are not correlated does not rule out the possibility of interaction or interdependence among the mech-anisms in question; the locus of interrelationships among interdependent per-ceptual processes may be at a cognitive or "executive" level of information-processing and not at the component level.

Second, there is relatively little evidence of individual differences, age-related or otherwise, in what is referred to as short-term memory, active or working memory, or the available work space in consciousness [Miller, 1956; Mandler, 1975]. It appears that there is a *subject-invariant limit* of "seven plus or minus two" items that can be held in active consciousness. Craik [1977] pointed out that age-related deficits arise primarily when the contents of consciousness need to be manipulated by the subject. That is, older subjects are at a disadvantage mainly when it comes to carrying out mental manipulations of the contents of active memory, but there appears to be no age differences in the amount or capacity of memory space [Craik, 1977].

Third, there is a wide range of interindividual differences in older age groups on perceptual and cognitive tasks [Baltes et al, 1979; Hoyer, 1974; Thomas et al, 1978; Schaie, 1980]. The high degree of interindividual variation along with the varying degree of intraindividual "plasticity" in perceptual functions points to the influence of experiential and life history factors on visual capacity and processing.

SELECTIVITY OF PROCESSING RESOURCES

In order for processing to be efficient, it is necessary that cognitive resources be allocated selectively to perceptual input. Attentional selectivity refers to the proportion of processing resources allocated to the targets vs the distractors in filtering and target detection tasks [Norman and Bobrow, 1975]. Some information should be ignored as irrelevant so that relevant information receives priority processing. It has been suggested by several authors [eg, Layton, 1975; Rabbitt, 1977; Schonfield, 1974] that there is an age-associated deficit in the ability to selectively extract relevant from irrelevant information. This observation has been derived from several studies of age differences in the processing of irrelevant information.

For example, Rabbitt [1965] used a visual search task to investigate adult age differences in the ability to ignore irrelevant information. Generally, as the number of nontarget items in a visual display is increased, the more difficult it becomes to detect a target within that display (ie, the *display size effect*). The magnitude of the display size effect is related to the subject's ability to ignore irrelevant display items while searching for relevant items. Rabbitt [1965] found that the magnitude of the display size effect was larger for elderly (average age, 67.4 years) than young adults (average age, 19.0 years). A card-sorting procedure having two conditions of relevancy was used: The first condition required a two-choice sort on the basis of whether one of the two targets was detected; in the second condition, there were eight targets to be discriminated. In both conditions targets appeared individually within four levels of irrelevancy: none, one, two, or eight distractor letters.

Age and irrelevancy interacted such that older adults were more slowed than young adults by the presence of nontarget letters. Rabbitt concluded that elderly adults have more difficulty than young adults in ignoring irrelevant stimuli. According to one hypothesis offered by Rabbitt, there is with increasing adult age a change in "perceptual sampling." Perceptual sampling is the way in which a visual display is parsed on initial exposure during a preattentive stage of processing [Neisser, 1967]. Young adults appear able to attend to perceptual samples in groups that can be ignored as a whole (provided the group contains no target), whereas the elderly cannot sample letters in displays in large groups and must, therefore, rely on a serial analysis in order to detect a target. The result is that in comparison to younger adults, the aged expend more limited cognitive resources while examining irrelevant information.

Layton's [1975] *perceptual noise hypothesis,* which attributes perceptual aging decrements to an increased presence of irrelevant and interfering stimuli (ie, noise) within the aging nervous system, can also account for Rabbitt's [1965] findings and the findings of other early studies [eg, Basowitz and Korchin, 1957]. However, later investigations by Wright and Elias [1979] and Farkas and Hoyer [1980] have suggested that Layton's perceptual noise hypothesis and Rabbitt's perceptual sampling hypothesis are oversimplifications.

Wright and Elias [1979] questioned whether nontargets in visual search tasks are truly "irrelevant." In visual search, irrelevant stimuli have to be discriminated from relevant stimuli and thus age differences in visual search may reflect difficulties in *discriminating* relevant from irrelevant information, not in *ignoring* irrelevant stimuli per se. In order to assess the age-related effects of irrelevant information that could be ignored, Wright and Elias [1979] modeled their study after Eriksen and Eriksen's [1974] nonsearch detection paradigm. Young (18–25 years) and older (60–82 years) adults were required to respond on the basis of a (relevant) target presented in the center of a horizontal display. On some trials, other (irrelevant) items bordered the target position. Both age groups were slowed by the presence of "neutral" irrelevant information, but the elderly were *not differentially* slowed by this factor.

Wright and Elias [1979] used a *selective focusing* task. In contrast, visual search tasks like Rabbitt's [1965] can be classified as *selective search* tasks. In the former, a subject must ignore or filter out information that is irrelevant to task performance, whereas in the latter, irrelevant stimuli must be discriminated from relevant stimuli. More recently, Farkas and Hoyer [1980] conducted two experiments that relate to the focusing-search distinction. In both experiments, the interfering effects of background (irrelevant) information either did or did not contrast with the orientation of targets. In the first experiment (selective search), the position of a target in the display varied over cards on a deck. Elderly adults (60–81 years) but not middle-aged (37–58 years) or young (18–30 years) adults were slowed by the presence of contrasting irrelevant information. All three age groups were slowed by the presence of irrelevant information in the same orientation as the target. In the second study (selective focusing), the position of a target did not vary over cards. No age group was slowed by contrasting irrelevant information, and only the oldest group was slowed by the presence of similar irrelevant information. These findings support the view that irrelevant information may have different age-associated effects depending on the nature of the processing demands of performance.

In summary, the studies reviewed in this section indicate that there are adult age differences in the selectivity of information-processing. In the previous section, we reviewed evidence indicating adult age differences in general processing capacity. One of many difficulties in studying adult developmental differences in perception and information-processing is the confounding of general processing capacity and attentional selectivity. Consider the following: Define S as the proportion of processing resources given to the target stimulus in a filtering task, and define C as the individual's total processing capacity. The quantity of resources allocated to the target stimuli (C_1) and to the distractor stimuli (C_2) can be written as:

$$C_1 = SC \tag{1}$$

$$C_2 = (1 - S)C \tag{2}$$

The quantity C should reflect age-related differences in total processing capacity, whereas S should reflect age-related differences in attentional selectivity. If performance is a monotonic function of the amount of allocated resources, then the performance differential for target items and distractor items should be

$$C_1 - C_2 = SC - (1 - S)C = C(2S - 1) \tag{3}$$

Clearly, age differences in target detection can be explained by differences in either C or S. In the next section we acknowledge the inseparability of selectivity and capacity functions, and propose a superordinate, conceptually driven view of resource allocation in aging.

ALLOCATION OF PROCESSING RESOURCES

Many of the limited capacity theories of attention have been replaced by resource allocation theories. From the resource allocation view have emerged a number of two-process models, which have their roots in Atkinson and Shiffrin's [1968] model of human memory. According to Atkinson and Shiffrin [1968], control processes direct the mechanisms and contents of sensory, short-term, and long-term memory structures.

Some perceptual tasks require "mental effort" whereas others may require little or no "mental effort." Processes related to performing tasks that demand attention or effort have been variously termed "effortful" [Hasher and Zacks, 1979], "controlled" [Schneider and Shiffrin, 1977], and "conscious" [Posner and Snyder, 1975]. If there is an age-related decrease in the capacity to control cognitive resources, then tasks requiring effortful processing are likely to yield greater magnitudes of age-associated decline than tasks that are performed automatically. For example, visual and memory search tasks have traditionally shown substantial age decrements in performance, but recent work has suggested that the magnitude of the age decrements depends on the automaticity of performance. Schneider and Shiffrin [1977] used a hybrid memory search-visual search task to study the differences between controlled and automatic aspects of information processing. Subjects who developed an automatic target detection strategy were unaffected by manipulations of information load (ie, target set size and display size), while subjects who had to rely on controlled processing (ie, scanning and selective attention) showed typical decrements as a function of load. The critical manipulation determining whether processing was controlled or automatic centered on the consistency of S-R mapping during an extensive training period. Under consistent stimulus mapping, subjects developed automaticity, while subjects in the varied mapping continued to rely on capacity-limited control processes [see Schneider and Shiffrin, 1977; Shiffrin and Schneider, 1977].

Adopting the Schneider and Shiffrin paradigm, Plude and Hoyer [1981] investigated adult age differences in effortful, controlled processing in a visual search task. Young (average age, 23.6 years) and elderly (average age, 75.0 years) searched either for an unchanging memory set (consistent mapping) or for changing memory sets (varied mapping) in displays containing a target letter and either none, three, or eight distractor letters. The main finding was that under the varied mapping condition, the traditional pattern of age-associated decrement in search was obtained. In the consistent mapping condition, adult age differences in processing irrelevant information were not found. This finding was taken as evidence that age-related decrements in visual search can be eliminated or at least minimized when the demand of information load on effortful processing is lessened by means of consistent stimulus mapping [see also, Plude et al, 1979].

In a related study, Madden and Nebes [1980] examined the acquisition of automaticity by young (18–25 years) and elderly (61–74 years) subjects. Again, a hybrid memory search-visual search paradigm was used, but here display size was kept constant at two items. Search was conducted for fixed memory sets containing one, two, or three targets. It was found that the slopes of the set size functions for both age groups decreased at equivalent rates over sessions, suggesting that elderly and young adults acquire automaticity at equivalent rates [see also Hasher and Zacks, 1979].

The main significance of the automatic-effortful distinction with regard to aging has to do with the role of life history and life experiences in information processing. There are many "real world" examples of highly efficient processing by older adults when executing well-practiced skills. Apparently, these well-automated skills, once acquired, are carried out with relatively little or no "mental effort."

In many respects, the acquisition of automaticity described in Madden and Nebes [1980] is analogous to the effects of familiarity on performance. It has been shown that familiarity plays an important role in determining the magnitude of age-related decline in memory scanning rate [Thomas et al, 1978] and naming latency [Poon and Fozard, 1978]. Much more needs to be known about how familiarity affects processing resources and selectivity and how familiarity factors interact with age. Further, it is important to determine how such factors as familiarity, expectancy, or context guide the operation of "lower-level" perceptual processes, and how the efficient use of available control processes might serve to offset some of the age-related decline in perceptual processing.

Several current theories of information processing include a perceiver component having to do with arousal [Anderson, 1976; Kahneman 1973], activation [Hayes-Roth, 1977; Quillian, 1968], alertness [Posner and Boies, 1971], or interest [Norman, 1976]. The main idea is that the allocation of resources depends on the level of arousal. However, there has been relatively little research devoted to this kind of component in perceptual aging research [but see Simon, 1979]. Anecdotally, many researchers are aware of "warm-up" phenomena that serve to facilitate access to the contents of memory. Empirically, information that has been recalled recently is more accessible than information that has been activated less recently [Simon, 1979]. Such "readiness" phenomena suggest the possibility that specific contents of information may exist at various levels of activation throughout the human processing system.

Some stimulus situations appear to affect the rate and type of perceptual processing. Depending on the perceiver-situation interaction, such events might either facilitate or debilitate stimulus processing. It can be argued that high arousal debilitates perceptual performance because processing resources are allocated to the stressful stimulus events (perhaps those that are not being experimentally manipulated in the laboratory). Mandler [1975] has suggested that arousal improves performance when the narrowing of attention serves to exclude irrelevant cues, but when effective action demands attention to a wide range of stimulus events, arousal serves to decrease processing efficiency. Older people are exposed to many stressful situations, and it has been suggested that an impaired ability to deal with stress is one of the main debilitating characteristics of aging [Jarvik and Russell, 1979; Schultz et al, 1980]. Eisdorfer and Wilkie [1977] suggested that older adults exhibit a generally lower level of cognitive performance because they are more anxious. The study of adult age differences in the effects of arousal on the allocation of processing resources is an important and relatively unexplored area of research.

Elsewhere we have suggested that higher-order processes may play a major role in differentiating the perceptual experiences of young and older adults [Hoyer and Plude, 1980]. Following Norman's [1976] *pertinence model,* we suggested that the establishment of stimulus precedence or dominance takes place early in the sequence of processing. According to a pertinence model, initial processing is parallel with capacity limitations occurring at later stages. However, it is suggested that the selection of one message over another is determined by the pertinence or relevance given to the messages early on in the processing sequence.

In a sense, pertinence is a function of the ongoing aim of the system [Solso, 1979]. Thus, that which receives priority processing is that which conforms to the goals of performance. Perceiver or system goals may vary depending on the perceiver's degree of skill and experience, task demands, and the interactions of perceiver characteristics and task demands.

Neisser and Becklen [1975] have provided some support for a pertinence model using a task that required visual monitoring of two superimposed events. Subjects had little difficulty in monitoring one event and ignoring the other, but both events could not be monitored simultaneously without sacrificing accuracy. The authors concluded that perception may be so organized that when a particular flow of information is being followed, perception cannot follow another flow [see also Neisser, 1976]. Consistent with Neisser's [1967] model of analysis-by-synthesis, perception is at once a constructive and deductive process. That which fits the constructed schema or percept is perceived.

Several experiments by de Groot [1965] can also be interpreted as support for an experience-based concept of pertinence. De Groot asked chess masters and chess beginners to reproduce arrangements of chess pieces on a board after only 5 seconds of viewing time. Chess masters had better memories than beginners of arrangements that could actually occur during a chess contest, but there were no differences in memory for random arrangements of chess pieces. Similarly, Chase and Simon [1973] reported that skill at chess can be attributed to the experience-based selectivity of perception and not to general capacity differences in the components of cognitive performance. Similarly, Charness [1981] examined aging and skill in chess players and found that older players are as efficient as equivalently skilled young players, even though the encoding component of visual short-term memory exhibited an age deficit.

According to Navon [1977], levels of structure in visual forms can be ordered from "global" to "local" where global levels encompass local elements. Frequently, global feature analysis takes precedence over local or component feature perception [Navon, 1977], especially for well-practiced perceivers. Reading words, for example, takes precedence over seeing letters or the component forms of letters for well-practiced readers [see LaBerge and Samuels, 1974]. Seeing an automobile as a global whole consisting of fenders, tires, bumpers, a windshield, and other local components is another example. Clearly, some units or configurations are processed more readily than others because of factors related to the stimulus and/or to the perceiver [Garner, 1970; Miller, 1979; Pomerantz, 1977]. Data from several lines of research also suggest the precedence of top-down over bottom-up perceptual analysis. Stevens [1972], for example, has interpreted *context effects* on perception as triggers of internally stored information. Further, the "word superiority effect" of Reicher [1969] and Wheeler [1970], the object superiority effect of Weisstein and Harris [1974], and the "forest before trees" research of Navon [1977] suggest that the detectability of stimuli is enhanced by perceptual analysis at the global level. However, Kinchla and Wolf [1979] examined the *global precedence hypothesis* under different letter display sizes, and found that the precedence of global analysis depends on an "optimal" perceptual size for the display [see also Miller, 1981].

Although there is converging evidence to suggest the roles of higher-order, top-down factors in controlling attention, there is little consensus among researchers as to the nature of the higher-order construct(s). Perhaps Abelson's [1976] concept of *script*, Minsky's [1975] *frame* concept, or other schema constructs could help to organize and explain some of the evidence concerning selectivity of processing. By *script*, Abelson meant coherent sequences of events expected by the individual. Similarly, *frames* refer to abstract knowledge structures that serve to organize generic expectations about objects or situations [Minsky, 1975]. That schemas serve to organize the perceptual world and that learned schemas or percepts influence what is seen is not a new notion. Although many theorists in many areas of psychology have postulated percept-type constructs, there are few if any systematic and testable percept-type models of top-down control of processing and aging.

Even though many contemporary investigators acknowledge the importance of conceptually driven processes, it is very difficult to systematically examine the operation of such processes. For example, *analysis-by-synthesis models* postulate that processing takes place as a match between the units of information in memory and the units of perceptual or sensory input [Neisser, 1967]. However, it has been difficult to test this analysis-by-synthesis model and other cognitive models because there is no precise way of identifying the units within memory or cognition. The higher-order system that presumably controls or guides perceptual and attentional processes needs to be described, and hypotheses regarding how such a system changes with advancing age need to be specified.

As an extension and integration of the research and theory to date, we propose a framework to explain and predict aging changes in human visual information-processing. Our position is that higher-order processing resources guide the quality and quantity of sensory and perceptual processing. Under conditions in which receptor function and sensory signal are adequate, adult age differences in visual function are attributed to interindividual differences and intraindividual change in the amount and allocation of processing resources. We hypothesize that perceiver expectations, stimulus demands, and perceptual development and learning affect the amount and allocation of processing resources.

For descriptive purposes, we propose that perceptual and sensory information is constructed and delineated in *percepts*. Percepts are defined as the smallest information units of perception that can be functionally described and identified. The amount and type of information held within a single percept changes over time due to the processing of new perceptual information. New information affects percept structure and content as follows: First, new information can be subsumed within an existing percept, thereby increasing the amount of information within the percept. Second, new information can lead to a decomposition or refinement of an existing percept, thereby changing the quality and decreasing the quantity of information in the percept. And third, new information can lead to the formation of a new percept. Thus, we propose that the smallest definable units of perception change over the course of (experience-based) development and (practice-based) learning. Changes in the quality and quantity of percepts require the allocation of processing resources; the amount and type of percept reorganization required determines the demand on the individual's supply of processing resources.

Several memory theorists [eg, Anderson, 1976; Collins and Loftus, 1975; Hayes-Roth, 1977; Schneider and Shiffrin, 1977] have proposed descriptive and predictive systems for the acquisition and development of knowledge within the human organism. One of the most testable of these frameworks is Hayes-Roth's [1977] knowledge-assembly theory. Her theory consists of 24 theoretical assumptions regarding knowledge acquisition, and these propositions are consistent with a large body of memory and perception research. For example, she reviewed evidence suggesting that the presence of interrelated ideas in memory causes interference in accessing parts of this information. These findings also suggest that memory search processes are slowed as a function of the number of related ideas (or percepts) in memory. These findings have obvious implications for the study of adult age differences in information-processing [see Hoyer, 1980].

SUMMARY

There is increased research interest in the characteristics of the perceiver in controlling perceptual experience [Erdelyi, 1974; Neisser, 1976]. Acquired knowledge determines perception, or at least some aspects of perceptual processing. Recent work on "top-down" systems suggests that more consideration needs to be given to the subject's control of attending, selecting, organizing, and retrieving "new" and "old" stimulus information. The search, filtering, and interpretation of stimulus information is to some extent an active (or constructive), perceiver-controlled process. Most of the work on perception and adult age differences gives emphasis to the "signal" or data-driven limits to processing, while the study of conceptually driven limits to processing have been relatively ignored until recently. One purpose of this chapter was to consider the role of processing resources in limiting (or controlling) perceptual performance. Such an approach appears particularly useful to explaining the wide range of interindividual variation and age-related intraindividual change in visual performance.

The study of age-related individual differences and intraindividual change in visual performance supplements our understanding of basic visual processes. Theories of visual function need to be consistent with knowledge of individual differences in processing. Developmental changes in vision can occur because of neurophysiological, genetic, and/or experiential factors. Factors within each of these broad categories of antecedents can be universally age-ordered, differentially age-ordered within cohorts or cultures, or non-normative (ie, individualized). The main concern of this chapter was to review research and theory related to normal aging changes in visual information-processing. Given that experiential factors lead to the development of processing selectivity and resource allocation, it is reasonable to suggest that for some older adults, higher-order executive functions can compensate for age-related losses in the quality of sensory input. How higher-order processes change with age offers a fruitful direction for future research on human visual function.

ACKNOWLEDGMENTS

Preparation of this chapter was supported in part by NIA Grant AG 02713 to WJH. We gratefully acknowledge the comments and suggestions of Don Kline, M. Elliot Familant, and David Madden, which have served to improve the clarity of this chapter.

REFERENCES

Abel M (1972) The visual trace in relation to aging. Ph.D. diss, Washington University, St. Louis, Missouri. (Cited in Botwinick, 1978.)

Abelson RP (1976) Script processing in attitude formation and decision making In Carroll JS, Payne JW (Eds) "Cognition and Social Behavior." Hillsdale, N.J.: Erlbaum.

Adler FH (1965) "Physiology of the Eye." St. Louis, Missouri: Mosby.

Anderson JR (1976) "Language, Memory, and Thought," Hillsdale, N.J.: Erlbaum.

Atkinson RC, Shiffrin RM (1968) Human memory: A proposed system and its control processes. In Spence KW, Spence JT, (Eds) "Advances in the Psychology of Learning and Motivation: Advances in Research and Theory," Vol. 2. New York: Academic.

Baltes PB, Willis SL, Bleiszner R, Lachman ME, Cornelius SW (1979) The Penn State Adult Development and Enrichment Project (ADEPT). Cognitive training research. Paper presented at the Gerontological Society Meetings, Dallas, TX.

Basowitz H, Korchin SJ (1957) Age differences in the perception of closure. J Abnormal Soc Psych 54:93–97.

Botwinick J (1978) "Aging and Behavior." New York: Springer.

Broadbent DE (1958) "Perception and Communication." New York: Pergamon.

Broadbent DE (1977) The hidden preattentive processes. Am Psych 32:109–118.

Cerella J, Poon LW, Williams DM (1980) Age and the complexity hypothesis. In Poon LW (Ed) "Aging in the 1980s: Psychological Issues." Washington, D.C.: American Psychological Association.

Charness N (1981) Visual short-term memory and aging in chess players. J Gerontol 36:615–619.

Chase WG, Simon HA (1973) Perception in chess. Cog Psych 4:55–81.

Collins AM, Loftus EF (1975) A spreading-activation theory of semantic processing. Psych Rev 82:407–428.

Craik FIM (1977) Age differences in human memory. In Birren JE, Schaie KW (Eds) "Handbook of the Psychology of Aging." New York: Van Nostrand.

Craik FIM, Jacoby LL (1979) Elaboration and distinctiveness in episodic memory. In Nilsson L (Ed) "Perspectives on Memory Research." Hillsdale, N.J.: Erlbaum.

Craik FIM, Simone (1980) Age differences in memory: The roles of attention and depth of processing. In Poon LW et al (Eds) "New Directions in Memory and Aging: Proceedings of the George A Talland Memorial Conference." New Jersey: Erlbaum.

Dark AJ, Streeten BW, Jones D (1969) Accumulation of fibrillar protein in the aging human lens capsule. Arch Ophthalmol 82:815–821.

de Groot AD (1965) "Thought and Choice in Chess." The Hague: Mouton.

Deutsch JA, Deutsch D (1963) Attention: Some theoretical considerations. Psych Rev 70:80–90.

Eisdorfer C, Wilkie F (1977) Stress, disease, aging, and behavior. In Birren JE, Schaie KW (Eds) "Handbook of the Psychology of Aging." New York: Van Nostrand.

Erdelyi MH (1974) A new look at the new look: Perceptual defense and vigilance. Psych Rev 81:1–25.

Eriksen BA, Eriksen CW (1974) Effects of noise letters upon the identification of a target letter in a nonsearch task. Percept Psychophys 16:143–149.

Farkas MS, Hoyer WJ (1980) Processing consequences of perceptual grouping in selective attention. J Gerontol 35:207–216.

Fozard JL, Bell B, McFarland RA, Podolsky S (1977) Visual perception and communication. In Birren JE, Schaie KW (Eds) "Handbook of the Psychology of Aging." New York: Van Nostrand.

Galton F (1869) "Hereditary genius: An Inquiry into its Laws and Consequences." London: Macmillan.

Garner WR (1970) Good patterns have few alternatives. Am Sci 58:34–42.

Grossberg S (1980) How does the brain build a cognitive code? Psych Rev 87:1–51.

Hasher L, Zacks RT (1979) Automatic and effortful processes in memory. J Exp Psych [Gen] 108:356–388.

Hayes-Roth B (1977) Evolution of cognitive structures and processes. Psych Rev 84:260–278.

Hirst W, Spelke ES, Reaves CC, Caharack G, Neisser U (1980) Dividing attention without alternation or automaticity. J Exp Psych 109:98–117.

Hoyer WJ (1974) Aging as intraindividual change. Dev Psych 10:821–826.

Hoyer WJ (1980) Information processing knowledge acquisition and learning: Developmental perspectives. Hum Dev 23:389–399.

Hoyer WJ, Plude DJ (1980) Attentional and perceptual processes in the study of cognitive aging. In Poon LW (Ed) "Aging in the 1980s: Psychological issues." Washington, D.C.: American Psychological Association.

Jarvik LF, Russell D (1979) Anxiety, aging, and the third emergency reaction. J Gerontol 34:197–200.

Kahneman D (1973) "Attention and Effort." Englewood Cliffs, N.J.: Prentice-Hall.

Kinchla RA, Wolf JM (1979) The order of visual processing: "Top-down," "bottom-up," or "middle-out." Percept Psychophys 25:225–231.

Kirchner WK (1958) Age differences in short-term retention of rapidly changing information. J Exp Psych 55:352–358.

Kline DW, Orme-Rogers C (1978) Examination of stimulus persistence as the basis for superior visual identification performance among older adults. J Gerontol 33:76–81.

LaBerge D, Samuels SJ (1974) Toward a theory of automatic information processing in reading. Cog Psych 6:293–323.

Layton B (1975) Perceptual noise and aging. Psych Bull 82:875–883.

Logan GD (1978) Attention in character-classification tasks: Evidence for the automaticity of component stages. J Exp Psych: [Gen] 107:32–63.

Logan GD (1979) On the use of concurrent memory load to measure attention and automaticity. J Exp Psych [Hum Percept Perform] 5:189–207.

Logan GD (1980) Short-term memory demands of reaction-time tasks that differ in complexity. J Exp Psych: [Hum Percept Perform] 6:375–389.

Madden DJ, Nebes RD (1980) Aging and the development of automaticity in visual search. Dev Psych 16:377–384.

Mandler G (1975) "Mind and Emotion." New York: Wiley.

McFarland RA (1968) The sensory and perceptual processes in aging. In Schaie KW (Ed) "Theory and Methods of Research on Aging." Morgantown: West Virginia University Press.

Miller GA (1956) The magic number seven, plus or minus two: Some limits on our capacity for processing information. Psych Rev 63:81–97.

Miller J (1979) Cognitive influences on perceptual processing. J Exp Psych [Hum Percept Perform] 5:546–562.

Miller J (1981) Global precedents in attention and decision. J Exp Psych [Hum Percept Perform] 7:1161–1174.

Minksy ML (1975) A framework for representing knowledge. In Winston P (Ed) "The Psychology of Computer Vision." New York: McGraw-Hill.

Navon D (1977) Forest before trees: The precedence of global features in visual perception. Cog Psych 9:353–383.

Navon D (1981) Do attention and decision follow perception? J Exp Psych [Hum Percept Perform] 7:1175–1182.

Navon D, Gopher D (1979) On the economy of the human-processing system. Psych Rev 86:214–255.

Neisser U (1967) "Cognitive Psychology." New York: Appleton-Century-Crofts.

Neisser U (1976) "Cognition and Reality." San Francisco: Freeman.

Neisser U, Becklen R (1975) Selective looking: Attending to visually significant events. Cog Psych 7:480–494.

Newell A (1973) Production systems: Models of control structures. In Chase WG (Ed) "Visual Information Processing." New York: Academic.

Norman DA (1976) "Memory and Attention," Second ed. New York: Wiley.

Norman DA, Bobrow DJ (1975) On data-limited and resource-limited processes. Cog Psych 7:44–64.

Plude DJ, Hoyer WJ (1981) Adult age differences in visual search as a function of stimulus mapping and information load. J Gerontol 36:598–604.

Plude DJ, Hoyer WJ (1982) Age differences in identifying and categorizing stimuli during visual search. Paper presented at the American Psychological Association Meetings, Washington, DC.

Plude DJ, Kaye DB, Hoyer WJ, Post TA, Saynisch MJ, Hahn MV (1979) Adult age differences in visual search as a function of information load and target mapping. Paper presented at the 32nd Annual Meeting of the Gerontological Society, Washington, D.C.

Pomerantz JR (1977) Pattern goodness and speed of encoding. Mem Cog 5:235–241.

Poon LW, Fozard JL (1978) Speed of retrieval from long-term memory in relation to age, familiarity, and datedness of information. J Gerontol 33:711–717.

Posner MI, Boies SJ (1971) Components of attention. Psych Rev 78:391–408.

Posner M, Snyder CRR (1975) Attention and cognitive control. In Solso RL (Ed) "Information Processing and Cognition: The Loyola Symposium." Hillsdale, N.J.: Erlbaum.

Quillian MR (1968) Semantic memory. In Minsky M (Ed) "Semantic Information Processing." Cambridge, Mass.: MIT Press.

Rabbitt PMA (1965) An age-decrement in the ability to ignore irrelevant information. J Gerontol 20:233–238.

Rabbitt PMA (1977) Changes in problem solving ability in old age. In Birren JE, Schaie KW (Eds) "Handbook of the Psychology of Aging." New York: Van Nostrand.

Reicher GM (1969) Perceptual recognition as a function of the meaningfulness of the material. J Exp Psych 81:275–280.

Said FS, Weale RA (1959) The variation with age of the spectral transmissivity of the living human crystalline lens. Gerontologia 3:213–231.

Schaie KW (1980) Intraindividual change in intellectual abilities. Paper presented at the Gerontological Society Meetings, San Diego, Ca.

Schnedier W, Shiffrin RM (1977) Controlled and automatic information processing: I. Detection, search, and attention. Psych Rev 84:1–66.

Schonfield D (1974) Translations in gerontology—From lab to life: Utilizing information. Am Psych 29:796–801.

Schultz NR Jr, Hoyer WJ, Kaye DB (1980) Trait anxiety, spontaneous flexibility, and intelligence in young and elderly adults. J Consult Clin Psych 48:289–291.

Shiffrin RM (1976) Capacity limitations in information processing, attention, and memory. In Estes WK (Ed) "Handbook of Learning and Cognitive Processes," Vol. 4. Hillsdale, N.J.: Erlbaum.

Shiffrin RM, Schneider W (1977) Controlled and automatic human information processing: II. Perceptual learning, automatic attending, and a general theory. Psych Rev 84:127–190.

Shulman HG, Greenberg SN (1971) Perceptual deficit due to division of attention between memory and perception. J Exp Psych 88:171–176.

Simon HA (1979) Information processing models of cognition. Annu Rev Psych 30:363–396.

Simon JR, Pouraghabagher AR (1978) The effect of aging on the stages of processing in a choice reaction time task. J Gerontol 33:553–561.

Smith A (1980) Age differences in encoding, storage, and retrieval processes. In Poon LW, Fozard JL, Cermak LS, Arenberg DL, Thompson LW (Eds) "New Directions in Memory and Aging." Hillsdale, N.J.: Erlbaum.

Solso RL (1979) "Cognitive Psychology." New York: Harcourt.

Spelke E, Hirst W, Neisser U (1976) Skills of divided attention. Cognition 4:215–230.

Sperling G (1960) The information available in brief visual presentations. Psych Mon 74:Whole No 11.

Stevens KN (1972) Segments, features, and analyses by synthesis. In Kavanagh JF, Mattingly IG (Eds) "Language by Ear and by Eye: The Relationship between Speech and Reading." Cambridge, Mass.: MIT Press.

Thomas JC, Waugh NC, Fozard JL (1978) Age and familiarity in memory scanning. J Gerontol 33:528–533.

Till RE (1978) Age related differences in binocular backward masking with visual noise. J Gerontol 33:702–710.

Walsh DA, Prasse MJ (1980) Iconic memory and attentional processes in the aged. In Poon LW, Cermak LS, Arenberg D, Thompson LW (Eds) "New Directions in Memory and Aging." Hillsdale, N.J.: Erlbaum.

Walsh DA, Till RE, Williams MV (1978) Age differences in peripheral perceptual processing: A monoptic backward masking investigation. J Exp Psych [Hum Percept Perform] 4:232–243.

Walsh DA, Williams MV, Hertzog CK (1979) Age-related differences in two stages of central perceptual processes: The effects of short duration targets and criterion differences. J Gerontol 34:234–241.

Weisstein N, Harris CS (1974) Visual detection of line segments: An object superiority effect. Science 186:752–755.

Welford AT (1964) Experimental psychology in the study of aging. Br Med Bull 20:65–69.

Welford AT (1977) Motor performance. In Birren JE, Schaie KW (Eds) "Handbook of the Psychology of Aging." New York: Van Nostrand.

Wheeler DD (1970) Processes in word recognition. Cog Psych 1:59–85.

Wolf E (1960) Glare and age. Arch Ophthalmol 64:502–514.

Wright LL, Elias JW (1979) Age differences in the effects of perceptual noise. J Gerontol 34:704–708.

V. METHODOLOGICAL ISSUES

Aging and Human Visual Function, pages 267–268
© 1982 Alan R. Liss, Inc., 150 Fifth Avenue, New York, NY 10011

Introduction

There is no doubt that aging exerts powerful and often pervasive effects on the structure and function of the visual system. Nevertheless, it is very difficult to determine the precise character and basis of such effects in a methodologically sound way. This is true for the study of age-related changes in particular visual processes as well as for the prevalence and incidence of such changes across individuals (ie, their epidemiology). The following chapters by Storandt and Greenberg and Branch examine these methodological difficulties in detail.

With increasing adult age there is a dramatic rise in the rate of visual impairment. For example, the prevalence of cataracts is about eight times greater in persons over 65 than in the general population, and glaucoma occurs about eight times more frequently and retinal disorders about six times more often. The human significance of these statistics is underscored by the realization that they occur in a group that is also more likely to experience increased physical vulnerability and economic hardship. However, as Greenberg and Branch make clear, because of methodological problems, the frequency of occurrence of these and other age-associated visual impairments cannot be estimated with any precision at present. In fact, they conclude that the net effect of these methodological limitations is to underestimate the prevalence and incidence of visual handicaps among the elderly. They argue compellingly for new epidemiological studies that use samples of greater size, include institutionalized persons, consider the insidious onset of many of the late-life visual disorders, and employ standardized testing and reporting procedures. The need for such systematic and well-controlled studies is attested to by the prevalence and human cost of visual disorders among the elderly.

However, as a research variable, the very nature of age challenges our ability to systematically study the causes and consequences of visual aging. Chronological age is an index only of the passage of time since an individual's birth. Manipulation of the variable of interest, a process fundamental to experimental science, is not possible in studying the effects of aging on vision. The visual scientist, like any other gerontologist, must either select for simultaneous comparison individuals who already differ in age or await the aging of some sample(s) under consideration. That is, the researcher must choose among the cross-sectional design, the longitudinal design, or some hybrid of the two.

As Martha Storandt makes clear in the second chapter in this section, the limitations in either of the major alternatives seriously challenge the investigator searching for the basic factors that underlie age-related change. The cross-sectional approach confounds age with cohort, the unique sociohistorical influences that groups of different age have experienced. The longitudinal design, on the other hand, confounds age with the changing constellation of factors associated with each new time of measurement. It is only with a full appreciation of these fundamental methodological issues that we will be able to make progress in furthering our understanding of basic visual aging as well as define the distribution of age-related disorders of sight.

Aging and Human Visual Function, pages 269–278

Concepts and Methodological Issues in the Study of Aging

Martha Storandt

In the study of age changes in vision, as in aging research in general, it is difficult but important to distinguish the events that are intrinsic to aging from those attributable to various other factors. For example, is the commonly observed decline with age in visual acuity an inevitable feature of aging or does it also reflect the particular type of test used or the health status and life history of the research population studied? Such research questions, although they typically appear in far more subtle and complex form, continually confront the visual scientist in the design of aging research.

BASIC DESIGNS

The two basic designs that are used to examine age-related differences and changes in a dependent variable are the *cross-sectional* and the *longitudinal* designs, respectively. As you will recall, in a cross-sectional design, individuals of different ages are measured at one time (see Table I). Note that the people of different ages are born in different years; they are of different *cohorts*. Thus in a cross-sectional design there is an intrinsic confound of the effect of age, or maturation, with the effect of cohort, or year of birth. That is, the two factors, age and cohort, vary together, and it is impossible to determine if observed differences in the various age groups are the result of the influence of maturation or the result of being born at different times and therefore belonging to different cohorts.

Generally, cohort differences are a function of changes in the culture or environment. Whereas our society is not a static one, the person born in 1900 has been exposed to a cultural milieu quite different from that of the person born in 1960—different practices of child-rearing, different health and sanitation practices, different cultural value systems. A classic example of cohort differences found in comparing young and old adults today is the difference in the number

TABLE I. Cross-Sectional Design. CONFOUND:
AGE AND COHORT

Year of Birth (Cohort)	Age
1900	80
1910	70
1920	60
1930	50

TABLE II. Longitudinal Design. CONFOUND: AGE AND TIME OF MEASUREMENT

	Year of Birth (Cohort): 1900			
Times of Measurement	1950	1960	1970	1980
Age	50	60	70	80

of years of formal schooling experienced by the two age groups. For the average person born in 1900, 8 years of education was, perhaps, the most that could be expected. For the person born in 1960, the expectation was 12 or more years of formal schooling. Maturation does not bring about a reduction in the number of years of formal education received; this is illogical. However, older people do have less education because they are from a different cohort. This could have an impact on their ability to identify some kinds of visual stimuli or even determine the difficulty they will experience in understanding the accompanying task instructions.

Notice that in the cross-sectional design we speak of group differences. We can say nothing of change, since measurement is conducted at only one time.

In the longitudinal design, individuals from only one cohort are examined at successive times of measurement (see Table II). Thus, the effect of cohort is held constant. Note that the sample is older at each successive interval of testing. In the longitudinal design there is a different intrinsic confound, this time between age and time of measurement. That is, age and time of measurement vary together; it is impossible to determine if differences at the various times of measurement are a function of increased maturation or if they are a function of the change in the time of measurement. A common example would be a practice effect. Performance of subjects is seen to improve at successive times of measurement. We have no way of knowing if we are examining an incremental phenomenon that occurs because of maturation or whether the improved performance is a function of practice. Other common factors related to time of measurement that may affect the performance of subjects in longitudinal studies are such things as improved equipment or cultural events that have occurred in the period intervening between the times of measurement. Think of the example of a test that asks subjects to define the word "watergate." In 1970, when the subjects were 70 years old, the word was defined as a gate through which water passes. In 1980, when the subjects are 80 years old, it was defined as a government scandal leading to the resignation of a president of the United States. An investigator from another solar system would not know if the change in the definition of the word was due to maturation or to some event that occurred between 1970 and 1980.

Similarly, one would have to be very careful in interpreting the results of a longitudinal examination of visual discrimination ability. Such variables as the subject's familiarity with the test materials or the general test environment, a change in the subject's glasses, or even a change of experimenter could contaminate an apparent age effect.

Both cross-sectional and longitudinal designs have their advantages and disadvantages. We have just seen that in both, the factor of age is confounded with another independent variable. In the case of the cross-sectional study, age is confounded with cohort; in the longitudinal design, age is confounded with time of measurement. A growing number of researchers now refer to "age/cohort" differences in cross-sectional studies and to "age/time-of-measurement" changes in longitudinal studies in order to remind us of the confounded nature of the age variable.

This intrinsic confound has been attacked in a number of ways, most notably by Schaie [1965], who proposed a system of sequential designs. However, it was later pointed out [Adam, 1978] that even these designs do not eliminate the essential and intrinsic confounds that exist in the study of the aging process. It is not possible for the investigator to randomly assign subjects to be the same age but from different cohorts in a cross-sectional design. In a longitudinal design, it is not possible to assign people from the same cohort to be of different ages at a particular time of measurement. Members of a cohort grow old together. The essentiality of these confounds arises from the very nature of the study of organismic variables.

The cross-sectional method has some practical advantages in comparison with the longitudinal design, especially in the study of later life. It is a much more feasible and practical method. The longitudinal design requires a long-term committment on the part of the research team and funding agency. Results are not immediately forthcoming. Data management is sometimes a problem. The longitudinal study does allow us to study changes within individuals as opposed to differences between individuals. However, advances in knowledge that occur during the period of the longitudinal study sometimes make the results of the effort less beneficial than we might wish. New advances in technology, new methods of measurement, and new insights about pertinent variables may render obsolete the results of a longitudinal study begun prior to the existence of such information. Some degree of precognition, in the extrasensory perception sense, would be helpful to the researcher undertaking a longitudinal study spanning more than a few years.

Sometimes the choice between a cross-sectional and a longitudinal design will be based on the researcher's "best guess" about the degree of impact of cohort-related variables as opposed to time-of-measurement-related variables; in one design age is confounded with cohort and in the other it is confounded with time-of-measurement. For example, if the researcher expects substantial differences in successive cohorts on a variable highly correlated with the dependent variable of interest, then a longitudinal design may be better. On the other hand, if substantial time-of-measurement differences are expected, a cross-sectional study would be more appropriate.

SAMPLING ISSUES

Another disadvantage of both cross-sectional and longitudinal designs arises from the fact that if we are interested in older adults, rarely can we obtain a truly representative sample. The major reason for this derives from the fact that some of the people who are born into a cohort die before others from the same cohort. We tend to be less concerned about this attrition when we study younger human beings, since the attrition is small. However, the problem is much more severe when older adults are the target of the research. Approximately two-thirds of those born in 1920 and now 60 years old are currently living, and only slightly more than one-half of those born in 1910 have survived to age 70. Research would indicate that those who do survive to age 70 or 80 are a superior group, at least in terms of some variables such as intelligence [Jarvik and Falek 1963]. Although little is known about the degree to which survivors are representative of their cohort in terms of visual function, it might be presumed that their visual abilities would also be characterized by superior health.

This *selective attrition* can be found in both cross-sectional and longitudinal studies. The older persons in cross-sectional studies are likely to represent a superior segment of their original cohort. Younger adults included in cross-sectional studies represent a wider range of their cohort. The same is true of those individuals who remain in a longitudinal study. Later and later times-of-measurement will include fewer and fewer persons; those who remain may well be those who represent the superior portion of the original distribution at the first time of testing.

Representatives of samples of older adults can be influenced in other ways as well. For example, many of the younger adults who participate in our research projects are college students; they are easily available to the large group of researchers based in universities. Convenient samples of older adults are found in nursing homes or institutions for the aged. These older adults, however, are often ill and have experienced a large degree of functional deterioration, whereas the college students to whom they are compared represent a highly superior, select group of young adults. This problem seems obvious to most researchers today but represents a severe limitation of many studies conducted in the past.

To avoid comparing highly superior young adults with sick old people, researchers have sought their older subjects from social groups organized for the old such as local chapters of the American Association of Retired Persons. However, these older adults, too, are selected. They are the outgoing, energetic, healthy ones, by and large, probably superior in many ways to the other survivors of their cohort.

Researchers interested in basic research on vision may have less fear of using such samples in their studies than do researchers involved in studies of, for example, attitudes, personality, or cognitive processes. However, an institutionalized sample of older adults should surely represent some concern for researchers interested in the visual processes, since many of these persons have numerous health problems that can influence vision as well as other bodily systems. Just obtaining responses may be a problem, given the drugged state of the residents of some nursing homes. Rarely do researchers obtain from the older adult a listing of current medications. Even more rarely are the effects of these medications considered in the analyses of the data. Often we just do not have the necessary sophistication about drug effects to consider their impact on our data in any meaningful way.

Samples of older adults in cross-sectional studies and those who remain in the successive waves of longitudinal studies will include individuals who are experiencing varying degrees of health problems. No one denies that the incidence of certain types of disease processes increases with age, just as the incidence of certain other types of disease processes declines with age. Thus, it behooves the researcher interested in aging to have some measure of the health of the sample involved in the study. Just how much impact health will have on the conclusions drawn from the results of the study varies greatly as a function of the dependent variable under examination. Political preferences may not be influenced at all; life satisfaction may be influenced substantially.

There are no easy solutions to the problems of subject selection in studies of the aging process. Some researchers have resorted to limiting their samples to those from highly select populations such as prisoners. At our institute, we tend to rely on newspaper advertisements for our subject solicitation. At least we know both our young and old subjects read the newspaper! Of course, more sophisticated random sampling procedures based on door-to-door solicitation are available, but these are costly and time-consuming. We would still not know if there were systematic factors biasing the participation of the young, the middle-aged, and the old. It is extremely difficult if not impossible to determine the exact characteristics of those who volunteer to participate in our studies as opposed to the characteristics of those who do not volunteer.

MATCHING VS ANALYSIS OF COVARIANCE

Since the researcher cannot randomly assign subjects to be various ages, many have resorted to two other procedures in order to reduce the systematic differences in related, or concommitant, variables in the age groups they wish to compare. One procedure is matching; the other is analysis of covariance. These two procedures are similar in that both require researchers to specify in advance the source of systematic variation they wish to "control for."

In describing these procedures let me use as an example the dissertation of one of our students, Warren Danziger [1979], in which differences among young, middle-aged, and old adults in a visual discrimination task involving Landolt rings were examined. It was suspected that performance on this task might be related to the intellectual ability of the subject. Therefore, the three age groups were matched on the basis of the Information subtest of the Wechsler Adult Intelligence Scale. Similarly, it was felt that visual acuity would influence performance on this visual discrimination task. Therefore, homogeneous samples of young, middle-aged, and old adults with good corrected acuity were employed. When all of this was done, no differences in visual descrimination performance at the eight levels of difficulty used in the study were observed. However, now we worry that perhaps we "threw out the baby with the bathwater." Perhaps previously reported age-related differences in visual discrimination were a function of differences in visual acuity or the intelligence of the different age groups used in the samples.

The alternate procedure, analysis of covariance, would have allowed the three different age groups of subjects to vary on the concommitant variables of intelligence and visual acuity. Both concommitant variables would have been measured, just as they were when the matching procedure was employed. The advantage of employing the analysis of covariance procedure, if we could meet the statistical assumptions, would have been that the differences in visual discrimination ability among the three age groups could have been examined with and without the corrections for the suspected covariates. If differences in visual discrimination ability were observed among the three age groups when no correction for differences in intelligence or visual acuity were employed, and if these differences disappeared when one or both of the covariates were included, then some estimation of the impact of the covariates would be possible.

The contrast of these two procedures demonstrates the difference among researchers who tend to employ analysis of variance models and those who tend to conceptualize their research problems in terms of regression analysis. Probably most basic scientists concerned with vision belong to the former group and tend to rely on *t*-tests and analyses of variance. It should be pointed out that analysis of variance is a specific case of the general linear model, and that regression analysis, especially when organismic variables such as age are of interest, may be the more useful procedure. Among the advantages of regression analysis is the use of all the quantitative information we have about our variable of greatest interest—age. Regression analysis does not require that we categorize our major independent variable into the gross groups of, for example, young, middle-aged, and old. Interactive models are possible and such procedures as trend analysis allow us to go beyond the first step of asking *if* a relationship exists between our independent and dependent variables to the second step of specifying the form of that function. However, many basic researchers in the behavioral and medical sciences received their formal methodological training at a time when ANOVA reigned supreme and regression models were used only by school psychologists and personnel managers. Perhaps this cohort effect will disappear as researchers trained to think in terms of the general linear model appear on the scene. Then the choice between analysis of variance and regression analysis can be made on the basis of the research questions to be answered rather than on the habits of the researchers.

AGE: A LEGITIMATE VARIABLE

There are those who would say that age is an infinitely eliminable variable. Aging is disease. Cure all diseases and human beings will not grow old. It may well be that the age-associated differences or changes observed in some psychological variables are the results of disease processes. However, the view that aging is identical to disease seems somewhat parochial. Even if all disease were to be eradicated, the older adult would have a history different from that of the younger person. The behavior of the immortal 60-year-old may not be identical to the behavior of the same immortal at 20 years of age. For example, much would be learned and experienced in the intervening 40-year period. And experience does influence behavior. Let us eliminate disease and sickness, but let us not expect that such successes will allow us to eliminate all age-related differences in people at the same time.

One example of such age-related differences that may be of special interest to visual scientists relates to what has been described as the increased cautiousness of older adults. It has been suggested that a portion of the difference in the performance of older adults on a variety of tasks may be related to their response bias. For example, in a threshold determination experiment the old person may wait until really "sure" that the signal is present before reporting it, whereas the younger person may act in a more impulsive manner. This response bias, of course, would result in different measured thresholds for the young and old observers.

Okun and Elias [1977] have suggested that the "cautiousness" of the older person is appropriate cautiousness in that it depends on the payoff structure. The incautious nature of the younger person results in fewer worthwhile successes. Those interested in the relationship of age to sensory as well as cognitive functions are beginning to employ theory of signal detection procedures in order to measure the impact of age-related response bias on the performance of young and old adults [Danziger and Botwinick, 1980].

MAGNITUDE OF EFFECT

Just what does a significant difference between young and old adults really mean? Too often researchers stop when they observe a significant F-ratio related to an age effect. They fail to ask the important question: How much variance in the dependent variable can be accounted for by the knowledge of a person's age? Everyone knows that even the most trivial difference between two means can produce a significant t- or F-ratio, given that the sample size is large enough. One of the difficulties that our reliance upon ANOVA models has produced is our fascination with significance levels rather than a concern about the proportion of explained variance. Modern concerns about effect size, as measured by R^2 or ω^2, for example, begin to bring us back to the question of how important an observed age difference really is. A significant t- or F-ratio represents the beginning, not the end, of the interesting aspect of the research process.

PRACTICAL PROBLEMS

Researchers interested in aging face a number of practical problems in working with older subjects. Older adults are often assumed to be quickly and easily fatigued by the rigors of the experimental process. This may be true for some, and scheduling breaks may be appropriate for them. Other older adults work hard for several hours on the boring, difficult cognitive problems we ask them to solve, refusing to give up before they finish. Fatigue may have little impact on performance [Cunningham et al, 1978]. In one study [Klodin, 1976] a woman spent 56 minutes on one item of the Block Design from the Wechsler Adult Intelligence Scale. The tester, a very patient young man, described it as one of the most painful experiences of his lifetime. Is the fatigue experienced in the experiment that of the subject or of the experimenter? Most research assistants, and researchers themselves, are bright, competent, efficient people who know how to do the task, having watched many others perform it. Do we become bored and project our boredom onto the subject, for whom the task is novel and challenging?

On the other hand, some older adults do refuse to continue a difficult task. Perhaps these old people truly cannot perform the task, or perhaps they are freer than young adults of social constraints to conform to the experimenter's expectations. Bright young college students may view experimental procedures as a challenge to their self-esteem. Perhaps older adults refuse such challenges because they measure their self-esteem in other ways.

Severe blows to the older adult's ego may come from well-intentioned research assistants who are unconsciously condescending in word and action. The old people who participate in research projects are not children; by and large they are a superior group of intelligent, knowledgeable, involved people. However, many younger adults, including research assistants, have certain stereotypes about older people, and these stereotypes can be communicated by word, action, and demeanor. An uncomfortable relationship between the experimenter and subject can result in the subject failing to return for subsequent sessions. Careful observation of the way research assistants deal with older subjects is important and may reveal a need for a few sensitivity training sessions. Most older subjects have inquisitive minds and appreciate an explanation of the research and debriefing after experiments. The social amenities, such as offering a cup of coffee or tea and a willingness on the part of the research assistant to chat for a while, seem to be relatively little to pay for the cooperation of those without whom we would have no data.

The older people who participate in research projects frequently have busy social lives and working in a trip to the laboratory is sometimes not as easy as researchers might think. Bringing the older person to the laboratory to participate in experiments is often troublesome. Sometimes the laboratory is located at the end of a complex maze of interlocking buildings and corridors in which the uninitiated soon become lost. Some older adults face severe transportation difficulties. They may not have a car, and the bus trip to the laboratory may be long and arduous, involving several transfers. Even the weather presents problems. A broken hip from a fall on the ice may be a death-dealing trauma for the older person.

Some of these practical difficulties can be overcome with ingenuity and forethought. Can the laboratory be set up in a room close to an easily identifiable outside door with a highly visible sign indicating that this is the place? Can one or more parking places be set aside for subjects on data collection days? In our own work we sometimes find it useful to meet our subjects in the parking lot. When all else fails, increasing the size of the payment made to the subject sometimes helps, especially in these inflationary times.

REFERENCES

Adam J (1978) Sequential strategies and the separation of age, cohort, and time-of-measurement contributions to developmental data. Psych Bull 85:1309–1316.

Cunningham WR, Sepkowski CM, Opel MR (1978) Fatigue effects on intelligence test performance in the elderly. J Gerontol 33:541–545.

Danziger W (1979) Adult age differences in sensitivity and response bias in a visual discrimination task. Ph.D. diss, Washington University, St. Louis, Missouri.

Danziger WL, Botwinick J (1980) Age and sex differences in sensitivity and response bias in a weight discrimination task. J Gerontol 35:388–394.

Jarvik LF, Falek A (1963) Intellectual stability and survival in the aged. J Gerontol 18:173–176.

Klodin VM (1976) The relationship of scoring treatment and age in perceptual-integrative performance. Exp Aging Res 2:303–313.

Okun MA, Elias CS (1977) Cautiousness in adulthood as a function of age and payoff structure. J Gerontol 32:451–455.

Schaie KW (1965) A general model for the study of developmental problems. Psych Bull 64:92–107.

Aging and Human Visual Function, pages 279-296

A Review of Methodologic Issues Concerning Incidence and Prevalence Data of Visual Deterioration in Elders

David A. Greenberg and Laurence G. Branch

BACKGROUND

A recent position paper of the National Institute of Aging, calling for more organized and enlightened attention to the health care of the elderly, states: "A more balanced view of the entire life cycle is in order, one which defines the biomedical, social and behavioral aspects throughout human development." [USDHEW, 1979].

Incentive for this attention is in one sense dictated by the extraordinary demographic alterations of this century. In 1900, 4% of the United States' population was over the age of 65. By 1970 this had increased to 10%, with projections for the year 2020 ranging from a low of 13% to a high of 20% [Kovar, 1977; USDHEW, 1979; USDHEW, 1978a; Besdine, 1979]. The elderly are clearly an increasing slice of an expanding pie. Perhaps a more vivid impression is drawn from considering that of all those people who have ever lived to the age of 65, fully one-half of them are alive today [Dans and Kerr, 1979].

One implication of these demographic trends is particularly sobering. The most costly diseases, in terms of both human suffering and dollars, develop and accrue in the later stages of life [Kovar, 1977; Adams, 1977; USDHEW, 1978a]. Given that the cost of caring for the elderly already far exceeds costs for other age groups, and that the fiscal encumbrance of major illness influences not only the affected individual and family unit but the larger society as well, the consequences of these demographic trends cannot be ignored [USDHEW, 1978b].

Furthermore, it is well documented that the elderly as a group must abide a variety of age-specific social and economic realities, not the least of which is significantly reduced income [USDHEW, 1968; USDHEW, 1980]. Additionally, the elderly are more frequently beset by visual anomalies that not only increase their vulnerability to physical injury but also restrict their self-sufficiency and thereby diminish their sense of self-reliance [U.S. Senate, 1978]. We all appreciate the freedom and enhanced enjoyment sight affords us as participants in the myriad activities life offers. To avoid the removal of older people from the field of play and relegation to the role of spectator in many of these activities, vision must, where possible, be maintained and enhanced.

The recognition of these broader considerations related to aging is beginning to be appreciated, and the difficult economic, humanistic, and technological issues surrounding geriatric care are serving as a catalyst for this new sensitivity. This volume is therefore timely. While the visual abilities of older people represent but one component of human aging, vision is extremely important.

The primary purpose of our review is to report the incidence and prevalence of visual deterioration associated with age. For our working definitions, "incidence" refers to the specific number of new cases of a particular disorder occurring within the study population during a specified time frame. "Prevalence" refers to the ratio of the total number of cases of a particular disorder present at a given time to the size of the population under consideration [Colton, 1974].

Our task has been facilitated by a 1976 report prepared for the National Eye Institute by the Westat Corporation and entitled "A Summary and Critique of Available Data on the Prevalence and Economic and Social Costs of Visual Disorders and Disabilities" [Westat, 1976]. The impetus for this study was the statement of the National Eye Institute that "the existing information was not satisfactory because it was 'conflicting, poorly documented, and ambiguous' " [Westat, 1976, p 1.1]. Westat "saw its role in this study to be threefold: (1) identification and location of data sources relevant to the purposes of the study; (2) methodological and general evaluation of existing data; and (3) estimation of the incidence and prevalence rates of visual disorders and cost factors associated with them" [Westat, 1976, p 1.2].

While not specifically geared to address the visual problems of the elderly, the Report's statistical stratification does provide a category for people aged 65 and over. We are not particularly enamored of the import attached to the 65th birthday, a legacy sometimes attributed to Chancellor Bismarck's enlightened policymaking [Butler, 1975]. However, we are less enchanted with reinventing a wheel (in this case, recollating existing data), and we thus elected to utilize the Westat Report as a baseline for our work.

METHODOLOGIC ISSUES

Of the pertinent areas reviewed, the Report states that the quality of available data was weakest for incidence rates. Two problems affecting even the most carefully executed studies have persisted. The first is that many of the most significant conditions, both in terms of disability produced and societal cost, tend to have an *insidious onset* and to become chronic. Therefore it is difficult to designate a specific time of onset or to calculate accurately the number of new cases during a particular time interval.

The second pervasive difficulty was the problem of *insufficient sample size* to permit a reasonably precise determination of disease incidence in the national population. This inadequacy produces large standard errors around the estimate. Intuitively we recognize that the potential for error decreases as the sample sizes increase. For example, let us consider disease X, which for our purpose is known to have a national incidence rate of 100,000 new cases per year. This certainly is not a rare disorder. Yet, this is only 1 case per 2,200 people per year. In other words, locating 1 case requires a sample size of 2,200 cases.

However, the luck of the draw for any particular sample of 2,200 people might include anywhere from 0 to 3 cases of disease X. (Author's computation of a basic formula for standard error of a proportion:

$$\text{s.e.}(P_{srs}) = \sqrt{\frac{p\,(1-p)}{n}}$$

Ninety-five out of 100 simple random samples of 2,200 each would identify 0 to 3 cases of disease X.) If we had only 1 sample to estimate the national incidence rate (and we did not know the true rate of 1 per 2,200) and if our 1 sample identified 3 cases, then our sample would overestimate the true rate by a factor of 3. In fact, with the small sample size of 2,200, we could expect to perhaps overestimate the magnitude of the problem at the national level by predicting 300,000 new cases per year when in fact there are only 100,000. The implications for planning, funding, and implementation are staggering. Through the marvel of mathematics in general (and the central limits theorem in particular), increasing the size of a simple random sample from 2,200 to 22,000 cases would substantially decrease the likelihood that our particular sample would be so much in error. With the larger sample of 22,000 cases and with 95% confidence, we could expect to overestimate maximally the magnitude of the problem at the national level with a prediction of 130,000 new cases when in fact there are only 100,000. The implications for potential error in planning, funding and implementation are much more reasonable. This increase in precision is due solely to the increase in sample size.

Additional methodological problems are also recognized in some existing studies. For example, some studies rely on incidence reporting by providers. This practice contains a number of uncontrolled variables. For example, it is not necessarily clear whether a particular patient (case) has been seen by another provider for the same condition. This sort of situation can lead to inflated incidence rates if several providers report the case during the same reporting period, or if the same case is reported in more than one period. Another problem of the timeliness of reporting a specific case can occur with chronic visual disorders such as open angle glaucoma, which frequently require several visits for definitive diagnosis. In these situations the problem of "insidious diagnosis" hinders the determination of a precise time of onset.

The critique in the Westat Report goes on to describe the variety of difficulties that arise from the use of various survey techniques such as household interviews, which have been utilized in the accrual of incidence data. In their summary opinion on available incidence data, the authors of the Westat Report stated that "available statistics on incidence that can make any claim to being nationally representative are not very satisfactory" [Westat, 1976, p 3.6].

The Westat Report also reviewed the quality of available prevalence data and noted that current prevalence data has primarily relied upon population surveys, either of the interview type or the examination and history variety. A potential shortcoming of the interview type of survey, such as the Health Interview Survey (HIS) of the National Center for Health Statistics, is the reliance upon the lay responder's ability to relate diagnostic information given by a provider. A major difficulty of the examination and history type of survey, such as the Health and Nutrition Examination Survey (HANES) of the National Center for Health Statistics, is the reliance placed on the single visit with no follow-up, which does not adequately deal with disorders with insidious onset.

Both types of population surveys additionally suffer from the problem of inadequate sample size as did the available incidence data. Furthermore, both the HIS sample and the HANES sample ignore the institutional population, an oversight that renders estimates of total population prevalence speculative at best.

An overriding concern of the Westat Report centered on the inexact classification of levels of visual disability (eg, severe, moderate, slight). These classifications contribute to the determination of both incidence and prevalence data. There exists an overall "lack of uniformity in classification" [Westat, 1976, p 4.11]. The Report quite candidly states "something better is needed in the way of objective criteria to define levels of visual impairment" [Westat, 1976, p 4.5]. The Report goes on to point out that "there are no statistics on the prevalence of the most severe degrees of visual impairment based on acceptable sampling techniques for representative samples of the U.S. population" [Westat, 1976, p 4.6].

Concerning visual disorders that cause lesser degrees of visual impairment, the available studies again suffer from inadequate sample sizes, the assessment problem that single-visit examinations can sometimes cause, bias due to non-responsiveness of particular age groups, and lack of uniformity and consistency in the examination procedures and environment. This latter problem is perhaps most pervasive and pernicious because it undermines the basic reliability (both *intrasite* and *intersite*) of the data upon which classification must be based.

After evaluating the state of affairs through 1976, the Report made a number of recommendations. Those that are germane to our discussion include

1. The sample sizes for both self-reported surveys and examination surveys should be increased in order to decrease errors in prevalence and incidence estimates.

2. The sampling frame for national surveys should be extended to include institutionalized populations.

3. In studies that estimate incidence or prevalence by means of office- or clinic-reported cases, standard procedures must be developed to insure that every case is in fact reported once, but only once, and during the appropriate reporting period.

4. The problems of estimating the prevalence or incidence of certain disorders that require clinical testing for accurate accounting should be addressed and standardized, and examining techniques should be developed and implemented.

5. Standardized procedures are necessary for the classification of levels of disability (eg, severe, moderate, or slight), which in turn are aggregated to report various incidence and prevalence rates.

6. Further refinement of measurement and interpretations is necessary to adequately reflect the individual's ability to perform those tasks necessary for his or her routine daily functioning, including occcupational considerations.

[Paraphrased from Westat, 1976, pp 8.1, 8.2, 8.3].

In light of these recommendations, let us briefly consider some of the incidence and prevalence data presented in the Westat Report. One purpose in our presenting these data is to satisfy the not insignificant demand of that part of the vision community that requires "some data, even if it is biased data." A more consequential purpose is to emphasize the care a reader must take in interpreting much of the existing incidence and prevalence data if one is to avoid planning, funding, and implementation difficulties. An accurate interpretation of these data requires a sensitivity to and awareness of the potentially tenuous methodologies used in some of their collection.

Table I presents an abridged version of the estimates of various acute conditions, injuries, and chronic conditions presented in the Westat Report. Please attend carefully to the explanations provided, which accompanied the table as originally presented in the Westat Report.

Table II presents an abridged version of estimates of *prevalence* for 15 categories of afflictions by degree of visual impairment. Again, please attend carefully to the explanations provided, which accompanied the original tables, and consider the following comments that the Westat authors felt compelled to provide:

. . . these notes [which accompany the tables—Eds] should not be detached from the tables since all users should be made aware of the limitations of the data.

The weakest part of the estimates has to do with prevalence in the institutional population. The numbers of cases in institutions are too large to be ignored (in contrast with incidence for which institutional cases can and have been ignored).

TABLE I. Abridged Estimates of Incidence (in Thousands of Cases Per Year) —U.S. 1972†

Diagnosis Group and Sex		All ages	Age 65 +
Acute Conditions[a]			
Infective & parasitic	Both sexes	4	1
disease of eye	Males	1	*
	Females	2	1
Allergic disorders	Both sexes	200	8
of eye	Males	78	2
	Females	121	7
Inflammations of	Both sexes	1,180	59
eye	Males	580	24
	Females	600	35
Ophthalmia neonatorum	Both sexes	22	2
and vision symptoms[e]	Males	12	1
	Females	10	1
All other acute	Both sexes	598	95
diseases of eye	Males	281	41
	Females	317	54
Injuries[b]			
Open wound of eye	Both sexes	198	5
	Males	173	4
	Females	25	*
Abrasion of cornea	Both sexes	446	39
and eye	Males	279	12
	Females	167	27
Foreign body in eye	Both sexes	1,014	30
and adnexa	Males	897	18
	Females	116	12
Other injury to eye	Both sexes	331	11
and optic nerve	Males	237	1
	Females	94	10
Chronic Conditions[c]			
Neoplasms of eye	Both sexes	7	1
	Males	4	1
	Females	3	*
Eye complications	Both sexes	46	18
of diabetes	Males	14	4
	Females	32	15
Corneal ulcer	Both sexes	104	19
and opacity	Males	55	10
	Females	49	9
Strabismus	Both sexes	403	20
	Males	189	9
	Females	214	11
Cataract	Both sexes	912	693
	Males	333	246
	Females	581	447

(Table continued on next page.)

TABLE I. Continued

Diagnosis Group and Sex		All ages	Age 65 +
Detachment of retina	Both sexes	25	9
	Males	13	7
	Females	11	2
Glaucoma	Both sexes	178	97
	Males	69	35
	Females	109	62
Congenital eye	Both sexes	49	2
disorders	Males	29	*
	Females	20	1
Special Group[d]			
Sarcoidosis,	Both sexes	13	*
histoplasmosis and	Males	5	*
toxoplasmosis	Females	7	*

†The basic source materials are statistics from the National Health Interview Survey, used to define the totals by age and sex for acute conditions and injuries, and first-visit statistics from the National Disease and Therapeutic Index, used for diagnostic distribution of acute conditions and injuries and for approximation of incidence of chronic conditions.

[a]Acute conditions include all conditions with abrupt onset and fairly short duration, plus a few minor chronic conditions in the residual group. All conditions must have involved medical care or one or more days of restricted activity. Totals agree with HIS averages for 1970–73.

[b]All injuries must have involved medical care or one or more days of restricted activity. Totals agree with HIS averages for 1970–73.

[c]Chronic condition incidence based on number of newly diagnosed cases. Age stated is age at which treatment began.

[d]This group included owing to expressed interest of NEI. Not restricted to cases involving eye because no distinction is made in the disease classification.

[e]Cases labeled ophthalmia neonatorum have been included here despite the fact that many are believed to be due to gonococcal infection. When such infection is not specified, classification practice is not to include the case with infectious diseases.

N.B. Totals may not agree with sums of subcategories owing to rounding of estimates. Asterisks indicate estimates of less than 500 cases. All estimates of less than 10,000 are subject to especially high chance of error owing both to small sample sizes and the method of estimation.

The estimates [in the present Table II] . . . are probably underestimates of the amount of blindness in the country meeting the legal blindness definition. This is because even the best of the State Registers of blindness (on which the National Society for the Prevention of Blindness basically relies) probably miss certain cases in the population. For example, we are told that the

TABLE II. Abridged Estimated of Prevalence of Conditions (in Thousands of Cases) U.S. 1972

Type of Eye Affection	Total (across all ages)	Age 65+ years								
		Impaired Vision[a]			Severe Visual Impairments[b]			Legal Blindness[c]		
		Total	Male	Female	Total	Male	Female	Total	Male	Female
Glaucoma	1,070	808	295	513	179	66	113	41	18	23
Cataract— prenatal	41	7	3	4	7	3	4	2	1	1
Cataract— other	1,670	1,314	460	853	162	46	115	36	13	23
Retinal disorder— prenatal	76	29	12	17	29	12	17	6	3	3
Retinal disorder— diabetic	138	85	21	64	49	10	39	11	3	8
Retinal disorder— other	601	404	139	264	217	66	150	48	18	30
Retrolental Fibroplasia	19	*	*	*	*	*	*	*	*	*
Myopia	715	148	53	95	20	7	13	5	2	3
Cornea or sclera	294	99	46	53	46	16	30	10	4	6
Uveitis	285	100	36	64	41	15	26	9	4	5
Optic nerve disease	121	65	32	32	58	29	28	14	8	6
Multiple affections	90	81	21	60	81	21	60	18	6	12
Refractive errors with lesser disability	1,662	314	113	201	0	0	0	0	0	0
Other	3,656	1,212	444	767	35	16	19	8	4	4
Unknown	221	166	56	110	138	46	92	31	13	18

[a]Based upon prevalence figures by age and sex from the Health Interview Survey and the 1973–74 Nursing Home Survey subdivided into more detailed eye affection categories using all-visit statistics from the National Disease and Therapeutic Index (for the lesser impairments) and the Model Reporting Area (for the more seriously impaired).

[b]Based upon prevalence figures by age and sex from the Health Interview Survey and the 1973–74 Nursing Home Survey subdivided into more detailed eye affection categories using statistics from the Model Reporting Area.

[c]Based upon prevalence figures published by the National Association for the Prevention of Blindness (see Hatfield: Sight-Saving Review, Vol. 43, No. 2) subdivided by age and sex and type of eye affection categories using statistics from the Model Reporting Area.

N.B. Columns may not always add owing to rounding. Asterisk means estimate of less than 500. Estimates are for the total civilian population. All estimates less than 25,000 are subject to large relative errors of sampling. The "All Other" estimates were made separately. Note that the cases in Disability Category B are included in Category A, a broader group; the cases in Disability Category C are almost entirely included in Category B, a broader group.

registers are intended to include some cases residing in institutions but could very well miss some. Furthermore, cases not requiring or requesting any assistance from the public and private programs of assistance would be less likely to be registered.

It should again be emphasized that the statistics [in the present Table II] . . . should not be used to draw epidemiological conclusions.

[Westat, 1976, pp 4.14, 4.15]

Notwithstanding these caveats, the incidence data presented in Table I require further explanation of some inherent shortcomings. Consider the first recommendation previously presented concerning the sample size necessary for establishing reasonably accurate estimates. The N.B. footnote in Table I unequivocally specifies that "all estimates of less than 10,000 are subject to especially high chance of error owing to both the small sample sizes and the method of estimation" [Westat, 1976, p 3.11]. Estimates of less than 10,000 are found in more than half of the cells (28 out of 54 total cells). For instance, the first cell of the table that represents infective and parasitic diseases of the eye for both sexes for people aged 65 or more estimated incidence at 1,000 cases per year. The second cell (same conditions for males aged 65 or more) estimated fewer than 500 cases per year, while the third cell (representing females aged 65 or more with the same condition) was reported as 1,000 cases per year. The estimates within all three cells fall substantially below the 10,000 cases required.

The merits of cautioning that estimates of fewer than 10,000 cases have an especially high chance of error and then presenting estimates that approached only 1,000 seems to us to invite planning, funding, and implementation difficulties. On the other hand, if the intent of reporting such data is simply to document that the population incidence rates are perhaps minuscule, then a more explicit format, simply stating that the rates are very small, is perhaps warranted.

Of the 54 cells of incidence rates for elders presented in Table I, 28 estimated fewer than 10,000 cases. Of the 19 cells for both sexes, 8 had under 10,000 cases. Eleven conditions for males and 9 for females out of 18 for each had estimated under 10,000 cases. Thus the minimum sample size recommended by Westat for statistical reliability failed to be achieved more often than it was.

Examining the instances of cells with over 10,000 cases in Table I, we see that the incidence of only two acute conditions (inflammation of the eye and all other acute conditions of the eye) contained sufficient numbers of cases for reasonable accuracy. However, the vagueness of the categories is another potential problem that will be addressed subsequently.

Examining the incidence of the various types of injury presented in Table I, we see that only two of the four presented (abrasion of cornea and eye, and foreign body in eye and adnexa) allow for reasonably accurate population estimates. Another (injury to eye and optic nerve) indicates a 10-times-greater incidence for women than for men, a difference that probably emphasized more the unreliability of rare case estimates from the sample size than any need for a gender-related theory to explain the result.

Examining the incidence estimates of the chronic conditions in Table I, we see two categories that occurred frequently enough among elders to be estimated with reasonable accuracy from samples of this size (National Health Interview Survey [HIS] includes approximately 134,000 people; National Disease and Therapeutic Index [NDTI] includes 2 days of office-visit reports from approximately 1,500 physicians). Cataracts were estimated at 693,000 cases per year for elders (246,000 among men and 447,000 among women) and glaucoma was estimated at 97,000 cases per year for elders (35,000 cases for men and 62,000 cases for women).

Let us next examine the incidence data from the perspective of the second recommendation previously noted, namely the need to include the institutionalized population in the sampling frame. The estimates of acute conditions and injuries came from the two surveys—HIS did not include any institutionalized respondents, and NDTI did. Therefore, at least part of the resulting estimates are misestimates because institutionalized people are underrepresented (unless one is willing to assume that the rates for institutional and noninstitutional elders do not differ statistically in any of these areas, an assumption that would seem exceedingly difficult to justify).

The estimates of chronic conditions, however, did not systematically exclude institutionalized people because these estimates came solely from the NDTI. This is not to suggest, however, that the estimates in the chronic condition cells with sufficient sample sizes are therefore beyond criticism as estimates of incidence. We need only examine the third recommendation previously listed—clinic- or office-visit reporting systems require special standard procedures to avoid undercounting or overcounting—to suggest additional criticisms.

The risk of undercounting any specific condition exists because only physicians are asked to report; other professionals who might diagnose chronic visual conditions, like optometrists or nonphysician staff in certain institutions, are automatically excluded from the sample frame. The risk of overcounting or double counting exists because one person conceivably might visit more than one physician about the same condition. In these situations, double counting can exist.

The fourth recommendation is also pertinent to the topic of clinic or office reporting of chronic conditions. Standardization of the examination tests and procedures is essential for interreporter reliability. Furthermore, the potential for inconsistent or ambiguous reporting exists especially for those conditions that might be presumptively diagnosed on the first visit but might still require multiple visits for definitive diagnosis. Should the physicians report the case with the presumptive diagnosis or the definitive diagnosis? Human nature being what it is, it is plausible that the personality of the reporter or the demands of one's workload rather than the design assumptions of the study might influence the decision of when to report this kind of case.

Examination of Table II (the prevalence data) reveals similar methodological shortcomings. The readers recall the previously mentioned N.B. footnote in Table I to the effect that "All estimates less than 25,000 are subject to larger relative errors of sampling" [Westat, 1976, p 4.16]. Estimates of fewer than 25,000 cases are found in over half of the cells (70 out of 135 total cells).

Inspection of the estimates in Table II by degree of impairment indicates that the sample sizes were adequate for those with "impaired vision" (the broadest category) in 35 out of 45 cells. The sample sizes were, however, inadequate for 40 out of 45 cells among the most seriously impaired—the legally blind. Unfortunately, the accuracy of available estimates diminishes considerably with increasing levels of visual deficit. The most fragile numbers exist for those with the most fragile vision, precisely those who need efficient and effective special services based on accurate program planning estimates.

Three additional methodological difficulties include (1) the systematic exclusion of institutionalized people from some of the data, (2) the risks of specific types of overcounting and undercounting that clinic- or office-visit reported data from physicians only exacerbates, and (3) the lack of standardized examination tests and procedures across individual practitioners' offices. These difficulties were already discussed with the incidence data but apply similarly to the reported prevalence data. In addition, the prevalence data as presented suffer from the two potential problems discussed in the original Westat Report recommendations.

Specifically, the standards or procedures used to define operationally an individual's level of impairment (eg, impaired vs severe visual impairment vs legal blindness) are not universally agreed on, and the relationship of these operational definitions to occupational or routine daily functioning requires refinement.

In order to determine whether the disturbing implications and the recommendations of the 1976 Westat Report had a positive impact, we initiated a computerized literature search that reviewed the published work in the intervening period. Our search unfortunately provided no indication that there had been much significant progress towards the production of incidence and prevalence data reflecting incorporation of the Westat recommendations. The data still often come from the HIS and NDTI and still suffer from

(1) insufficient sample sizes to estimate accurately prevalence or incidence rates of visual disorders other than cataracts and glaucoma;

(2) lack of representation of institutionalized older people in HIS;

(3) the potential of variable overreporting and underreporting associated with the office-reporting procedures from physicians only used in NDTI;

(4) lack of standardized tests and procedures across the practitioners' offices;

(5) lack of consensus on operational definitions for the classification of levels of visual disability;

(6) lack of sensitivity to the interrelationship between visual dysfunction and the requirements for routine daily functioning.

Through this point we have specified in some detail (we hope not in laborious detail) some of the common methodological problems that compromise much of the available prevalence and incidence data concerning visual impairments among the elderly in this country.

Fortunately, some recent efforts, such as those of Kirchner et al in the Statistical Brief Series prepared by the Social and Behavioral Analysis Division of the American Foundation for the Blind, have recognized certain of these problems and indeed point out their "concern that statistics should be used appropriately— which usually means they should be used with caution" [Kirchner et al 1978b, p 419]. Perhaps of equal import is the fact that Kirchner et al have begun to address the issue of the lack of uniformity in the definition of terms defining visual loss, stating that "there are a number of distinct but related concepts that refer to visual loss. Unfortunately, the terms commonly used to designate these concepts are often used interchangeably, or to represent more than one concept leading to confusion in research and program planning" [Kirchner et al, 1978a, p 329]. As attested to by this series, the American Foundation for the Blind appears to be committed to the development of statistically sound as well as policy-relevant data bases. Examples of their particular work to date are referenced in Kirchner et al [1978a, 1978b].

Two ongoing, nationally known studies have addressed the issue of visual deficits as related to aging, but, unfortunately, have done so from perspectives that do not readily lend themselves to the development of incidence and prevalence generalizations. Both the Duke Longitudinal Study of Aging [Palmore, 1970, p 178] and the Framingham Study [Kahn et al, 1977] dealt, by design, with the interrelationships between or among specific variables at the expense of generalizability. The Duke Study was quite specific in identifying this conscious decision on their part.

> With appropriate misgivings, the research group at Duke University decided to continue the practice of recruiting volunteers rather than attempting to involve a randomly drawn sample of elderly non-institutionalized subjects in research that would require intensive clinical evaluation. . . . One consequence of the decision to use volunteer subjects was obvious. Generalizations from the data would necessarily be limited to statements concerning the relationship among factors in the aging process under specified conditions. Statements about elderly persons in general would not be warranted.
>
> [Palmore, 1970, p 178]

What generalizations can be made concerning the rates of visual impairment among the elderly? We have seen that in general the available national data do not support exact prevalence and incidence estimates of the kind that have been necessary for focused policy discussion in other allied health areas. Nevertheless, it is possible to draw some conclusions about the proportions of older people with various kinds of visual impairments, if not the more exact prevalence rates. Furthermore, it is also possible to appreciate the changes in the order of magnitude of visual impairments associated with changes in age.

Let us now re-examine some of the prevalence data presented in Table II in order to draw estimates of proportion of occurrence. As we proceed, however, bear in mind that more of the methodological inadequacies previously discussed logically would result in *undercounting* or underestimating a problem rather than overcounting.

By converting the total number of cases of impaired vision (column 2 of Table II) for specific types of eye affection into the percentage of older people affected (by dividing the figure in Table II by 21,300,000, the 1973 census estimate of people aged 65 or older in the United States), some interesting estimates can be derived.

There are three specific conditions that affect more than one percent of people aged 65 or more:

(1) Cataracts (other then prenatal) affect in the order of 5% to 7% (6.17%) of elders, or more than 1 out of every 20 people aged 65 or more.

(2) Glaucoma affects in the order of 3% to 5% (3.79%) of elders, or 1 out of 20.

(3) Retinal disorders other than diabetic retinopathy affect in the order of 1% to 3% (1.90%) of elders, or approximately 1 out of 50 older people.

Several other conditions affect 2 to 8 elders per 1,000:

(1) Myopia affects in the order of 6 to 8 per 1,000 elders.
(2) Uveitis affects in the order of 4 to 6 per 1,000 elders.
(3) Cornea or sclera problems affect in the order of 3 to 5 per 1,000 elders.
(4) Diabetic retinopathy affects in the order of 3 to 5 per 1,000 elders.
(5) Optic nerve disorders affect in the order of 2 to 4 per 1,000 elders.

It is also interesting to examine how age might have influenced the magnitude of the three most prevalent visual impairments among elders (cataracts, glaucoma, and retinal disorders other than diabetic retinopathy).

With the information presented in Table II, we calculated that approximately 8 per 1,000 people across all ages had cataracts, compared with 62 per 1,000 people aged 65 or more. Therefore cataracts are approximately eight times more prevalent among elders.

Glaucoma also appears to be nearly eight times more prevalent among elders, with approximately 5 cases per 1,000 in the general population compared with the 38 cases per 1,000 elders.

The risk of retinal disorders other than diabetic retinopathy is about six times greater for elders than the general population. Three cases per 1,000 in the general population are presented, compared with 19 cases for every 1,000 people aged 65 or more.

Not only are these three visual impairments the most prevalent among the aged, but the risk of having any one of them is increased six to eight times as a function of aging.

A RESEARCH ILLUSTRATION OF DATA COLLECTION PROBLEMS WITH POLICY IMPLICATIONS

Increased awareness of the problems associated with nonstandardized tests and procedures across practitioners' offices might also be considered another constructive addition to the goal of reliable and valid incidence and prevalence data. The development of such awareness might be facilitated by considering the operative integration of research and clinical care.

While many research efforts acknowledge the need for corroboration in clinical practice, there appears to be an appreciable delay in the incorporation of certain conceptual changes into the everyday clinical armamentarium. Additionally, many clinicians are reluctant to participate in organized research efforts, perhaps in response to the operating constraints of a research regimen.

From the other perspective, researchers frequently hesitate to use clinical data, not because the data are necessarily invalid, but rather because they frequently exist in a form that precludes the objective coding required for a reliable data base. This observation should not be construed as a negative comment on the quality of clinical care. We are simply noting that, for the most part, clinicians have had only the responsibility for encoding information for their own retrieval, buoyed by the knowledge that, should another provider become involved in the care of a particular patient, the opportunity for verbal or written amplification of the record exists.

The clinician is often simply preparing a case note. The researcher often would like to be able to use the "case note" as "research data," but the requirements of the two currently exist at different levels. Resolution could occur if clinicians began to adopt standardized recording techniques geared to criteria that render clinical notations suitable for retrieval, and if researchers participated in the design of the standardized recording instrument.

The impact of this coordinated approach would be increased if the issue selected for collaboration had the potential for influencing social and governmental policy as well as delivery of care to the individual.

Fortunately, in the field of vision, there is an issue that can benefit from increased attention to uniform measurement from both clinicians and researchers. We refer to that routine clinical measure of visual function, acuity. Unfortunately, "routine" as a modifier applies not only to the regularity with which the measurement is taken but also to the automatic way in which it is often measured and recorded. Herein lies the danger: It is all too easy to lose sight of the fact that this routine procedure has varied and critical implications for the patient. Whether it is the renewal of a driver's license, qualification for particular disability benefits, or, perhaps of greater import, the potential ineligibility for such programs, codification for bureaucratic purposes has made acuity measure the fulcrum upon which livelihoods and lifestyles may balance.

By convention, the visual acuity measure has developed as a standard notation for distance vision. Most modern eye examination lanes utilize projection systems to arrive at the appropriate measure. We hypothesize, however, that only a small minority of these examination lanes are regularly evaluated as to their adherence to pertinent test variables, such as exact testing distance between patient and screen, letter size projected on screen, and ambient illumination on the lane.

We also suggest that this inadvertent lack of attention to testing detail has been a source of frustration to both clinicians and researchers alike. One example would be the re-examination of referred patients or research subjects who demonstrate an acuity considerably different from the level at which they were referred.

We must also consider that sources of error in obtaining the acuity measure likely go beyond physical testing variables to include the often-neglected area of doctor-patient communication. We refer specifically to the content of the instructions for task compliance and the manner in which they are delivered. It might, for instance, be interesting to compare the results of acuity assessments when a patient is first simply instructed to "Read the lowest line you can" as opposed to receiving the added reinforcement of "Try just one more line—you can do it."

We have considered three areas of potential difficulties in obtaining reliable and valid data from clinical settings: (1) the clinician's "case notes" are often rather abbreviated for "research data," (2) the physical testing variables are often not standardized in the clinical setting, and (3) the psychological testing variables are not uniform.

To get some indication of the pervasiveness of these kinds of potential problems, we reviewed 200 randomly selected records from the first decade of an ongoing clinic-based study of normal aging. Each record contained multiple eye-care entries made over a 10-year span. We found considerable intra- and inter-patient inconsistencies in the extent and thoroughness of the eye-care entries in general. Examples of the inconsistencies both within a record and across records existed most glaringly in the area of acuity notations. While all of the entries were probably useful for patient care at the time they were made, their utility for subsequent investigation by the third party researcher left much to be desired. In short, these acuity notations provided a most suitable example of clinicians' habits of encoding information in such a way as to hinder subsequent research.

Our original goal of trying to present reliable and valid incidence and prevalence data concerning causes of visual deterioration with age is becoming increasingly illusive. We have examined in considerable detail some of the problems associated with existing data. Since a large part of the existing data come from clinical settings, and since we have seen that the information available from clinical settings is not necessarily consistent, we propose to examine in more detail the degree of comparability across sites.

Specifically, we propose to study the process of measuring visual acuity and its notation as performed at approximately six different clinical sites in a repeated measures design on the same subjects. We shall examine the manner of notation as well as the accuracy of the acuity itself. In other words, we propose to study the influences of the data collection methods on the data collected. We shall first recruit approximately 30 subjects and carefully measure the visual acuity of each in a manner most frequently utilized in clinical settings but under the most rigorous and controlled of circumstances. All physical testing variables and psychological testing variables will be uniform and in accordance with accepted practice. We then propose to have each subject tested for visual acuity at several stations in each of several sites in a randomized order. (Of course, the site testors will be blind to the purposes of the study, and the cooperation of the site administrators will be necessary for such a project.)

The study design will thus enable us to examine and identify some basic elements of the measurement process itself, which might require more rigorous attention and standardization. Such increased attention will be necessary if we are ever to reach a point at which clinic-based information could be used to produce reliable and valid incidence and prevalence rates.

Specifically, we can test *intrasite reliability* by calculating an index of reproducibility across stations within each site for each individual. Obviously this kind of intrasite reliability must exist at a statistically high level before the validity of incidence and prevalence data can be achieved.

Second, we can test *intersite reliability* by calculating correlation coefficients across sites for each individual. Again, this form of reliability must also precede the validity of incidence and prevalence data.

Third, we can calculate the average difference between the criterion acuity measure and the acuity measures from each particular site for all subjects *(criterion-validity)*. In this fashion, we can assess the degree to which the differences obtained are statistically significant, and a panel can judge in what context the observed differences between criterion and site begins to focus on the *validity* of clinic-based information.

After these examinations of the differences in recorded acuity measures, we would attempt to understand why the obtained differences might exist by evaluating the process of measurement at each site. Specifically, we would examine and note both the physical and psychological testing variables. As part of the consideration of physical testing variables, we would document the frequency and process of standardizing the equipment used in each testing lane within each site. As part of the consideration of psychological testing variables, each participant-subject would record *any* and *all* verbal instructions given to him or her by the tester as soon as possible after the testing.

To recapitulate, then, the purposes of this kind of proposed investigation are (1) to examine quantitatively the reliability and validity of the acuity measures typically obtained in clinics (and therefore typically used in the development of incidence and prevalence rates), and (2) to describe qualitatively the standards and procedures typically used in clinical settings to obtain these acuity measures.

Presumably, an examination of this type will highlight the need for standardized procedures. Once uniform methods are adopted, attention can then be focused on the functional and social implications of these measurements.

SUMMARY

We have discussed previously some methodological sampling artifacts that can encourage *underreporting* of visual problems (eg, including only physicians in the NDTI sample). At this juncture, we might similarly consider that all clinically-based incidence and prevalence data are affected by the monetary and physical limitations of the elderly. These limitations exacerbate *underreporting* of a different nature. Various surveys have indicated that, because of such constraints, as many as 45% of the elderly did not go to an eye specialist the last time they experienced difficulty [U.S. Senate, 1978]. Until the implications of such issues as these are considered, there will continue to be serious problems with incidence and prevalence data for the elderly.

Preliminary evidence suggests that the prevalence of visual impairments such as cataracts, glaucomas, and retinal disorders is six to eight orders of magnitude higher among elders than among people under age 65. If social policy is formulated even in part on the existing data, the implications for potential hardships resulting from the underestimations are considerable. This nation's visually impaired elders at the very least deserve a social policy predicated upon an accurate statement of the magnitude of their problem.

In this volume, we have heard a great deal about the visual deterioration and underlying pathophysiology that accompany the aging process. This type of information and associated research is essential for comprehending the effects of aging on the visual system, but it is our opinion that not until we are able to complement such knowledge with reliable and valid incidence and prevalence data can we hope for noteworthy clinical intervention.

REFERENCES

Adams, G. (1977) "Essentials of Geriatric Medicine." New York: Oxford University Press.

Besdine, R. (1979) "Observations on Geriatric Medicine." U.S. Department of Health, Education and Welfare, Public Health Service, DHEW Publication No. (NIH) 79–162.

Butler, R. (1975) "Why Survive? Being Old in America." New York: Harper & Row.

Colton, T. (1974) "Statistics in Medicine." Boston: Little, Brown.

Dans, P.E., Kerr, M.R. (1979) Gerontology and geriatrics in medical education. N Eng J Med 300:228.

Kahn et al (1977) The Framingham Eye Study—Outline and major prevalence findings. Am J Epidemiol 196.

Kirchner et al (1978a) Visual Handicaps: Statistical Data on a Social Process. Statistical Briefs on Visual Impairment and Blindness. American Foundation for the Blind.

Kirchner et al (1978b) Sources of Variation in the Estimated Prevalence of Visual Loss. Statistical Briefs on Visual Impairment and Blindness.

Kovar, M.D. (1977) Health of the elderly and use of health services. Pub Health Rep, 92(1).

Palmore, E. (Ed.) (1970) "Normal Aging." Reports from the Duke Longitudinal Study, 1955 to 1969. Durham, N.C.: Duke University Press.

U.S. Department of Health, Education and Welfare. (1968) "Demographic Characteristics of the Aged." Social Security Administration, Office of Research and Statistics, DHEW Publication No. (SSA) 75-11802.

U.S. Department of Health, Education and Welfare (1978a) Fact Book on Aging.

U.S. Department of Health, Education and Welfare (1978b) Health—United States, Part B, Section IV, Public Health Service.

U.S. Department of Health, Education and Welfare (1979) "Recent Developments in Clinical Research in Geriatric Medicine: The NIA Role." Public Health Service, National Institute of Health.

U.S. Department of Health, Education and Welfare. (1980) "Income and Resources of the Aged." Social Security Administration, Office Of Policy, Office of Research and Statistics, DHEW Publication No. 13-11727.

U.S. Senate Special Committee on Aging. (1978) "Vision Impairments Among Older Americans." Ninety-fifth Congress, August 3, 1978.

Westat Corporation. (1976) "Summary and Critique of Available Data on the Prevalence and Economic and Social Costs of Visual Disorders and Disabilities." For the National Eye Institute of the Public Health Service, U.S. Department of Health, Education and Welfare.

VI. THE HUMAN IMPACT OF VISUAL CHANGES WITH AGE

Aging and Human Visual Function, pages 299–300
© 1982 Alan R. Liss, Inc., 150 Fifth Avenue, New York, NY 10011

Introduction

Deterioration of visual functions hampers the efforts of older people to work, take care of themselves, and enjoy life. The extent and rate of deterioration varies considerably among individuals but it is a universal process; even in the absence of pathology, all of us who live long enough can expect some loss in vision. For many individuals the loss is severe enough to interfere with important visual activities such as reading and driving.

How can the scientific community help ameliorate the problems with vision people encounter as they get older? The preceeding chapters illustrate what has been learned about the mechanisms of vision and perception and how they change with age. There is considerable data about molecular changes affecting transmission of light through the eye, cellular changes in the retina and brain, and perceptual changes in processing of visual information. However, it is not sufficient to study these changes in isolation; there is an urgent need to understand how these processes alter the integrated functioning of the visual system and the ability of human beings to perform in their normal environments as they get older. Unfortunately, in this respect we have not made much progress; only in a crude way are we able to characterize the visual requirements for a task such as automobile driving, and assessing the functional impact of visual deterioration is more an art than a science. Consequently we have not made great strides in developing devices to compensate for visual deterioration or procedures for training individuals to use their residual vision.

This last section of our book is included with the hope of stimulating scientists and clinicians to think about the human impact of the age-related changes in vision that they study piece-meal in laboratories. In order to effectively apply the knowledge generated by biological and psychological research to the solution of human problems, those doing research must have a good sense of what the problems are. Conversely, consideration of social needs will reveal new opportunities for research.

One approach to understanding people's problems is to put ourselves in their shoes. In his paper in this section, Leon Pastalan describes such an approach, in which contact lenses were used to simulate the visual deterioration typically occurring with age. The degree of deterioration simulated was probably an underestimate, but the personal impact of visual loss is brought home in a way that graphs and prose cannot match. These contact lenses are being used in training programs to sensitize people to the needs of the elderly: For instance, they have been used in architecture courses in the hope of stimulating architects to think about designs that will reduce the visual problems the elderly face. Perhaps if scientists and clinicians who deal with the effects of age on vision would spend some time wearing these lenses they would discover new research and service delivery opportunities.

The papers by Eleanor Faye and William Padula point out the urgent need for more effective service-delivery systems for elderly patients who have severe visual impairment. For instance, the eye examination of partially sighted patients must include an assessment of visual function far more comprehensive than simple measurement of central acuity and field as conventionally determined. This need for comprehensive assessment is also an exciting opportunity for research.

Psychophysical research in recent years has shown that traditional measures of central acuity and field give a quite limited characterization of the visual information-extraction processes of human beings. For instance, Sekuler points out earlier in this book that the ability to identify minute objects does not necessarily predict how well people can discern larger targets. Similarly, conventional measurement of visual field gives the clinician quite limited information about an aspect of the visual system that is crucial for orientation, movement, and avoidance of oncoming subjects. Psychophysicists have developed laboratory techniques for characterizing the visual system's ability to extract spatial information; these and other psychophysical techniques might prove useful in assessing the visual status of elderly patients.

Opportunities for research related to service delivery are not limited to psychophysics. We know, for instance, that sensory loss tends to isolate older individuals in a way that contributes to declining mental acuity and social functioning, but we have not given much attention to ways of offsetting this effect. There is also an urgent need for demographic studies of the effects of age on vision and social functioning and a need for social policy analysis of service delivery for the elderly.

Perhaps the most important message of this section is the one with which Barry Robinson concludes: The elderly are not a special population requiring our sympathy; they are quite simply ourselves, their vision is ours, and their condition is our future.

Aging and Human Visual Function, pages 301–313
© 1982 Alan R. Liss, Inc., 150 Fifth Avenue, New York, NY 10011

The Older Low-Vision Patient: Visual Function and Human Factors

Eleanor E. Faye

INTRODUCTION AND DEFINITIONS

A common assumption in defining low vision is that the condition can be described numerically; groups of people of all ages and widely disparate conditions who have visual acuities of 20/70 to 5/200 are lumped together and called "low-vision patients." Such a superficial definition does injustice to a complex field of visual rehabilitation known as "low vision."

There are many types of physical impairments; low vision deals specifically with the eye and its diseases and their effect on the manner in which a person functions. Impairment can occur at birth or at any time thereafter and the degree of impairment can range from minimal to profound. A person born with low vision has different rehabilitation requirements from persons who develop low vision during the vocational years or during the retirement years [Faye, 1970].

Vision impairment implies either a permanent reduction of central visual acuity that cannot be corrected to the normal standard with conventional eyeglasses, a reduction and/or extinction of a portion of the field of vision, reduction or loss of color vision, abnormal light and dark adaptation, or reduced focus. The most significant of these are loss of central vision and loss of peripheral field of vision.

The macula and fovea are responsible for seeing details; impairment of this relatively small but sensitive area causes reduction of visual acuity. Loss of macular tissue does not cause total blindness; the degree of reduction of central vision depends on the type of tissue damage.

Impairment of one or more of the functions of the eye usually leads to visual disability. The term "visual disability" is applied when a person's impairment prevents him or her from performing accustomed tasks that require either gross or detailed vision. Visual disability may also be based on the individual's or society's expectations of performance as well as actual ability to perform a visual task.

What can be done to help a low-vision patient function visually or to improve visual performance after the eye disease has been diagnosed and treated with medical and/or surgical procedures and it has been explained to the patient that this is the best restoration of vision that can be expected? For this patient the next step is optical therapy: a low-vision examination, prescription of low-vision aids, and instruction in the use of the aids.

Low-Vision Aids

Because the human eye is limited in its ability to resolve details, many optical devices have been invented for people with normal vision who must see details, eg, opera glasses, microscopes, telescopes, handheld loupes. Whereas a normal person may need occasional magnification for unusual tasks, the patient with subnormal vision needs magnification all of the time for usual tasks. Low-vision aids are optical devices or systems that enlarge images to the extent required by the injured eye. These aids may consist of a lens, a combination of lenses, a prism, a mirror, or an electronic system; they all use optical means to raise the level of visual performance of impaired patients.

Low-vision aids do not restore normal vision for either distance or close work, such as reading. For distance, one or more types of telescopic lenses are used. If the person must read or do close work, a variety of convex lens devices (spectacles, hand magnifiers, stand magnifiers) or reading telescopes are available. To date, no one lens has been designed that can replace all of the functions of the normal eye. A patient who has many tasks and interests usually receives more than one prescription. To date, most low-vision lenses have been adapted from a variety of industrial loupes; very little advanced work in the fields of optics and space technology has been applied to the problems of visual impairment.

Optical or visual aids must not be given on a hit-or-miss basis or through trial and error to individuals with impaired vision. The examination and prescription is a complex process that must take into consideration the medical status, ophthalmological condition, socioeconomic background, and current life situation and objectives of the patient.

The Low-Vision Examination

The low-vision examination is the mechanism by which low-vision aids are prescribed, taking into consideration the eye disorder, the functional visual acuity, and the patient's objectives and abilities. There are three stages in the examination: (1) taking a detailed history of medical and eye problems and pertinent background information, particularly about tasks and interests of the patient, (2) making the actual eye examination and detailed analysis of the visual function and strength of optical aid needed, and (3) prescribing the aid and giving the training and instruction necessary for correct, effective use of the aid(s). This paper is particularly concerned with the function of the older individual with low vision and will demonstrate the way in which the diagnosis influences the prescription of low-vision optical aids.

Function vs Diagnosis

The customary orientation of current medical care is to do diagnostic tests, gather data, and treat the disorder if it is treatable. Medical data are used to treat a patient's disorder, but the life management is often left to the patient, who must adjust to the functional disability alone or with the help of well-meaning friends and family. Unfortunately, this hit-or-miss system has been the usual path to low-vision care; both ophthalmology and optometry have been slow to move toward effective programs for low-vision patients.

A more effective approach to managing low-vision cases is to use all of the historical and diagnostic data and place special emphasis on function. With this approach, diagnostic tests assume another dimension; for example, the eye diagnosis, in addition to its primary role, tells us to look for certain responses and behavior in learning to use magnifying devices. Visual acuity tests give us a base from which to select the appropriate magnification for distant, intermediate, or near tasks. Visual field tests tell us what to expect from a person's ability to travel and to use reading aids and telescopes. Color vision tests help us to predict what color cues a patient can use in daily life related to vocation and to home and outdoor communities. Binocular function and light tolerance assessment furnish cues for mobility when the patient wishes to continue independent travel. The history tells us what the patient expects, and what abilities and attitudes he or she brings to the examination. The visual problems are presented for our solution, usually a prescription of optical aids. In low-vision work, we use all of the information we collect in order to understand the functional impact of visual loss and the needs of our patients. Only then are we doing a complete low-vision examination and rendering low-vision care.

Defining the Older Low-Vision Patient

The responses of older people to disabling eye problems have aspects not encountered with younger people with the same diseases. For example, we must consider

(1) Diminished neurological function, reflected in diminished performance in motor function, loss of agility, and diminished ability to sustain physical stress.

(2) Loss of higher brain (cortical) functions, demonstrated by decrease in sensory awareness, slower thought processes, and increased time needed to learn new things.

We must also keep in mind that aging does not affect all systems or all people uniformly and adapt treatment to individual patients accordingly. There are a number of other considerations for management of low-vision patients, eg:

(1) the eye diagnosis;

(2) type, location, and severity of field defects;

(3) presence of medical illnesses such as diabetes, which affect function;

(4) arthritis, orthopedic, and neurological disorders that affect handling aids;

(5) intelligence and perceptual awareness of the patient;

(6) reading ability;

(7) ability to travel alone;

(8) customary interests, whether many or few; and

(9) the person's expectations.

In low-vision work with old people, diagnosis is the key to understanding function and low-vision aid prescription. It is best to discuss the diseases in a format that classifies the conditions according to the *pattern of field defect* [Faye, 1979]. In this way it is easier to see what the conditions have in common. We will consider first those diseases that have no gross field defect, second those that have central field defects, and finally those that have peripheral field defects [Faye, 1979].

NO FIELD DEFECT

In this category, there are three subgroups, depending upon whether the disease affects the refractive media, the pupil, or the macula.

Diseases of the Refractive Media

The largest group of these diseases involves the cornea, lens, and vitreous. Any opacity or disturbance of the normally transparent structures produces aberrations in light transmissions to the retina. Patients complain of reduction of acuity outdoors, variability of vision, glare, and lack of contrast. There is, however, no visual field impairment to restrict traveling; object perception and depth perception (if the person is binocular) are intact. Color perception also will be normal although less intense. The type of vision a patient might experience with a media opacity is hazy, blurred, and glarey throughout most of the field, although no segment of the field will actually be missing. The basic optical problem is poor contrast and glare. The visual acuity in these cases may be nearly normal to nearly blind, and function is usually directly related to the level of visual acuity. Visual acuity tests are useful if they are related to function, which must include both indoors and outdoors conditions. The patient's ability to function in outdoor lighting conditions may differ greatly from his ability under the indoor conditions in which acuity is usually measured.

Examples of the more common conditions affecting the refractive media are listed below. There are, of course, many other such diseases but they have similar effects on vision and require similar approaches to case management as those listed.

Corneal diseases:
   scarring from an inflammation
   corneal dystrophy or edema
Types of cataract:
   posterior subcapsular opacity
   senile nuclear opacity
   mixed posterior and cortical cataract
Vitreous disturbances:
   bleeding from any cause, commonly from diabetes
   turbidity from uveitis with membrane formation,
     including vitreous bands

How do these conditions affect function? Indoors, most people will have less trouble in familiar surroundings than outdoors. Depending on their acuity and conditions of lighting and contrast, they can orient themselves in spite of the hazy or blurred nature of their visual world. Most of their problems are related to lighting—too much or too little—so lighting conditions need to be regulated to suit the person. Lights should be placed at the correct angle to prevent glare and at the correct distance from the object that is being viewed.

Contrast presents a problem that can be solved by having the person use contrasting colors, for example, with plates and food. Work spaces can be arranged so that dark objects show up clearly against a light background or vice versa and furniture shows up against wallpaper, rugs, and so forth. This strategy should be discussed with other family members so they will understand the problem. Bold or enlarged print can be used for reading and writing. Black on white offers the best contrast.

Visual acuity, which may test close to normal in indoor test situations, may be reduced to near-blindness by glare out-of-doors. Patients who function well indoors may say that they are "blind" out on the street. Light, illumination, and glare are an ever-present problem because there are so many uncontrollable variables, such as street lighting, time of year, time of day, and weather.

Disorders of the refractive media can often be corrected by surgery: grafts of the cornea, implants of the cornea and lens, cataract extraction, or vitrectomy. When feasible, surgical intervention is preferable, but not all people are able to have surgery, and not all surgery is successful in restoring visual function. Those patients who cannot undergo surgery require an optical approach to treatment, which may include control of illumination, prescription of corrective lenses, and/ or use of magnifiers or large print. Absorptive lenses are needed to control glare, although visors and hat brims are also useful simple aids to block overhead light.

Standard refraction with conventional lenses is emphasized in *all* refractive media problems, particularly corneal and lens problems. Contact lenses including extended-wear and toric contacts play a major role in treating media problems.

Laminated lenses with an artificial iris are used in aniridia and in coloboma of the iris.

Magnification aids used out-of-doors may be less effective in cases of hazy vision or veiling glare. Magnification degrades the image in cases where there is an initial lack of contrast. Glare may be intensified with a telescope unless one is deliberately selected with a small objective or with a filter cap or coated lenses. (All of the optical aids mentioned in the text are available from the New York Lighthouse *Catalogue of Optical Aids* [New York Lighthouse, 1980]. Write to request a copy.) The patient with this kind of vision may use indoors a simple monocular or binocular telescope like the Selsi Sportscope to watch TV, movies, or the theater. The help requested most often is for reading. Reading is difficult if print appears hazy and contrast is poor. Magnification with spectacles or handheld lenses may be ineffective because it further reduces contrast; thus modification of illumination or use of large print may be more effective.

Lighting and contrast are equally important. For example, a patient with uveitis may be able to read only in the morning with venetian blinds carefully adjusted and a large-print book. This affords ideal lighting conditions and incidentally, illustrates the usefulness of large print. Illumination control may also be achieved by effective placement of lamps. If there is too much glare from reading surfaces, a typoscope (masking device) would be the most valuable aid to give.

Enlarged book print and numbers such as the large-print telephone dial are well-accepted simple devices. Many patients prefer to use large-scale print at a fairly normal reading distance rather than normal-scale print held very close, so that they can adjust the light more accurately.

Diseases Affecting the Pupil

The transmission of light to the retina is controlled mechanically by the size of the pupil. In disease conditions there may be too little or too much light, depending on the pupillary area.

Some examples of pupillary conditions are

(1) Aniridia—there may be severe photophobia because there is little or no iris tissue to block light entering the eye.

(2) Coloboma—in these cases only the lower sector of the iris is missing and the patient may have no complaints of excessive light.

(3) Surgical iridectomy—some large-sector iridectomies for cataract extraction cause severe photophobia.

(4) Miosis—glaucoma medication with miotics such as pilocarpine often affects function. For example, the side effects of miosis may turn the patient with a normal macula into a low-vision patient. High-intensity illumination often helps, as does the typoscope for masking glare, but we must remember that the side effects of an excessively small pupil influence patient cooperation and may

account for noncompliance and eventual loss of visual field and acuity. Some of the newer glaucoma medications may be introduced by the ophthalmologist after discussion with the patient, eg, a mild mydriatic, Timolol, or a diuretic.

Diseases Affecting the Macula

This subgroup consists of diseases that affect the macula but do not produce a scotoma; they usually result from maldevelopment or suppression. The commonest examples in old people are albinism; aniridia; achromatopsia (color blindness); amblyopic macula resulting from suppression, sensory deprivation, uncorrected or high refractive errors; high myopia with a posterior staphyloma; and diabetes resulting in macular edema but without scotoma.

In considering the visual function of this group it is important to realize how different the visual picture is from that of refractive media disease. In this group the peripheral field of vision is essentially clear (unless there is an uncorrected refractive error). The only abnormality is the lack of a developed fovea. The effect is poor resolution rather than dimness or blur. The affected person comments that it is a simple matter to see things clearly by moving closer to the object, much as we all do when we cannot see a movie marquee three blocks away and walk closer for better resolution. There certainly is no scotoma and no overall blur. When indoors these patients have few specific functional problems with vision.

Management of specific conditions in this group warrants comment. For example, not all albinos are light sensitive, depending on the amount of pigment they have and whether Ty-negative or Ty-positive. They respond well to standard eye glasses with moderate degrees of magnification in a bifocal or magnifier. They might like mildly or moderately tinted lenses, depending on subjective evaluation and preference [Faye, 1979]. Achromats are the reverse, being pathologically photophobic. The treatment for this is dense absorptive lenses, usually with 1–2% light transmission, or welding goggles, which cut out all extraneous light. NoIR lenses are also acceptable.

A surprisingly large number of older patients are seen for low-vision help when an amblyopic eye from childhood must be used after the "good" eye loses vision (often from a vascular accident). This underlines the importance of early discovery and treatment of amblyopia. The response of the amblyopic eye even at an advanced age is interesting and worth further study of the reversal of suppression in an old eye.

Cases of myopia should be refracted carefully, since increasing myopia due to lenticular change is often overlooked. Before prescribing a stronger lens, a trial application for a press-on Fresnel minus lens to the patient's correction should be made.

Edema of the macula, particularly when secondary to diabetes, may be improved by photocoagulation of the peripheral retinas, but this is a matter of preference, belief, and experience among retinal specialists. Patients do not respond as well to magnification once the peripheral retina has been heavily treated.

In summary there are many conditions among this varied group, but the visual function is affected in much the same way: Lighting and contrast affect this whole group very much, refraction is basic, control of light is basic, and high magnification is not always successful but is worth trying, as in all low vision cases.

CENTRAL FIELD LOSS

This is quite a straightforward group, which includes the greatest numbers of cases seen in the elderly. Any type of posterior pole disease would come under this heading, including atrophic degenerative macular lesions, hemorrhagic exudative macular lesions, infectious diseases such as histoplasmosis, chorioretinitis, cystoid edema of the macula, macular "hole," and pathological myopia with Fuch's spot. Typically, this group will have a central scotoma, and ophthalmoscopy will reveal demonstrable pathology. Into this category fall 75% of the cases seen in the low-vision clinic at the New York Lighthouse. Similar figures have been reported at other centers, with the exception of rehabilitation-oriented clinics that service a younger group [Faye, 1979].

Functionally, scotomas are not always uniformly dense, varying from slight distortion in foveal disease to a 20° central field loss in advanced macular disease. In macular disease, many cells remain functional within the macula so that visual acuity may range from 20/40 to 20/200. In advanced cases, acuities of 20/400 are common but may fall as low as 3/200, depending on the severity of the case. Total blindness is rare.

Measurement of scotomas is important for several reasons. The #1 plate of the Amsler grid is ordinarily used diagnostically, but it can also be used prognostically, to determine the position and density of scotomas [Faye, 1979]. This allows us to predict how much interference to expect from the defect. It also helps to teach the patient where the scotoma is, and to learn to move it away from the center of the field of gaze. It is important for the clinician to show the patient that the scotoma is the result of the macular pathology, and that it represents only a small portion of the whole field. The average scotoma is usually only 5° to 10° out of the entire field of 180° binocularly (140° monocularly). Using the grid to demonstrate the scotoma's location, the clinician or instructor can help the patient move the eyes or head to a position that places the scotoma out of the reading field. Many patients have learned to do this spontaneously but appreciate reinforcement that they are not harming their eyes.

How do patients with macular disease function? Indoors, patients usually have no difficulty doing tasks that do not require very detailed vision. They sit close to the TV; they arrange objects in their houses to increase contrast. There are many accessory, or nonoptical aids that help with household activities, for example, large-print telephone dials, bold pens for lists and telephone numbers, high-intensity lamps. Travel ability is excellent unless the central scotoma exceeds 20°. Central visual acuity may be reduced because of a scotoma, but the peripheral photoreceptors are still there to provide serviceable visual acuity. Most people spontaneously learn to view eccentrically and substitute a paramacular area for their defective macula. Patients who don't realize that they see better from the peripheral retina can easily be taught at the time of their visual acuity test to scan or view eccentrically, thus converting the chart test to a functional learning experience.

Refraction should not be neglected just because the macular elements are disturbed. Improved image quality can be appreciated by patients using the peripheral retina. Patients can also use telescopes and binoculars effectively if they want them for specific tasks, although they tend to prefer their unaided peripheral vision for traveling.

Reading difficulty is a major complaint in cases of macular degeneration because the scotoma blocks the area normally used for this critical vision activity. Fine details of letters and words are blocked out as the eye moves along a line of print. Low-vision magnifying aids bring a surprising amount of visibility to print reading and other near tasks.

Spectacles, hand magnifiers, and stand magnifiers are the most commonly prescribed low-vision aids for elderly people. Magnification with optical aids is effective in central scotomas because when the patient brings the print closer, the scotoma becomes relatively smaller. The aids are familiar to any person who has ever used a magnifier or field glasses and can be mastered with relative ease. There are only four basic types of optical aids: three of them are types of convex lens in spectacle, hand magnifier or stand magnifier mountings, and the fourth type consists of hand-held or spectacle-mounted telescopic devices.

Each type of lens has its advantages and disadvantages; each is prescribed in relation to the type of disorder, the type of reading aid formerly used by the patient, and, most important, the task the patient wishes to perform. Probably the most commonly prescribed device is the high-power spectacle correction, with handheld magnifiers a close second. Basically, any of the major types of aids can be used, depending on the motivation and intellectual capacity of the patient and on the experience and preference of the examiner.

Many productive older people develop macular degeneration but often they do not get prompt low-vision care, sometimes as the result of the attitude of the primary care physician. Supportive care should include an adequate explanation of the patient's condition, an examination to determine the appropriate optical aids, and instruction in their use. Patients need reassurance and encouragement once the diagnosis of macular degeneration has been made. They pick up on words like "degeneration" and are sensitive to any attitude of the ophthalmologist that suggests theirs to be "hopeless" cases. Even though there may be no medical or surgical treatment, there is optical treatment and the physician can dispel fears of blindness, loss of independence, stroke, and senility that patients associate with their eye disease. Once they have been reassured by the physician, patients can tackle their adjustment and the substitution of visual aids for their once normal vision. After the correct magnifying aid has been prescribed, the patient has several instructional visits to learn the new technique of reading with magnification. These visits may be handled by office staff members trained to work with low vision patients.

In summary, management of the patient with a central scotoma depends on the mental condition of the patient, on motivation, the size and location of the scotoma, and its effect on visual acuity. Proper prescription of aids requires allotting adequate time to instruction and training of the patient. If motivation and intelligence are normal, as they are in most elderly patients, low vision prescriptions work effectively. Basically, the intact person with this type of field defect functions nearly normally, unless the scotoma covers the posterior pole, as it sometimes does. In advanced cases in which optical aids do not help, the low-vision patient may need a referral to an agency for the visually impaired for recreation and rehabilitation and to learn techniques for daily living skills [American Foundation for the Blind, 1980].

PERIPHERAL FIELD DEFECT

This final group is potentially the most difficult to manage because field loss in the periphery affects the ability to travel safely. The peripheral retina normally provides all of the cues for action, location, and warnings of danger and is responsible for night vision.

In this category are retinal pigmentary degenerations such as retinitis pigmentosa and allied degenerations; optic atrophy from glaucoma; neurological disease head trauma; and cerebral vascular disease such as stroke, localized vascular problems, ischemic optic atrophy, and retinal vessel occlusion. Toxicity from drugs may also cause peripheral field constriction. Detached retina is another common cause. One of the hardest types of cases to work with is the proliferative diabetic retina.

There are four basic types of defects in this group. However two types, small arcuate and perimacular defects, are not so serious because their location does not create serious dysfunction, and they will not be considered here. This discussion will be confined to two conditions: those that permanently constrict visual field to a central (or eccentric area) of 20° or less, and those that reduce peripheral acuity to less than 3/200. It should be kept in mind that the smaller the remaining central field becomes, the more difficulty the patient experiences.

Field constrictions typical of retinitis pigmentosa, end-stage glaucoma, optic nerve disease, and homonymous hemianopias cause severe disability and loss of independence. Improving visual function with optical devices is not always feasible in these cases. In these patients, measured visual acuity often remains normal if macular function is undisturbed, but *blurred* vision may indicate not just disease in the macula but also an uncorrected refractive error. All low-vision patients should have a careful refraction to rule out ordinary myopia, hyperopia, or astigmatism that would further blur peripheral vision.

Almost all people with large peripheral field defects have difficulty in walking around independently. These defects are absolute; there is no incoming information about motion, contrast, spatial cues, or objects in the environment. A field of 5° or less contains such limited information that the patient is forced to scan his surroundings constantly. These patients learn spontaneously to scan; however, most people with progressive disease benefit from professional orientation/mobility training in the maximal use of visual and auditory cues.

The reading field is reduced even more than the distance field in these conditions, since the central field is cone shaped with the apex towards the eye. The closer the patient brings reading material, the smaller the area encompassed and the reading rate slows down even if there is normal acuity. The usefulness of magnifying optical aids depends on the size of the patient's central field. If high magnification is prescribed, the reading material has to be held close; the near field gets progressively smaller as the material is brought to the eye. The enlarged symbols may go outside of the field area and detail is lost.

The Amsler grid is an invaluable test for constricted field. It demonstrates the exact size of the reading field and indicates how much magnification can be tolerated in each case. The field of the *aid* can also be plotted on the grid so that the two may be matched. Hand magnifiers or stand magnifiers are more useful than other aids in these cases because objects can be held farther from the eye and adjusted by the patient for minimal effective magnification in the field. Also, closed circuit television makes scanning easier although the magnification factor remains in the same ratio.

Hemianopia

Patients with hemianopia seem to be unresponsive to magnifiers and prisms that shift the available field. In these cases we must keep in mind that there may be systemic complications such as diabetes, hypertension, or organic brain damage that make adjustment to aids even more difficult for these patients whose behavior is altered by their disease state.

Field Expansion

Reverse (minifying) telescopic systems have been developed to compress more information into the available field, but elderly patients have not been able to adjust to the sensory distortion of existing devices. More work remains to be done to develop undistorted minification of images and to evaluate how well patients can use this kind of aid.

Fresnel press-on prisms (base toward the field defect) have been used in both right and left hemianopias to allow the patient to bring a portion of the blocked field into view. Here too, results have been inconclusive. It may be more productive to teach patients to scan or turn their heads without special aids.

A closed circuit television system is the best type of visual aid for patients with small fields who can view projected print material on a television monitor and scan more easily at a distance where the field is larger.

In summary, it is generally difficult to manage patients with peripheral field constriction in a way that significantly improves their visual function. The success of optical aids, particularly high magnifying spectacles and telescopes, is guarded in these cases because magnified images disappear into the scotoma. It is, therefore, important to measure the actual size of the scotoma in inches or feet to compare the size of the patient's field to the field of the aid. The aid should not reduce the patient's field. Light control is important, as is a good refraction. Minification of the field, while theoretically a good idea, has not worked particularly well and awaits the invention of a better wide-angle lens. Mobility and other rehabilitation services may be needed, or referral to special agencies for the visually impaired or to private mobility teachers.

CONCLUSION

There is much discussion of human factors in aging but there are few standards by which we can define, judge, or improve the lot of the elderly and few practical methods of resolving the problems of old age. However, much of visual impairment responds to intervention, so it should not be a secret that low-vision care offers something concrete that can be prescribed to keep the visually impaired person independent and functioning. There is a well-defined body of knowledge currently in wide use at a grassroots level. The eye-care professions as well as concerned federal and state agencies should support low-vision care standards and methods of financing aid for all low-vision patients. Clinicians and clinical assistants should be able to attend regional training courses to learn the skill of prescribing for the low-vision patient [New York Lighthouse, 1981].

Not all clinicians can incorporate low-vision work into their practices; however, there is a network of low-vision referral sources throughout the United States that is listed in the American Foundation for the Blind's Manual of Services [American Foundation for the Blind, 1980]. Basically, low-vision patients who function well other than when reading can be handled in an average office practice. Patients with more complicated conditions needing services such as mobility instruction, daily living skill training, and social services are best managed in a specialized agency setting geared for the needs of partially sighted persons, who may have many other difficulties.

REFERENCES

American Foundation for the Blind (1980) "Directory of Agencies Serving the Visually Handicapped in the United States," 21st Ed. Lists low-vision clinics. (15 West 16th St, New York, NY 10011.)
Faye, EE (1970) "The Low Vision Patient." New York: Grune and Stratton.
Faye, EE (1979) "Clinical Low Vision." Boston: Little Brown.
New York Lighthouse (1981) "Low Vision Training and Continuing Education Center Brochure."
New York Lighthouse (1980) "A Catalogue of Optical Aids." (111 East 59th St, New York, NY 10022.)

Aging and Human Visual Function, pages 315–322

Low Vision Related to Function and Service Delivery for the Elderly

William V. Padula

Demographic studies consistently show that age is the best predictor of blindness and visual impairment [Hatfield, 1973; Trovern-Trend, 1968]. Aging contributes to visual impairment through both normal deterioration of eye tissues and increased incidence of eye pathology.

According to the National Center for Health Statistics (NCHS) Health Interview Survey of 1977, [Kirchner and Peterson, 1979], an estimated 1.4 million individuals in the United States have severe visual impairments (inability to read normal newspaper-size print with conventional glasses). Estimated as legally blind (20/200 visual acuity or less and/or less than a 20° visual field) are 500,000 individuals. The U.S. Bureau of the Census projects that by the year 2000, the population of the United States will increase by 20% to over 260 million people. The number of people aged 65 and over is expected to increase disproportionately, rising from 23 million in 1977 to 32 million by the year 2000 [Lowman and Kirchner, 1979].

Kirchner and Peterson [1979] have reported that the estimated prevalence of legal blindness for those over 65 is approximately 230,000 and that, according to the 1977 NCHS survey, there are 990,000 elderly individuals with severe visual impairment. These estimates may be undercounts (see Greenberg and Branch, this volume). The projection for the year 2000 is that there will be between 272,000 and 376,000 elderly individuals who are legally blind and 1,760,000 elderly individuals with severe visual impairment. These statistics indicate that while the overall legally blind population will increase by 14%, the population of persons over 65 with severe visual impairment is expected to approximately double.

This increase in visual impairment is projected from a major increase expected in the population over 65. According to 1977 Bureau of Census projections, there will be a 20% increase of persons between 65 and 74, a 56% increase of persons between 75 and 84, and an 84% increase of persons aged 85 and over. It was assumed, in Lowman and Kirchner's [1979] projections, that the rates of visual impairments within those age categories would remain the same, as would the underlying causes. For example, the most common cause of blindness in the United States at present is glaucoma, which in 1962 accounted for 13.5% of all blindness, occurring predominantly in individuals over 40 years of age. Therefore, with the statistical projections for the year 2000, the over-65 age group is expected to increase considerably and the incidence of blindness or sight impairment caused by glaucoma may be assumed to rise proportionately. Also, the rates of sight impairment in older groups may increase, so these projections may be conservative. It is speculated that because of continued advances in medical and surgical technology and treatment regimens, sight loss will less often be total and the relative proportion of partial loss will be greater.

Sight impairment can greatly interfere with the performance of aging individuals. For the purposes of this paper, sight impairment is loss of acuity and/or restriction of field and may be analyzed by taking acuity and/or field measurements. However, these measurements alone do not indicate the severity of interference with performance and function. Visual impairment must be characterized by the degree to which behavior is affected. In other words, visual impairment is defined as interference with the processing of information received through the sense of sight that in turn impedes performance and function.

Recent psychophysical research indicates that measurement of visual acuity gives only a very limited indication of overall visual functioning. For example, acuity, which refers to the ability to resolve minute objects or separations, is a function of the visual system's sensitivity to high spatial frequencies but not low and intermediate frequencies. Thus, measuring an individual's visual acuity can give an indication of his ability to distinguish small print but would not necessarily predict his ability to recognize faces and distinguish forms from background, tasks involving low and intermediate spatial frequency information-processing. Aging appears to produce a selective loss in sensitivity to lower spatial frequencies (Sekuler, this volume).

For the aging person, the effects on life style of a visual impairment can be quite profound. Since vision is the dominant mode of processing information about the environment and leading motor movement [Gesell, 1949], impairment can cause a variety of problems such as inaccurate visual-motor coordination, reduced depth judgment, wide stance and gait, head tilt and/or turn, moving the head close to working material, and eccentric viewing. The frustration of having visual impairment may also lead to depression, irritability, disorientation, dizziness, lack of continuity of thought, memory loss, etc. Ultimately, these problems can result in a loss of independence. It must be realized that these behaviors are symptoms and that the cause lies in the inability to visually adapt to the impaired and relate visual information to deeper psychophysical processes.

Sight impairments traditionally have been divided into four classes: (1) central acuity reduction, (2) central field loss, (3) peripheral field loss, and (4) combinations of these three. It has been a common clinical observation that not all people are affected the same by acuity and/or field losses [Genensky, 1976], and that performance and functional abilities can vary considerably. Elderly individuals with impaired sight may or may not experience interference with function and performance, depending on their habitual mode of visual operation. An individual who depends heavily on central acuity (eg, a jeweler) may be expected to be more profoundly affected by a loss of foveal vision than by loss of peripheral function, whereas another person, perhaps an actor, might be more seriously affected by peripheral loss.

The functional impact of losses in different parts of the visual field may be considered in terms of the concept of two fundamental modes of processing of visual information: focal and ambient [Leibowitz and Post, 1982; Trevarthen, 1973]. Focal vision subserves visual attention (conscious), object recognition, and identification. The ambient mode is a general awareness state of vision (conscious or unconscious). It is spatially oriented and involved with locomotion and posture. Focal vision primarily involves the central field, whereas the ambient system involves the entire visual field. Typically, the individual is well aware of the operation of focal functions but can process ambient information with little conscious awareness. The focal and ambient functions are mediated by eye and brain. Although the two systems can be distinguished on the basis of retinal location, effective visual functioning is dependent on the sharing of information between the two systems through higher-order perceptual processes. For example, stereopsis (a focal process) involves the fusion of the two visual fields, using such skills as differentiating figure from ground and maintaining strong object or perceptual constancies. The perception of depth involves the spatial projection from disparate retinal points (ambient function) in relation to central function. A full appreciation of visual space is made possible by the integration of information from these two systems.

The relationship between vision and the individual's overall situation is complex. Arteriosclerosis and deterioration of neurons and muscle fibers gradually erode psychological, emotional, physical, and psychological functions; however, my own clinical experience has been that the effects of visual impairment are especially profound. Visual impairment has many ramifications. Loss of independence may result from interference with simple tasks such as reading labels on medicine bottles and walking to the store. Extreme frustration and failure can lead to social isolation and the development of a myriad of psychological defenses and neuroses [Gilbert, 1968]. The impaired person's loss of independence places burdens on his family's time and finances. An economical burden is also placed on community, state, and federal programs to deliver alternative support programs, varying from driving services to living care programs, to the elderly visually impaired individual.

Historically, compensatory care services for the elderly visually impaired have been oriented toward compensating for their loss of independence. This approach is symptom-oriented and does not attempt to deal with the cause of the loss of independence by rehabilitating the person's functional abilities. Unfortunately, the majority of visually impaired individuals in the United States are served only through such alternative support means and are never referred for low-vision services, which are oriented around the individual's impairment and his/her rehabilitation. Kirchner and Phillips [1980] estimated that in 1976 only 35,000 of the approximately 1,700,000 visually impaired people in this country received low-vision services. The elderly visually impaired are no exception to these general statistics.

THE LOW-VISION SERVICE APPROACH

Low-vision services are multidisciplinary and utilize special visual examination techniques and optical aids to improve the individual's vision, thereby rehabilitating functional abilities and skills. The primary objective of low-vision services is to increase independence. The low-vision examination is a specialized form of vision analysis, differing from routine eye examinations in that special methods of testing must be used to determine refractive status, acuities (near and far), visual field, and eye health of individuals with substantial impairment. On the basis of this analysis, lens prescriptions and special optical aids of various types are prescribed to improve acuity levels.

Unlike the routine eye examination, the low-vision service ideally should begin with a functional assessment of the individual in his normal environment. Functional assessment is important because it allows the low-vision doctor to better evaluate the individual's abilities and needs: the extent to which the sight loss may be interfering with visual functioning, the areas with which testing should begin, and, in general, the type(s) of optical aids that may help the person meet his or her needs. Since the optometrist or ophthalmologist performing the low-vision examination is usually unable to go to the visually impaired individual's home or place of employment, other professionals such as social workers, orientation mobility specialists, or educators involved in the rehabilitative program should evaluate the patient's abilities and needs in the field. These professionals can provide the low-vision doctor with information regarding typical lighting conditions, architectural barriers, and educational activities, and with behavioral observations of visual functioning (ie, how well the person negotiates stairways, travels, recognizes faces at distances; the lighting conditions he prefers; how the person interacts socially).

The next phase of the service is the low-vision examination, which the doctor begins by analyzing functional abilities the moment the person walks into the office. This continued behavioral analysis, in conjunction with assessment of function, adds meaning to the measurements of sight that the doctor will make during the examination. An in-depth history is taken, and social workers, educators, and other professionals may need to confer to further assess needs and abilities.

When examining elderly visually impaired persons, the doctor should take special care to display a positive attitude and adapt the examination procedure to bring out the visual abilities the patient retains. I have found that elderly people have generally experienced greater frustration and failure from sight impairment than have younger patients. The examiner can stimulate motivation, interest, and cooperation by designing the examination so that the patient can perform successfully. For example, instead of taking acuities at 20 feet with the standard Snellen acuity chart, a special low-vision acuity chart with larger letters and numbers can be used at any distance that the patient can see. Lighting conditions should be adapted to maximize the patient's visual functioning. In general, the normal procedures for field testing, refractive analysis, eye health examination, etc., should be altered to emphasize the particular abilities the patient retains. (See Faye, this volume, for an in-depth description of the low-vision examination.)

After the examination, optical aids are chosen on the basis of both the functional assessment and the refractive analysis. These aids may include handheld or spectacle-mounted telescopes, microscopes, telemicroscopes, handheld magnifiers, stand magnifiers, etc., as well as special spectacle lenses. Optical aids improve visual acuity, thereby directly improving sight, but improvement of performance and function depends on how the patient utilizes his enhanced sight.

The prescribed aids are often loaned to the patient on a trial basis, but before he takes them home he must be trained in their use. Training may be provided by either the prescribing doctor or other professionals within the office or clinic. The elderly individual with sight impairment may need only demonstration of the use of the aid; however, if he also has a visual (performance) impairment, training must be more involved. In the latter case training may require several office visits utilizing special techniques to improve the patient's ability to match and reinforce visual information with input from other sensory and motor channels.

After the patient has demonstrated efficient use of the aid and the final prescription has been made, he or she may be referred to other professionals for continuation of the low-vision service. For example, social workers may provide counseling on emotional, family, or financial difficulties; rehabilitation counselors can help develop useful work skills utilizing the optical aids prescribed; and orientation and mobility specialists may provide training in navigational skills using the optical aids. Communication between the doctor prescribing the optical aid and the professionals in the field is essential for successful rehabil-

itation of the elderly visually impaired. Follow-through by rehabilitation professionals can determine the degree of improvement of the patient's functional
abilities and training in the field can further improve use of the optical aid.

ECONOMIC CONSIDERATIONS

Delivering low-vision services is more economical than providing only compensatory care services. Hospital care costs for a person over 65 average $125.00
a day, not including special services (R. Jose, personal communication); nursing
home care is $30–35 a day, not including special services. A year's nursing
home care would cost approximately $11,000. Compensatory care services are
designed to provide care for individuals who cannot function effectively in their
normal environments; many elderly people end up in nursing homes because of
the functional impairment resulting from their sight loss. The 1976 Survey of
Institutionalized Persons (SIP) reported that 48% of the people in nursing homes
(572,000) have trouble seeing and that 14% are "severely disabled" or "unable
to see" [Peterson and Kirchner, 1980]. Of this population, one-quarter of those
under 65 years of age have trouble seeing, and one-half of those over 65 have
difficulty seeing.

Many elderly visually impaired individuals in nursing homes could benefit
from low-vision services and might be rehabilitated. The cost of delivering low-
vision services in a clinical setting would be between $800–1600 (R. Jose,
personal communication) less the cost of optical aids. The costs of low-vision
services vary widely because individual needs differ considerably. An elderly
visually impaired individual who also has other handicaps may require additional
professional services, such as physical and/or occupational therapy.

The cost of optical aids also varies greatly depending on need. A handheld
magnifier may cost as little as $10, whereas a closed circuit television may be
$1,200. The average cost for optical aids per person at the Low Vision Clinic
at the Lighthouse for the Blind in New York is $67 (C. Hood, personal com-
munication), which includes optical aids such as handheld magnifiers, stand
magnifiers, spectacle-mounted magnifiers, microscopes, and telescopes, but not
closed circuit televisions and driving telescopes. Obviously, the cost of services
and optical aids together is considerably less than that of providing compensatory
care services. Follow-up services for the visually impaired cost considerably less
than initial costs of low-vision services; in contrast, compensatory care programs
usually require continuing care at an increasing yearly cost.

SUMMARY

For the elderly person, low-vision services are a means to redevelop effective
visual functioning; the purpose of the service is to increase the independence

and improve the self-concept of the aging person. Low-vision services enable federal, state, and individual costs to be reduced by actively dealing with the cause of the problem, vision loss, and not simply reacting to the symptom; loss of independence. Thus, these services both reduce the economic burden on society and help us fulfill our obligations to the elderly by assisting them to maintain their independence through rehabilitative health care.

REFERENCES

Arden GD (1968) Importance of measuring contrast sensitivity in visual impairment. Br J Ophthalmol 62.

Campbell FW (1974) Contrast and spatial frequency. Sci Am 221.

Dartmouth Medical School (1947) "A Study and Development of Optical Devices to Aid Persons with Subnormal Vision: A Final Report to the National Research Council, Committee on Sensory Devices." Eye Institute, Hanover, New Hampshire.

Faye EE (1965) Management of the low vision patient. Internat Ophthalmol 5:495.

Faye EE (1975) Low vision services in an agency. New Outlook 4:241–248.

Genensky S (1976) Acuity Measurements—Do They Indicate How Well a Partially Sighted Person Functions or Could Function? New Outlook (January).

Genensky S (1978) Data Concerning the Partially Sighted and Functionally Blind. J Vis Impair Blindness 72(5):177–180.

Gesell Arnold (1949) "Vision, Its Development in Infant and Child." New York: Harper and Row.

Gilbert Jeanne (1968) "The Psychological Implications of Severe Visual Impairment in Older Persons." Proceedings on the Research Conference on Geriatric Blindness and Severe Visual Impairment. American Foundation for the Blind, New York, 43–45.

Gnade M (1965) Low vision services. Sight-Saving Rev 35:216.

Hatfield EM (1973) Estimates of blindness in the United States. The Sight-Saving Rev 43:69–80.

Jose R, Cumming J, McAdams L (1975) A model of low vision clinical service: An interdisciplinary vision rehabilitation program. New Outlook 5:249–54.

Kirchner C, Lowman C (1978) Services of variation in estimated prevalence of visual loss. J Vis Impair Blindness 72(8):329–332.

Kirchner C, Peterson R (1979) The latest data on visual disability from NCHS. J Vis Impair Blindness 73(4):151–153.

Kirchner C, Peterson R (1980) Prevalence of blindness and visual impairment among institutional residents. J Vis Impair Blindness 74(8):323–326.

Kirchner C, Phillips B (1980) Report of a survey of U.S. low vision services. J Vis Impair Blindness 74(3):122–124.

Leibowitz HW, Post RB (1982) The two modes of processing concept and some implications. In Beck JJ (Ed) "Organization and Representation in Perception." Hillsdale, N.J.: Erlbaum (in press).

Lowman C, Kirchner C (1979) Elderly blind and visually impaired persons: Projected numbers in the year 2000. J Vis Impair Blindness 73(2):73–74.

Lowrey A (1965) Plan for a low vision clinic. New Outlook for the Blind 59(8):275–277.

National Center for Health Statistics (1971) Prevalence of selected impairments: United States, Vital and Health Statistics Series 10, No 111, DHEW, Pub No 77-1537, Washington, D.C.

Padula, WV (1979) Philosophy, definition and a model of low vision services. American Foundation for the Blind, New York (unpublished).

Padula WV (1980) Low vision services. American Foundation for the Blind, New York.

Trevarthen CB, Sperry R (1973) Perceptual unity of the ambient visual field in human commissurotomy patients. Brain 96:547–570.

Trovern-Trend (1968) Blindness in the United States: A review of the available statistics with estimates of the prevalence of blindness and its economic impact. Hartford, Conn. Travelers Research Center.

Aging and Human Visual Function, pages 323–333

Environmental Design and Adaptation to the Visual Environment of the Elderly

Leon A. Pastalan

Since an organism can respond directly only to those aspects of the environment experienced through the sense organs, age-related changes in sensory and perceptual mechanisms alter the world in which the aging individual lives. The Empathic Model [for a general description see Pastalan et al, 1973] is a technique that simulates selected age-related visual changes while an observer engages in various everyday environmental tasks. This paper discusses some environmental design principles and adaptations developed using this model.

A technical description of the age-related visual loss simulated by the Empathic Model will not be given here; suffice it to say that the crystalline lenses of our eyes typically lose their elasticity and gradually become more dense as we get older. The condition usually becomes noticeable when one reaches the mid-fifties and continues to progress with age until the lens becomes totally opaque. Along with opacification, there is an increase of light scattering within the lens, degrading the retinal image.

We simulated a combination of reduced retinal illumination and degraded retinal image with specially designed lenses that younger observers could wear. These spectacle lenses had a coating that both diffused and attenuated (by 25%) the light passing through. The lenses reduced the acuity of a wearer who had normal vision to the 20/40 level. The preparation and coating of the spectacle lenses was developed after extensive consultation with eye-care specialists and after several trials and errors. Obviously there is considerable individual variability in the rate at which vision changes with age, but it is likely that most people will eventually be reduced to the condition we have simulated, if they live long enough. Some might experience it in their 60s or 70s, and others much later. The reduction simulated by these lenses may underrepresent the extent of deterioration actually experienced by many older people. Weale [1963, 1965] has estimated that as a result of lenticular and pupillary (senile miosis) changes combined, the 65-year-old retina receives only about one-third of the light received by its 20-year-old counterpart. (Also see the papers of Carter, Pitts, and Weale in this volume for discussion of related changes in visual function).

STUDIES ON THE EFFECTS ON DAILY LIFE OF WEARING THE LENSES

A series of experiments were run to evaluate the impact on young subjects of wearing the lenses in daily life settings. The first study involved five people, four of whom were male graduate students in architecture specializing in gerontology. The fifth person was the author, who was in his late 30s at the time. The study participants wore the lenses in three standard settings: a dwelling unit, a multipurpose senior center, and a shopping center. They remained for at least 1 hour in a given setting on one day and then went to the second setting the next day and went to the third setting on the final day of the cycle. The 3-day cycle was repeated throughout a 6-month period; in later studies the period was reduced to 3 months with comparable results.

Each participant kept a log of his or her daily living experiences during the study, recording observations on legibility of printed information (street signs, directories, labels, etc.); effects of lighting, colors, and textures of building interiors on personal activities; hazards, barriers, and safety factors; and accessibility of buildings and subunits.

Throughout the study, the participants met regularly to compare observations and reactions. A number of observations were shared by all participants in this first study and by another 30 participants in subsequent studies. These consensus observations are

(1) Glare from uncontrolled natural light and from unbalanced artificial light sources was the single most ubiquitous difficulty encountered. For instance, when participants walked up an aisle toward the front of a supermarket, the typical vast expanse of plate glass across the front of the store obliterated most of the detail in surrounding objects on bright days. Single intense artificial light sources produced more uncomfortable glare than combinations of less intense sources.

(2) Colors all tended to fade—the cool colors such as green and blue faded most and red the least.

(3) Contouring presented problems. Perceiving the boundary between two contrasting surfaces was most difficult when two intense colors such as red and green bounded each other. The boundary becomes visually unstable because the intensity of the colors seem to overlap and as one focuses on the boundary it appears to shift. In contrast, closely related colors such as blues and greens tend to fade and blend into each other. This created problems in distinguishing wall and floor surfaces. For example, light green walls and blue-green carpets become

virtually impossible to distinguish. These problems with perceiving boundaries can cause hazards such as stumbling into walls and tripping on stairs.

(4) Depth perception was affected, making it difficult to judge risers and treads going down a flight of stairs, particularly when stairs were carpeted with a floral print carpet or painted the same color.

(5) Adjusting to changes in illumination was difficult when moving from a lighted area to a dark area or vice versa. The abrupt movement from an area having too much light to an area having too little should be avoided, perhaps with transitional lighting arrangements. Dark wall surfaces bounded immediately by windows admitting bright sunlight make it difficult to see objects located near the walls. Here too extreme contrast should be avoided.

(6) The ability to discriminate fine visual detail was seriously impaired. Reading printed information such as medicine bottle labels, names on doors, and directional signing in hallways of public buildings was a continual burden.

These observations are partially illustrated by Figures 1 through 6, which consist of common scenes photographed with and without filtering by the Empathic Model lens. Unfortunately, it was not feasible to reproduce these photographs in color in this book, so some of the impact is lost.

Considerable thought was given to the issue of participants' adaptation to their altered visual environments. In the initial study, an adjustment period of 6 weeks was necessary before all five participants felt comfortable carrying out the study on a rigorous daily schedule; it took this much time before they were able to adequately concentrate on what *could* be perceived rather than on the bewilderment of sensory deprivation. One reason for spending 6 months observing the same three settings was to observe the adaptation to the sensory changes as well as to determine what elements in the environment impeded or facilitated activities.

There does not seem to be any ready way of determining how closely the participants' adaptation corresponded to that of persons getting older; however, the participants felt that the experience gave them some intuition about the adaptations made by older people. Some of the coping strategies older people use to compensate for sensory losses were also used by the participants—for example, reducing the distance between oneself and the person one is talking to, speaking face to face, slowing down the speed of conversations, and crossing streets only when others are doing so. A systematic investigation of adaptive behaviors would be most useful.

IMPLICATIONS FOR ENVIRONMENTAL DESIGN

The Empathic Model illustrates the difficulties older people commonly experience in their environments because of the normal changes in the lens of the eye that occur with age. To date there are no clinical procedures that can correct

Fig. 1 (a) Without lens and (b) with lens. Veiling glare from uncontrolled natural light flooding through a window and reflecting off a highly polished wooden floor can obscure important cues necessary for negotiating the environment. Notice that the edges of individual stairs disappear in the top half of the stairway. Also the toy on the bottom stair vanishes, as does most of the furniture.

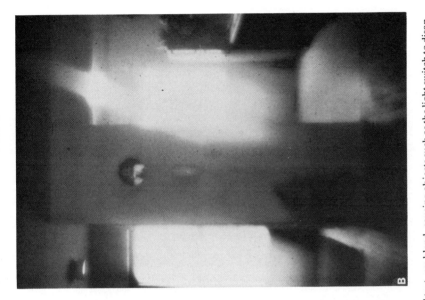

Fig. 2 (a) Without lens and (b) with lens. Closely related colors and textures blend, causing objects such as the light switch to disappear. Cool colors such as the blue throw rug at the bottom left of the picture will essentially become a black or undifferentiated dark color.

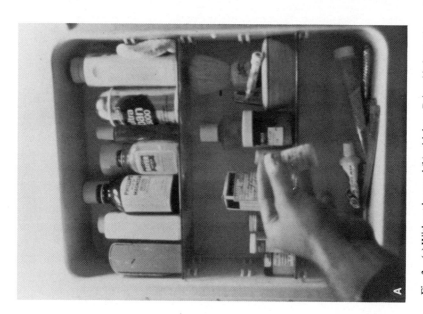

Fig. 3   (a) Without lens and (b) with lens. Printed information on items such as packaged goods and medications is obscured. The only clue to the contents of the medicine bottle is the print on the label; if the label cannot be read, there is no way of determining the contents.

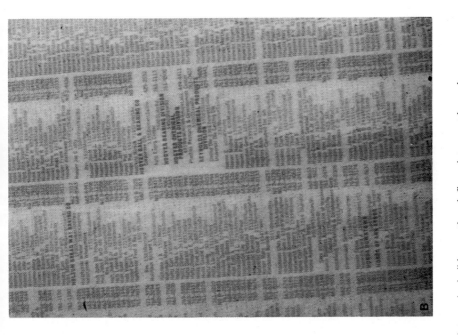

Fig. 4   (a) Without lens and (b) with lens. The large bold print remains legible even though fine print cannot be read.

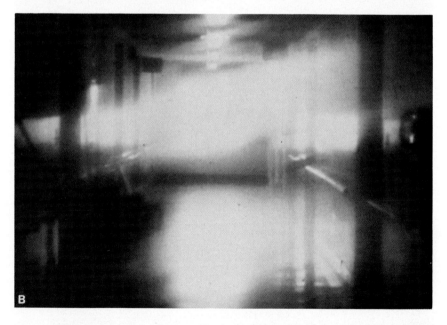

Fig. 5 (a) Without lens and (b) with lens. The corridor painted blue and green is dark even in the clear photo, despite lights and a large window. The filtering of the lens of course makes matters much worse, completely obliterating objects such as the mop bucket and making the surfaces between walls and floor indistinguishable.

Fig. 6 (a) Without lens and (b) with lens. Depth perception is reduced and the edge of the curb is obscured.

or alleviate these changes; however a great deal can be done to design the environment in a way that minimizes the problems people encounter because of either normal visual deterioration with age or visual impairment due to pathology or trauma. A major reason for developing this model was to sensitize designers and to explore approaches to compensatory environmental design.

The model helped make apparent a number of implications for specific designs, but these will not be listed in detail here. Instead I will suggest organizing principles for classes of design solutions, in the hope of enlisting the creative talents of interested designers and others to develop their own specific sets of solutions.

There are two basic principles that emerge from our experience; these concern organized space as stimulus and organized space as orientation. Organized space as stimulus involves the principles of getting the message or environmental cue across through stimulation. Our visual environment is organized as intricately and systematically as any spoken language. It has a system of cues that tells us how to respond to specific situations, but these cues work only if they can be received and perceived by an individual. If vision or hearing has deteriorated to the point that the message comes through only very weakly, the person may respond inappropriately. Organized space as stimulus involves a design concept called redundant cuing, which refers to making a message available through more than one sensory modality. An example of this kind of redundancy is getting the cue that one is in the kitchen by hearing the clatter of pots and pans, smelling the aroma of food cooking, and seeing kitchen appliances. This brings three senses into action, all saying the same thing: "You are in the kitchen."

Organized space as orientation is a design concept that seeks to organize space for predictive value. The idea is that in general a space should have a singular and unambiguous definition and use, because blunted senses are less able to resolve ambiguities. The space should be cued with landmarks that act as focal points for functionally different zones. For example, surfaces can be color coded to visually signal functionally different spaces and, similarly, they can be textured for the tactile sense. The objective is to sensorally load the spaces so that they may more effectively serve as points of reference and obviate ambiguous messages. For the visually impaired, subtle and complex architectural statements are dysfunctional and probably unappreciated anyway; thus designing for these people requires an emphasis on simplicity and clarity.

Many of the observations described above have been incorporated as part of the American National Standards Institute Consensus Standards; they have also been used by state and local housing authorities. One architectural firm in Southfield, Michigan, used the Empathic Model to aid in the design of a retirement community. All the members of the firm on this project used the Model extensively to develop personal empathy and to gather data; it was also used as a cross-validation tool in the programming and design phases. This direct experience with the Model under a variety of conditions gave the design team a group cohesion during critical stages of the design process and a means of testing their conceptions during the progression from observations to programming to schematics to working drawings.

The resulting final design for the retirement community took into account the sensory deficits of elderly persons by improving sensory input with lighting, color, texture, and sound. Compensation for the reduced sensitivity of elderly residents to sensory stimuli was provided through redundant cuing of environmental messages. An orderly hierarchy of personal, social, and public spatial zones was established. Spaces were cued with landmarks or focal points to facilitate orientation and were designed to have singular, unambiguous definition and use. Buildings were scaled and organized to compensate for the elderly residents' decreased ability to deal with large numbers of people and complex spaces.

The model has proved to be a very powerful training tool for designers and others who work with physically vulnerable people, and it provides a link between researchers and designers. It has been used extensively with planning and design professionals, educators, social services personnel, housing managers, and community service personnel such as firemen, policemen, and telephone operators who frequently deal with the elderly in emergency situations. Graduate students from a large number of disciplines have also worked with the model.

In addition to its use in training, we feel that this model has considerable potential for field testing of design concepts; it also offers wide-ranging opportunities for research on the effects of visual impairment on the performance and well-being of both old and young people.

REFERENCES

Pastalan LA, Mantz RK, Merrill J (1973) The simulation of age-related sensory losses: A new approach to the study of environmental barriers. In Preiser WFE (Ed) "Environmental Design Research," Vol. 1. Stroudsberg, Pa.: Dowden, Hutchinson & Ross.

Weale, RA. (1963) "The Aging Eye." London: Lewis.

Weale, RA (1965) On the eye. In Welford A. T., Birren J.E. (Eds). "Aging, Behavior, and the Nervous System." Springfield, Il.: Charles C Thomas, pp 307–325.

Aging and Human Visual Function, pages 335–338
© 1982 Alan R. Liss, Inc., 150 Fifth Avenue, New York, NY 10011

The Vision of Aging: Sight and Insight

Barry Robinson

In concluding this book's examination of the deterioration that often takes place in the vision of middle-aged and older adults, it seems appropriate to ask: "Why is this sight different from all other sight?"

Actually it is not. It is simply our sight, but our sight grown older in the same sense that, when referring to the growing middle-aged and older population that will make up a major part of the total population by the year 2000, we are really talking to a very great extent about ourselves.

Old people, after all, are not so very different from you and me. In fact, with the passage of sufficient time, they are you and me, or, rather, we become them. We should only live so long! Consequently, we need to begin thinking about today's old people, and also about our aging selves, as the ultimate consumers of the results of our research. Greater emphasis needs to be placed upon what can be done to cure or cope with the changes that occur toward the end of the natural life cycle.

Much of this book is devoted to reporting research that has sought to determine how and why people's vision changes as they grow older. This is a good beginning since this type of basic research establishes the factual foundation upon which applied research can be built. However, while we can easily appreciate that inescapable truth, there are nonetheless some 24 million Americans over age 65 who may recognize the need for pure research but who are in a very great hurry to receive the applicable results of that research. These people cannot wait patiently for results to develop through the normal research process because their time is quite simply running out, as someday our time will also be running out.

Considerable thought must be given to these people and, to start with, it is important to realize that there is no one single universal older person. Thus, there is no way we can even begin to devise a single strategy or total therapy, no matter how brilliant, for treating the problems of "the older American" since there is, after all, no such person. There are many different individual older

Americans, and we need to keep their diversity in mind when considering their circumstances and conditions.

Although introductory social gerontology textbooks allude to the growing recognition of socioeconomic diversity among older Americans, relatively little is known about the specific ways in which today's elders differ from one another. For example, only in recent years has serious consideration been given to the implications of the varied ethnic backgrounds of today's older population [Gelfand and Kutzik, 1979; Fujii, 1980].

When today's older Americans were in their years of prime interest to the business community, demographic and psychographic research techniques were far less sophisticated and employed than they are now. In fact, no one really expected older citizens to be around for as long as they have and will undoubtedly continue to be. The children whose lives were saved by improved pediatric care during the early 1900s [Dowd, 1980] grew up to become today's old people. Consequently, socioeconomic researchers are now playing catch-up in their efforts to learn more about today's unexpected population of elders.

It seems safe to assume that the same dearth of data will not exist for tomorrow's elders. To assess their potential as consumers, their preferences as purchasers, their attitudes as voters, and their needs for services they are currently being studied extensively. Thus, a substantial baseline has been established for those who will become the older Americans of the year 2000 and beyond.

Even though our knowledge of the diversity of today's older population is inadequate, we must start using what *is* known about the effects of aging on vision to work on behalf of today's and tomorrow's older people. Basic research must, of course, continue, but there is an inescapable need to begin screening the results of research, both completed and in progress, for findings that might be usefully applied now. We do not have to wait for major breakthroughs; the lives of millions of older people would be improved immeasurably by having their visual coping ability improved even slightly.

In this volume, Padula describes the decline in the ability of older people to function that can result from visual deterioration; this decline is especially tragic when it occurs unnecessarily because services that should be available have not been obtained. A number of factors interfere with the availability of needed services; for instance, many people do not notice the gradual loss of their visual abilities until the deterioration is well advanced. We need to develop appropriate outreach capabilities for locating people with visual impairments and intervening while there is still time to make a meaningful difference. This of course will be difficult, especially since neither Medicare nor most private health insurors provide coverage for eye examinations and corrective lenses. There is currently no financial incentive for instituting an effective large-scale program of preventive screening and therapy, and, without funding, any outreach effort would depend largely on the perceptive observations of social service providers and the *pro bono* generosity of eye care professionals.

Another factor is that for many older people there is an inherent double stigma in wearing glasses. The first stigma is simply one of being old. We live in a society in which oldness is not always considered particularly admirable, especially by those who are old and who have thus suffered the slings and arrows of the outrageous discrimination known as ageism [Butler 1975]. Instead of hating those who discriminate against them, many old people fall victim to self-hatred and to these people perhaps more than anyone else, wearing glasses connotes being old. In addition, there are still some who feel that wearing glasses denotes loss of manliness or femininity, although one hopes that this attitude is dying out.

Old age is for most a time of multiple losses and adaptations, the latter often more forced than voluntary. People lose their vocations, the income derived from them, their roles in their communities, and their comfortable familiarity with a world that often seems to be changing as fast or faster than they can adjust. Friends die, spouses die, sometimes their adult children die. Thus, their vision is deteriorating at a time when older people experience all of their physical and perhaps mental functions as becoming "not so good."

Within this context, an individual's self-image may suffer considerably if he or she is saddled with implements, no matter how beneficial, that symbolize lessened status. Thus, there is sometimes seemingly illogical resistance to devices that can help a person compensate for the losses accompanying aging. However, if devices and designs now available only to the elderly or disabled individuals were to become an integral part of the so-called normal environment throughout the lifespan, there would be much greater acceptance of them. In addition, these innovations and modifications, which may be necessary for older people or those with physical impairments, can confer important benefits on the rest of the population. For example, the architectural modifications espoused by Leon Pastalan (this volume) would not only make building interiors more suitable for older people, but would also make life far more pleasant for people of all ages. Widespread implementation would also lower the cost of such innovations.

There is reason to believe that this concept of increased utility could be applied to all environments inhabited by young and old, weak and strong, disabled and what members of the growing corps of militant handicapped individuals refer to as TBAs—the temporarily able-bodied. For example, ramps for by-passing stairs need not be reserved exclusively for paraplegics in wheelchairs or arthritics supporting themselves with walkers; they can also provide comfortable access to mothers pushing baby carriages, furniture movers, and young lovers leisurely strolling hand-in-hand. Necessity or amenity or both; it all depends on how you look at it during the design process.

Unfortunately, for the most part, our society is busy building a world fit only for people who can walk and talk and hear and see; impaired individuals are effectively shut out. This atrocious state of affairs stems not from malicious intent, but from a lack of intent, more specifically a lack of thought and prescience.

To some extent these oversights can be corrected, often at great expense, but the most effective solution is prevention. If we want to be a part of the world we are helping to build today when we grow older, we had better start making that world accessible to physically impaired and/or elderly people now. If we do not, we will most likely find ourselves locked out of the environments we helped create, and we will be left with the shattering realization that we have only ourselves to blame for building the insurmountable walls, turning the keys in the locks, and marooning ourselves forever on the wrong side of the closed doors.

REFERENCES

Butler RN (1975) "Why Survive? Being Old in America." New York: Harper & Row.

Dowd JJ (1980) "Stratification among the Aged." Monterey, Ca.: Brooks/Cole.

Fuji SM (1980) Minority group elderly: Demographic characteristics and implications for public policy. In Eisdorfer C (Ed), "Annual Review of Gerontology and Geriatrics," Vol. I. New York: Springer.

Gelfand DE, and Kutzik AJ (Eds) (1979) "Ethnicity and Aging: Theory, Research and Policy." New York: Springer.

Index